23 Legal Defenses to Foreclosure

How to Beat the Bank

By Troy Doucet

http://www.foreclosure-fight.com

A1

For bulk sales information, contact the author at www.foreclosure-fight.com.

ISBN1438278195
EAN-139781438278193

Custom Books Publishing
Scotts Valley, CA 95066 USA

Disclosure

The author is not an attorney and is not rendering legal, financial, or other professional services.

THE AUTHOR MAKES NO REPRESENTATIONS OR WARRANTIES WITH RESPECT TO THE INFORMATION CONTAINED IN THIS BOOK OR ITS CONTENTS. THE AUTHOR DISCLAIMS ALL WARRANTIES, EXPRESS OR IMPLIED, INCLUDING WITHOUT LIMITATION THE IMPLIED WARRANTIES OF MERCHANTABILITY AND FITNESS FOR A PARTICULAR PURPOSE. THE AUTHOR MAKES NO REPRESENTATIONS OR WARRANTIES THAT THE SERVICES PROVIDED BY THESE PAGES ARE ACCURATE, COMPLETE, CURRENT, OR ERROR-FREE, THAT DEFECTS WILL BE CORRECTED, OR THAT THE INFORMATION IS FREE FROM INACCURATE STATEMENTS, INCLUDING THOSE THAT MAY BE HARMFUL TO YOUR FORECLOSURE DEFENSE.

The information in this book is subject to change without notice and does not represent a commitment by the author to notify or provide updates to the purchaser. Author is not obligated to notify purchaser of any updates to this book.

IN NO EVENT SHALL THE AUTHOR, HIS EMPLOYEES OR AGENTS, OR ANYONE ELSE WHO HAS BEEN INVOLVED IN THE CREATION, PRODUCTION, OR DELIVERY OF THIS BOOK OR THE INFORMAITON CONTAINED THEREIN BE LIABLE FOR ANY DIRECT, INCIDENTAL, OR CONSEQUENTIAL DAMAGES, SUCH AS, BUT NOT LIMITED TO, LOSS OF ANTICIPATED PROFITS, BENEFITS, USE, OR LEGAL DEFENSES RESULTING FROM THE USE OF THIS BOOK.

THE LIABILITY OF THE AUTHOR, RETAILERS, OR DISTRIBUTORS SHALL NOT EXCEED THE PURCHASE PRICE OF THIS BOOK.

This book is not a substitute for personalized advice from a knowledgeable attorney.

TABLE OF CONTENTS

INTRODUCTION

This book gives the reader a good starting point for their foreclosure defense research. Most of the topics covered in this book have entire volumes of legal work dedicated to them in law libraries so this book is a condensed, easy to follow version of foreclosure defense. Several topics, such as the Truth in Lending Act, have multiple volumes of work available in law libraries, spanning thousands of pages. This book boils each topic down into their most understandable format so the reader may quickly ascertain whether each defense is worthy of more research. Always use other sources for more complete information concerning each of the defenses contained in this book.

This publication is designed to provide a basic understanding of some of the legal defenses available to attorneys defending foreclosure actions. It is a guide – not a final authoritative source for case law or statute. The interpretation of laws will vary from state to state, and jurisdiction to jurisdiction. You should consult your local rules and local legal interpretations of the law when planning any litigation strategy. Not all the defenses contained in this book may be available in every jurisdiction, so conduct further research when warranted. Non-attorneys should consult the skills and independent judgment of an attorney or other professional before embarking on defending foreclosure themselves. This book is not a substitute for the skill and expertise of an attorney.

Every state has its own consumer protection laws. Many states have laws specifically designed to protect homeowners in foreclosure. You are urged to research state laws that may be beneficial in your particular circumstance. You will likely find many websites offering advice on where to begin researching state laws. State laws are not covered in detail in this book.

PART I

A BASIC UNDERSTANDING OF FORECLOSURE DEFENSE

THE HOME BUYING PROCESS & LEGAL DEFENSES

The process for buying or refinancing a home is lengthy and very paperwork intense. There are rules and regulations governing every step of the process. These rules are designed to ensure the homebuyer (or homeowner that is refinancing) is getting a fair deal. There are rules associated with appraisals, credit reporting, loan application, document preparation, closing, and post-closing.

The federal laws governing the home buying process include the Real Estate Settlement Procedures Act (RESPA), its implementing rule called Regulation X, the Truth in Lending Act (TILA) and its implementing rule called Regulation Z, and the Home Owners Protection Act (HOEPA), also a part of TILA. These laws cover everything from proper annual percentage rate (APR) disclosures to prohibiting the mortgage broker from paying kickbacks to real estate agents.

In addition to federal laws, may states have their own rules and regulations that come into play with real estate finance. They may include specific rules on interest rates and disclosures, but will also include rules on real estate appraiser and mortgage broker licensing. Each state has its own set of laws, so it would be wise to check your state's regulations in addition to the defenses discussed in this book.

The "meat and potatoes" of this book enables a homeowner or attorney walk through their loan documents to ensure their accuracy with federal law. This book contains several chapters on TILA defenses because TILA offers the most substantial ability to obtain damages. Several common violations of TILA enable the homeowner to rescind the entire mortgage transaction and obtain damages plus costs and attorneys fees. Rescission means the entire mortgage transaction is unwound – all fees, closing costs, and down payment for the home is refunded to the homeowner. Additionally, all principal and interest payments are also refunded to the homeowner – putting the homeowner in the position he or she would have been if the loan never existed. Rescission is clearly an enormously powerful tool for foreclosure defense so TILA is discussed the most here.

HOW THIS BOOK WORKS

Each defense provides the homeowner specific damages and remedies. The scale of remedies varies from complete rescission of the loan transaction to statutory damages (money the court is required by law to award the homeowner) of a few hundred dollars or more. These types of damages give the homeowner a means to mitigate any losses they may suffer, with some defenses offering greater protection than others.

Beating the bank in foreclosure is accomplished in varying degrees. The highest degree of prevailing in a foreclosure action is causing the lender to have to refund every penny paid on the loan (through rescission). The next level of beating the bank in foreclosure would be in obtaining money damages. Finally, beating the bank may be in raising a solid defense to prevent the bank from being able to remove you from the property, whether it be for a few extra months or a few extra years.

Each chapter is dedicated to one defense or **counter claim** (a lawsuit against the lender). Each chapter is broken down into parts as follows, but not every chapter contains every one of these parts:

Defined
The first section in each defense provides a brief explanation as to what the defense is. It provides the reader with the ability to quickly understand the basics of the defense and evaluate whether or not it may apply in their particular situation.

Spot it!
This section shows the reader how to quickly spot whether the defense applies to their situation.

Limitations
If the defense has any major limitations or drawbacks, this section of the chapter will identify each.

Potential Recovery
What is the defense worth? Is it a tool that enables rescission of the loan, or is the defense worth a few hundred dollars? This section tells the reader what the defense or counter claim provides.

Strategy

Some defenses have strategies to obtain the maximum benefit for the homeowner defending foreclosure. This section lays out in detail how to operate a litigation strategy, if applicable.

Applicable law or Civil Rule

If the defense is available because Congress specifically created the ability to sue the lender, this section will provide the specific statute. If a civil rule applies, it will be stated in this section. The reader can then reference the exact section of law using this information.

Elements

Some defenses have been created over time through the court system, like breach of contract. These defenses have elements, or requirements, to meet in order to prove the claim. This section of the chapter will provide the reader with the elements of the defense, if elements apply.

Factors

Some defenses have factors in addition to elements, like "unconscionability." If factors are present, this section provides some factors to consider.

Worksheets / Formulas

If the defense requires some calculations by the reader, this section provides the exact formula with directions on how to calculate whether a defense is present. This section may also be used to calculated potential damages, if applicable.

Checklists

This section breaks down the defense into an easy to follow checklist, walking the reader through each step of the defense.

Defenses

Defenses is the section where the nuts and bolts of the legal defense are laid out in specific detail, with precise copy-and-paste language that can be copied directly into an "Answer." (See Appendix D.) The defenses section is broken down into two categories: Defenses, and Affirmative Defenses. These are the two sections most Answers contain.

Discovery

Discovery is the process whereby the homeowner can get access to the records of the bank, and whereby the homeowner can obtain information from the bank, or force it to admit or deny certain facts. Each discovery section includes a sub-section on interrogatories (questions to ask the bank), requests for admissions (to get the bank to admit or deny facts), and requests for the production of documents (where the bank is asked to deliver specific mortgage records). This book includes suggested discovery forms (Appendices H, I, and J), and each chapter has suggested discovery questions that are copy-and-paste ready.

Counter Claims

When a homeowner's property is foreclosed upon using judicial process, the homeowner has the ability to counter-sue the lender. This is called filing a "counter claim." The book contains a series of counter claims that are available to the home owner, with copy-and-paste language for each that can be easily put into the Answer for filing with the court. (See Appendix D.)

Third Party Claims

Sometimes the homeowner might want to sue the mortgage broker or originator in the case, say when fraud was involved. This section provides information on how that is done, with some suggested language for doing so.

WHAT STATES DOES THIS BOOK COVER?

The material covered in this book can be used in every state. It includes specific federal law, state common law, and the rules of civil procedure. The federal laws covered in this book are valid in every state of the United States. The common law defenses are universally available in each state. The rules of civil procedure used in this book follow the numbering system used by the federal courts, as adopted by nearly every state.

Many states have slightly modified their version of the civil rules away from the federal version, but most use the federal rules as their model. Some states, like Florida, using an entirely different numbering system, but the substance follows the federal system. For example, questioning whether the lender foreclosing is the actual owner of the mortgage is a rules-based procedural defense that can be raised in any state, irrespective of where it is located in the rules.[1] For ease of reference, a copy of the Federal Rules of Civil Procedure are in included in Appendix L.

The initial part of the book is written to explain the legal process in plain English. The second part of the book includes each legal defense, and the third part contains an appendix of useful information.

JUDICIAL SALE VERSUS NON-JUDICIAL SALE STATES

This book is written to defend against foreclosure actions filed in court, which will always happen in judicial states. In a judicial state, the lender must look to the courts for the ability to sell the property. That is, the homeowner must be served with a foreclosure lawsuit and the judicial process run its course before the lender is entitled to remove the homeowner from the property and sell it to pay off the mortgage. The judicial states are Connecticut, Delaware, Florida, Hawaii, Illinois, Indiana, Iowa, Kansas, Kentucky, Louisiana, Maine, Nebraska, New Jersey, New Mexico, New York, North Dakota, Ohio, Oklahoma, Pennsylvania, South Carolina, Vermont, and Wisconsin.

In non-judicial states, the lender may proceed in selling the property without having to file a lawsuit first. Yet, even in these states, lenders regularly file lawsuits in court because this is a means of obtaining a deficiency judgment against the homeowner (the difference between what the home is sold for at auction and the amount owed on the loan).

---

[1] ABC lender may be foreclosing, but XYZ lender really owns the mortgage. In this example, XYZ should be the one foreclosing – not ABC lender. This defense attacks the plaintiff's "standing" as not the "real party in interest."

The defenses in this book are valid against every foreclosure, even in non-judicial states, but the book is written as a defensive tool for use when the lender files the foreclosure lawsuit first. If the lender does not file a foreclosure lawsuit in court, the homeowner will need to file her own injunctive lawsuit to prevent the bank from selling the property. This type of action is beyond the scope of this book. However, the defenses included in this book will still apply, just the form they are applied will be different. For example, a claim of predatory lending would not be used as a defense (as indicated in this book), but would be an actual claim against the lender in a homeowner's lawsuit.

Most law libraries have state recognized forms for filing injunctive lawsuits against lenders to prevent foreclosure sales pending the outcome of the lawsuit.[2] In non-judicial states, sometimes a bond (a type of insurance policy) is required be placed with the clerk of court prevent the sale pending the lawsuit's outcome.

WHAT THIS BOOK DOES NOT COVER

This book is primarily designed as a tool to defend foreclosure litigation after a foreclosure action has been filed in court by the lender. The process for filing a pre-emptive court action to prevent a sale in a non-judicial state is beyond the scope of this book, although the defenses offered here are valid defenses to any foreclosure action (whether in a judicial or non-judicial sale state).

Additionally, this book does not cover loss mitigation, short sales, restatements, repayment plans, assumptions, or deeds in lieu of foreclosure. These foreclosure "tools" are covered by a number of sources elsewhere. This book is written so most anyone can understand the basic foreclosure concepts, with a focus on the specific laws and legal regulations available to defend foreclosure actions.

The book also does *not* look at reverse mortgages and the potential for homeowner's over 62 years old to secure a reverse mortgage to avoid foreclosure. The author recommends contacting a local lender specializing in reverse mortgages if you think a reverse mortgage would help.

---

[2] Call your local library to find out where the closest law library is located.

WHAT ARE YOUR GOALS?

The first question you must answer in defending a foreclosure action is: "What is my goal?" This is an important question because how you proceed depends on what you want to get out of putting up a fight. For example, you could be defending foreclosure because you felt you were taken advantage of by a lender when you obtained the loan, or feel the lender is incorrectly foreclosing on the property. Others might have put their life savings into buying the property and wish not to see their savings disappear. Yet others might be looking for a way to prolong the foreclosure process while they look for alternative housing arrangements. Some might be considering bankruptcy, but want to postpone that decision until the time is necessary. Each situation will dictate different goals in defending foreclosure.

Deciding on goals are important because someone looking to work-out their loan with a lender might not want to put up a vigorous foreclosure defense if it means the lender will be adding greater attorneys fees, interest, and costs to their loan. These homeowners might want to just prolong the foreclosure long enough to avoid a sale and save the house.

Others might want to drag out the foreclosure process as long as possible, at all costs. They may not be as worried about the costs they incur, instead focusing on staying in the home long enough to make other arrangements.

Some of the defenses in this book will take some time to employ, like calculating whether your mortgage loan violates TILA. However, the benefit of having a TILA violation cannot be understated. If the finance charge is only $35 understated, the entire loan is unraveled and the homeowner walks away with every penny put into the loan. Imagine not only walking away from the foreclosure with no liability, but also having no negative mark on your credit and a check for tens of thousands of dollars. It is well worth investing a couple hours in reviewing the TILA chapters carefully.

Raising the defenses in this book will likely cost lenders considerable sums to fight - which might mean greater end costs for the borrower if your state permits the lender to obtain attorneys fees. Keep in mind that the courts do not like when homeowners frivolously fight a foreclosure (or defend any action frivolously, for that matter) just to rack up a lender's costs. However, employing defenses due to bona fide wrongs is more than a valid reason to defend a foreclosure action – it is a constitutional right.

QUICK & IMPORTANT DEFINITIONS

The party filing the foreclosure lawsuit is the **Plaintiff**.

The party defending the lawsuit is the **Defendant**.

The borrower is the **Mortgagor**.

The lender is the **Mortgagee**.

If the lender sells the mortgage to another company, the lender is the **Assignor**.

The company that buys the mortgage from the original lender is the **Assignee**.

The transfer of the mortgage to another party is called an **assignment**; or **assigning** the mortgage.

The **United States Code** is how federal laws are codified, abbreviated as **U.S.C.** Sometimes, **U.S.C.A** or **U.S.C.S** is used, which reflects versions maintained by companies that keep current on the changes to the Code. They each will point to the same material. **15 U.S.C. § 1601** refers to Title 15 of the United States Code, section (§) 1601. **15 U.S.C. § 1601** is shorthand for locating the pertinent section of the law.

The **Code of Federal Regulations** is a compilation of all agency and executive decisions that are also law, but were not passed by Congress or signed by the President (like FDIC regulations for banks). References to the Code of Federal Regulations are abbreviated as **C.F.R.**

The **note** is the financial obligation that requires you to pay back money over a period of time. It is the "contract" for the payment of money.

The **mortgage** or **deed of trust** is the document that ties your obligation under the note to the property you are buying. That is, the mortgage is the document whereby you give the lender a right to sell the property if the note is not paid.

For a good review of what a mortgage and note are, see Professor Cyril A. Fox's "A Mortgage Primer," at http://faculty.law.pitt.edu/fox/common/Mtgprim.htm (last visited July 23, 2008).

RULES OF CIVIL PROCEDURE

Every court has a set of rules it follows in criminal and civil lawsuits. In civil lawsuits, the rules are called the "Rules of Civil Procedure." The rules lay out what can and cannot be done when prosecuting or defending a lawsuit. There are rules on time, form, and substance, among other things. The federal courts use the "Federal Rules of Civil Procedure," and many states have adopted the general layout of these rules for their own state versions. Thus, in many states, state rule eight will be very similar to federal rule eight. Because the majority of states follow the numbering system used by federal courts, this book will always refer to the federal rule number. You will need to ensure that rule number corresponds directly to your state's own rules if you intend on citing to it in any legal **pleading** (any legal motion or memorandum filed with the court).[1] Use the copy of the Federal Rules of Civil Procedure are found in Appendix L to compare your state's rules.

Important! Locate and print your state's Rules of Civil Procedure, usually found at the state's Supreme Court website. A copy of the Federal Rules are Appendix L.

When aware of a differing state rules, the difference in the federal rule number to that state's rule number may be pointed out in this book. For example, Florida uses a different numbering system than the federal rules, to where Federal Rule 8 is Florida Civil Rule 1.110. You will notice the substance between the two rules is very similar, just the rule numbering is different. You will absolutely want to locate a copy of your state rules of civil procedure and print out a copy to use. These are available online from most state Supreme Court websites. Just look for "Rules of Civil Procedure." Additionally, each local court may have their own special rules to follow, which are called "Local Rules." It would be wise to obtain a copy of the local rules when feasible. Finally, when appealing decisions, there is another set of rules, called the Appellate Rules of Procedure, which are only used when appealing a court's decision.

---

[1] Pleadings are technically the Complaint (the lawsuit) and the Answer. Motions and Memoranda are sometimes lumped into the term "pleadings" by lawyers, as has been done here.

ANSWERING A FORECLOSURE LAWSUIT

DEFINED

A lawsuit is a legal action filed by a party seeking to enforce his or her legal rights. A foreclosure action is one whereby a lender seeks to enforce its legal rights by foreclosing on the mortgage,[2] taking the property, selling the property, and recouping the money the owed under the mortgage.[3] When the amount recouped by the sale of the property is less than the amount owed on the mortgage, the lender will look to the borrower pay the difference. This difference – the amount the borrower must pay after the sale – is called a **deficiency.** When ordered to pay this amount by a court, it is called a **deficiency judgment**. Depending on the sale price of the property, this deficiency judgment can be substantial.

THE ANSWER

The answer is exactly what is appears to be – a borrower's answer to the allegations made in the foreclosure lawsuit. The lender is the "plaintiff" and the borrower is the "defendant" when the lender files a foreclosure lawsuit against the borrower. The answer contains three sections: answers to the allegations, defenses, and affirmative defenses.

It is very important all defenses known to the borrower at the time the answer is filed are included within the Answer. Civil Rule 12(b) requires "every defense to a claim...must be asserted in the [Answer]…" Not including the defenses in the Answer can cause the borrower to waive his or her ability to raise the defenses later. If a rough Answer has already been filed in the lawsuit, the borrower may be able to file an Amended Answer. See the next section called "Filing an Amended Answer" if this applies in your situation. (An Answer is in Appendix D, and an Amended Answer is in Appendix E.)

TIMING

It is critical that an answer be filed within the required time frame under the rules of your state. Most states require the lender state within the lawsuit paperwork (within the Complaint, or on a cover sheet) how long a borrower has to file his or her Answer. Whether a date is stated or not, the Answer **usually must be filed within 20-30 days from the date served with the lawsuit.** If an Answer is not filed, the lender can move for **default judgment**, which means the borrower does not disagree with the foreclosure, even

---

[2] Technically, the lender is foreclosing your right of redemption (foreclosing your right to keep the property) in most states, but this is unnecessarily complicated for the practical purposes of this book.

[3] In some states, this is accomplished through a judicial proceeding, in other states this is done without a judicial proceeding.

though he or she was given an opportunity to do so. If it is nearing the deadline or the lender has not requested a default judgment yet, it is generally appropriate to file a **Motion for Extension of Time**. (See Appendix B.)

Instead of filing an Answer, the borrower may file a **Motion to Dismiss**, which stops the clock running on the need to file an Answer until the Motion to Dismiss is ruled upon by the Court. If you believe a defense is present that warrants a Motion to Dismiss, this will stop the foreclosure clock until the court decides whether dismissal is warranted. Defenses #9, #12, #13, #14, and #15 can be used in a motion to dismiss. (Also See Appendix C.)

THINGS TO CONSIDER WHEN BEGINNING A FORECLOSURE DEFENSE

The most significant item to consider is the impact fighting a foreclosure will have on the amount you might be obligated to pay post-foreclosure via deficiency judgment.

The amount owed at the end of the foreclosure action generally includes the amount of interest and penalties accumulated between the default date and the date of final judgment, as well as (in most states) attorney's fees.[4] If the borrower thinks he or she might end up in bankruptcy if the foreclosure defense fails, then these accumulating costs might be less of a concern.

Next, consider if you wish to have a jury trial or a trial in front of a judge. This designation should be made within the Answer, usually by writing "JURY TRIAL DEMANDED" under the title of the document, then add a section after any Counter Claims titled "JURY TRIAL DEMANDED" and write "Defendant hereby demands a trial by jury." It is usually a good idea to demand a jury trial, or one judge will be making all of the decisions.

WHAT AN ANSWER MUST CONTAIN

The Answer has three major parts to it: 1) A statement admitting or denying the allegations made in the Complaint, 2) A list of defenses to the foreclosure lawsuit, and 3) A list of affirmative defenses to the foreclosure lawsuit. Sometimes, there is a section called "Counter Claims," which acts like a counter-lawsuit, suing the lender for its own violations of the law. Each is discussed below. (An Answer is in Appendix D.)

---

[4] The author suggests any mortgage defense include a defense that awarding lenders' attorneys' fees are against the public policy of your state. Some states have found attorneys fees contrary to public policy, like Ohio.

Important! Most states are "notice pleading" states, which means an answer only needs to put the other side on notice of your defenses. An answer generally does not require a laundry list of facts supporting each defense, just enough information to put the other side on notice of how you intend to defend the lawsuit at trial[5]. However, counterclaims, as discussed below, should contain each of the "elements" that establish that particular counterclaim.

ADMITTING OR DENYING ALLEGATIONS

The first section of the "Answer" admits or denies each allegation of the lender, paragraph by paragraph of the complaint. For example, paragraph #2 of the complaint may *allege* you have not made a payment since January 1. If you actually stopped making your payments on March 1, then you would deny the allegation in paragraph #2. Your denial would appear like this in the Answer: "1. Defendant denies the allegation contained in paragraph number 2 of the complaint."[6] (See an example Answer in Appendix D.)

DEFENSES

The defenses section of the lawsuit is the section where the defendant-borrower states the reasons why the lawsuit should never have been filed because the plaintiff-lender is flatly wrong. Each defense only needs to be a short and plain statement of the defense raised, unless fraud is one of the defenses, in which case the grounds of the fraud must be stated with particularity. Generally, most of the defenses raised in this book will not fall under this section, but rather under the "Affirmative Defenses" section, as described below.

A defense would include a statement to the effect of "you got the wrong guy." Formally, this would be defense entitled, "Failure to State a Claim."[7] The purpose of this book is to outline defenses and affirmative defenses available in foreclosure actions.

Worth Repeating! It is very important all defenses known to the borrower at the time the answer is filed are included within the Answer. Civil Rule 12(b) requires "every defense to a claim...must be asserted in the [Answer]..." Not including the defenses in the Answer can cause the borrower to waive his or

---

[5] See rule 8(a) and (b) of the federal rules and your corresponding state rule.
[6] Alternatively, you can admit the paragraph in part (that you defaulted), but deny in part (the date of default).
[7] See generally outlined in most states and federal court as Civil Rule 12(b).

her ability to raise the defenses later. If a rough Answer has already been filed in the lawsuit, the borrower may be able to file an Amended Answer. See the section called "Filing an Amended Answer" if this applies in your situation. (Appendix E.)

AFFIRMATIVE DEFENSES

Affirmative defenses are the rough equivalent of "yeah, but…" That is, the lender is not flatly wrong in filing the foreclosure action, *but* there is some legal reason to avoid judgment in the lender's favor. For example, the lender might have sued the right person, but failed to mail a required Notice of Acceleration, which most mortgages/deeds of trusts require occur *before* the lender files foreclosure. (See Defense #12: Conditions Precedent for more information on this.) Or, the lender might be the cause of the default if it forced-placed insurance on the homeowner, causing the payments to be impossible.

COUNTER CLAIMS

Counter claims are mini-lawsuits filed back at the lender. Instead of filing a separate lawsuit against the lender, you may include a section within the Answer that alleges claims against the bank. If you think a counter claim is applicable, you *must* file it in the foreclosure action, or be forever barred from bringing it.[8]

Civil Rule 13(a) requires the Answer you file include as a counterclaim any claim that – at the time of the lawsuit's service – arises out of the transaction that is the subject matter of the opposing party's claim. In a foreclosure lawsuit, this means any claims the homeowner has against the lender due to a defect in the mortgage must be filed with the Answer. This is called a compulsory counterclaim. If you lose the foreclosure lawsuit and later find out the mortgage is defective, then you most likely will barred from suing the lender for the defect (so it must be brought as a counter claim).

---

[8] See rule 13(a), compulsory counter claims, and your state's corresponding rule.

FILING AN AMENDED ANSWER

When the borrower has already filed an Answer that does not contain all the defenses he or she seeks to include, the borrower will file an Amended Answer with the court. If the Answer was filed more than 20 days ago,[1] the borrower will need to ask for permission from the court to file an amended answer, and state the reasons why the court should allow the late filing.

An Amended Answer is important because most defenses to the lawsuit must be stated within the Answer or are considered waived.[2] Thus, if the borrower intends on raising any of the defenses in this book, it is likely necessary the borrower file a corrected (amended) Answer to put the lender on notice of the defenses he or she now intends to raise. It is critical the lender is put on notice through the Answer because it cannot defend against what it is not aware of (and because the rules say defenses must be in the Answer). While it might seem like an exciting idea to bring up a TILA violation at last minute to catch the lender off guard, you can be rest assured the judge will likely not permit a borrower to do this. The lender must be notified of the defenses a borrower intends to raise, and be given the opportunity to conduct discovery on the defenses, as the borrower can conduct discovery on the lender. (See Appendix E.)

Filing an "Amended Answer" and a "Motion for Leave" are only necessary if an Answer has already been filed in the case. If the borrower already responded to the lawsuit with any type of letter to the court, the court will consider that letter an Answer, making the filing of an Amended Answer appropriate.

---

[1] See Federal Civil Rule 15(a)(1)(B) and your state's corresponding rule.
[2] See Federal Civil Rule 12(b) and your state's corresponding rule.

A Few Words on the Form of Memos: IRAC

After the "Answer" stage of the lawsuit, each party will have an opportunity to file motions and discovery. A motion is a document that requests the court take some kind of action, like when a borrower would ask the court for more time to file an Answer. A "Memorandum in Support" of the motion or a "Memorandum in Opposition" are almost always attached to the motion and outline the factual reasons why the motion should be granted. These memoranda outline the legal argument supporting or opposing the motion. To be effective, the memoranda must be based on solid legal principles and be supported by the facts. Using the "IRAC" form in writing the memoranda enables the court to follow a legal argument in a manner it is used to seeing.

Law students are taught to write memoranda in the IRAC form from the very first class. IRAC stands for Issue, Rule, Application, and Conclusion. The "Issue" is a brief statement of the dispute. The "Rule" is the section that contains any elements or statutory requirements that must be proven, and should be followed by a citation of the statute in question, or citation to a case from that court's jurisdiction that explains the elements of rule. The "Application" is how the facts support or oppose the particular Rule elements. This is where the persuasive selling of the argument comes into play. The application part of IRAC should start with the word "Here," to tell the court the writer is moving into the application stage. The "Conclusion" is a brief sentence summing up what was said. Here is an example of a brief IRAC argument:

For ease of reading, each IRAC part is highlighted differently:

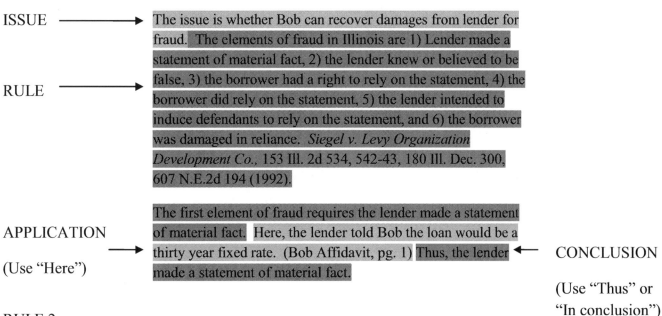

ISSUE → The issue is whether Bob can recover damages from lender for fraud. The elements of fraud in Illinois are 1) Lender made a statement of material fact, 2) the lender knew or believed to be false, 3) the borrower had a right to rely on the statement, 4) the

RULE → borrower did rely on the statement, 5) the lender intended to induce defendants to rely on the statement, and 6) the borrower was damaged in reliance. *Siegel v. Levy Organization Development Co.*, 153 Ill. 2d 534, 542-43, 180 Ill. Dec. 300, 607 N.E.2d 194 (1992).

The first element of fraud requires the lender made a statement of material fact. Here, the lender told Bob the loan would be a thirty year fixed rate. (Bob Affidavit, pg. 1) Thus, the lender made a statement of material fact.

APPLICATION

(Use "Here")

CONCLUSION ←

(Use "Thus" or "In conclusion")

RULE 2

APPLICATION 2 →

CONCLUSION 2 →

The second element of fraud requires the lender knew or believed the statement to be false. Here, the paperwork the lender presented to Bob for signing indicated the loan was a two year "adjustable rate mortgage" (ARM). As evidenced by the lender's broker, Patty Jones, the lender never intended to provide Bob a thirty year fixed loan. (Patty Jones Affidavit, pg 1.) Thus, the lender made a statement it knew to be false.

….after each element is discussed in its own paragraph, an overall conclusion is stated at the end

CONCLUSION →

…In conclusion, Bob is entitled to recover damages from the lender for common law fraud.

Motion for Extension of Time to File Responsive Pleading

After being properly served with a foreclosure lawsuit, the defendant must respond within a specific amount of time or risk immediately forfeiting his or her case. When first served with a foreclosure lawsuit, it may be very wise to file a motion to extend the time to file a response. This buys the borrower time to gather their wits and decide how to proceed. Generally, the courts will be receptive to this type of motion. Many times the plaintiff does not even file an objection.

Whether or not the court rules on the motion, make sure that any response to the lawsuit (a responsive pleading) is filed within the time frame requested in this motion. That is, if the defendant asks for an additional 30 days, make sure the response is actually filed within those 30 days.

A copy of a motion for an extension is Appendix B.

It is important to note that upon the expiration of the time requests, the defendant must either file an Answer or Motion to Dismiss. It is this authors opinion that if grounds to dismiss are present, this motion should be filed. Usually, filing this motion enables the defendant more time to file his or her answer, as the motion to dismiss must be ruled upon first.

MOTION TO DISMISS

A motion to dismiss is a way to quickly dispose of the lawsuit without spending time writing and filing an Answer. A motion to dismiss attacks the very ability of the lender to bring the foreclosure lawsuit. Civil Rule 12(b)(6) governs the filings of motions to dismiss, and states that it is not necessary to file an Answer in the lawsuit until the motion to dismiss is ruled upon. Thus, filing this motion not only attacks the lender's ability to bring the lawsuit, but it also buys you time.

A motion to dismiss the lawsuit can be brought for a number of reasons. Several are discussed in this book, and include:

a. Defense #9: Real Party in Interest.
b. Defense #12: Failure to Establish Conditions Precedent.
c. Defense #13: Failure to Comply with FHA Pre-Foreclosure Requirements.
d. Defense #14: Mortgage or Note not Attached to Complaint.
e. Defense #15: Insufficiency of Process

A motion to dismiss is sometimes called a Demurrer (in California and Virginia) or a Preliminary Objection (Pennsylvania). Some defenses **must** be raised in a motion to dismiss or they are waived forever.[1] Compare your state's civil rules against the federal rules located in Appendix L of this book to determine which defenses must be raised immediately by motion under rule twelve.

---

[1] See Federal Rule 12(b) and your state's corresponding rule.

THE DISCOVERY PROCESS

After a lawsuit is filed, each side is permitted to obtain information and documents from the other side. This process is referred to as "discovery." There are several methods of obtaining information – tools in the discovery tool belt. The methods covered in this book are those that are the least costly and easiest to employ: Interrogatories, Requests for Admissions, and Requests for the Production of Documents. The discovery methods not covered are written and oral depositions.

SERVING THE LENDER WITH DISCOVERY

A defendant may usually commence discovery as soon as he or she has been served the complaint (the written document containing information about the lawsuit). Sometimes, as is the case in federal court, there are mandatory disclosures that must be provided by each side without being asked.[2]

INTERROGATORIES

Interrogatories are simply questions asked of the other party. For example, an interrogatory might say, "State the date and amount of each and every payment received by the plaintiff in payment of the mortgage or note since May 1, 2005." They can be questions, or directed statements, such as this one is, telling the other side to provide specific written information you seek.

Usually, interrogatories are preceded by a list of definitions so the other side is clear on what you mean when you use a particular term. For example, in the suggested definitions in Appendix J, "document" has a very specific (and extensive) definition. These are usually used so the other side's attorney can not avoid answering the question based on a limited definition.

One of the most important things to remember about interrogatories is that they are generally limited in how many can be asked. In the Federal Rules of Civil Procedure, each party is limited to asking just 25 interrogatories, and they can only be directed to parties.[3] A "party" is someone or some organization who is suing or being sued in a lawsuit. This means interrogatories cannot be served on the mortgage broker who took the borrower's loan application, unless he or she is first brought into the lawsuit as a party (accomplished

---

[2] See Federal Civil Rule 26 for more information about mandatory disclosures if your foreclosure is in federal court.
[3] Fed. R. 33(a)(1). You can request more from the judge using a motion.

by filing a third party complaint).[4] Federal Rule 33 governs interrogatories in federal court. Look at your state's rules for a heading called "Interrogatories."

Many chapters will have a section that suggests some interrogatories based on that particular defense. This assumes you will be using the model interrogatory form and adding in the suggested interrogatories as paragraphs where indicated. (See Appendix J.) Take a moment to review the interrogatory form now.

Here are some general rules to follow with respect to interrogatories:

1. Leave several spaces below each interrogatory for an answer.
2. Some courts require the interrogatory form be provided on diskette or CD to the other party.
3. You must mail a copy of your interrogatories to every other party in the lawsuit (everyone suing or being sued), even if the questions are only directed to the bank.
4. You will usually need to mail a copy of the interrogatories to the court, to be filed with the case.
5. You most likely must double space this document; it is single spaced here to save space.

REQUESTS FOR ADMISSIONS

Requests for admissions are simple statements that requires the other party to either admit or deny the truth of the statement. A request for admission to the lender might be, "Admit on May 5, 2006, plaintiff purchased the mortgage from ABC Corporation." The lender would then respond in writing with a simple "Admit" or "Deny." If the lender objects to the request, it may state something similar to, "Plaintiff objects to this request for admission because…." It may state it does not have sufficient information to form a belief, or refuse to answer on other grounds.

The purpose of requests for admissions is that they narrow the scope of what is contested for trial. If the parties can admit that certain facts are true, then these facts do not generally need to be litigated later. These must be presented in a manner where the other side can either admit or deny each. If you seek to ask questions with open ended responses, then using interrogatories or depositions might be more useful. Depositions are beyond the scope of this book, but well-crafted interrogatories might get you the information you seek. In federal court, Rule 36 governs requests for admissions. Like interrogatories, they can only be served on parties.

One of the most important facts to remember about requests for admissions is that in many states failing to respond to requests within the time limit (30 days in federal court) is

---

[4] Also by subpoena. See Appendix K.

equivalent to admitting the statement's truthfulness. **Be very careful** if you are served with requests for admissions so your failure to respond does not equate to admitting each! Do *not* be late filing your responses, or you may find them deemed admitted.

Many chapters will have a section that suggests some requests based on that particular chapter. This assumes you will be using the model request for admission form (see Appendix H), and adding in the suggested requests as paragraphs where indicated.

Here are some general rules to follow with respect to requests for admissions:

1. Leave a couple of spaces below each for an answer.
2. Some courts require the requests be provided on diskette or CD to the other party.
3. You must mail a copy of your requests to every other party in the lawsuit (everyone suing or being sued), even if the questions are only directed to the bank.
4. You should file a copy of the requests to the court, to be filed with the case.
5. You most likely must double space this document; it is single spaced here to save space.

REQUESTS FOR THE PRODUCTION OF DOCUMENTS

Requests for the production of documents or other tangibles (like records) are a right afforded to litigants during a lawsuit. You may ask the lender in a formal document (see Appendix I) to produce the original mortgage and note, as well as any other physical thing that relates to the lawsuit. Civil rule 34 governs these requests.

It would be wise to get copy of the closing documents from the title company, lender, broker, real estate agent, and whoever else is involved in the transaction that may have copies. You may also want obtain copy of the invoice and appraisal via subpoena to ensure the amount showing on the settlement statement is correct. If the party you want information from is not a party to the lawsuit, you may have to subpoena them for the information. (See Appendix K for an example of a subpoena.)

When served with this type of discovery, you will *not* mail a copy of your responses to these requests to the court (again, do *not* mail documents in response to this type of discovery request to the court), although the court may want you to file a *Notice* that you did, in fact, respond.

GETTING SERVED WITH DISCOVERY

Be very mindful that failing to respond to discovery within the time period prescribed by the rules can get you into trouble. Answering untruthfully can also get a party into trouble, opening up them to sanctions or attorneys fees and costs for trying to avoid a bona fide question.

SUMMARY JUDGMENT

Summary (final) judgment is a motion that asks the court to rule on the case without going to trial. The party requesting summary judgment asks the court to review the case using the evidence before it to come to a conclusion. Summary judgment will almost always be used by the bank sometime after the Answer is filed and before trial.

This is one of the most critical motions filed in court, as it can end the borrower's rights to the property. It grants a bank finality as to the lawsuit. Defending a summary judgment motion takes time, attention to detail, and a focus on the law and facts – and how they apply to the lawsuit. The party defending summary judgment will not only need to tell a court why the motion should be denied, but also point to the specific cases or written law that show the court why the motion should be denied. This is where the information in this book becomes very important in the case. The information in this book provides you a basis of defending against summary judgment, and even provides you enough information to file your own summary judgment motion.

The following is a good legal description of how a court will decide whether summary judgment is warranted in any particular case. While this was taken from a federal court in Pennsylvania, you will likely find the standard of review in your state very similar. The **movant** is the party *moving* the court (by filing a motion) to grant it summary judgment. The **non-moving party** is the party that is defending against the summary judgment motion.

> "In considering a motion for summary judgment, the court must determine whether 'the pleadings, depositions, answers to interrogatories, and admissions on file, together with the affidavits, if any, show that there is no genuine issue of material fact and that the moving party is entitled to judgment as a matter of law.' Fed. R. Civ. P. 56(c); Anderson v. Liberty Lobby, Inc., 477 U.S. 242, 247 (1986); Arnold Pontiac-GMC, Inc. v. General Motors Corp., 786 F.2d 564, 568 (3d Cir. 1986). Only facts that may affect the outcome of a case are 'material.' Anderson, 477 U.S. 248. All reasonable inferences from the record are drawn in favor of the non-movant. See id. at 256.

> "Although the movant has the initial burden of demonstrating the absence of genuine issues of material fact, the non-movant must then establish the existence of each element on which it bears the burden of proof. See J.F. Feeser, Inc. v. Serv-A-Portion, Inc., 909 F.2d 1524, 1531 (3d Cir. 1990) (citing Celotex Corp. v. Catrett, 477 U.S. 317, 323 (1986)), cert. denied, 499 U.S. 921 (1991). A plaintiff cannot avert summary judgment with speculation or by resting on the allegations in his

pleadings, but rather must present competent evidence from which a jury could reasonably find in his favor. Anderson, 477 U.S. at 248; Ridgewood Bd. of Educ. v. N.E. for M.E., 172 F.3d 238, 252 (3d Cir. 1999); Williams v. Borough of West Chester, 891 F.2d 458, 460 (3d Cir. 1989); Woods v. Bentsen, 889 F. Supp. 179, 184 (E.D. Pa. 1995).[1]

In plain English, the party moving the court for summary judgment is asking the court to find that there are no genuine issues that need to be decided at trial. The moving party is asking the court to save everyone the time and expense of proceeding with the litigation, and ending the lawsuit now in their favor. For example, if your answer to the lawsuit does not contain a defense, then the lender will point to the existence of the note, the default on the note, and its right under the mortgage to sell the property to recover its money in moving for summary judgment. Without a defense, the court will be required to grant summary judgment in the lender's favor.

Your ability to win using summary judgment exists when you establish a genuine defense to the foreclosure action. For example, if the notice of rescission is not correctly filled out (see Defense #5: TILA Notice of Rescission), your motion for summary judgment will point to the existence of the defective notice and the federal law that grants you rescission. These facts, if undisputed, would force the court to rule in your favor in summary judgment. However, if your copy of the Notice is not filled out, but the lender's copy is filled out, then there may be a "genuine issue of material fact" that would preclude the court from granting summary judgment. In that case, the lawsuit would need to go to trial.

---

[1] *Robert Craig Attig v. DRG, Inc.*, Civ. Act. No. 04-CV-3740 (E.D. Pa., March 30, 2005).

FILING AN APPEAL

Appeals are beyond the scope of this book. If a borrower intends on filing an appeal, it will be necessary to obtain a copy of the Appellate Rules of Procedure from whichever court you will be appealing to. There will be strict format requirements and stricter deadlines to follow. Making a mistake in an appellate filing could spell the end of your legal options, so proceed carefully.

FILING A COMPLAINT WITH A REGULATORY AGENCY

If you want to lodge a complaint with a federal regulatory agency, the following information is provided directly by the FDIC:[1]

COMPLAINT FILING PROCESS

The agency will usually acknowledge receipt of a complaint letter within a few days. If the letter is referred to another agency, the consumer will be advised of this fact. When the appropriate agency investigates the complaint the financial institution may be given a copy of the complaint letter.

The complaint should be submitted in writing and should include the following:

- Complainant's name, address, telephone number;
- The institution's name and address;
- Type of account involved in the complaint--checking, savings, or loan--and account numbers, if applicable;
- Description of the complaint, including specific dates and the institution's actions (copies of pertinent information or correspondence are also helpful);
- Date of contact and the names of individuals contacted at the institution with their responses;
- Complainant's signature and the date the complaint is being submitted to the regulatory agency.

The regulatory agencies will be able to help resolve the complaint if the financial institution has violated a banking law or regulation. They may not be able to help where the consumer is not satisfied with an institution's policy or practices, even though no law or regulation was violated. Additionally, the regulatory agencies do not resolve factual or most contractual disputes.

The following information will help in determining which agency to contact.

National Bank
The Word "National" appears in the bank's name, or the initials N.A. appear after the bank's name.
Agency to Contact: Comptroller of the Currency

State-Chartered Bank, Member of the Federal Reserve System

---

[1] Cited verbatim from: http://www.fdic.gov/consumers/consumer/rights/index.html (last visited July 23, 2008).

Two signs will be prominently displayed on the door of the bank or in the lobby. One will say "Member, Federal Reserve System." The other will indicate deposits are insured by the Federal Deposit Insurance Corporation and/or "Deposits Federally Insured to $100,000--Backed by the Full Faith and Credit of the United States Government." The word "National" does not appear in the name; the initials N.A. do not appear after the name.

Agency to Contact: Federal Reserve Board for federal laws; State Banking Department for state laws.

State Non-Member Bank or State-Chartered Savings Bank, Federally Insured

A sign will be prominently displayed at each teller station that indicates that deposits are insured by the Federal Deposit Insurance Corporation and/or "Deposits Federally Insured to $100,000--Backed by the Full Faith and Credit of the United States Government." There will not be a sign saying "Member, Federal Reserve System." The word "National" or the initials N.A. will not appear in the name.

Agency to Contact: Federal Deposit Insurance Corporation for federal laws; State Banking Department for state laws.

Federal Savings and Loan Association or Federal Savings Association, Federally Insured

Generally, the work "Federal" appears in the name of the savings and loan association or its name includes initials such as "FA" which indicate its status as a federal savings and loan association. A sign will be prominently displayed at each teller station that says "Deposits Federally Insured to $100,000--Backed by the Full Faith and Credit of the United States Government."

Agency to Contact: Office of Thrift Supervision

Federal Savings Bank, Federally Insured

Generally, the work "Federal" appears in the name of the savings bank or its name includes the initials such as "FSB" which indicate its status as a federal savings bank. A sign will prominently displayed at each teller station that says "Deposits Insured to $100,000--Backed by the Full Faith and Credit of the United States Government."

Agency to Contact: Office of Thrift Supervision

State-Chartered Federally Insured Savings Institution

There will be a sign prominently displayed at each teller station that says "Deposits Federally Insured to $100,000--Backed by the Full Faith and Credit of the United States Government."

Agency to Contact: Office of Thrift Supervision.

State Chartered Banks or Savings Institutions without Federal Deposit Insurance

Institution has none of the above described characteristics.

Agency to Contact: State Banking Department for state laws; Federal Trade Commission for federal laws.

Federally Chartered Credit Union

The term "Federal credit union" appears in the name of the credit union.

Agency to Contact: National Credit Union Administration

State-Chartered, Federally Insured Credit Union

A sign will be displayed by stations or windows where deposits are accepted indicating that deposits are insured by NCUA. The term "Federal credit union" does not appear in the name.

Agency to Contact: State Agency that regulates credit unions or Federal Trade Commission.

State-Chartered Credit Unions without Federal Insurance

The term "Federal credit union" does not appear in the name.

Agency to Contact: State Agency that regulates credit unions or Federal Trade Commission.

Other

Institutions have none of the characteristics described. Agency to Contact: Appropriate State

Agency for state laws; Federal Trade Commission for federal laws.

COMPLAINTS

Complaints should be mailed to the appropriate agency with copies of all relevant documents. Original documents or currency should not be sent. Addresses for the federal agencies are:

Board of Governors of the Federal
Reserve System
Division of Consumer and Community
Affairs
20th & Constitution Avenue, NW
Washington, DC 20551

Federal Deposit Insurance Corporation
Division of Supervision and Consumer
Protection
550 Seventeenth Street, NW
Washington, DC 20429

Office of Thrift Supervision
Consumer Affairs Office
1700 G Street, NW
Washington, DC 20552

National Credit Union Administration
Office of Public and Congressional
Affairs
1775 Duke Street
Alexandria, Virginia 22314-3428

Office of the Comptroller of the Currency
Customer Assistance Group
1301 McKinney Street
Suite 3710
Houston, TX 77010

Federal Trade Commission
Bureau of Consumer Protection
Office of Credit Practices
Washington, DC 20580

PART II

FORECLOSURE DEFENSES

LITIGATION STRATEGY

Follow the following steps in defending your foreclosure action:

1. Decide what your litigation goals are. What are you trying to accomplish?
    a. Rescission of the loan.
    b. Mitigating some of the money you will need to pay the lender.
    c. Drawing out the process long enough to make other living arrangements.
2. Print your state's "Rules of Civil Procedure." These rules are available on your state's Supreme Court website. The federal rules are in Appendix L.
3. File a Motion for Extension of Time to buy some additional time. (See Appendix B.)
4. Walk through the 23 legal defenses of this book to determine which defenses apply in your case. Use the checklists found in most chapters to quickly determine if the defense applies in your situation.
5. Pay special attention to the chapters that are most powerful:
    a. Defense #1, #2, and #4: Truth in Lending Act.
    b. Defense #3: HOEPA.
    c. Defense #9: Real Party in Interest.
6. File a Motion to Dismiss, if a defense supports it. (See Appendix C for the form.) Use:
    a. Defense #9: Real Party in Interest.
    b. Defense #12: Failure to Establish Conditions Precedent.
    c. Defense #13: Failure to Comply with FHA Pre-Foreclosure Requirements.
    d. Defense #14: Mortgage or Note not Attached to Complaint.
    e. Defense #15: Insufficiency of Process
7. After the Motion is ruled on, file an Answer. (See Appendix D and E.)
8. At any time, you may start filing discovery, including:
    a. Interrogatories. (See Appendix J.)
    b. Requests for Admissions. (See Appendix H.)
    c. Requests for the Production of Documents. (See Appendix I.)
9. File a Motion for Summary Judgment, or
10. Go to Trial.
11. If necessary, file an appeal.

POTENTIAL THIRD PARTY DEFENDANTS

The following are parties involved in the mortgage transaction that may be brought in as third party defendants (people you can sue), if claims against these parties can be identified:

Original Lender

Originator (Mortgage Broker). Almost every state requires mortgage brokers maintain a surety bond for the benefit of consumers. Check your state law, as you may be able to collect against this bond even if the broker is out of business.

Real Estate Broker

Appraiser

Closing Agent

Servicer

Seller

Building contractor

Seller's attorney

Home inspector

Underwriter of the loan as a security.

Holder of the mortgage or note. (This should be the party foreclosing.)

The trustee for the securitized debt

DEFENSE #1: TRUTH IN LENDING ACT (TILA) VIOLATIONS ENABLING RESCISSION

TRUTH IN LENDING ACT (TILA) VIOLATIONS ENABLING RESCISSION

DEFINED

Congress enacted the Truth in Lending Act (TILA) to standardize the way credit is disclosed to consumers. TILA covers both closed-ended credit, like mortgages, and open-ended credit, like credit cards and home equity loans. Before TILA, lenders could (and did) disclose finance charges on monthly, weekly, or daily basis, making credit appear cheaper than it really was. For example, a car dealership might have advertised financing at 1% per week and not include within that interest rate a list of fees that had to be paid at closing. Thus, 1% per week would turn into 52% annually, plus charges that might bring the actual cost of credit to 70% or more. TILA changed this by requiring credit offerors disclose finance charges in terms of an Annual Percentage Rate, or APR. It also requires the finance charge be disclosed as a dollar figure, amongst a litany of other disclosures. TILA is federal law that covers most consumer credit transactions.

The penalties for non-compliance can be stiff, including rescission of the loan transaction. Rescission means the entire mortgage transaction is unwound – all fees, closing costs, and down payment for the home is refunded to the homeowner. Additionally, all principal and interest payments are also refunded to the homeowner – putting the homeowner in the position he or she would have been if the loan never closed.[1] However, rescission is not available for loans used to purchase a property (rescission is primarily available in refinances only).[2]

Rescission makes for a good incentive for lenders to comply with this regulation. TILA has many parts to it and this book focuses on four. This chapter and the next are devoted to accurate presentation of the finance charges under Regulation Z of TILA because these violations are the most common. The following chapters discuss the TILA required disclosures, notice of rescission in refinances, and high cost loans under the Home Ownership Equity Protection Act (HOEPA).

TILA is remedial legislation, designed for consumers to correct lender errors after the transaction is consummated. When there is a dispute about whether an action rises to a violation TILA, TILA requires that the law be interpreted in favor of the consumer.[3] Liability will flow from even minute deviations from requirements of the statute.[4]

---

[1] 15 U.S.C. § 1635(b).
[2] 12 C.F.R. § 226.23(a)(1).
[3] *Morning v. Family Publications Service, Inc.,* 411 U.S. 356, 363-365, 377 (1973).
[4] *Shroder v. Suburban Costal Corp.,* 729 F.2d 1371, 1380 (11th Cir. 1984).

Technical or minor violations of TILA impose liability on the creditor and entitle the borrower to rescind. To insure that the consumer is protected by TILA, it must be absolutely complied with and strictly enforced.[5]

LIMITATIONS

For mortgage purposes, TILA applies to loans on properties with 4 units or less, but includes transactions for individual condominium units, cooperative units, mobile homes, and trailers, if used as a residence.[6] TILA does **not** apply to business, commercial, agricultural, or organizational credit (investment purchases are also excluded).[7] The right to rescind **only** applies to transactions secured by the borrower's principal dwelling, and *not* loans use to purchase a property (rescission is primarily available in **refinances** only).[8] There is a 3 year statute of limitations, so if your loan closed over 3 years ago, this defense would not apply.[9]

As soon as it is clear the borrower has a right to rescind the transaction, it is critical notice of the rescission is mailed to all lenders, assignees, and servicers immediately.[10] An example notice is in Appendix A. The right to rescission ends when the creditor cures the violation (unless you already mailed the rescission notice) by providing new disclosures and permits the three days to elapse, the property is sold, or three years expire.[11] Rescission is effective when mailed.[12]

At least two courts have stated rescission is not necessarily automatic, and may require a court ruling before the rescission is effective (such as would be the case in a foreclosure action).[13]

---

[5] *Semar v. Platte Valley Federal Savings & Loan*, 791 F.2d 699, 702 (9th Cir. 1986), *citing Mars v. Spartanburg Chrysler Plymouth, Inc.*, 713 F.2d 65, 67 (4th Cir. 1983).

[6] 12 C.F.R. § 226.2(a)(19).

[7] 12 C.F.R. § 226.3(a).

[8] 12 C.F.R. § 226.23(a)(1).

[9] 15 U.S.C. § 1635(f).

[10] Although the case law indicates filing a complaint is sufficient notice, indicating notice within an Answer would suffice as notice, the author recommends taking the extra step as outlined here. *See, Taylor v. Domestic Remodeling, Inc.*, 97 F.3d96, 100 (5th Cir. 1996).

[11] *Beach v. Ocwen Fed. Bank*, 523 U.S. 410 (1998).

[12] 12 C.F.R. § 226.23(a)(2).

[13] We agree that a borrower's notice of intent to rescind his loan transaction does not in and of itself automatically void the transaction. Rather, a rescission occurs under §1635 either when the creditor acknowledges the consumer's right to rescind or, in a contested case, such as this, when a court determines that the consumer is entitled to rescission. *Yamamoto v. Bank of New York* (C.A.9, 2003), 329 F.3d 1167" *Bank of New York v. Jordan*, 2007-Ohio-4293 (Ohio Ct. App. 8th Dist.)

SPOT IT!

TILA requires the disclosure of several pieces of information to the borrower at the time of closing. This information must be grouped together on one form. The TIL statement is used by most lenders, and is easily identified by the four blocks of information at the top of the page, as indicated in this image.

ANNUAL PERCENTAGE RATE The cost of my credit as a yearly rate.	FINANCE CHARGE The dollar amount the credit will cost me.	Amount Financed The amount of credit provided to me or on my behalf.	Total of Payments The amount I will have paid after I have made all payments as scheduled.
%	$	$	$

My Payment Schedule will be:

Number of Payments	Amount of Payments	When Payments Are Due

Security: You will have a security interest in the following described property: (property description) _____

Late Charge: If any part of a payment is unpaid for 10 days after it is due, I may be charged 5% of the amount of payment.
Prepayment: **(Scheduled Installment Earnings Method):** If I pay off early, I may be entitled to a refund of part of the Finance Charge and I will not have to pay a penalty. **(True Daily Earnings Method):** If I pay off early, I will not have to pay a penalty.
Additional Information: See the contract documents for any additional information about nonpayment, default, any required repayment in full before the scheduled date, and prepayment refunds and penalties.

THE FINANCE CHARGE DEFINED

The "finance charge" is "the dollar amount the credit with cost you."[14] This chapter is dedicated to ensuring that number is accurate because there are substantial benefits to the borrower if it is wrong by $35 or more.[15]

The finance charge is an important figure in these calculations, as the lender only has a $35 margin of error, or it faces potential rescission by the borrower up to three years after the closing.[16] The finance charge is actually a total dollar amount of a number of smaller charges associated with the loan. Federal law specifies a number of different fees and loan costs that must be included in the calculation of finance charge. Federal law also specifies which fees may be excluded from this calculation. Although the law specifies many costs, there are gray areas that developed over time with respect to some of the fees. These

---

[14] 12 C.F.R. § 226.18(d).
[15] 15 U.S.C. § 1635(i); 12 C.F.R. § 226.23(h).
[16] Id.

include how excess title insurance premiums, yield spread premiums, and inflated credit report or notarizing fees are factored into the finance charge.

In calculating the finance charge associated with the loan in foreclosure, paying close attention to the calculations and individual fees are important. You will need to compare the Settlement Statement with the worksheets below in order to ascertain the *real* finance charge associated with your loan. The key here is to find at least $35 in fees that should have been disclosed in the TIL, but were not.

WHAT TO INCLUDE AS A FINANCE CHARGE

There is an extensive spreadsheet towards the end of this chapter that describes, line by line, what should be included in any finance charge calculation. It includes the corresponding federal law for each line for ease of reference.

Some of the fees in the spreadsheet do not have to be included in the finance charge calculation. While these are not included on their face, some further investigation will be needed to determine the full extent of their exclusion from the list. The following sub sections highlight this need.

If the charge could go either way, case law supports narrowly reading the regulation in favor of consumers to ensure proper disclosure of the costs of credit.[17]

TITLE INSURANCE PREMIUMS: ONLY THOSE BONA FIDE & REASONABLE

Title Insurance Premiums are excluded from the finance charge calculation only if they are bona fide and reasonable.[18] Some courts have found this means the rates charged should not exceed those prescribed under state law, especially with respect to any manuals of title insurance.[19] In *Oscar*, the court looked at the Manual of Title Insurance Rating Bureau of Pennsylvania to determine the maximum title insurance rates permitted under Pennsylvania law. The court determined failing to provide the refinance rates (which are cheaper than the purchase rates) in a refinance was beyond the reasonable title insurance amounts that would be excluded from finance charges.[20] It found the excess over the reasonable or bona fide amount for these fees should be treated as part of the finance charge.[21]

---

[17] *De Luz Ranchos Inv., Ltd. V. Coldwell Banker & Co.*, 608 F2d 1297, 1302 (9th Cir. 1979).

[18] 12 C.F.R. § 226.4(c)(7)(i).

[19] *Oscar v. Bank One, N.A.*, Civ.A. No. 05-5928, 2006 U.S. Dist. LEXIS 6410 at *9 (E.D.Pa. Feb.17, 2006).

[20] Id. *See, Johnson v. Known Fin. Group,* 2004 WL 1170335 (E.D. Pa. May 26, 2004).

[21] *Id., quoting Guise v. BWM Mortgage, L.L.C.,* 377 F.3d 795, 800 (7th Cir. 2004). "("An allegedly partial overcharge does not convert the entire title insurance transaction into a finance charge, it only demonstrates that some amount of the fee was not eligible from exclusion from the finance charge computation."); *Walker v. Gateway Fin. Corp.*, 286 F. Supp. 2d 965, 966-67 (N.D. Ill. 2003) (noting that the "excess over what is treated for present purposes as the 'bona fide and reasonable amount' chargeable for title insurance is treated as an undisclosed finance charge for TILA purposes"); *Quinn v. Ameriquest Mortgage Co.*, No. 03-CV-5059, 2004 WL 316408, at *4 (N.D. Ill. Jan. 26, 2004) ("[W]e must discern how much of the total cost of the title insurance

YIELD SPREAD PREMIUMS (YSP): NOT FINANCE CHARGE

Yield Spread Premium is: "a bonus paid to a broker when it originates a loan at an interest rate higher than the minimum interest rate approved by the lender for a particular loan. The lender then rewards the broker by paying it a percentage of the 'yield spread' (i.e., the difference between the interest rate specified by the lender and the actual interest rate set by the broker at the time of origination) multiplied by the amount of the loan."[22]

Oscar continues: "While the YSP is a finance charge, the Federal Reserve Board has concluded that it should **not** be disclosed as a pre-paid finance charge pursuant to 15U.S.C. § 1605(a)(6) because it is already included in the interest rate: 'Fees paid by the funding party to a broker as a 'yield spread premium,' that are already included in the finance charge, either as interest or as points, should not be double counted.[23] Each of the federal circuit courts have held the same, save for the 6th circuit, that has not yet faced the question. Thus, YSP should not be included in the finance charge when doing finance charge calculations.

CREDIT REPORT / COURIER FEES

The credit report and courier fees are only excluded up to the *actual* cost of each.[24] If the lender or broker inflates these charges on the settlement statement (very common), then the amount in excess of the actual amount must be disclosed as a finance charge. For example, a $15 credit report may be showing a cost of $55 on the HUD-1 Settlement Statement. This $40 difference would need to be disclosed as part of the finance charge.

---

was made up of a finance charge. In order to do so, we must subtract from the amount charged a reasonable rate for title insurance. To do otherwise would be to penalize the defendants for the portion of the entire title insurance cost that actually went to providing the plaintiffs with title insurance."); *In re Strong*, Civ.A.No. 04-4699, 2005 WL 1463245, at *4 (E.D. Pa. June 20, 2005) (finding that the bankruptcy court properly included only the unreasonable portion of a title insurance premium as a finance charge); Johns*on v. Know Financial Group L.L.C.*, Civ.A.No. 03-378, 2004 WL 1179335, at *8 (E.D. Pa. May 26, 2004) ("Several courts have held, . . . that only the unreasonable portion of a charge deemed not to be 'reasonable in amount,' 12 C.F.R. § 226.4(c)(7), should be included as a finance charge.") (listing cases).

[22] *Oscar v. Bank One, N.A.*, Civ.A. No. 05-5928, 2006 U.S. Dist. LEXIS 6410 at *9 (E.D.Pa. Feb.17, 2006); In re Bell, 309 B.R. 139, 153 n.9 (Bankr. E.D. Pa. 2004) (citing Noel v. Fleet Finance, Inc., 971 F. Supp. 1102, 1106-07 (E.D. Mich. 1997)).

[23] 61 F.R. 26126, 26127 (1996); see also 61 F.R. 49237, 49238-49239 (1996); 12 C.F.R. § 226, Supplement I, sec. 4(a)(3)-3. *Oscar* continues further: Also see, "*Stump*, 2005WL 645238, at *4 (finding that a $1,100 YSP was properly excluded from the itemized pre-paid finance charge on the TILA Disclosure Statement even though a YSP is a finance charge because 'the cost to the Plaintiffs is not imposed at settlement, but is instead paid out as interest over the course of the . . . mortgage'); *Strang*, 2005 WL 1655886, at *5 ("[C]ourts in the Eastern District of Pennsylvania have held that the yield spread premium is properly excluded . . . . Specifically, courts have found that the yield spread premium is already incorporated into the total finance charge as a higher interest rate and therefore should not be double-counted.") (citing *Stump*, 2005 WL 645238, at *4); *In re Bell*, 309 B.R. at 153. The Court finds, accordingly, that the YSP was properly excluded from the pre-paid Finance Charge disclosed to Plaintiffs in the TILA disclosure statement."

[24] 12 C.F.R. § 226.4(c)(7)(iii).

NOTARY FEES

Like the credit report and courier fees, the notary fees must not be in excess of the actual cost of the notary. Check your state's maximum permitted fee, and add an excess beyond that fee to the finance charge calculations. (In 2003, Pennsylvania limited the fee to $2.00 under 57 Pa. Stat. § 167; California is limited to $10 for each signature taken under CA Civil Code 8211.)

APPRAISALS

Check the HUD-1 Settlement Statement see if the appraisal was paid directly to an appraiser, or if the funds went to the mortgage broker for distribution. This number could be inflated, and need to be included in the finance charge.

Also, check to see if the appraisal is an update from a previous appraisal completed several months earlier (in refinance transactions). Was the amount charged reasonable if it was redone by the same company?

Finally, check to see if the appraisal was an interior or exterior appraisal. That is, did anyone go inside the property, or was it a "drive by." If it was just a "drive by" exterior-only appraisal, check the customary fees to ensure you were not charged for a full interior appraisal.

MULTIPLE INSURANCE POLICIES

TILA states the homeowner may chose their own insurance agent, and then that dollar amount does not need to be included in the finance charge. Additionally, the lender may sell you an insurance policy from their agent, but they must disclose certain things to the homeowner in writing to exclude the fee from the finance charge.[25] If the lender sells the policy and does not provide the necessary disclosures, then the charge must be included in the finance charge. The necessary disclosures for lender directed home-owners insurance are as follows:[26]

> (2) Premiums for insurance against loss of or damage to property, or against liability arising out of the ownership or use of property, may be excluded from the finance charge if the following conditions are met:
>
> (i) The insurance coverage may be obtained from a person of the consumer's choice, and this fact is disclosed.
>
> (ii) If the coverage is obtained from or through the creditor, the premium for the initial term of insurance coverage shall be disclosed. If the term of insurance is less than the term of the transaction, the term of insurance shall also be disclosed. The

---

[25] 12 C.F.R. § 226.4(d).
[26] 12 C.F.R. § 226.4(d)(2).

premium may be disclosed on a unit-cost basis only in open-end credit transactions, closed-end credit transactions by mail or telephone under § 226.17(g), and certain closed-end credit transactions involving an insurance plan that limits the total amount of indebtedness subject to coverage.

Please note that these disclosures only kick in if the policy was sold to the homeowner at closing. If the lender later decides to force-place insurance, that would not be a finance charge problem (although it may raise other legal claims, like breach of contract).

DOCUMENT PREPARATION

RESPA prohibits any servicer provider from charging for preparing the TILA and RESPA documents. [27] Therefore, charges for document preparation that include the preparation of these documents are not *bona fide* charges and must be included in the finance charge.[28] The entire charge does not need to be provided, just that portion of the charge that went to the preparation of TILA and RESPA documents.[29]

POTENTIAL RECOVERY

A TILA violation may be brought against a lender at any time as a defense to collecting the debt (offset, including in a foreclosure action), but there is a one year statute of limitations if seeking to bring an independent TILA action outside of foreclosure.[30] A borrower facing foreclosure has special rights and can rescind the transaction up to three years after the loan is closed if material disclosures are not provided, including the misrepresentation of the finance charge beyond $35.

If multiple loan transactions are involved and interrelated, the borrower should be permitted to rescind both transactions.[31]

FOR A LOAN WHERE A MORTGAGE BROKER FEE WAS NOT INCLUDED IN THE FINANCE CHARGE

This law has a unique provision whereby rescission is possible and all of the aforementioned damages are triggered if *any* mortgage broker fee was not included in the closing documents as a finance charge.[32] However, this remedy is only available if the property is currently in foreclosure.[33]

---

[27] 12 U.S.C. § 2610; 24 C.F.R. § 3500.12.
[28] *Layell v. Home Loan and Inv. Bank, F.S.B.*, 244 B.R. 345 (E.D.Va 1999).
[29] *Id.*
[30] 15 U.S.C. § 1640(e).
[31] *Arnold v. W.D.L. Investments, Inc.,* 703 F.2d 848 (5th Cir. 1983).
[32] 15 U.S.C. § 1635(i)(1)(A).
[33] Id.

The author would expect that this would most likely occur when a mortgage broker fails to report in the HUD-1 Settlement Statement a fee the borrower paid directly to it earlier in the transaction (like an application fee). Look for old cancelled checks from the borrower to establish a fee was not included in the HUD-1 Settlement Statement. Alternatively, if the broker received a kickback from the title company in exchange for sending it business, this might be a fee subject to this regulation.

An application fee paid to the broker must be disclosed in the finance charge unless that application fee is charged to every applicant who applies for credit with that broker, whether or not credit is extended.[34] The author would note that in today's mortgage marketplace it is near impossible to charge such a fee to every applicant, especially if credit is not extended, so you will likely find every mortgage fee needs to be in the finance charge.

WHEN THE FINANCE CHARGE IS UNDERSTATED BY $35 OR MORE.

If the finance charge was understated by more than $35, then a borrower fighting foreclosure might be able to rescind.[35]

IF RESCISSION IS AVAILABLE

If rescission is available *all* of the following layers of relief kick in:[36]

1) A right to immediately rescind the transaction,
2) A refund of all principal and interest payment made to the lender,
3) A refund of all closing costs paid at the time of closing,
4) A refund of any down payment made in connection with the loan,
5) Termination of the mortgage,
6) Keep the property if you have already paid it off, and
7) A borrower able to rescind the loan is also able to also secure damages for general TILA violations, as described in the next chapter.[37]

In addition to rescission, the lender is also liable for statutory damages, as set forth below[38]:

1. An amount equal to the sum of the greater of: 1) any actual damage sustained by such a person as a result of the failure to comply;[39]
2. Not less than $200 or greater than $2,000 if the home loan is not a home equity loan;[40] and

---

[34] 12 C.F.R. § 226.24(c)(1); 226 Supp I § 4(a)(3).
[35] 12 C.F.R. § 226.23(h)(2)(i); 15 U.S.C. § 1635(i).
[36] 15 U.S.C. § 1635(b).
[37] 15 U.S.C. § 1635(g).
[38] *White v. WMC Mortgage*, 2001 U.S. Dist. LEXIS 15907, at * 5 (E.D. Pa. July 31, 2001); *Williams v. Gelt*, 237 B.R. 590, 598-99 (E.D. Pa. 1999).
[39] 15 U.S.C. § 1640(a)(1).

3. Costs of the action, together with reasonable attorney's fees.;[41]

A TILA violation may be brought against a lender at any time as a defense to collecting the debt (including foreclosure), however there is a one year statute of limitations if seeking to bring an independent TILA action outside of the foreclosure process. [42]

The lender MUST act within 20 days after receipt of the notice of rescission to affect the rescission, or the borrower may keep the property without further obligation.[43]

STRATEGY

For a loan used in a refinance, the benefit to having a TILA violation is in rescission. In other transactions, violations of the finance charge may go to establishing a continual pattern of bad dealing by the lender.

Pay attention to the three years statute of limitations, as it begins to run with the consummation of the transaction (the closing).

APPLICABLE LAW OR CIVIL RULE

TILA is located at 15 U.S.C. § 1601, et seq. TILA is implemented by regulation according to the Board of Governors of the Federal Reserve System (the "Board").[44] The Board has issued several regulations, including Regulation Z, which implements TILA for homeowners. Regulation Z begins at 12 C.F.R. § 226.

Rescission is not a common law remedy. It is a statutory remedy which means the law prescribes rescission when a violation is found.[45]

Supplement I to Regulation Z provides definitions and additional information on how Regulation Z is implemented. This is part of regulation Z and is definitive as to Regulation Z's meaning and purpose.

---

[40] 15 U.S.C. § 1640(a)(2)(A)(iii).
[41] 15 U.S.C. § 1640(a)(3).
[42] 15 U.S.C. § 1640(e). Some courts require a judicial order before the clock starts to run.
[43] 15 U.S.C. § 1635(b).
[44] 15 U.S.C. § 1602(b).
[45] 12 C.F.R. § 226.23. *Semar v. Platte Valley Federal Savings & Loan*, 791 F.2d 699 (9th Cir. 1986).

KNOW THE HUD-1 SETTLEMENT STATEMENT

The HUD-1 is the document that contains the charges that must be included in the finance charge. This is where our analysis begins.

The HUD-1 Settlement Statement has two pages, with the second page looking like the image below. In a purchase transaction, this page will have two columns, while a refinance will have only one column. The 700 series goes to pay the real estate agents involved with the transaction. Generally, the 800 series block are fees that go to the broker, lender, and appraiser. The 900 series is for pre-paid interest, while the 1000 block contains room for escrow accounts. The 1100 and 1200 blocks are used for title company charges, while any charges in the 1300 or 1400 blocks (sometimes with addendums attached) represent extra fees associated with the loan.

		PAID FROM BORROWER'S FUNDS AT SETTLEMENT	PAID FROM SELLER'S FUNDS AT SETTLEMENT
700. TOTAL SALES/BROKER'S COMMISSION based on price $ @ %=			
Division of Commission (line 700) as follows:			
701. $ to			
702. $ to			
703. Commission paid at Settlement			
704.			
800. ITEMS PAYABLE IN CONNECTION WITH LOAN			
801. Loan Origination Fee %			
802. Loan Discount %			
803. Appraisal Fee to			
804. Credit Report to			
805. Lender's Inspection Fee			
806. Mortgage Insurance Application Fee to			
807. Assumption Fee			
808.			
809.			
810.			
811.			
900. ITEMS REQUIRED BY LENDER TO BE PAID IN ADVANCE			
901. Interest from to @$ /day			
902. Mortgage Insurance Premium for months to			
903. Hazard Insurance Premium for years to			
904. years to			
905.			
1000. RESERVES DEPOSITED WITH LENDER			
1001. Hazard Insurance months @ $ per month			
1002. Mortgage Insurance months @ $ per month			
1003. City property taxes months @ $ per month			
1004. County property taxes months @ $ per month			
1005. Annual assessments months @ $ per month			
1006. months @ $ per month			
1007. months @ $ per month			
1008. Aggregate Adjustment months @ $ per month			
1100. TITLE CHARGES			
1101. Settlement or closing fee to			
1102. Abstract or title search to			
1103. Title examination to			
1104. Title insurance binder to			
1105. Document preparation to			
1106. Notary fees to			
1107. Attorney's fees to			
(includes above items numbers:)			
1108. Title Insurance to			
(includes above items numbers:)			
1109. Lender's coverage $			
1110. Owner's coverage $			
1111.			
1112.			
1113.			
1200. GOVERNMENT RECORDING AND TRANSFER CHARGES			
1201. Recording fees: Deed $; Mortgage $; Releases $			
1202. City/county tax/stamps: Deed $; Mortgage $			
1203. State tax/stamps: Deed $; Mortgage $			
1204.			
1205.			
1300. ADDITIONAL SETTLEMENT CHARGES			
1301. Survey to			
1302. Pest inspection to			
1303.			
1304.			
1305.			
1400. TOTAL SETTLEMENT CHARGES *(enter on lines 103, Section J and 502, Section K)*			

ELEMENTS

To **rescind** the transaction for a violation of 15 U.S.C. § 1635, et seq. for improper disclosure of the finance charge in a foreclosure action, a borrower must demonstrate:

1) The property subject to the loan is used as the principal dwelling of the person to whom credit is extended;[46]
2) The loan was not used to purchase or construct the property subject to the loan.
3) The loan was a refinance of a previous loan either:
    a. held by a different lender than the original, (the borrower switched lenders), or
    b. the borrower refinanced with the original lender and took cash-out of the property.
4) It has not been 3 years since the loan's closing date,[47] and
5) One of the following apply:
    a. The loan is currently in foreclosure and a*ny* mortgage broker fee was not included in the finance charge,[48]
    b. The loan is currently in foreclosure and the finance charge was understated by more than $35.[49]
        i. Use the following worksheet to determine if $35 has been exceeded. Remember to look for charges paid to the broker or lender that may be inflated. Seek invoices and receipts during discovery, or
    c. A material disclosure was not provided to the borrower.[50] These include:
        i. Disclosing the correct APR.[51]
        ii. Disclosing the correct finance charge.
        iii. Disclosing the total payments
        iv. Disclosing the payment schedule.
        v. Disclosing the existence of a variable rate feature, if applicable.[52]
        vi. Disclosing the necessary information with respect to the notice of the right to rescind (See Defense #4: TILA Notice of Right to Rescind).
    d. The loan is *not* in foreclosure and the finance charge exceeds .50% of the loan amount or $100, whichever is greater.[53]
        i. Must be a refinance with a new lender, or the same lender with cash-out to the borrower.[54]

---

[46] 12 C.F.R. § 226.3(a).
[47] 15 U.S.C. § 1635(i)(1).
[48] 15 U.S.C. § 1635(i)(1)(B).
[49] 12 C.F.R. § 226.23(i)(2).
[50] 12 C.F.R. § 226.23(a)(3).
[51] 12 C.F.R. § 226.21(a)(2).
[52] *In re Hopkins*, 372 B.R. 734 (Bkrcy.E.D.Pa., 2007).
[53] 12 C.F.R. § 226.23(g)(1).
[54] 12 C.F.R. § 226.23(g)(2)(i).

TILA RESCISSION WORKSHEET: WHAT IS MY LOAN'S *REAL* FINANCE CHARGE?

1) Transfer all fees from the HUD-1 Settlement Statement to the "Finance Charge" worksheets on the next few pages. Pay close attention to those fees that may be inflated, as described earlier.

    a. Note: You may get help from the title company's closing instructions that break down the specific charges for you. Look for a statement that has the closing charges split into two groups; the top group will likely be the figures included in the finance charge. This form is not always included.

2) Start by filling out the following spreadsheet, which are all the fees that are NOT included in the APR. Go line by line on your settlement statement and move each of the fees into this spreadsheet. Notice the appraisal and credit report fees go in this spreadsheet and are NOT finance charges (unless inflated).

    a. Only include those fees listed on the second and third page of the HUD-1 (if you have a third page), in the column labeled "Paid from borrowers funds at settlement." Do not include those fees located on the first page.

    b. Note that most fees have standard names, although your lender may use a variation on the HUD-1 settlement statement. This is normal. Keep these rules in mind when deciding whether to put a fee in the finance charge:

        i. Most mortgage broker and lender fees will be included in the finance charge.

        ii. About half of the title company charges are included in the finance charge.

        iii. Appraisal, credit report, flood insurance, and other third party fees are generally not included in the finance charge.

        iv. None of the real estate agent fees are included in the finance charge.

Before going through the work on the following worksheets, check to make sure this defense applies in your situation (a more detailed checklist follows the worksheets):

☐ Is the property subject to the loan used as the principal dwelling of the person to whom credit is extended?[55] (Must be Yes.)

☐ Has it been less than 3 years since the loan's closing date?[56] (Must be Yes.)

☐ Was the loan used to purchase the property?[57] (Must be No.)

---

[55] 12 C.F.R. § 226.3(a).
[56] 15 U.S.C. § 1635(i)(1).
[57] 15 U.S.C. § 1635(e).

Fees that should NOT be included in the Finance Charge

Amount Charged in Loan	Fees that should NOT be included in the Finance Charge	CFR Section
	Abstract of title (Bona fide & reasonable)	12 C.F.R. § 226.4(c)(7)(i)
	Application Fee, if charged to everyone who applies.	12 C.F.R. § 226.4(c)(1)
	Appraisal Fees (if performed pre-close) *(Get invoice!!)	12 C.F.R. § 226.4(c)(7)(iv)
	Credit Report Fees *(Get invoice!)	12 C.F.R. § 226.4(c)(7)(iii)
	Debt Cancellation coverage not included in APR so long as consumer is told in writing not required by the creditor, the fee or premium is disclosed, and consumer signs or initials in the affirmative his understanding of such.	12 C.F.R. § 226.4(d)(3)
	Deed Preparation	12 C.F.R. § 226.4(c)(7)(ii)
	Flood Determination/Monitoring Fees *(should be no more than about $35)	12 C.F.R. § 226.4(c)(7)(iv)
	Real Estate Agent Fees	12 C.F.R. § 226.4(a)(1)
	EPA or other type of endorsements (Bona fide & reasonable) *(Usually about $75 each)	12 C.F.R. § 226.4(c)(7)(i)
	Home Owner's Insurance. Includes insurance imposed by lender, so long as lender discloses coverage can be obtained from someone of his choosing, and premium for initial term is disclosed.	12 C.F.R. § 226.4(d)(2)
	Insurance Premiums for voluntary credit life, accident, health, loss-of-income. IF DISCLOSED IN WRITING THAT THESE ARE NOT MANDATORY, and told the amount of premiums, and sign a statement. If disclosure, do NOT count in APR.	12 C.F.R. § 226.4(d)(1)
	Loan Preparation (actually preparing the document)	12 C.F.R. § 226.4(c)(7)(ii)
	Mortgage Preparation (actually preparing the document)	12 C.F.R. § 226.4(c)(7)(ii)
	Notary Fees* (Check your state maximums!!)	12 C.F.R. § 226.4(c)(7)(iii)
	Property Inspection Fees (if performed pre-close)	12 C.F.R. § 226.4(c)(7)(iv)

Amount Charged in Loan	Fees that should NOT be included in the Finance Charge	CFR Section
	Property Taxes (Escrow Amounts) **NOTE: If there is an aggregate adjustment in line 1011, subtract the adjustment from the taxes amount before placing in this column.	12 C.F.R. § 226.4(c)(7)(v)
	Property Survey (Bona fide & reasonable)	12 C.F.R. § 226.4(c)(7)(i)
	Reconveyance Preparation	12 C.F.R. § 226.4(c)(7)(ii)
	Seller's Points paid.	12 C.F.R. § 226.4(c)(5)
	Settlement Doc Preparation	12 C.F.R. § 226.4(c)(7)(ii)
	Similar Purposes (Bona fide & reasonable)	12 C.F.R. § 226.4(c)(7)(i)
	Streamline Valuation Fee, if bona fide property appraisal related.	12 C.F.R. § 226.4(c)(7)(iv)
	Tax Escrow Amounts	12 C.F.R. § 226.4(c)(7)(v)
	Recording Fees: taxes actually paid to officials for determining the existence of or for perfecting, releasing, or satisfying a security instrument. If there is any credit back to the borrower, subtract that credit from the cost.	12 C.F.R. § 226.4(e)(1)
	Taxes on Security Instruments	12 C.F.R. § 226.4(e)(3)
	Title examination (Bona fide & reasonable)	12 C.F.R. § 226.4(c)(7)(i)
	Title Insurance (Bona fide & reasonable) *(Check to see if the refinance rate was issued!)	12 C.F.R. § 226.4(c)(7)(i)

Total fees NOT in APR: _____

After you have entered all of the fees NOT included in the APR, then complete the following checklist by moving over all of the fees that ARE included in the APR.

NEXT Worksheet: Fees that SHOULD be included in the Finance Charge

Amount Charged in Loan	Fees that SHOULD be included in the Finance Charge (paid by borrower)	CFR Section
	Administration Fee	12 C.F.R. § 226.4(b)(2)
	Amortization Schedule Fee	12 C.F.R. § 226.4(a)(3)
	Any fees in excess of those actual costs	12 C.F.R. § 226.4(b)(2)
	Appraisal Desk Review	12 C.F.R. § 226.4(b)(4)
	Assignment Recording Fee (to the lender)	12 C.F.R. § 226.4(b)(2)
	Assumption Fee	12 C.F.R. § 226.4(b)(3)
	Attorney Fee	12 C.F.R. § 226.4(a)(2)
	Broker Fee	12 C.F.R. § 226.4(a)(3)
	Broker Loan Discount Fee	12 C.F.R. § 226.4(a)(3)
	Broker Origination Fee	12 C.F.R. § 226.4(a)(3)
	Broker Underwriting Fee	12 C.F.R. § 226.4(a)(3)
	Buydown Fee Paid by Borrower	12 C.F.R. § 226.4(b)(1)
	Closing Agent Courier Fee	12 C.F.R. § 226.4(a)(2)
	Closing Agent Fee	12 C.F.R. § 226.4(a)(2)
	Closing Fee (or settlement fee)	12 C.F.R. § 226.4(a)(1)
	Closing Fee (to lender or broker)	12 C.F.R. § 226.4(a)(3)
	Commitment Fee	12 C.F.R. § 226.4(b)(2)
	Condo/Homeowner Association Approval Fee	12 C.F.R. § 226.4(a)(1)
	Construction Administration Fee	12 C.F.R. § 226.4(b)(2)
	Courier Fee	12 C.F.R. § 226.4(a)(2)
	Courier Fee By Title Company	12 C.F.R. § 226.4(a)(2)
	Credit Report Fee in excess of actual cost	12 C.F.R. § 226.4(a)(1)
	Desktop Underwriter Fee	12 C.F.R. § 226.4(b)(2)

Amount Charged in Loan	Fees that SHOULD be included in the Finance Charge (paid by borrower)	CFR Section
	Discount Fee (or Loan Discount Fee)	12 C.F.R. § 226.4(b)(1)
	Document Preparation Fee	12 C.F.R. § 226.4(a)(3)
	Escrow Fee	12 C.F.R. § 226.4(b)(2)
	Escrow Holdback Administration Fee	12 C.F.R. § 226.4(b)(2)
	Escrow Waiver Fee	12 C.F.R. § 226.4(b)(2)
	Fax Fee By Title Company	12 C.F.R. § 226.4(a)(1)
	FHA MIP	12 C.F.R. § 226.4(b)(5)
	FHA MIP Impounds	12 C.F.R. § 226.4(b)(5)
	FHLMC REO Delivery Fee	12 C.F.R. § 226.4(a)(1)
	Funding Fee	12 C.F.R. § 226.4(b)(2)
	Inspection Fees	12 C.F.R. § 226.4(b)(4)
	Interest (Prepaid)	12 C.F.R. § 226.4(b)(1)
	Jumbo Pool Fee	12 C.F.R. § 226.4(b)(2)
	Lender Courier Fee	12 C.F.R. § 226.4(a)(1)
	Lender Origination Fee	12 C.F.R. § 226.4(b)(2)
	Lender Underwriting Fee	12 C.F.R. § 226.4(b)(2)
	Lender's Attorney Fee	12 C.F.R. § 226.4(a)(1)
	Lender's Inspection Fee	12 C.F.R. § 226.4(b)(2)
	Loan Discount	12 C.F.R. § 226.4(b)(1)
	Loan Fee	12 C.F.R. § 226.4(b)(3)
	Loan Origination Fee	12 C.F.R. § 226.4(b)(3)
	Lock-In Fee	12 C.F.R. § 226.4(b)(2)
	Master Service Administration Fee	12 C.F.R. § 226.4(a)(1)
	MERS Fee	12 C.F.R. § 226.4(a)(1)
	Miscellaneous Broker/Lender Fees (not including the Yield Spread Premium)	12 C.F.R. § 226.4(b)(3)
	Mortgage Insurance (MI or PMI) fees	12 C.F.R. § 226.4(b)(5)
	Mortgage Insurance Impounds/PMI Impounds	12 C.F.R. § 226.4(b)(5)
	Mortgage Insurance Premium and Impound Cushion	12 C.F.R. § 226.4(b)(5)
	Mortgage Insurance Premium/PMI Premium	12 C.F.R. § 226.4(b)(5)
	NCHFA Processing Fee	12 C.F.R. § 226.4(a)(1)
	Other service related fees	12 C.F.R. § 226.4(b)(2)
	Plan Review Fee	12 C.F.R. § 226.4(a)(3)
	Prepaid Interest	12 C.F.R. § 226.4(b)(1)
	Processing Fee	12 C.F.R. § 226.4(b)(3)
	Processing Fee paid to third party	12 C.F.R. § 226.4(a)(1)
	Processing Fee to Bond Authority	12 C.F.R. § 226.4(a)(1)

Amount Charged in Loan	Fees that SHOULD be included in the Finance Charge (paid by borrower)	CFR Section
	Recording Fees (NOT to tax recording authority)	12 C.F.R. § 226.4(a)(1)(i)
	Redraw Fee	12 C.F.R. § 226.4(a)(2)
	RHS Guarantee Fee	12 C.F.R. § 226.4(a)(1)
	Settlement Fee	12 C.F.R. § 226.4(a)(2)
	Shipping and Handling	12 C.F.R. § 226.4(a)(1)
	Signing Fee	12 C.F.R. § 226.4(a)(2)
	Statement Fee	12 C.F.R. § 226.4(a)(3)
	Sub Escrow By Title Company To Pay Off Existing Liens On Loan	12 C.F.R. § 226.4(a)(2)
	Subordination Fee	12 C.F.R. § 226.4(a)(2)
	Sub-Title Fee	12 C.F.R. § 226.4(a)(2)
	Supplemental Origination Fee	12 C.F.R. § 226.4(a)(3)
	Table Funding Fee	12 C.F.R. § 226.4(a)(3)
	Tax Service or Tax Contract Fee	12 C.F.R. § 226.4(a)(1)
	Title Binder Fee[58]	12 C.F.R. § 226.4(a)(1)
	Title examination (Excess beyond bona fide & reasonable)[59]	12 C.F.R. § 226.4(c)(7)(i)
	Title Insurance/ endorsements (Excess beyond bona fide & reasonable)	12 C.F.R. § 226.4(c)(7)(i)
	Transfer Fee (if paid to lender or broker)	12 C.F.R. § 226.4(a)(3)
	Underwriting Fee	12 C.F.R. § 226.4(a)(3)
	VA Funding Fee	12 C.F.R. § 226.4(a)(1)
	Verification of Deposit (VOD) Fee	12 C.F.R. § 226.4(a)(3)
	Verification of Employment (VOE) Fee	12 C.F.R. § 226.4(a)(3)
	VHDA Bond Loan Fee	12 C.F.R. § 226.4(a)(1)
	Warehouse Fee	12 C.F.R. § 226.4(a)(3)
	Wire Fee to Lender	12 C.F.R. § 226.4(a)(2)
	Wire Transfer Fee	12 C.F.R. § 226.4(a)(1)

Then, add in any fees the borrower paid in cash to the mortgage broker (like any application fees):[60] + _____

Total fees that *are* included in the APR: _____ .

---

[58] A binder fee that actually went to purchase a title insurance binder policy would not be included in the finance charge. However, if no policy was obtained, then this is a junk fee that would need to be included in the finance charge.

[59] See section above titled, "Title Insurance Premiums" for explanation.

[60] The broker likely did not charge an application fee to every person walking into their office, whether or not credit was granted, making this fee likely a finance charge under TILA. 12 C.F.R. § 226.4(c)(1).

3) Next, state the amount of fees that you *think* are questionable: _____
4) State your grand total of finance charge fees here: _____
5) Then, turn to the *Truth in Lending Disclosure Statement*, provided at closing, and copy the information from the table into this grid and do the following multiplication:

NUMBER OF PAYMENTS	AMOUNT OF PAYMENTS	TOTAL PAID (MULTIPLY THE NUMBER OF PAYMENT BY THE AMOUNT OF PAYMENTS
Example: 364 Payments x	$700 =	$254,800
TOTAL	Add up next column =	

6) State the total amount of all payments (from Answer 5 directly above) here:_____ [61]
7) Re-state the number from line 4 here: +_____
8) State the total amount of the loan here: -_____
9) Subtract the number on line 8 from line 6, then add the number in line 7, and finally state the total here:_____. (This is likely your loans *real* finance charge – just verify the questionable charges).
10) Next, do some comparisons.
    a. Compare this dollar amount to the amount disclosed in the "Finance Charge" box located in the *Truth in Lending Disclosure Statement* provided at closing.
    b. Is your *real* finance charge more than the amount disclosed in the "Finance Charge" box by at least $35? If so, you may have finance charges than were **not** included within the finance charge and the loan may be rescindable.
    c. If the numbers are the same, then look to see if any of the fees stated in the Settlement Statement were inflated. If you can locate at least $35 in inflated fees, the excesses must have been disclosed as part of the finance charge. If they were not disclosed, the loan may be rescindable.
    d. If any of the inflated amounts went to the mortgage broker, the loan may be rescindable, even if the dollar amount was under $35.

---

[61] This number should be the same as the "Total of Payments" box on the TIL statement.

TILA RESCISSION CHECKLIST

Complete the preceding "NAME" before completing this checklist.

- ☐ Is the property subject to the loan used as the principal dwelling of the person to whom credit is extended?[62] (Must be Yes)
- ☐ It has not been 3 years since the loan's closing date.[63] (Must be Yes)
- ☐ The loan was not used to purchase the property.[64]
- ☐ Is the property in foreclosure?[65]
  - o If no, were all the material disclosures provided?[66] These include:
    - ▪ Disclosing the APR.
    - ▪ Disclosing the correct finance charge.
    - ▪ Disclosing the total payments
    - ▪ Disclosing the payment schedule.
    - ▪ Disclosing the existence of a variable rate feature, if applicable.[67]
  - o If yes, continue with this checklist.
- ☐ Did the mortgage broker charge any fee that was paid in cash by the borrower and not disclosed on the HUD?[68]
- ☐ Check to see if a copy of the credit report is enclosed in the loan file, and whether or not it has a price on it.
  - o Price on the credit report is: _____
  - o Amount charged on the settlement statement is: _____
  - o Amount borrower was overcharged, to be added to finance charge: _____
- ☐ State your state's maximum charge for notary services:[69] _____
  - o State the amount charged on the Settlement Statement for notary services: _____
  - o State the difference between the charges, to be added to the finance charge: _____
- ☐ State the amount charged on the settlement statement for the appraisal: _____
  - o State the amount actually charged for the appraisal (look for invoice): _____

---

[62] 12 C.F.R. § 226.3(a).

[63] 15 U.S.C. § 1635(i)(1).

[64] 15 U.S.C. § 1635(e).

[65] 12 C.F.R. § 226.23(h)(2(i).

[66] 12 C.F.R. § 226.23(a)(3).

[67] *In re Hopkins*, 372 B.R. 734 (Bkrcy.E.D.Pa., 2007).

[68] To avoid the application fee being included in the finance charge, every person walking into their office, whether or not credit was granted, would have needed to be charged the same fee. 12 C.F.R. § 226.4(c)(1).

[69] You may need to do some online research. Try searching, "maximum notary fees in [state]" to locate references to the particular state code that describes notary fees. Use the statute (code) as your guide.

- State the difference between the charges, to be added to the finance charge:_____
- State the amount charged on the settlement statement for the courier fee:_____
  - State the amount actually charged for the courier (look for invoice, or obtain a copy from the title company by subpoena):_____
  - State the difference between the charges, to be added to the finance charge:_____
- State this state's maximum permitted title insurance charge for this loan amount at the full purchase rates: _____
  - If this transaction was a refinance, state the maximum permitted title insurance charge for a "reissue" refinance rate:_____
  - State the title insurance premium charged for this loan, located on the settlement statement: _____
  - If the amount charged in this loan was in excess of the maximum permitted, state how much should be added to the finance charge:_____
- Complete the "What is My Loan's *Real* Finance Charge" worksheet, preceding this checklist.
- Transfer all charges listed in the loan's "Settlement Statement" to the spreadsheet below.
  - State the *real* finance charge here: _____
  - Add any finance charge amounts left out for inflated credit reports, notary services, and title insurance: _____
  - The TOTAL *real* finance charge is: _____
  - The difference between the *real* finance charge and the finance charge listed on the TILA statement is: _____
    - Is it over $35? Understating the finance charge is by this amount is grounds for rescission.[70]

Checklist for Rescission if a mortgage broker was involved in the transaction:[71]

- Was the credit report fee exaggerated, not included in the finance charge, and paid to the mortgage broker?
- Was any other fee exaggerated, not included in the finance charge, and paid to the mortgage broker?
- Ask the borrower if he or she paid any fee to the broker that wasn't disclosed at closing.
  - Get cancelled checks if possible.

---

[70] 12 C.F.R. § 226.23(h)(2)(i).
[71] 15 U.S.C. § 1635(i)(1)(A)

- ☐ Ask the borrower if the broker kept any of the loan proceeds after closing.
  - o Get cancelled checks; subpoena the cancelled checks from the title agency or bank.
- ☐ Check to see if *any* mortgage broker fee was charged, but not included in the finance charge.
  - o Rescission is possible under for missing even one dollar,[72] but the loan must be in foreclosure.
  - o Rescission only available for three years after the date of closing.
  - o Was there a broker and realtor involved, and possibly any kickbacks paid to the mortgage broker?
- ☐ State laws may also afford rescission to the borrower in addition to TILA, and TILA permits states to do so.[73]

DEFENSES

AFFIRMATIVE DEFENSES

Properly included as an affirmative defense, and survives even when counterclaim dismissed.[74] Add these affirmative defenses to your "Answer" under the affirmative defenses section. (See Appendix D.) Use paragraph numbers where indicated.

[paragraph no.] The mortgage and note are void for lack of compliance with the Truth in Lending Act, 15 U.S.C. § 1601, et seq. and Regulation Z, 12 C.F.R. § 226.1, et seq.;

[paragraph no.] The defendant is entitled to, and hereby exercises *[his/her]*, right to rescind the loan transaction for lack of compliance with the Truth in Lending Act, 15 U.S.C. § 1601, et seq. and 12 C.F.R. § 226.1, et seq.;

---

[72] 15 U.S.C. § 1635(i)(1)(A).
[73] 15 U.S.C. § 1635(i)(3).
[74] "We first address the Bank's argument that Jordan cannot argue rescission, because the trial court dismissed her counterclaims, which included a claim for damages under §1640, as a sanction for her failure to comply with its discovery order. We note that although Jordan's counterclaims were dismissed, she also asserted rescission as an affirmative defense. Those defenses remain valid even after the dismissal of her counterclaims. Accordingly, although Jordan is precluded from pursuing any claim for damages based upon her right to rescind, she is entitled to assert rescission as an affirmative defense to the Bank's foreclosure action." *Bank of New York v. Jordan*, 2007-Ohio-4293 (Ohio Ct. App. 8th Dist.)

STARTER DISCOVERY

INTERROGATORIES

Add these interrogatories to your "Request for Interrogatory Responses" form. (See Appendix J.) Use paragraph numbers where indicated.

[paragraph no.] State the method the finance charge was calculated.

[paragraph no.] State each charge on the settlement statement that was included in the finance charge.

[paragraph no.] State each charge on the settlement statement that was not included in the finance charge.

REQUESTS FOR ADMISSIONS

Add these requests to your "Requests for Admissions" form. (See Appendix H.) Use paragraph numbers where indicated.

[paragraph no.] Admit the *[name of fee]* charge was not included in the finance charge.

[paragraph no.] Admit the *[name of fee]* charge should have been included in the finance charge.

[paragraph no.] Admit the finance charge is understated by at least $35.

[paragraph no.] Admit the *[name of fee]* charge was paid to the mortgage broker in this transaction.

[paragraph no.] Admit the defendant has a statutory right to rescind the loan transaction under the Truth in Lending Act, 15 U.S.C. § 1601, et seq. and Regulation Z, 12 C.F.R. § 226.1, et seq

REQUESTS FOR THE PRODUCTION OF DOCUMENTS

Get absolutely every invoice for every fee charged on the settlement statement that you can locate.

Subpoena the entire mortgage record from the mortgage broker involved in the transaction, as well as the title company and real estate. (See Appendix K.) If you can locate the name of the appraiser, or credit bureau retailer for this transaction, subpoena all of their records for this transaction. The idea is to obtain every document possible and to look for inconsistencies.

Make sure all fees are accurately reflected on the settlement statement and that there were no up charges, especially on the appraisal, title, notary, and courier. A request for production to the lender might look like this (See the form in Appendix I):

[paragraph no.] Provide a copy of the invoice for the property appraisal completed on *[date]*.

[paragraph no.] Provide a copy of the invoice for the credit report dated *[date]*.

COUNTER CLAIMS

Because there are statutory damages associated with a rescission, you may chose to include a counterclaim seeking payment of those damages.

COUNT ONE

[paragraph no.] Defendant alleges the *[mortgage/deed of trust]* and note are void for lack of compliance with the Truth in Lending Act, 15 U.S.C. § 1601, et seq. and Regulation Z, 12 C.F.R. § 226.1, et seq.;

[paragraph no.] Defendant alleges *[he/she]* is entitled to rescind the loan transaction for lack of compliance with the Truth in Lending Act, 15 U.S.C. § 1601, et seq. and 12 C.F.R. § 226.1, et seq.;

[paragraph no.] Defendant alleges Plaintiff is liable to *[him/her]* in an amount equal to the sum of *[dollar amount]*, which represents Defendant's actual damages sustained as a result of the failure to comply with the Truth in Lending Act, 15 U.S.C. § 1601, et seq. and Regulation Z, 12 C.F.R. § 226.1, et seq.;

[paragraph no.] Defendant alleges Plaintiff is liable to *[him/her]* in an amount of $2,000 for statutory damages under the Truth in Lending Act, 15 U.S.C. § 1601, et seq. and Regulation Z, 12 C.F.R. § 226.1, et seq.;

THIRD PARTY CLAIMS

Rescission is brought against the holder of the loan, the holder (as assignee) is liable for the rescission.[75] Thus, no third party claim is necessary to rescind. An action against a third party for damages under the TILA sections discussed in this chapter must be brought in one year.

---

[75] 15 U.S.C. § 1641(c).

Bonus!

For an extra spin on TILA rescission, several courts have determined that the borrower's right to rescind survives a refinance. That is, even though the lender no longer has a security interest in the loan, the borrower may *still* rescind the loan. The sixth circuit says it best:[76]

> "No doubt, the imposition of a security interest as part of the loan transaction is necessary for the right of rescission to attach to a transaction—what in the words of the regulations "giv[es] rise" to the right. 12 C.F.R. § 226.23(d)(1); 12 C.F.R. § 226, Supp. I, at 226.23; *see also* 15 U.S.C. § 1635(a). But neither the Act nor the regulations say that the right persists only as long as the security interest does, and of course the right applies to the "transaction," not just the security interest. Nor does the Ninth Circuit's decision in *King v. California*, 784 F.2d 910 (9th Cir. 1986), prompt us to reach a different conclusion. The entirety of *King*'s analysis on the point is this: "The loan of March 1981 cannot be rescinded, because there is nothing to rescind. King refinanced that loan in November 1981, and the deed of trust underlying the March 1981 loan has been superseded." *Id.* at 913. Not only does *King* of course not bind us, but it does not address the provisions of the Truth in Lending Act that undermine its conclusion. Only one other court of appeals to our knowledge has considered the issue. In an equally brief (and unpublished) analysis, the D.C. Circuit offered this drive-by rejection of the *King* approach: "[W]e disagree with [the creditor's] contention that the refinancing of the 1994 loan rendered unavailable [the Act's] statutory rescission remedy, notwithstanding the Ninth Circuit's terse suggestion to the contrary in *King*." *Duren v. First Gov't Mortgage and Investors Corp.*, No. 99-7026, 2000 WL 816042, at *2 (D.C. Cir. June 7, 2000) (per curiam).
>
> "Some district courts, it is true, have followed *King*. *See, e.g., Jenkins v. MercantileMortgage Co.*, 231 F. Supp. 2d 737, 745–46 (N.D. Ill. 2002) ("[I]f a loan has been paid off, there is nothing to rescind because the mortgage that the plaintiff wants rescinded has been released and no longer exists.") (internal quotation marks and brackets omitted); *Coleman v. Equicredit Corp. of Am.*, No. 01-C-2130, 2002 WL 88750, at *2 (N.D. Ill. Jan. 22, 2002) ("[T]here is nothing to rescind because the mortgage they want rescinded has been released and no longer exists.").
>
> "Most district courts, however, have not. *See, e.g., McIntosh v. Irwin Union Bank and Trust, Co.*, 215 F.R.D. 26, 30 (D. Mass. May 13, 2003) ("This Court rejects [the] argument that it should apply *King*. . . . [A]s several courts have noted, a serious flaw in *King*'s approach is that the implementing regulations of [the Truth in Lending Act] never state that paying off a loan in full cuts off unexpired rescission rights."); *In re Wright*, 127 B.R. 766, 770–71 (Bankr. E.D. Pa. 1991) ("*King* . . . reaches [its] conclusion without the analysis that we believe that this

---

[76] *Barrett et al. v. JP Morgan Chase Bank*, Nos. 05-5035/5146 (6th Cir. Apr. 18, 2006). http://caselaw.lp.findlaw.com/data2/circs/6th/055035p.pdf (last visited June 28, 2008).

issue deserves.") (citation omitted); *In re Steinbrecher*, 110 B.R. at 166 ("[G]iven that the [the Truth in Lending Act] is to be favorably construed toward borrowers, and that provisions such as 15 U.S.C. § 1635(d) and 12 C.F.R. § 226.23(e) limit a borrower's ability to waive his rescission rights, the loss of a borrower's ability to rescind a loan transaction that has later been refinanced, due solely to refinancing, is questionable."); *Payton v. New Century Mortgage Corp.*, Nos. 03-C-333, 03-C-703, 2003 WL 22349118, at *2 & n.1 (N.D. Ill. Oct. 14, 2003) ("Given the absence of . . . analysis by the Ninth Circuit in *King*, this court agrees with the courts which have held refinancing does not bar a suit for rescission."); *Pulphus v. Sullivan*, No. 02-C-5794, 2003 WL 1964333, at *17 (N.D. Ill. Apr. 28, 2003) ("The *King* court's conclusion, however, is at odds with [the Truth in Lending Act] and its regulations."); *Nichols v. Mid-Penn Consumer Disc. Co.*, No. A-88-1253, 1989 WL 46682, at *6 (E.D. Pa. Apr. 28, 1989) (finding unpersuasive the lender's argument that because a loan "was paid in full as a result of [a later] refinancing [the lender] could have done nothing in response to the debtor's demand for rescission" of the refinanced loan), *judgment aff'd*, 893 F.2d 1331 (3d Cir. 1989); *see also Abele v. Mid-Penn Consumer Disc.*, 77 B.R. 460, 464–65 (E.D. Pa. 1987).

The bank, finally, complains that this approach will allow borrowers to "avoid any period of repose by simply contriving a colorable notice issue that could give rise to the right to rescind." Bank One Br. at 21. "Financial institutions," according to the bank, "could be forced to defend a [ ] rescission claim long after the transaction is finished." *Id.* at 22 n.6. But the same is already true if the borrower chooses *not* to refinance the loan. Under those circumstances, all agree, the borrower has three years in which to rescind the transaction if (as alleged here) the bank failed to satisfy the notice requirements of the Act. The statute itself in other words describes the rules for repose—three days if the bank satisfies its disclosure requirements and three years if it does not. *See Beach*, 523 U.S. at 419. To the extent banks wish to avoid a three-year window for bringing rescission claims, the Act offers them a fail-safe way for doing so: satisfy the disclosure requirements. *See, e.g.*, 15 U.S.C. § 1635(a); *id.* § 1635(f); 12 C.F.R. § 226.23(a)(3); *id.* § 226.23(b)(4); *see also Cox v. First Nat'l Bank of Cincinnati*, 751 F.2d 815, 818 (6th Cir. 1985) ("When there is a failure to make all material disclosures, the consumer has a continuing right of rescission."); *Davis v. Fed. Deposit Ins. Corp.*, 620 F.2d 489, 492 *amended on rehearing* 636 F.2d 1115 (5th Cir. 1980) ("[T]he borrowers' right of rescission under § 1635(a) and (f) continues for more than three days after the extension of credit only if the lender has failed to make 'material disclosures required under this part' . . . , and continues, for up to three years, only so long as the lender fails to make such material disclosures."); *Eby v. Reb Realty, Inc.*, 495 F.2d 646, 648 (9th Cir. 1974) ("When the creditor fails to disclose any item of the requisite information, the right to rescind is not limited by the normal three day period but continues until all the disclosures are made [or the right expires]."). Nor has the bank supplied us with any indication that the numerous district court decisions embracing this approach have prompted a flood of rescission claims premised on a "colorable notice issue." Bank One Br. at 21.

DEFENSE #2: TRUTH IN LENDING ACT (TILA) VIOLATIONS FOR DAMAGES

Truth in Lending Act (TILA) violations for damages

Defined

TILA's purpose is to ensure the proper disclosure of credit. Violations of TILA give rise to strict liability, so there is no "technical" violation of TILA that does not create liability.[1] The significant remedy available to consumers is that of rescission, as discussed in the previous chapter. Rescission means the entire mortgage transaction is unwound – all fees, closing costs, and down payment for the home is refunded to the homeowner.[2] Additionally, all principal and interest payments are also refunded to the homeowner – putting the homeowner in the position he or she would have been if the loan never occured. Rescission is clearly an enormously powerful tool for foreclosure defense, so it is discussed the most here.

When a lender violates TILA in a manner that does not rise to rescission, the lender is still liable for damages under the act. For example, if the finance charge is incorrect by $20, instead of the $35 required for rescission, the borrower can still obtain damages. Alternatively, a violation in a purchase transaction yields damages under TILA if the finance charge is not understated by more than $100.[3] TILA also outlines a series of disclosures that must be provided to the homeowner. A failure to provide these disclosures triggers liability under TILA.

Spot it!

Spotting TILA violations requires walking through the checklists provided at the end of this chapter. Each section of TILA has its own rules and corresponding liability. Spotting a TILA violation takes time and patience, but as mentioned, can pay big dividends.

Limitations

For mortgage purposes, TILA applies to loans on properties with 4 units or less, but includes transactions for individual condominium units, cooperative units, mobile homes, and trailers, if used as a residence.[4] It does **not** apply to business, commercial, agricultural, or organizational credit (investment purchases are also excluded).[5] The right to rescind

---

[1] *Adams v. Nationscredit Financial Services Corp.*, 351 F. Supp.2d 829 (N.D. Ill. 2004).
[2] 15 U.S.C. § 1635(b).
[3] 12 C.F.R. § 226.18(d)(1)(i).
[4] 12 C.F.R. § 226.2(a)(19).
[5] 12 C.F.R. § 226.3(a).

only applies to transactions secured by the borrower's principal dwelling.[6] If a loan is modified due to the consumer's delinquency or default, the lender need not provide new TILA disclosures.[7] However, a consumer that is assuming a loan must be provided TILA disclosures.[8]

POTENTIAL RECOVERY

A creditor who fails to comply with any requirement imposed under TILA is liable in an amount equal to the sum of the following: 1) any actual damage sustained by such a person as a result of the failure, and 2) damages not less than $200 or greater than $2,000 if the home loan is not a home equity loan.[9] Recovery is not cumulative, so the borrower is only able to recover for one set of damages (even if there are multiple disclosure failures).[10]

In addition to TILA damages, many states may also provide for recovery under state law.

STRATEGY

It is well worth the time and energy to carefully review your loan documents for violations of TILA. While the violations in this chapter will secure you a small amount of damages, your research may very well lead to damages that enable rescission. TILA rescission is detailed in the previous chapter.

APPLICABLE LAW OR CIVIL RULE

TILA is located at 15 U.S.C. § 1601, et seq. TILA is implemented by regulation according to the Board of Governors of the Federal Reserve System (the "Board").[11] The Board has issued several regulations, including Regulation Z, which implements TILA for homeowners. Regulation Z begins at 12 C.F.R. § 226.

Supplement I to Regulation Z provides definitions and additional information on how Regulation Z is implemented. This is part of regulation Z and is definitive as to Regulation Z's meaning and purpose.

---

[6] 12 C.F.R. § 226.23(a)(1).
[7] 12 C.F.R. § 226.20(a)(4).
[8] 12 C.F.R. § 226.20(b).
[9] 15 U.S.C. § 1640(a)(1), (2).
[10] 15 U.S.C. § 1640(g).
[11] 15 U.S.C. § 1602(b).

ELEMENTS

Any violation found in the previous chapter will create liability for the lender, as well as any violation found in the next two chapters. The violations discussed in this chapter allow for damages. The basic elements of a TILA damages claim are as follows:

1) The property subject to the loan is used as the principal dwelling of the person to whom credit is extended.[12]
2) It has not been 1 years since the loan's closing date, or the loan is in foreclosure.[13]
3) One of the following apply:
   a. A disclosure was not provided to the borrower,[14] or not updated after the information became inaccurate or outdated before closing.[15] These include:
      i. The APR.[16]
         1. The finance charge and APR must be more conspicuous than any other disclosure, except the creditor's identity.[17]
      ii. The correct finance charge.
         1. The finance charge must be accurate within $100.[18]
         2. The finance charge and APR must be more conspicuous than any other disclosure, except the creditor's identity.[19]
      iii. The total payments.[20]
      iv. The payment schedule.[21]
      v. The amount financed.[22]
      vi. Disclosing the necessary information with respect to the notice of the right to rescind (see that chapter in this book).[23]
      vii. The identity of the creditor.[24]
      viii. Whether the loan has a variable rate.
      ix. Whether the loan has a demand feature.
      x. If the loan has a prepayment penalty.

---

[12] 12 C.F.R. § 226.3(a).

[13] 15 U.S.C. § 1635(e).

[14] 12 C.F.R. § 226.23(a)(3).

[15] 12 C.F.R. § 226.17(e)

[16] 12 C.F.R. § 226.18(e); 12 C.F.R. § 226.23(a)(3). This failure enables rescision. The "annual percentage rate" is "a measure of the cost of credit, expressed as a yearly rate, that relates the amount and timing of value received by the consumer to the amount and timing of payments made." 12 C.F.R. § 226.22(a)(1).

[17] 12 C.F.R. § 226.17(a)(2). A violation here triggers normal TILA damages.

[18] 12 C.F.R. § 226.18(d)(1)(i). See the previous chapter for these calculations.

[19] 12 C.F.R. § 226.17(a)(2). A violation here triggers normal damages.

[20] 12 C.F.R. § 226.23(a)(3). This failure enables rescision.

[21] 12 C.F.R. § 226.23(a)(3). This failure enables rescision.

[22] 12 C.F.R. § 226.23(a)(3). This failure enables rescision. The "amount financed" is "the amount of credit provided to you or on your behalf." 12 C.F.R. § 226.18(b).

[23] 12 C.F.R. § 226.23(a)(3). This failure enables rescision..

[24] The following disclosures are all required by 12 C.F.R. § 226.18.

      xi.   The amount of the fee for paying late.

     xii.   The fact that the lender will have a security interest in property.

    xiii.   A reference to the contract that tells borrowers where to look for information about nonpayment, default, and rights to accelerate.

    xiv.   A statement on whether assumption of the loan is possible.

     xv.   The total sale price, using that term, and a descriptive explanation such as "the total price of your purchase on credit, including your down payment of $___."

    xvi.   An itemization of the amount financed, that may be provided as the HUD-1 Settlement Statement.[25] This document must be provided separately from every other form.[26]

   xvii.   The foregoing disclosures must be in writing, in a form the consumer may keep. The disclosures must be grouped together, segregated from everything else, and not contain any information not related to the disclosures.[27]

b.   A good faith estimate was not provided within three days of the loan application.

c.   For variable rate loans, the booklet titled Consumer Handbook on Adjustable Rate Mortgages was not provided to the consumer within three days of the loan application.[28]

    i.   Also, disclose the loan program guidelines for any variable-rate program that the consumer expresses an interest, including:[29]

       1.   The fact that the interest rate, payment, or term of the loan can change.

       2.   The index or formula used in making the adjustments.

       3.   An explanation of how the interst rate and payment will be determined, including an explanation of how the index is adjusted, such as by the addition of a margin.

       4.   A statement that the consumer should ask about the current margin value and current interest rate.

       5.   The fact that the interest rate will be discounted, and a statement that the consumer should ask about the amount of the interest rate discount.

       6.   The frequency of interest rate and payment changes.

       7.   Any rules relating to changes in the index, interest rate, payment amount, and outstanding loan balance including, for

---

[25] 12 C.F.R. § 226.18(c).

[26] 12 C.F.R. § 226.17(a)(1).

[27] Id.

[28] 12 C.F.R. § 226.17(b); 12 C.F.R. § 226.19(b)(1).

[29] 12 C.F.R. § 226.17(b); 12 C.F.R. § 226.19(b)(2).

example, an explanation of interest rate or payment limitations, negative amortization, and interest rate carryover.

8. At the option of the creditor, a historical example illustrating how payments would have been affected by interest rate changes, or an example using the maximum interest rate and maximum adjustment for the loan.

9. An explanation of how the consumer may calculate the payments for the loan amount to be borrowed based on either:

   (A) The most recent payment shown in the historical example in paragraph (b)(2)(viii)(A) of this section; or

   (B) The initial interest rate used to calculate the maximum interest rate and payment in paragraph (b)(2)(viii)(B) of this section.

10. The fact that the loan program contains a demand feature.

11. The type of information that will be provided in notices of adjustments and the timing of such notices.

12. A statement that disclosure forms are available for the creditor's other variable-rate loan programs.

d. Any advertisement for TILA loans must clearly and conspicuously disclose all of the following, if any of the following are used in an advertisement:[30]

   i. The amount or percentage of any down payment.

   ii. The number of payments or period of repayment.

   iii. The amount of any payment.

   iv. The amount of any finance charge.

WORKSHEETS / FORMULAS

Use the TILA worksheet in the previous chapter to calculate finance charge figures.

---

[30] 12 C.F.R. § 226.24(d).

TILA DAMAGES CHECKLIST

☐ Check to see if the following disclosures were provided to the consumer at closing:

- o The APR.[31]
  - ▪ The finance charge and APR must be more conspicuous than any other disclosure, except the creditor's identity.[32]
- o The correct finance charge.
  - ▪ An error under $35 in a foreclosure action enables damages.
  - ▪ An error in excess of $35 enables rescission.[33]
  - ▪ The finance charge and APR must be more conspicuous than any other disclosure, except the creditor's identity.[34]
- o The total payments.[35]
- o The payment schedule.[36]
- o The amount financed.[37]
- o Disclosing the necessary information with respect to the notice of the right to rescind (see that chapter in this book).[38]
- o The identity of the creditor.[39]
- o Whether the loan has a variable rate.[40]
- o Whether the loan has a demand feature.
- o If the loan has a prepayment penalty.
- o The amount of the fee for paying late.
- o The fact that the lender will have a security interest in property.
- o A reference to the contract that tells borrowers where to look for information about nonpayment, default, and rights to accelerate.
- o A statement on whether assumption of the loan is possible.
- o The total sale price, using that term, and a descriptive explanation such as "the total price of your purchase on credit, including your down payment of $__."
- o An itemization of the amount financed, that may be provided as the HUD-1 Settlement Statement.[41] This document must be provided separately from every other form.[42]

---

[31] 12 C.F.R. § 226.18(e); 12 C.F.R. § 226.23(a)(3). This failure enables rescission. The "annual percentage rate" is "a measure of the cost of credit, expressed as a yearly rate, that relates the amount and timing of value received by the consumer to the amount and timing of payments made." 12 C.F.R. § 226.22(a)(1).

[32] 12 C.F.R. § 226.17(a)(2). A violation here triggers normal TILA damages.

[33] 15 U.S.C. § 1635(i). See the previous chapter for these calculations.

[34] 12 C.F.R. § 226.17(a)(2). A violation here triggers normal damages.

[35] 12 C.F.R. § 226.23(a)(3). This failure enables rescission.

[36] 12 C.F.R. § 226.23(a)(3). This failure enables rescission.

[37] 12 C.F.R. § 226.23(a)(3). This failure enables rescission. The "amount financed" is "the amount of credit provided to you or on your behalf." 12 C.F.R. § 226.18(b).

[38] 12 C.F.R. § 226.23(a)(3). This failure enables rescission..

[39] The following disclosures are all required by 12 C.F.R. § 226.18.

[40] *In re Hopkins*, 372 B.R. 734 (Bkrtcy.E.D.Pa. 2007) (this violations enables rescission in a refinance).

- o The foregoing disclosures must be in writing, in a form the consumer may keep. The disclosures must be grouped together, segregated from everything else, and not contain any information not related to the disclosures.[43]
- ☐ A good faith estimate was not provided within three days of the loan application.
- ☐ For variable rate loans, the booklet titled Consumer Handbook on Adjustable Rate Mortgages (CHARM) was not provided to the consumer within three days of the loan application.[44]
  - o Also, disclose the loan program guidelines for any variable-rate program that the consumer expresses an interest, including:[45]
    - o The fact that the interest rate, payment, or term of the loan can change.
    - o The index or formula used in making the adjustments.
    - o An explanation of how the interest rate and payment will be determined, including an explanation of how the index is adjusted, such as by the addition of a margin.
    - o A statement that the consumer should ask about the current margin value and current interest rate.
    - o The fact that the interest rate will be discounted, and a statement that the consumer should ask about the amount of the interest rate discount.
    - o The frequency of interest rate and payment changes.
      - o Any rules relating to changes in the index, interest rate, payment amount, and outstanding loan balance including, for example, an explanation of interest rate or payment limitations, negative amortization, and interest rate carryover.
      - o At the option of the creditor, a historical example illustrating how payments would have been affected by interest rate changes, or an example using the maximum interest rate and maximum adjustment for the loan.
      - o An explanation of how the consumer may calculate the payments for the loan amount to be borrowed based on either:

---

[41] 12 C.F.R. § 226.18(c).
[42] 12 C.F.R. § 226.17(a)(1).
[43] Id.
[44] 12 C.F.R. § 226.17(b); 12 C.F.R. § 226.19(b)(1).
[45] 12 C.F.R. § 226.17(b); 12 C.F.R. § 226.19(b)(2).

- o The most recent payment shown in the historical example in paragraph (b)(2)(viii)(A) of this section; or
- o The initial interest rate used to calculate the maximum interest rate and payment in paragraph (b)(2)(viii)(B) of this section.
  - o The fact that the loan program contains a demand feature.
  - o The type of information that will be provided in notices of adjustments and the timing of such notices.
  - o A statement that disclosure forms are available for the creditor's other variable-rate loan programs.
- ☐ Any advertisement for TILA loans must clearly and conspicuously disclose all of the following, if any of the following are used in an advertisement:[46]
  - o The amount or percentage of any down payment.
  - o The number of payments or period of repayment.
  - o The amount of any payment.
  - o The amount of any finance charge.

DEFENSES

Use the defenses outlined in the previous chapter.

STARTER DISCOVERY

Use the discovery in the previous chapter. You may wish to include a request for admission along these lines when disclosure is inaccurate or missing:

"*[paragraph no.]* Admit the lender did not provide *[state required disclosure here]*.

---

[46] 12 C.F.R. § 226.24(d).

DEFENSE #3: HOME OWNERSHIP AND EQUITY PROTECTION ACT (HOEPA)

HOME OWNERSHIP AND EQUITY PROTECTION ACT (HOEPA)

DEFINED

The Home Ownership and Equity Protection Act (HOEPA, pronounced "hoe-pa") is a section within Regulation Z of TILA that contains stringent rules associated with refinance loans considered high cost. These high-cost loans require an extra layer of disclosure under HOEPA.

If the loan is subject to HOEPA, the lender must provide the following notices in addition to the other disclosures required by TILA:[1]

> "You are not required to complete this agreement merely because you have received these disclosures or have signed a loan application."

> "If you obtain this loan, the lender will have a mortgage on your home. You could lose your home, and any money you have put into it, if you do not meet your obligations under the loan."

When HOEPA is triggered, the lender not only needs to provide these disclosures at closing, but also must provide them *three days before closing*.[2] Additionally, the lender must disclose the following three days before closing:[3]

> Annual percentage rate:

> (A) In the case of a credit transaction with a fixed rate of interest, the annual percentage rate and the amount of the regular monthly payment; or

> (B) In the case of any other credit transaction, the annual percentage rate of the loan, the amount of the regular monthly payment, a statement that the interest rate and monthly payment may increase, and the amount of the maximum monthly payment, based on the maximum interest rate allowed pursuant to section 3806 of title 12.

Even if you do not think your loan is approaching the thresholds to trigger the HOEPA requirements, it is well worth spending the time to do the calculations to find out. This is especially true if your initial home loan amount is below $120,000, or if your interest rate was above 10% at closing. HOEPA not only entitles the borrower to rescind the mortgage transaction (if the loan qualifies) up to three years after the closing,[4] but also provides

---

[1] 15 U.S.C. § 1639(a)(1); 12 C.F.R. § 226.32(c)(1)
[2] 15 U.S.C. § 1639(b)(2).
[3] 15 U.S.C. § 1639(b)(1).
[4] 12 C.F.R. § 226.23(a)(3).

statutory damages an amount **equal to the sum of all finance charges and fees paid by the consumer**, unless the creditor demonstrates the failure to comply is not material.[5] HOEPA does *not* use the same calculations as the other TILA sections. Therefore, a lender who might properly have disclosed the finance charge to the consumer might be running afoul of HOEPA without realizing it. This is most likely to occur when the consumer purchases credit life insurance with the mortgage (listed on the HUD-1 Settlement Statement) because this type of insurance policy must be included in the HOEPA calculation, irrespective of the disclosures provided. Use the worksheet in this chapter to calculate whether the loan triggers HOEPA.

SPOT IT!

If the loan's interest rate was above 10% at closing, or if the loan amount is below $120,000, it is wise to carefully review the loan with the worksheets provided in this chapter. Additionally, if your settlement statement indicates credit life insurance was sold, you should review the loan for HOEPA violations.

If the loan was closed by Countrywide Home Loans, Inc. and the fees near HOEPA's threshold, then absolutely complete the HOEPA worksheet. Countrywide owns LandSafe Inc., LandSafe Credit, LandSafe Flood Determination, Inc., and LandSafe Services, Inc., amongst other companies.[6] HOEPA, unlike the normal provisions of TILA, requires all fees paid in connection with title, appraisals, credit reporting, and flood certifications be included in the HOEPA calculations if the service provider is an affiliate of the lender.[7]

LIMITATIONS

HOEPA, as a TILA defense, applies to loans on properties with 4 units or less, but includes transactions for individual condominium units, cooperative units, mobile homes, and trailers, if used as a residence.[8] It does **not** apply to business, commercial, agricultural, or organizational credit (investment purchases are also excluded).[9] The right to rescind **only** applies to transactions secured by the borrower's principal dwelling.[10] Rescission is only available in refinance transactions.[11]

---

[5] 15 U.S.C. § 1640(a)(4).
[6] Countrywide Financial Corp.'s 12/31/2007 Form 10-K filed with the SEC on 2/29/2008, as reported at http://www.secinfo.com/dVut2.t21n.n.htm (last visited August 10, 2008).
[7] 12 C.F.R. § 226.32(b)(1)(iii).
[8] 12 C.F.R. § 226.2(a)(19).
[9] 12 C.F.R. § 226.3(a).
[10] 12 C.F.R. § 226.23(a)(1).
[11] 12 C.F.R. § 226.32(a)(2)(i).

As soon as it is clear the borrower has a right to rescind the transaction, it is critical notice of the rescission is mailed to all lenders, assignees, and servicers immediately.[12] The right to rescission ends when the creditor cures the violation (unless you already mailed the rescission notice) by providing new disclosures and permits the three days to elapse, the property is sold, or three years expire.[13] Rescission is effective when mailed.[14]

At least two courts have stated rescission is not necessarily automatic, and may require a court ruling before the rescission is effective (such as would be the case in a foreclosure action).[15]

POTENTIAL RECOVERY

If the loan is subject to HOEPA and the lender does not provide the required notices, including those required to be given 3 days before the closing date, then the lender has failed to provide a "material disclosure" and the homeowner may rescind the loan up to three years after closing. [16]

If rescission is available, *all* of the following layers of relief kick in:[17]

1) A right to immediately rescind the transaction,
2) A refund of all principal and interest payment made to the lender,
3) A refund of all closing costs paid at the time of closing,
4) A refund of any down payment made in connection with the loan,
5) Termination of the mortgage,
6) Keep the property if you have already paid it off, and

in addition to rescission, the lender is also liable for statutory damages in an amount equal to the sum of: [18]

---

[12] Although the case law indicates filing a complaint is sufficient notice, indicating notice within an Answer would suffice as notice, the author recommends taking the extra step as outlined here. *See, Taylor v. Domestic Remodeling, Inc.*, 97 F.3d96, 100 (5th Cir. 1996).

[13] *Beach v. Ocwen Fed. Bank*, 523 U.S. 410 (1998).

[14] 12 C.F.R. § 226.23(a)(2).

[15] "We agree that a borrower's notice of intent to rescind his loan transaction does not in and of itself automatically void the transaction. Rather, a rescission occurs under §1635 either when the creditor acknowledges the consumer's right to rescind or, in a contested case, such as this, when a court determines that the consumer is entitled to rescission." *Yamamoto v. Bank of New York* (C.A.9, 2003), 329 F.3d 1167" *Bank of New York v. Jordan*, 2007-Ohio-4293 (Ohio Ct. App. 8th Dist.)

[16] 12 C.F.R. § 226.23(a)(3).

[17] 15 U.S.C. § 1635(b).

[18] *White v. WMC Mortgage*, 2001 U.S. Dist. LEXIS 15907, at * 5 (E.D. Pa. July 31, 2001); *Williams v. Gelt*, 237 B.R. 590, 598-99 (E.D. Pa. 1999).

a. any actual damage sustained by such a person as a result of the failure to comply;[19]

b. Not less than $200 or greater than $2,000 if the home loan is not a home equity loan;[20]

c. Costs of the action, together with reasonable attorney's fees;[21] *and*

d. **An amount equal to the sum of all finance charges and fees paid by the consumer,** unless the creditor demonstrates the failure to comply is not material.[22] An assignee of the mortgage is liable for *all* claims that could be brought against the original lender.[23]

A TILA violation may be brought against a lender at any time as a defense to collecting the debt (including foreclosure), however there is a one year statute of limitations if seeking to bring an independent TILA action.[24]

The lender MUST act within 20 days after receipt of the notice of rescission to affect the rescission, or the borrower may keep the property without further obligation.[25]

STRATEGY

Look for credit life insurance in the settlement statement, as this must be included in the HOEPA calculations, although it is *not* required under normal TILA finance charges if the proper disclosures are given. Under HOEPA, it does not matter that disclosures were provided. Also look for affiliated business disclosure statements among the closing documents. (See Appendix R.) If Countrywide was the original lender, look for LandSafe, which is a wholly owned subsidiary of Countrywide Home Loans.[26] You may want to look at the extensive list of wholly owned Countrywide subsidiaries that can be found as part of its Form 10-K filing with the SEC if Countrywide was involved with your loan.

(See http://www.secinfo.com/dVut2.t21n.n.htm)

---

[19] 15 U.S.C. § 1640(a)(1).
[20] 15 U.S.C. § 1640(a)(2)(A)(iii).
[21] 15 U.S.C. § 1640(a)(3).
[22] 15 U.S.C. § 1640(a)(4).
[23] 15 U.S.C. § 1641(d)(1).
[24] 15 U.S.C. § 1640(e).
[25] 15 U.S.C. § 1635(b).
[26] Countrywide Financial Corp.'s 12/31/2007 Form 10-K filed with the SEC on 2/29/2008, as reported at http://www.secinfo.com/dVut2.t21n.n.htm (last visited August 10, 2008).

APPLICABLE LAW OR CIVIL RULE

TILA begins at 15 U.S.C. § 1601. TILA is implemented by regulation according to the Board of Governors of the Federal Reserve System (the "Board").[27] The Board has issued its regulations, calling them Regulation Z, which implements TILA for homeowners. Regulation Z begins at 12 C.F.R. § 226. HOEPA is at 12 C.F.R. § 226.32.

ELEMENTS

To **rescind** the transaction for a violation of HOEPA, a borrower must demonstrate:

1) The property subject to the loan is used as the principal dwelling of the person to whom credit is extended;[28]
2) The loan was *not* used to purchase or construct the property subject to the loan;[29]
3) The loan was a refinance of a previous loan either:
   a. held by a different lender than the original, (the borrower switched lenders), or
   b. the borrower refinanced with the original lender and took cash-out of the property;
4) It has not been 3 years since the loan's closing date for rescission;[30]
   a. Damages other than rescission, including damages in an amount equal to the sum of all finance charges and fees paid, may be brought at anytime as a defense as recoupment/set-off for the lender's damages.[31]
5) One of the two apply:
   a. The annual percentage rate will exceed by more than 8 percentage points for first lien loans or 10% for subordinate-lien loans the H-15 rates posted by the Federal Reserve ,[32] **or**
   b. The total points and fees payable by the consumer exceed the greater of 8 percent of the total loan amount, *or* the dollar amount stated in the following chart:[33]

---

[27] 15 U.S.C. § 1602(b).

[28] 12 C.F.R. § 226.3(a).

[29] 12 C.F.R. § 226.32(a)(2)(i).

[30] 15 U.S.C. § 1635(a); *Beach v. Ocwen*, 523 U.S. 410 (1998). Note that some state laws may strengthen the ability to use this violation as an offset in a foreclosure action at any time. For example, see 735 ILCS 5/13-207.

[31] 15 U.S.C. § 1640(e).

[32] 12 C.R.F. § 226.32(a)(1)(i). http://www.federalreserve.gov/releases/h15/ (last visited June 20, 2008) Look for the interest rate "as of the fifteenth day of the month immediately preceding the month in which the application for the extension of credit was received by the creditor." *Id.*

[33] While often overlooked, the maximum dollar amount is *not* $400. 12 C.F.R. § 226.32(a)(1)(ii). Instead, it starts at $400 and is adjusted each year with the rate of inflation, as indicated by the CPI. The Federal Reserve publishes the annual adjustments in the staff notes to Official Staff Commentary to 12 C.F.R. § 226.32(a)(1)(ii). Use the figures from the year your loan closed – not the current years figures.

Year of Loan Closing	Percent Increase	Max Fee Amount Charged for that Year
1995	0	$ 400
1996	3.00%	$ 412
1997	2.90%	$ 424
1998	2.50%	$ 435
1999	1.40%	$ 441
2000	2.30%	$ 451
2001	3.10%	$ 465
2002	3.27%	$ 480
2003	1.64%	$ 488
2004	2.22%	$ 499
2005	2.29%	$ 510
2006	3.51%	$ 528
2007	3.55%	$ 547
2008	2.56%	$ 561

6) If the loan qualifies under HOEPA, then the following disclosures must have been given to the consumer:

    a.   "You are not required to complete this agreement merely because you have received these disclosures or have signed a loan application."[34]

    b.   "If you obtain this loan, the lender will have a mortgage on your home. You could lose your home, and any money you have put into it, if you do not meet your obligations under the loan."[35]

    c.   *Annual percentage rate.* The annual percentage rate.[36]

    d.   *Regular payment; balloon payment.* The amount of the regular monthly (or other periodic) payment and the amount of any balloon payment.[37]

    e.   *Variable-rate.* For variable-rate transactions, a statement that the interest rate and monthly payment may increase, and the amount of the single maximum monthly payment, based on the maximum interest rate required to be disclosed under § 226.30.[38]

    f.   *Amount borrowed.* For a mortgage refinancing, the total amount the consumer will borrow, as reflected by the face amount of the note; and where the amount borrowed includes premiums or other charges for optional credit insurance or

---

[34] 15 U.S.C. § 1639(a)(1); 12 C.F.R. § 226.32(c)(1).
[35] 15 U.S.C. § 1639(a)(1); 12 C.F.R. § 226.32(c)(1).
[36] 15 U.S.C. § 1639(a)(2); 12 C.F.R. § 226.32(c)(2).
[37] 12 C.F.R. § 226.32(c)(3).
[38] 12 C.F.R. § 226.32(c)(4).

debt-cancellation coverage, that fact shall be stated, grouped together with the disclosure of the amount borrowed. The disclosure of the amount borrowed shall be treated as accurate if it is not more than $100 above or below the amount required to be disclosed.[39]

7) Additionally, if the loan qualifies under HOEPA, then the lender must have provided the following disclosures to the borrower *three days prior to the loan closing*:[40]

    a. "You are not required to complete this agreement merely because you have received these disclosures or have signed a loan application."

    b. "If you obtain this loan, the lender will have a mortgage on your home. You could lose your home, and any money you have put into it, if you do not meet your obligations under the loan."

    c. *Annual percentage rate.* The annual percentage rate.

8) Also, if a loan qualifies under HOEPA, the loan may not include any of the following terms:

    a. Balloon payments, unless it is a construction bridge loan with less than a one year term.[41]

    b. Negative amortization.[42]

    c. Advance payments. (A payment schedule that consolidated more than two periodic payments and pays them in advance from the proceeds.[43]

    d. An increase in the interest rate after default.[44]

    e. Rebates. (A refund calculated by a method less favorable than the actuarial method for rebates of interest arising from a loan acceleration due to default.[45]

    f. Prepayment penalty, unless limited to the first five years, the source of funds is not a refinancing by the creditor, and the consumers total monthly debts do not exceed 50% DTI.[46]

9) Finally, the following practices are prohibited in connection with a HOEPA loan:[47]

    a. Home improvement contracts. Pay a contractor under a home improvement contract from the proceeds of a mortgage covered by HOEPA, other than:

        i. By an instrument payable to the consumer or jointly to the consumer and the contractor; or

---

[39] 12 C.F.R. § 226.32(c)(5).
[40] 15 U.S.C. § 1639(b)(1).
[41] 12 C.F.R. § 226.32(d)(1)(i)-(ii).
[42] 12 C.F.R. § 226.32(d)(2).
[43] 12 C.F.R. § 226.32(d)(3)
[44] 12 C.F.R. § 226.32(d)(4).
[45] 12 C.F.R. § 226.32(d)(5).
[46] 12 C.F.R. § 226.32(d)(7).
[47] 12 C.F.R. § 226.34. The list that follows is taken directly from the code.

      ii. At the election of the consumer, through a third-party escrow agent in accordance with terms established in a written agreement signed by the consumer, the creditor, and the contractor prior to the disbursement.

b. Notice to assignee. Sell or otherwise assign a mortgage subject to HOEPA without furnishing the following statement to the purchaser or assignee: ``Notice: This is a mortgage subject to special rules under the federal Truth in Lending Act. Purchasers or assignees of this mortgage could be liable for all claims and defenses with respect to the mortgage that the borrower could assert against the creditor."

c. Refinancings within one-year period. Within one year of having extended credit subject to Sec. 226.32, refinance any loan subject to Sec. 226.32 to the same borrower into another loan subject to Sec. 226.32, unless the refinancing is in the borrower's interest. An assignee holding or servicing an extension of mortgage credit subject to Sec. 226.32, shall not, for the remainder of the one-year period following the date of origination of the credit, refinance any loan subject to Sec. 226.32 to the same borrower into another loan subject to Sec. 226.32, unless the refinancing is in the borrower's interest. A creditor (or assignee) is prohibited from engaging in acts or practices to evade this provision, including a pattern or practice of arranging for the refinancing of its own loans by affiliated or unaffiliated creditors, or modifying a loan agreement (whether or not the existing loan is satisfied and replaced by the new loan) and charging a fee.

d. Repayment ability. Engage in a pattern or practice of extending credit subject to Sec. 226.32 to a consumer based on the consumer's collateral without regard to the consumer's repayment ability, including the consumer's current and expected income, current obligations, and employment. There is a presumption that a creditor has violated this paragraph (a)(4) if the creditor engages in a pattern or practice of making loans subject to Sec. 226.32 without verifying and documenting consumers' repayment ability.

WORKSHEETS / FORMULAS

To calculate whether the fees charged are in excess of the permitted HOEPA charges, first add all of the fees included in the following chart (this will give you the total HOEPA "points and fees").[48]

HOEPA Calculations

	Amount of finance charges appearing on the **HUD-1 Settlement Statement** (calculate from the TILA chapter), *including those charges you have estimated should have been included in the finance charge.*[49] Do not include the entire amount of the finance charge calculated in the previous chapter. Instead, just include those fees appearing on the HUD-1 Settlement Statement. For example, if the total HUD-1 fees show $8,000, but only $6,500 of the fees are finance charge fees, then only use $6,500 here.
-	Subtract pre-paid interest[50]
-	Subtract loan interest (if needed).[51]
+	Any mortgage broker fees not already included in the finance charge.[52]
+	*Add any of the following fees *if the fee goes to an affiliate of the creditor* (e.g., Countrywide owns LandSafe title/credit): title examination, abstract of title, endorsements, title insurance, property survey, fees for preparing documents, loan-related documents, deeds, mortgages, reconveyance or settlement documents, notary and credit reporting fees, property appraisal fees, property inspection fees, pest inspection fees, flood cert. fees.[53]
+	*All premiums or other charges for credit life, accident, health, or loss-of-income insurance, or debt-cancellation coverage (whether or not the debt-cancellation coverage is insurance under applicable law) that provides for cancellation of all or part of the consumer's liability in the event of the loss of life, health, or income or in the case of accident, written in connection with the credit transaction.[54]
=	TOTAL "Points and Fees"

---

[48] 12 C.F.R. § 226.32(b)(1); *Jones v. Aames Funding Corp.*, Civil Action No. 04-CV-4799, 2006 WL 2845689 (E.D.Pa.)
[49] 12 C.F.R. § 226.32(b)(1)(i).
[50] Id.
[51] Id.
[52] 12 C.F.R. § 226.32(b)(1)(ii).
[53] 12 C.F.R. § 226.32(b)(1)(iii).
[54] 12 C.F.R. § 226.32(b)(1)(iv).

After you have added up each of the fees, next calculate the "total loan amount," as provided in the next worksheet.[55] The total loan amount is *not* the face value of the loan, but may be a lower number if the creditor charged you any of the fees in the worksheet above (that are asterisked). This is good for the consumer, as it makes the division more consumer-friendly.

In plain English, the statute allows the consumer to decrease the total loan amount by the amounts asterisked in the worksheet above. Thus, a $10,000 loan yields a $9,600 "total loan amount" if the "*" fees listed above equal $400. After the "total loan amount" is determined, divide the two numbers to obtain the loan's HOEPA percentage.[56] If this number exceeds .08, or 8%, then the loan violates HOEPA.[57]

The "total loan amount" is determined as follows:[58]

	"Total Loan Amount" Calculations
	Start with the "Amount Financed," as indicated toward the top of the Truth in Lending Statement
-	Subtract those fees listed in the above worksheet from the first "*" (fees going to a creditor affiliate), that were financed into the loan (not paid in cash by borrower).
-	Subtract those fees listed in the above worksheet from the second "*" (fees for credit life, etc.) that were financed into the loan (not paid in cash by borrower).
=	This is the "total loan amount."

After completing both worksheets, divide the two numbers to obtain the loan's HOEPA percentage.[59] If this number exceeds 8%, then the loan violates HOEPA.[60]

The total "points and fees" for this loan are: _____ The total "loan amount" is: _____ .

Dividing these numbers yields the following percentage: _____

An example:

---

[55] Official Staff Commentary to 12 C.F.R. § 226.32(a)(1)(ii); *Jones v. Aames Funding Corp.*, Civil Action No. 04-CV-4799, 2006 WL 2845689 (E.D.Pa.)

[56] 12 C.F.R. § 226.32(a)(1)(ii).

[57] Id.

[58] Official Staff Commentary to 12 C.F.R. § 226.32(a)(1)(ii); *Jones v. Aames Funding Corp.*, Civil Action No. 04-CV-4799, 2006 WL 2845689 (E.D.Pa.)

[59] 12 C.F.R. § 226.32(a)(1)(ii).

[60] Id.

If the loans total points and fees equal $700, and the total loan amount equals $10,000, then dividing $700 / 10,000 yields .07 or 7.0%. That loan would not violate HOEPA.

If the percentage of the fees to the loan is in excess of 8%, then the loan triggers the disclosure requirements of HOEPA.

Please see the Official Staff Commentary to 12 C.F.R. § 226.32(a)(1)(ii) and *Jones v. Aames Funding Corp.*, Civil Action No. 04-CV-4799, 2006 WL 2845689 (E.D.Pa.) for additional information and examples concerning the calculation of HOEPA figures.

HOEPA CHECKLIST

- ☐ The property subject to the loan is used as the principal dwelling of the person to whom credit is extended;[61]
- ☐ The loan was *not* used to purchase or construct the property subject to the loan;
- ☐ The loan was a refinance of a previous loan either:
  - o held by a different lender than the original, (the borrower switched lenders), or
  - o the borrower refinanced with the original lender and took cash-out of the property;
- ☐ It has not been 3 years since the loan's closing date for rescission;[62]
  - o Damages other than rescission, including damages in an amount equal to the sum of all finance charges and fees paid, may be brought at anytime as a defense as recoupment/set-off for the lender's damages.[63]
- ☐ One of the two apply:
  - o The annual percentage rate will exceed by more than 8 percentage points for first lien loans or 10% for subordinate-lien loans the H-15 rates posted by the Federal Reserve[64] **or**
  - o The total points and fees payable by the consumer exceed the greater of 8 percent of the total loan amount, *or* the dollar amount stated in the chart in the elements section of this chapter.[65]

---

[61] 12 C.F.R. § 226.3(a).

[62] 15 U.S.C. § 1635(a); *Beach v. Ocwen*, 523 U.S. 410 (1998). Note that some state laws may strengthen the ability to use this violation as an offset in a foreclosure action at any time. For example, see 735 ILCS 5/13-207.

[63] 15 U.S.C. § 1640(e).

[64] 12 C.R.F. § 226.32(a)(1)(i). http://www.federalreserve.gov/releases/h15 (last visited June 23, 2008) Look for the interest rate "as of the fifteenth day of the month immediately preceding the month in which the application for the extension of credit was received by the creditor." *Id.*

[65] While often overlooked, the maximum dollar amount is *not* $400. 12 C.F.R. § 226.32(a)(1)(ii). Instead, it starts at $400 and is adjusted each year with the rate of inflation, as indicated by the CPI. The Federal Reserve publishes the annual adjustments in the staff notes to Official Staff Commentary to 12 C.F.R. § 226.32(a)(1)(ii). Use the figures from the year your loan closed – not the current years figures.

- ☐ If the loan qualifies under HOEPA, then the following disclosures must have been given or the loan violates HOEPA:
  - ○ "You are not required to complete this agreement merely because you have received these disclosures or have signed a loan application."[66]
  - ○ "If you obtain this loan, the lender will have a mortgage on your home. You could lose your home, and any money you have put into it, if you do not meet your obligations under the loan."[67]
  - ○ *Annual percentage rate.* The annual percentage rate.[68]
  - ○ *Regular payment; balloon payment.* The amount of the regular monthly (or other periodic) payment and the amount of any balloon payment.[69]
  - ○ *Variable-rate.* For variable-rate transactions, a statement that the interest rate and monthly payment may increase, and the amount of the single maximum monthly payment, based on the maximum interest rate required to be disclosed under § 226.30.[70]
  - ○ *Amount borrowed.* For a mortgage refinancing, the total amount the consumer will borrow, as reflected by the face amount of the note; and where the amount borrowed includes premiums or other charges for optional credit insurance or debt-cancellation coverage, that fact shall be stated, grouped together with the disclosure of the amount borrowed. The disclosure of the amount borrowed shall be treated as accurate if it is not more than $100 above or below the amount required to be disclosed.[71]
- ☐ Additionally, if the loan qualifies under HOEPA, then the lender must have provided the following disclosures to the borrower *three days prior to the loan closing* or the loan violates HOEPA: [72]
  - ○ "You are not required to complete this agreement merely because you have received these disclosures or have signed a loan application."
  - ○ "If you obtain this loan, the lender will have a mortgage on your home. You could lose your home, and any money you have put into it, if you do not meet your obligations under the loan."
  - ○ *Annual percentage rate.* The annual percentage rate.
- ☐ If a loan qualifies under HOEPA, the loan may not include any of the following terms:
  - ○ Balloon payments, unless it is a construction bridge loan with less than a one year term.[73]

---

[66] 15 U.S.C. § 1639(a)(1); 12 C.F.R. § 226.32(c)(1).
[67] 15 U.S.C. § 1639(a)(1); 12 C.F.R. § 226.32(c)(1).
[68] 15 U.S.C. § 1639(a)(2); 12 C.F.R. § 226.32(c)(2).
[69] 12 C.F.R. § 226.32(c)(3).
[70] 12 C.F.R. § 226.32(c)(4).
[71] 12 C.F.R. § 226.32(c)(5).
[72] 15 U.S.C. § 1639(b)(1).
[73] 12 C.F.R. § 226.32(d)(1)(i)-(ii).

- o Negative amortization.[74]
- o Advance payments. (A payment schedule that consolidated more than two periodic payments and pays them in advance from the proceeds.[75]
- o An increase in the interest rate after default.[76]
- o Rebates. (A refund calculated by a method less favorable than the actuarial method for rebates of interest arising from a loan acceleration due to default.[77]
- o Prepayment penalty, unless limited to the first five years, the source of funds is not a refinancing by the creditor, and the consumers total monthly debts do not exceed 50% DTI.[78]

DEFENSES

AFFIRMATIVE DEFENSES

Properly included as an affirmative defense, and survives even when counterclaim dismissed.[79] Use the same paragraphs as in the defenses:

[paragraph no.] The mortgage and note are void for lack of compliance with the Truth in Lending Act, 15 U.S.C. § 1601, et seq. and The Home Ownership and Equity Protection Act (HOEPA), 12 C.F.R. § 226.32;

[paragraph no.] The defendant is entitled to, and hereby exercises [his/her], right to rescind the loan transaction for lack of compliance with the Truth in Lending Act, 15 U.S.C. § 1601, et seq. and HOEPA, 12 C.F.R. § 226.32;

---

[74] 12 C.F.R. § 226.32(d)(2).
[75] 12 C.F.R. § 226.32(d)(3)
[76] 12 C.F.R. § 226.32(d)(4).
[77] 12 C.F.R. § 226.32(d)(5).
[78] 12 C.F.R. § 226.32(d)(7).
[79] "We first address the Bank's argument that Jordan cannot argue rescission, because the trial court dismissed her counterclaims, which included a claim for damages under §1640, as a sanction for her failure to comply with its discovery order. We note that although Jordan's counterclaims were dismissed, she also asserted rescission as an affirmative defense. Those defenses remain valid even after the dismissal of her counterclaims. Accordingly, although Jordan is precluded from pursuing any claim for damages based upon her right to rescind, she is entitled to assert rescission as an affirmative defense to the Bank's foreclosure action." *Bank of New York v. Jordan*, 2007-Ohio-4293 (Ohio Ct. App. 8th Dist.)

STARTER DISCOVERY

INTERROGATORIES

Interrogatories asking the plaintiff to produce the mathematical calculations used in the loan may prove futile in the plaintiff is not the original lender, even if the plaintiff is subject to all defenses as the original lender. It may be more straight forward to use requests for admissions on each individual part of the mathematical equations to get the plaintiff to admit a violation exists.

However, if the original lender is also named as a defendant, it would be wise to serve a series of interrogatories on it to ascertain how it made its HOEPA calculations. Additionally, you would certainly want to ask for it to disclose all of its affiliated businesses to determine if your HOEPA calculations can be boosted. (All affiliated business agreements must be included in the calculations.)[80]

REQUESTS FOR ADMISSIONS

Requests for admissions may be very effective in getting the lender to admit each step in the mathematical equation that yields the HOEPA violation. This will also significantly narrow the issues necessary for the court to resolve with respect to a HOEPA violation. For example, the violation may turn on one specific fee that the lender claims should not be included in the calculation and the borrower claims should be included. The requests for admissions should be specifically tailored to the particular math you want admitted.

REQUESTS FOR THE PRODUCTION OF DOCUMENTS

You may seek to discover the manuals used by the lender in calculating HOEPA if it is a named defendant. You may also seek to use a subpoena duces tecum, if appropriate, or bring the original lender into the lawsuit via third party complaint. The documents requested would include any training manuals, memoranda, and policies with respect to HOEPA calculations. Many times the broker involved in the transaction will communicate with the lender on HOEPA, if the fees are nearing HOEPA's threshold. Seek that communication through discovery also.

---

[80] 12 C.F.R. § 226.32(b)(1)(iii).

COUNTER CLAIMS

Because there are statutory damages associated with a rescission, you may chose to include a counterclaim seeking payment of those damages. This counter claim may be heavy on the legal assertions, but it puts the plaintiff on notice of your claim and gives it an opportunity to admit or deny each.

COUNT ONE

[paragraph no.] Defendant alleges the *[mortgage/deed of trust]* and note are void for lack of compliance with the Truth in Lending Act, 15 U.S.C. § 1601, et seq. and The Home Ownership and Equity Protection Act (HOEPA), 12 C.F.R. § 226.32, et seq.;

[paragraph no.] Defendant alleges [he/she] is entitled to rescind the loan transaction for lack of compliance with the Truth in Lending Act, 15 U.S.C. § 1601, et seq. and HOEPA, 12 C.F.R. § 226.32, et seq.;

[paragraph no.] Defendant alleges Plaintiff is liable to *[him/her]* in an amount equal to the sum of *[dollar amount]*, which represents Defendant's actual damages sustained as a result of the failure to comply with the Truth in Lending Act, 15 U.S.C. § 1601, et seq. and HOEPA, 12 C.F.R. § 226.32;

[paragraph no.] Defendant alleges Plaintiff is liable to *[him/her]* in an amount of $2,000 for statutory damages under the Truth in Lending Act, 15 U.S.C. § 1601, et seq. and HOEPA, 12 C.F.R. § 226.32.;

[paragraph no.] Defendant alleges Plaintiff is liable to *[him/her]* in an amount of $XXX, which is equal to the sum of all finance charges and fees paid by the consumer, for statutory damages under the Truth in Lending Act, 15 U.S.C. § 1601, et seq. and HOEPA, 12 C.F.R. § 226.32, pursuant to 15 U.S.C. § 1640(a)(4).;

THIRD PARTY CLAIMS

Rescission is brought against the holder of the loan, as the holder (as assignee) is liable for the rescission.[81] The assignee "shall be subject to all claims and defenses with respect to that mortgage that the consumer could assert against the creditor."[82] Thus, you do not need to bring this claim against a third party because the holder inherits *all claims and defenses* that could be asserted against the original lender.

---

[81] 15 U.S.C. § 1641(c).
[82] 15 U.S.C. 1641(d)(1).

DEFENSE #4: FAILURE TO PROVIDE A CORRECT NOTICE OF THE RIGHT TO RESCIND

FAILURE TO PROVIDE A CORRECT NOTICE OF THE RIGHT TO RESCIND

DEFINED

In a refinance, the Truth in Lending Act requires every qualified customer be provided an accurate and correct notice of his or her right to rescind the transaction within three business days after the closing. If the lender fails to provide the notice, the borrower can rescind the entire transaction up to three years later, subject to the rules stated below.[1]

The borrower can also rescind the transaction up to three years after closing if the rescission notice "is not the appropriate form of written notice published and adopted by the Board or a comparable written notice…"[2]

A signed statement to the effect that the consumer received the required notices creates a rebuttable presumption only.[3] A borrower cannot sign a document at closing stating he does *not* wish to rescind the loan.[4] Additionally, the lender may not provide a correct notice to the borrower, but contradict the information in the notice contained elsewhere.[5]

SPOT IT!

The document you should look for is among the closing documents provided on the day of closing. It may be titled something similar to, "NOTICE OF RIGHT TO CANCEL." It does not need to be signed by you, although it may have an acknowledgment of receipt at the bottom with your signature on it.[6] Compare this document with the requirements set forth below in the checklist.

The following states consider property gained during mortgage to be community property: Arizona, California, Idaho, Louisiana, Nevada, New Mexico, Texas, Washington, Wisconsin. In these states, the borrower's spouse arguably has a security interest in the transaction, necessitating the need for the spouse to receive a copy of the notice also.

In these states, beyond rescission, see an attorney about the doctrine of tenancy by the entirety (whereby property is automatically owned by both married partners).

---

[1] *Westbank v. Maurer*, 658 N.E.2d 1381 (Ill.App. 2nd Dist. 1995).
[2] 15 U.S.C. § 1635(i)(1)(B).
[3] 15 U.S.C. § 1635(c). *Bryant v. Mortgage Capital Resource Corp.*, 2002 U.S. Dist. LEXIS 1566, at **11-17 (N.D. Ga. Jan. 2002).
[4] *Rodash v. AIB Mortgage Co.*, 16 F.3d 1142 (11th Cir. 1994).
[5] *Jenkins v. Landmark Mtge. Corp.*, 696 F.Supp. 1089 (W.D.Va. 1988); *Apaydin v. Citibank Federal Savings Bank*, 201 B.R. 716, 723-24 (Bankr.E.D.Pa.1996).
[6] 15 U.S.C. § 1635(c).

LIMITATIONS

A borrower's right to bring a lawsuit based on this section, or use it in the defense of a foreclosure action, expires three years after the date the loan was consummated (3 years after the closing date).[7] A lawsuit based on this section does not apply to refinance loans done with the original lender, unless taking cash-out.[8] A lawsuit based on this section cannot be brought if the loan was used to purchase or construct the property subject to the loan.[9] However, if the loan on the primary residence was a refinance to obtain cash to purchase another property, that loan may be subject to rescission rights.

The general TILA requirements still apply. For mortgage purposes, TILA applies to loans on properties with 4 units or less, but includes transactions for individual condominium units, cooperative units, mobile homes, and trailers, if used as a residence.[10] It does not apply to business, commercial, agricultural, or organizational credit.

> *Worth Repeating: As soon as it is clear the borrower has a right to rescind the transaction, it is critical that Notice of Rescission is mailed to the lenders and servicers immediately. This is because the right to rescission ends when the creditor cures the violation (unless you have already mailed a signed notice of rescission) by providing new disclosures and permits the three days to elapse, the property is sold, or three years expire.[11] Rescission is effective when mailed.[12]*

POTENTIAL RECOVERY

FOR A LOAN USED TO ACQUIRE OR CONSTRUCT A PROPERTY

A loan used to acquire or construct a property is not eligible. "Cash-out" refinances on the primary residence used the proceeds to buy another property are eligible. Then the loan on the primary residence might be subject to this section as a qualified refinance.

---

[7] 15 U.S.C. § 1635(f).
[8] 15 U.S.C. § 1635(e)(2).
[9] 15 U.S.C. § 1635(1).
[10] 12 C.F.R. § 226.2(a)(19).
[11] *Beach v. Ocwen Fed. Bank*, 523 U.S. 410 (1998).
[12] 12 C.F.R. § 226.23(a)(2).

FOR A LOAN USED TO REFINANCE A PROPERTY

This section is specifically designed for people that refinanced their *primary residence* with a different lender than the original, or with the original lender taking cash-out.[13] Failing to provide a valid notice of your right to rescind triggers **all** of the following layers of relief:[14]

1) A right to immediately rescind the transaction,
2) A refund of all principal and interest payment made to the lender,
3) A refund of all closing costs paid at the time of closing,
4) A refund of any down payment made in connection with the loan,
5) Termination of the mortgage,
6) Keep the property if you have already paid it off, and
7) A borrower able to rescind the loan is also able to also secure damages for general TILA violations, as described in the previous chapter.[15]

Additionally, TILA permits a person who successfully enforces their right to rescission to be entitled to the costs of the action, together with a reasonable attorney's fee.[16]

Further, the lender is liable in an amount equal to the sum of the following: 1) any actual damage sustained by such a person as a result of the failure, and 2) statutory damages not less than $200 or greater than $2,000 if the home loan is not a home equity loan.[17]

After the lender repays the borrower, the borrower must tender the home to the lender at the property's address. The lender MUST act within 20 days to act, or you keep the property.[18] The borrower may obtain damages if the lender fails to honor a valid rescission.

FOR SECOND MORTGAGES AND HELOCS

Home equity Lines of Credit (HELOC) are covered, as are second mortgages, when the loans are not used as part of the property's purchase or construction.[19] However, each advance after an initial advance on a HELOC is not subject to an individual notice, if treated as a single transaction.[20]

---

[13] 15 U.S.C. § 1635(a).
[14] 15 U.S.C. § 1635(b).
[15] 15 U.S.C. § 1635(g).
[16] 15 U.S.C. § 1640(a)(3).
[17] 15 U.S.C. § 1640(a)(1), (2); *White v. WMC Mortgage*, 2001 U.S. Dist. LEXIS 15907, at * 5 (E.D. Pa. July 31, 2001); *Williams v. Gelt*, 237 B.R. 590, 598-99 (E.D. Pa. 1999).
[18] 15 U.S.C. § 1635(b).
[19] 15 U.S.C. § 1640(e); 12 CFR § 226.23(f). Some courts start the clock once you have a judicial ruling stating rescission is granted.
[20] 12 CFR § 226.23(c)(6); 12 CFR § 226.23(f)

STRATEGY

If the lender realizes it needed to send you a proper notice or material disclosures and attempts to deliver a corrected version of the documents to you, make sure you sign the rescission notice where it indicates to rescind, make copies, and send back via registered mail to the lender (mail with tracking number). This author would take the preemptive step of mailing a notice of rescission as soon as an error is recognized to ensure it is received within the three year statute of limitations. The rescission notice is effective when mailed.[21] If mailing, it would be wise to send the notice certified mail.

APPLICABLE LAW OR CIVIL RULE

TILA's rescission rights can be found at 15 U.S.C. § 1635 and 12 C.F.R. § 226.23. The requirements of the rescission forms, as described in the checklist below, are found within the Board's regulations at 12 C.F.R. § 226.23.

ELEMENTS

To prove a violation of TILA, a borrower must demonstrate:

1) The property subject to the loan is used as the principal dwelling of the person to whom credit is extended.
2) The loan was not used to purchase or construct the property subject to the loan.
3) The loan was a refinance of a previous loan either:
    a. held by a different lender than the original, (the borrower switched lenders), or
    b. the borrower refinanced with the original lender and took cash-out of the property.
4) It has not been 3 years since the loan's closing date, and
5) The notice of your right to rescind was incorrect (use checklist on the next page).[22]

---

[21] 12 C.F.R. § 226.23(a)(2).
[22] 15 U.S.C. § 1635(a).

NOTICE OF RIGHT TO RESCIND CHECKLIST

To determine if a notice of the right to rescind is correct or valid, look to the following:[23]

- ☐ Ask the borrower if he or she was told anything about their right to cancel at closing which was inconsistent with the three-day rescission period.[24]
- ☐ Determine if the elements can be established that might impose duty to provide notice to consumer:
  - o The property subject to the loan is used as the principal dwelling of the person to whom credit is extended.
  - o The loan was *not* used to purchase or construct the property subject to the loan.
  - o The loan was a refinance of a previous loan either:
    - ▪ held by a different lender than the original, (the borrower switched lenders), or
    - ▪ the borrower refinanced with the original lender and took cash-out of the property.
  - o It has not been 3 years since the loan's closing date.
  - o The notice of your right to rescind was incorrect (use checklist below).[25]
- ☐ Each consumer entitled to rescind must have been given two copies of the notice.[26]
  - o Not limited to a borrower, but also any "natural person in whose principal dwelling a security interest is or will be retained or acquired, if that person's ownership interest in the dwelling is or will be subject to the security interest."[27]
  - o The following states consider property gained during mortgage to be community property, which means the spouse likely has a security interest in the home and must receive their own copy of the notice.
    - ▪ Arizona, California, Idaho, Louisiana, Nevada, New Mexico, Texas, Washington, Wisconsin.
- ☐ The notice must identify the transaction and must be on a separate document.[28]
- ☐ The notice must conspicuously disclose: the retention or acquisition of a security interest in the consumer's principal dwelling.[29]
- ☐ The notice must conspicuously disclose the consumers right to rescind.

---

[23] 12 C.F.R. § 226.23.

[24] *Jenkins v. Landmark Mtge. Corp.*, 696 F.Supp. 1089 (W.D.Va. 1988); *Apaydin v. Citibank Federal Savings Bank*, 201 B.R. 716, 723-24 (Bkrtcy.E.D.Pa. 1996).

[25] 15 U.S.C. § 1635(a).

[26] 12 C.F.R. § 226.23(b)(1).

[27] 12 C.F.R. § 226.2(a)(11).

[28] 12 C.F.R. § 226.23(b)(1).

[29] 12 C.F.R. § 226.23(b)(1)(i); *Williams v. Lafferty*, 698 F.2d 767 (1983); *Reynolds v. D &N Bank*, 792 F.Supp 1035 (E.D.Mich. 1992).

☐ The notice must conspicuously disclose: how to exercise the right to rescind, designating the address of the creditor's place of business to mail the notice.[30]

☐ **The date the rescission period ends.**[31] The rescission period lasts until midnight of the third business day following the consummation of the transaction.[32] This date must be accurate! (Either exactly accurate, or too much time given.)[33]

    o **The date must be present!** Failing to state the date is grounds for rescission.[34]

    o Check the date indicated on the notice against the date the HUD-1 Settlement statement was signed. Sometimes signing at a borrower's home may cause incorrect dates to be recorded.

    o Look back to a calendar from the day the loan closed, and count three days after the closing date. If any of the following days is included in the dates, then skip that date and continue counting thereafter.

        ▪ The following days are NOT included in any count:[35]

        ▪ **Sundays**

        ▪ New Year's Day, January 1.

        ▪ Birthday of Martin Luther King, Jr., the third Monday in January.

        ▪ Washington's Birthday, the third Monday in February.

        ▪ Memorial Day, the last Monday in May.

        ▪ Independence Day, July 4.

        ▪ Labor Day, the first Monday in September.

        ▪ Columbus Day, the second Monday in October.

        ▪ Veterans Day, November 11.

        ▪ Thanksgiving Day, the fourth Thursday in November.

        ▪ Christmas Day, December 25.

☐ The notice must conspicuously disclose: The effects of rescission, as follows:[36]

    o When a consumer rescinds a transaction, the security interest giving rise to the right of rescission becomes void and the consumer shall not be liable for any amount, including any finance charge.[37]

---

[30] 12 C.F.R. § 226.23(b)(1)(iii).

[31] 12 C.F.R. § 226.23(b)(v).

[32] 15 U.S.C. § 1635(a).

[33] If the form is missing a date, the loan is rescindable. *Semar v. Platte Valley Federal Savings & Loan*, 791 F.2d 699, 702 (9th Cir. 1986). If the form is misdated, the loan is rescindable. *Taylor v. Domestic Remodeling, Inc.*, 97 F.3d 96, 99 (5th Cir. 1996) (incorrect rescission date combined with disbursement of loan constitutes violation of TILA). However, the time provided for in the notice may be longer than 3 days. *Hawaii Community Federal Credit Union v. Keka*, supra, 94 Haw. 213, 11 P.3d 1 (2000).

[34] *Semar v. Platte Valley Federal Savings & Loan*, 791 F.2d 699, 702 (9th Cir. 1986) (failing to provide the date rescission ends on the notice is grounds for rescission; there is no equitable discretion for the courts – rescission is required under the code).

[35] 12 C.F.R. § 226.2(a)(6):

[36] 12 C.F.R. § 226.23(b)(1)(iv).

[37] 12 C.F.R. § 226.23(d)(1).

- o Within 20 calendar days after receipt of a notice of rescission, the creditor shall return any money or property that has been given to anyone in connection with the transaction and shall take any action necessary to reflect the termination of the security interest.[38]
- o If the creditor has delivered any money or property, the consumer may retain possession until the creditor has met its obligation under paragraph (d)(2) [last bullet point] of this section. When the creditor has complied with that paragraph, the consumer shall tender the money or property to the creditor or, where the latter would be impracticable or inequitable, tender its reasonable value. At the consumer's option, tender of property may be made at the location of the property or at the consumer's residence. Tender of money must be made at the creditor's designated place of business. If the creditor does not take possession of the money or property within 20 calendar days after the consumer's tender, the consumer may keep it without further obligation.[39]
- o The procedures outlined in this paragraphs (d)(2) and (3) of this section may be modified by court order.[40]
- ☐ Determine if the consumer waived the right to rescind when the loan closed by documenting a bona fide personal financial emergency.[41]
  - o Must be a signed written statement bearing the signature of all the consumers entitled to rescind.[42]

DEFENSES

DEFENSES

A defense under this section to rescind applies to foreclosure actions, and is specifically permitted, subject to the 3 year time limitation.[43]

AFFIRMATIVE DEFENSES

[paragraph no.] The mortgage and note are void for lack of compliance with the Truth in Lending Act, 15 U.S.C. § 1601, et seq. and 12 C.F.R. § 226.1, et seq.;

---

[38] 12 C.F.R. § 226.23(d)(2).
[39] 12 C.F.R. § 226.23(d)(3).
[40] 12 C.F.R. § 226.23(d)(4)
[41] 12 C.F.R. § 226.23(e).
[42] 12 C.F.R. § 226.23(e)(1).
[43] 15 U.S.C. § 1635(i).

[paragraph no.] The mortgage and note are void for lack of providing a proper notice of rescission in compliance with the Truth in Lending Act, 15 U.S.C. § 1601, et seq. and 12 C.F.R. § 226.1, et seq.;

STARTER DISCOVERY

INTERROGATORIES

A failure to disclose under TILA can easily be established on the face of the documents, which might be better suited to Requests for Admissions rather than Interrogatories.

REQUESTS FOR ADMISSIONS

The objective here is to get the plaintiff to admit the existence of a problem within the notice, and then to admit that problem is a material violation of the statute. Actual deficiencies in disclosures are fairly straight forward to identify. If the plaintiff can admit the deficiencies exist, the road to judgment in the borrower's favor is paved.

[paragraph no.] Admit the *[Notice of Right to Rescind]* fails to state *[whatever is required and it does not include]*.

[paragraph no.] Admit the *[Notice of Right to Rescind]* should have disclosed *[state the correct date the notice should have indicated as the rescission ending date, as properly calculated for Sundays and holidays, i.e., May 10, 2007]* as the date upon which the defendant's right to rescission ended.

[paragraph no.] Admit the *[Notice of Right to Rescind]* states a date sooner than *[state correct date here, i.e., May 10, 2007]*.

REQUESTS FOR THE PRODUCTION OF DOCUMENTS

This is a statutory provision that requires the documents be proven, on their face, to be incorrect. If that can be accomplished, there may not be a need to request calendars or other materials as to how the lender calculated or created the notices. Also note that many times the foreclosing party is not the lender who drew the documents, so a request for production wouldn't even be appropriate against the successor-in-interest to the mortgage or note. Of course, if the original lender is brought in as a third party defendant, then document requests can be had.

COUNTER CLAIMS

Rescission may be properly raised as an affirmative defense. However, here is an example of a detailed allegation if used as a counter claim.[44]

COUNT ONE

[paragraph no.] Defendant realleges as if set forth in this document paragraphs *[1-25]* of the Answer;

[paragraph no.] Defendant alleges defendant was required to be provided a notice of his/her right to rescission in accordance with the Truth in Lending Act, 15 U.S.C. § 1601, et seq. and 12 C.F.R. § 226.1, et seq.;

[paragraph no.] Defendant alleges defendant was required to be provided a notice of his/her right to rescission in accordance with 15 U.S.C. § 1635 and 12 C.F.R. § 226.23;

[paragraph no.] Defendant alleges the right to rescission received by him/her was defective because *[state the reasons why it was defective]*;

[paragraph no.] Defendant alleges that due to the defect in the notice of his/her right to rescind, her/his right to rescind has not expired under 15 U.S.C. § 1635 and/or 12 C.F.R. § 226.23;

[paragraph no.] Defendant alleges the defective notice of his right to rescind is apparent on the face of the loan documents.

[paragraph no.] Defendant alleges liability for the defective notice of his right to rescind and for any TILA claims for monetary damages runs against the plaintiff, as assignee, because the violations are apparent on the face of the loan documents under 15 U.S.C. § 1641(a).

[paragraph no.] Defendant alleges Plaintiff is liable to Defendant for damages for the defective notice of his/her right to rescind.

[paragraph no.] Defendant alleges Plaintiff is liable to Defendant for equitable and statutory damages for the defective notice of the right to rescind.

PRAYER FOR RELIEF

WHEREFORE, Defendant prays this court:

---

[44] Several of these allegations may be matters of law not suited for a counter claim, but these allegations give the plaintiff an opportunity to admit or deny each.

[paragraph no.] Grant defendant rescission of the mortgage transaction in accordance with his rights under the Truth in Lending Act, 15 U.S.C. § 1601, et seq. and 12 C.F.R. § 226.1, et seq.;

[paragraph no.] Grant defendant a refund of all principal and interest payment made to the lender in accordance with 15 U.S.C. § 1635(b);

[paragraph no.] Grant defendant a refund of all closing costs paid at the time of closing in accordance with 15 U.S.C. § 1635(b);

[paragraph no.] Grant defendant a refund of any down payment made in connection with the refinance loan in accordance with 15 U.S.C. § 1635(b);

[paragraph no.] Order the termination of the mortgage in accordance with 15 U.S.C. § 1635(b);

[paragraph no.] Grant defendant costs of the action, together with a reasonable attorney's fee in accordance with 15 U.S.C. § 1640(a)(3);

[paragraph no.] Grant defendant actual damages sustained by the defendant in accordance with 15 U.S.C. § 1635(b);

[paragraph no.] Grant defendant statutory damages not less than $200 or greater than $2,000 if the home loan is not a home equity loan in accordance with 15 U.S.C. § 1640(a)(1), (2); and

[paragraph no.] Grant defendant any other just and equitable remedy.

THIRD PARTY CLAIMS

A third party claim seeking the original lender indemnify the borrower from any losses he or she incurs in not being able to rescind may be appropriate. If the violations of this chapter are *not* evident on the face of the loan documents, then suing the original lender will be necessary to avoid Holder-in-Due Course defenses by the plaintiff.[45] However, liability for TILA claims for monetary damages runs against assignees where the violation is apparent on the face of the loan documents.[46]

---

[45] 15 U.S.C. § 1641(a). But, consider the F.T.C. Holder in Due Course Rule, 16 C.F.R. § 433, whereby consumers' claims and defenses against seller survive against holder of contract. With respect to the F.T.C. rule, see, *Brown v LaSalle Northwest National Bank*, 820 F Supp 1078 (ND Ill 1993) (claim against lender survives when lender is a participant ". . . the defendant can be part of a scheme to defraud consumers even if the regulation does not directly apply to lenders.")

[46] 15 U.S.C. § 1641(a).

BONUS!

For an extra spin on TILA rescission, several courts have determined that the borrower's right to rescind survives a refinance. That is, even though the lender no longer has a security interest in the loan, the borrower may *still* rescind the loan.[47]

---

[47] *Barrett et al. v. JP Morgan Chase Bank*, Nos. 05-5035/5146 (6th Cir. Apr. 18, 2006). http://caselaw.lp.findlaw.com/data2/circs/6th/055035p.pdf (last visited June 28, 2008). See the previous chapter on TILA rescission for an excerpt of this decision.

DEFENSE #5: BREACH OF CONTRACT

BREACH OF CONTRACT

DEFINED

"Breach of contract" developed as a means of excusing a party's performance under a contract when the other party breaches its obligations.

Contracts are formed when parties make an agreement and something a value is exchanged by each party.[1] In mortgage transactions, the lender agrees to provide money, in exchange for the borrower's promise to repay the money, and a promise that the loan will be secured by real property. The contract between the parties is extensive, with both the Note and Mortgage (or Deed of Trust) setting conditions between the parties. When one of the parties breaches a condition of the contract, then the other party will seek to enforce its rights. For example, when the borrower stops making payments, the lender forecloses.

Neither party may interfere with the other party's ability to perform under the contract without risking their own breach of contract. If a party does interfere, that interference may be an excuse for the other's non-performance. In mortgage lending, the lender may not interfere with the borrower's ability to make his or her payments within the confines of the contract. For example, if a lender begins to force-place insurance on the property at an excessive rate against the covenants of the mortgage, the lender would be in breach of the contract. If the cost of that insurance is the cause of the borrower's inability to make his or her payments, then the borrower's default was caused by the lender's breach of contract. This is a defense to foreclosure. The borrower can claim the lender's breach of contract is the cause of his breach, and therefore his default should be excused. (Note: this type of breach forgives the default, but the normal payments will still need to be made up by the borrower.)

The borrower should use breach of contract to supplement his or her other defenses under other laws in an attempt to nullify the contract. The courts usually have broad discretion to remedy breaches of contract, so it is wise to include it if the borrower appears to have grounds.

To show breach of contract, a party claiming breach must generally demonstrate as a matter of law that a valid contract exists, including its essential terms, that the other party breached a duty imposed under the contract, and that damages resulted.[2]

---

[1] A contract is technically mutual assent to the exchange with consideration. Unilateral contracts are beyond the scope of this book and are not discussed here.

[2] As described as Pennsylvania's common law: *Omicron Systems v. Weiner,* 860 A.2d 554, 564 (Pa.Super.Ct.2004); *Robert Craig Attig v. DRG, Inc.,* Civ. Act. No. 04-CV-3740 (E.D. Pa., March 30, 2005);

SPOT IT!

If the borrower includes a claim under a different chapter of this book, the borrower may be well served to include a claim for breach of contract, in addition to an affirmative defense for breach of contract. Law students spend a year or more on contract law alone, so a detailed look into breach of contract is not possible here.[3]

POTENTIAL RECOVERY

The courts have great leeway in providing remedies for breach of contract. A court can order the contract void, can order specific performance, or can order damages be paid.

STRATEGY

A breach of contract claim gives the court great leeway as to the remedy it can award, so a borrower would be wise to raise breach of contract where he or she can.

APPLICABLE LAW OR CIVIL RULE

Each state has its own set of laws on what constitutes a breach of contract. These laws will include elements, such as the ones listed below under "Elements." Federal courts will use the state law of the state in which the contract was formed, which would likely be the state in which the property and borrower resides.[4]

ELEMENTS

Pennsylvania law (and generally): To show breach of contract, a party claiming breach must demonstrate as a matter of law that:

1. A valid contract exists, including its essential terms,
2. That the other party breached a duty imposed under the contract, and
3. That damages resulted.[5]

---

[3] For more on understanding contracts, visit your local law library. A book some law students find helpful is Understanding Contracts by Ferriell and Navin (2004), ISBN-10: 0820554502

[4] While things can get complicated when a borrower lives in, or signed the contract in, another state. However, for all intents and purposes, use the state law of whatever state the borrower was sued in. If there are concerns here, look towards the end of the mortgage, which may state which state laws shall govern.

[5] *Robert Craig Attig v. DRG, Inc.*, Civ. Act. No. 04-CV-3740 (E.D. Pa., March 30, 2005); *Omicron Systems v. Weiner,* 860 A.2d 554, 564 (Pa.Super.Ct.2004).

Illinois law: "(1) the existence of a valid and enforceable contract; (2) its performance of the contract; (3) breach of contract by the other party; and (4) resulting injury."[6]

Florida law: "(1) the existence of a contract, (2) a breach of the contract, and (3) damages resulting from the breach."[7] "In addition, in order to maintain an action for breach of contract, a claimant must also prove performance of its obligations under the contract or a legal excuse for its nonperformance."[8]

Ohio law: in order to succeed on a breach of contract claim, the plaintiff must show (1) the existence of a binding contract; (2) that the plaintiff performed its contractual obligations; (3) that the defendant failed to fulfill its contractual obligations without legal excuse; and (4) that the plaintiff suffered damages as a result of the breach.[9]

Searching the internet may not yield a current version of the elements. Going to a *law* library (any librarian will tell you the closest law library – usually at the local court house or law school) and using Lexis or Westlaw would provide the most current cases on point.

DEFENSES IN GENERAL

Breach of Contract can be used as a shield or a sword, depending on your objectives. In a foreclosure action, the borrower would (if he or she has grounds), want to list a breach of contract defense under the affirmative defenses section. Placing it here would put the bank on notice that it did something wrong that caused it to breach the contract, thus excusing the borrower's performance under the contract. (i.e., the borrower wasn't obligated to make payments any longer due to the bank's error.)

Breach of contract can also be added as a counterclaim, using it to secure damages for the borrower from the bank. As a counterclaim, the borrower is suing the bank for its errors. Here, the borrower is saying the banks errors are so egregious that they constitute a material breach of the contract.[10] If the borrower is alleging any TILA, HOEPA, RESPA, or other similar claims, he or she should also allege breach of contract in an attempt to nullify the contract and recover all money paid. Even if the TILA violations don't amount

---

[6] *Preibe v. Autobarn, Ltd.*, 240 F.3d 584, 587 (7th Cir. 2001).

[7] *Rollins v. Butland*, 951 So.2d 860 (Fla. 2d DCA 2006), *citing Knowles v. C.I.T. Corp.*, 346 So.2d 1042, 1043 (Fla. 1st DCA 1977).

[8] *Rollins*, 951 So.2d 860, *citing Old Republic Ins. Co. v. Von Onweller Constr. Co.*, 239 So.2d 503, 505 (Fla.2d DCA 1970).

[9] *S&S Pallet Co., Inc. v. Delta Asphalt Co., Inc.* (Apr. 11, 2001), 9th Dist. No. 20170, citing *Garofalo v. Chicago Title Ins. Co.* (1995), 104 Ohio App.3d 95, 108.

[10] Material breach is one that can excuse performance. A non-material breach would be one that is not critical to the performance of the contract, like when yellow colored installation is installed inside the walls of a house instead of pink colored installation. While damages might be available, installing the wrong color installation would *not* be a material breach.

to rescission, a breach of contract finding might enable damages equivalent to rescission (and possibly rescission itself).

DEFENSES

Place this defense under the heading "Affirmative Defenses."

AFFIRMATIVE DEFENSES

An affirmative defense for breach of contract might read like this:[11]

[paragraph no.] Defendant's performance under the contract is excused due to plaintiff's breach of contract.

STARTER DISCOVERY

You may wish to obtain information surrounding the breach of contract that is alleged, such as training manuals, manuals of loan closing procedure, or other materials that may support an allegation that the bank breached its contract with the borrower. If the breach feeds from a breach under another chapter of this book, you may wish to reference the suggested discovery within those sections.

REQUESTS FOR ADMISSIONS

[paragraph no.] Admit the mortgage creates a binding contract between the plaintiff and the defendant.

[paragraph no.] Admit the plaintiff materially breached the contract between the parties when it…. *[state what the bank did, such as "failed to disclose XXX, as required by TILA, 15 U.S.C. § 1601, et seq.]*

[paragraph no.] Admit the plaintiff materially breached the contract between the parties when it…. *[use as many of these as necessary within the admissions limit set by your state or local rules.]*

[paragraph no.] Admit the defendant sustained damages in an amount equal to all costs of this transaction, including his/her down payment, closing costs, taxes, insurance, fees, and costs, due to plaintiff's breach of contract.

[paragraph no.] Admit the defendant performed all of his/her obligations up until the plaintiff's breach of contract *[on May 1, 2005. You may wish to leave out the date.]*

---

[11] An Answer only needs to contain a "short and plain" statement its defenses to each claim asserted. Fed. Civ. R. 8(b)(1)(A). (Check your state rules for the corresponding rule.)

COUNTER CLAIMS

The counterclaim must allege each of the elements of breach of contract, and is state specific. For example, a breach of contact counterclaim under Florida law will need to allege: (1) the existence of a contract, (2) a breach of the contract, and (3) damages resulting from the breach, (4) performance of its obligations under the contract or a legal excuse for its nonperformance.

A counterclaim for breach of contract under Florida law may look something like this:

COUNT ONE

[paragraph no.] Defendant realleges as if set forth in this document paragraphs *[1- all paragraphs]* of the Answer;

[paragraph no.] Defendant alleges a mortgage contract exists between the parties;[12]

[paragraph no.] Defendant alleges Plaintiff forced placed hazard, wind, fire, and/or flood insurance upon Defendant about April, 2007 and again in October, 2007, requiring Defendant to pay the premium for said insurance;

[paragraph no.] Defendant alleges said forced placed insurance was substantially more expensive than similar insurance available on the market;

[paragraph no.] Defendant alleges said forced placed insurance was unnecessary because Defendant had sufficient insurance in place;

[paragraph no.] Defendant alleges she repeatedly communicated with Plaintiff about the said forced placed insurance, specifically demonstrating her insurance was sufficient under the terms of the parties' contract;

[paragraph no.] Defendant alleges Plaintiff breached its contract with Defendant when it forced placed said insurance upon Defendant in an amount in excess of that required under the contract's "Hazard Insurance Authorization & Requirements";[13]

[paragraph no.] Defendant alleges her inability to make the payments under the contract actually and proximately caused the present action in foreclosure, damaging Defendant's credit, causing her to incur late fees, compounded interest, attorney's fees, and other damages arising from the breach;[14]

---

[12] *Element one is alleged here.*
[13] *After alleging some general facts surrounding the breach, element two is alleged here.*
[14] *Element three is alleged here.*

[paragraph no.] Defendant alleges Plaintiff's breach of contract actually and proximately caused Defendant to no longer be able to make her payments under the contract;[15]

[paragraph no.] Defendant alleges Plaintiff was unjustly enriched by force placing said unnecessary insurance and is liable to Defendant for damages;[16] and

[paragraph no.] Defendant alleges Plaintiff's breach of contract by force placing said insurance upon Defendant causes Plaintiff to be liable to Defendant for damages.[17]

THIRD PARTY CLAIMS

A claim and request for relief can be levied against a third party if that party has breached a contract existing between the borrower and it. However, filing a lawsuit against another party for breach of contract is not necessary (you can sue them separately).

---

[15] *Element four is alleged here; the borrower's inability to make the payments is excused because of bank's breach.*

[16] *This allegation lays the foundation for seeking restitution damages from the court. That is, asking the court to give the borrower back all the extra money paid for the unnecessary insurance.*

[17] *This is a catch all allegation for damages.*

DEFENSE #6: REAL ESTATE SETTLEMENT PROCEDURES ACT (RESPA)

REAL ESTATE SETTLEMENT PROCEDURES ACT (RESPA)

DEFINED

The Real Estate Settlement Procedures Act (RESPA), 12 U.S.C. § 2601, et seq., was first passed in 1974. It is designed to help consumers shop for settlement services (including broker and title company services), and eliminates kickbacks and referral fees from loans.[1] RESPA's implementing rule is known as Regulation X, which begins at 24 C.F.R. § 3500.

Each section of RESPA has its own set of damages, with several sections providing no civil liability. If a particular section does not provide damages under federal law, look to state consumer protection laws for liability. Some state laws provide civil liability for violations of federal laws like RESPA.[2]

For ease of reading, the "potential recovery" section is included after the definition of each section. The sections are as follows:

Information Booklet.[3] The information booklet contains information about the settlement of the loan and must be mailed within 3 days of the loan application.[4] The information booklet must include:[5]

1. A description and explanation of the nature and purpose of each cost involved in the transaction;
2. A description and explanation of the nature and purpose of escrow accounts when used in connection with the loan;
3. An explanation of the choices available to buyers of residential real estate in selecting persons to provide necessary services incident to a real estate settlement; and
4. An explanation of the unfair practices and unreasonable or unnecessary charges to be avoided by the prospective buyer with respect to a real estate settlement.

Damages. There is no civil liability under RESPA for failing to provide the information booklet. However, failing to provide the CHARM booklet (Consumer Handbook on Adjustable Rate Mortgages) when a variable rate loan is at issue is a violation of TILA.[6] (Violations of TILA are covered in Defense #2.)

---

[1] 12 U.S.C. § 2615(b)(1),(2).
[2] For example, Ohio's Consumer Sales Practices Act requires the court look at specific federal rules and guidelines when determining whether a federal violation equals a violation of Ohio's law, triggering damages under state law. R.C. § 1345.02(C) (F.T.C. Rules).
[3] 12 U.S.C. § 2604(b); 24 C.F.R. § 3500.6(a)
[4] 12 U.S.C. § 2604(d); 24 C.F.R. § 3500.6(a)(1).
[5] 12 U.S.C. § 2604(d).
[6] 12 C.F.R. § 226.17(b); 12 C.F.R. § 226.19(b)(2).

Good Faith Estimate.[7] Within 3 days of taking the mortgage application,[8] the lender must mail the consumer a good faith estimate of the amount or range of charges for specific settlement services the borrower is likely to incur in connection with the settlement.[9] Yield Spread Premium (YSP) and other payments made to affiliated or independent settlement service providers must be shown as P.O.C. (Paid Outside Closing) on the Good Faith Estimate.[10] If a mortgage broker is involved, and that broker is not the exclusive agent of the lender, then the lender is responsible for ascertaining that the good faith estimate was delivered.[11] If the lender requires the borrowers use and pay for certain service providers in conjunction with the loan, the lender must disclose who that provider is, describe the relationship between the parties, and an estimate of charges for that provider.[12]

Damages. There is no civil liability under RESPA for failing to provide a GFE.[13] However, failing to provide a GFE triggers regular statutory damages under TILA.[14] (Violations of TILA are covered in Defense #2.)

Use of HUD-1 (Settlement Statement). Every loan subject to RESPA must use the HUD-1 form as the settlement statement.[15] If the borrower requests a copy of the HUD-1 before settlement, it must be provided for inspection the day before settlement.[16] A copy of the completed HUD-1 must be provided at or before settlement,[17] unless the borrower waives delivery in writing or does not attend the settlement.[18]

Damages. There is no civil liability under RESPA for failing to provide a HUD-1 settlement statement. However, failing to provide the HUD-1 settlement statement does trigger regular statutory damages under TILA if this statement was relied on to provide the consumer a written itemization of the amount financed (a breakdown of costs).[19] (Violations of TILA are covered in Defense #2.)

---

[7] 12 U.S.C. § 2604(c); 24 C.F.R. § 3500.7(a).

[8] 12 U.S.C. § 2604(d); 24 C.F.R. § 3500.6(a)(1).

[9] 24 C.F.R. § 3500.7(d).

[10] 24 C.F.R. § 3500.7(a)(2).

[11] 24 C.F.R. § 3500.7(b).

[12] 24 C.F.R. § 3500.7(e).

[13] The statute does not provide for damages. *Also see, Collins v. FmHA-USDA*, 105 F.3d 1366 (11th Cir. 1997).

[14] 12 C.F.R. § 226.17(b); 12 C.F.R. § 226.19(b)(2).

[15] 24 C.F.R. § 3500.8(a).

[16] 24 C.F.R. § 3500.10(a)

[17] 24 C.F.R. § 3500.10(b).

[18] 24 C.F.R. § 3500.10(c), (d). Appendix A to Part 3500 outlines the procedures of calculating the HUD-1.

[19] 12 C.F.R. § 226.18(c). This violation triggers normal TILA damages, not rescission. See Chapter 3 of this book.

No fee for preparing HUD-1 or TILA statements. A lender or servicer cannot charge a fee for the preparation of the HUD-1 settlement statement, escrow account statement, or statements required by TILA.[20]

Damages. There is no civil liability under RESPA for charging to prepare a HUD-1 or TILA statement. ***However***, charging for this service may cause a fee normally excluded from the finance charge be included in the finance charge. For purposes of TILA and rescission under 15 U.S.C. § 1635(i), this charge may cause the loan to be rescindable if the amount charged can be established as in excess of $35.[21]

Notice on Servicing. At the time of application, a lender who makes loans subject to RESPA must disclose to the applicant whether the servicing of the loan may be assigned, sold, or transferred to any other person at any time while the loan is outstanding.[22] If an existing loan will be transferred to another servicer, the current servicer must notify the borrower in writing of the assignment not less than 15 days before the effective date of the transfer.[23] Then, the transferee of the servicing must provide notice not more than 15 days after the transfer.[24] Payments made to the transferor during the 60 days immediately following the effective date may not be considered late.[25] Each party must provide a notice than contains the following information:[26]

    a. The effective date of transfer of the servicing described in such paragraph.
    b. The name, address, and toll-free or collect call telephone number of the transferee servicer.
    c. A toll-free or collect call telephone number for (i) an individual employed by the transferor servicer, or (ii) the department of the transferor servicer, that can be contacted by the borrower to answer inquiries relating to the transfer of servicing.
    d. The date on which the transferor servicer who is servicing the mortgage loan before the assignment, sale, or transfer will cease to accept payments relating to the loan and the date on which the transferee servicer will begin to accept such payments.
    e. Any information concerning the effect the transfer may have, if any, on the terms of or the continued availability of mortgage life or disability insurance or any other type of optional insurance and what action, if any, the borrower must take to maintain coverage.

---

[20] 12 U.S.C. § 2610; 24 C.F.R. § 3500.12.
[21] 15 U.S.C. § 1635(i).
[22] 12 U.S.C. § 2605(a).
[23] 12 U.S.C. § 2605(b)(1),(2)(a). But See, § (b)(2)(B) (exception for termination of the contract or bankruptcy).
[24] 12 U.S.C. § 2605(c).
[25] 12 U.S.C. § 2605(d).
[26] 12 U.S.C. § 2605(b)(3), (c)(3) (direct quote from code).

    f.   A statement that the assignment, sale, or transfer of the servicing of the mortgage loan does not affect any term or condition of the security instruments other than terms directly related to the servicing of such loan.

Damages. RESPA provides for recovery of a sum equal to the amount of: (A) any actual damages to the borrower, (B) additional damages, in the case of a pattern or practice of noncompliance in an amount not to exceed $1,000.[27] RESPA also provides for attorneys fees in a successful action under RESPA.[28] The statute of limitations for a violation of this section is 3 years.[29]

Qualified Written Request (QWR). A qualified written request is a letter sent to the lender to correct an error or obtain information about the loan.[30] An example of a QWR is included in Appendix G. If the borrower sends a QWR to a servicer for information relating to the servicing of the loan, the servicer must provide the borrower:[31]

    a.   Written acknowledgement of receipt of the correspondence within 20 days (excluding legal public holidays, Saturdays and Sundays), unless the requested action is taken with the time period.

    b.   Not later than 60 days (excluding legal public holidays, Saturdays, and Sundays) after the receipt of a QWR and, if applicable, before taking any action with respect to the inquiry of the borrower, the servicer must:

        i.   Make appropriate corrections in the account of the borrower, including the crediting of any late charges or penalties, and transmit to the borrower a written notification of such correction (which shall include the name and telephone number of a representative of the servicer who can provide assistance to the borrower);

        ii.   After conducting an investigation, provide the borrower with a written explanation or clarification that includes (i) to the extent applicable, a statement of the reasons for which the servicer believes the account of the borrower is correct as determined by the servicer; and (ii) the name and telephone number of an individual employed by, or the office or department of, the servicer

           who can provide assistance to the borrower; or

        iii.   After conducting an investigation, provide the borrower with a written explanation or clarification that includes (i) information requested by

---

[27] 12 U.S.C. § 2605(f)(1).

[28] 12 U.S.C. § 2605(f)(3).

[29] 12 U.S.C. § 2614.

[30] A QWR is written correspondence, other than notice on a payment coupon, that 1) includes, or otherwise enables the servicer to identify, the name and account of the borrower, and 2) includes a statement of the reasons for belief of the borrower that the account is in error or provides sufficient detail to the servicer regarding other information sought by the borrower. 12 U.S.C. § 2605(e).

[31] 12 U.S.C. § 2605(e)(2),(e)(2)(A),(B),(C).

the borrower or an explanation of why the information requested is unavailable or cannot be obtained by the servicer; and (ii) the name and telephone number of an individual employed by, or the office or department of, the servicer who can provide assistance to the borrower.

c. During the 60-day period beginning on the date of receipt of a QWR, the servicer may not report the account as overdue to a credit reporting agency.

Damages. RESPA provides for recovery of a sum equal to the amount of: (A) any actual damages to the borrower, (B) additional damages, in the case of a pattern or practice of noncompliance in an amount not the exceed $1,000.[32] RESPA also provides for attorneys fees in a successful action under RESPA.[33] QWR violations may also trigger liability under the Fair Credit Reporting Act (FCRA) if the servicer reports negative information about the account to a credit reporting bureau before responding to the QWR.[34] The statute of limitations for a violation of this section is 3 years.[35]

Failing to provide a response to a QWR does *not* stop the lender's ability to foreclose, or from pursuing any other remedy against the borrower.[36]

Kickbacks and Unearned Fees. No person may give or receive any fee, kickback, or thing of value pursuant to any agreement or understanding, oral or otherwise, as part of a real estate settlement on a loan covered by RESPA.[37] This prohibits referral arrangements between mortgage brokers and real estate agents, as well as between title companies and real estate agents or brokers.[38] The service providers may not split fees (divide the fees generated by a service) unless actual services were performed in connection with that fee.[39] Payments do *not* include employee salaries, payments to agents of title companies, attorney fees, and real estate agent splits with their agent firm.[40]

---

[32] 12 U.S.C. § 2605(f)(1).

[33] 12 U.S.C. § 2605(f)(3).

[34] RESPA specifically prohibits credit reporting when a QWR is outstanding. 12 U.S.C. § 2605(e)(3). A violation of this act could trigger liability under 15 U.S.C. 1681a.

[35] 12 U.S.C. § 2614.

[36] 24 C.F.R. § 3500.21(e)(4)(ii). RESPA imposes an award of damages for violating this section of REPSA; failing to provide a QWR does not prevent foreclosure. *In re Schlupp*, No. 05-16879DWS, 2005 WL 2483209 (Bkrtcy.E.D.Pa. 2005); *Johnstone v. Bank of America, N.A.*, 173 F.Supp.2d 809, (N.D.Ill. 2001); *Cardiello v. Money Store*, 2001 WL 604007, at *9 (S.D.N.Y. 2001).

[37] 12 U.S.C. § 2607. "Things of value" is broadly defined and encompasses just about any conceivable arrangement under Regulation X. 24 C.F.R. § 3500.14(d).

[38] Id.

[39] 24 C.F.R. § 3500.14(c).

[40] 12 U.S.C. § 2607(c); 24 C.F.R. § 3500.14(g).

Exceptions to the kickback rule. Money that is exchanged is not subject to the kickback provision if an affiliated business arrangement exists, *and* proper disclosures were provided.[41] Affiliated business arrangement conditions are as follows:[42]

a. The party making the referral must provide to *each* person whose business is referred with a written disclosure in the form of the Affiliated Business Arrangement Disclosure Statement provided for under RESPA.[43] That form is included in Appendix R.

b. The party making the referral may not force the buyer to use the service, unless the party is a lender requiring the use of a particular credit reporting agency, attorney, or real estate appraiser chosen by the lender to represent its interests. Only an attorney may force the use of a particular title insurance policy if arranging for a client that the attorney actually represents in the real estate transaction.[44]

c. The only thing of value that is received from the arrangement is a return on an ownership interest or franchise relationship.[45] This essentially writes out the possibility for cash or other money to be exchanged directly between the parties. Instead, there must be a bona fide legal entity created that establishes an actual affiliated business between the parties.

Damages. A violation of this section of RESPA creates a right of action against all wrongdoers (jointly and severally liable for all damages) in an amount equal to three times the amount of any charge paid for such settlement service,[46] and court costs and attorneys fees.[47] The statute of limitations for a violation of this section is 1 year.[48]

Yield Spread Premium (YSP) Exception. Succinctly stated, Yield Spread Premium is not illegal under RESPA in the vast majority of cases. YSP is: "a bonus paid to a broker when it originates a loan at an interest rate higher than the minimum interest rate approved by the lender for a particular loan. The lender then rewards the broker by paying it a percentage of the 'yield spread' (i.e., the difference between the interest rate specified by

---

[41] 12 U.S.C. § 2607(c); 24 C.F.R. § 3500.15. The term ``affiliated business arrangement'' means an arrangement in which (A) a person who is in a position to refer business incident to or a part of a real estate settlement service involving a federally related mortgage loan, or an associate of such person, has either an affiliate relationship with or a direct or beneficial ownership interest of more than 1 percent in a provider of settlement services; and (B) either of such persons directly or indirectly refers such business to that provider or affirmatively influences the selection of that provider. 12 U.S.C. § 2602(7).

[42] 24 C.F.R. § 3500.15(b).

[43] 24 C.F.R. § 3500.15(b)(1).

[44] 24 C.F.R. § 3500.15(b)(2).

[45] 24 C.F.R. § 3500.15(b)(3).

[46] 12 U.S.C. § 2607(d)(2).

[47] 12 U.S.C. § 2607(d)(5).

[48] 12 U.S.C. § 2614.

the lender and the actual interest rate set by the broker at the time of origination) multiplied by the amount of the loan."[49] HUD has issued a policy statement that states YSP is not illegal, per se.[50]

Instead, HUD requires two questions be answered to determine whether the YSP is permissible under Section 8 of RESPA.[51] "…the first question is whether goods or facilities were actually furnished or services were actually performed for the compensation paid." Then, "the second question is whether the payments are reasonably related to the value of the goods or facilities that were actually furnished or services that were actually performed.[52] In 2001, HUD clarified the two question test as follows:[53]

> "The First Part of the HUD Test: Under the first part of HUD's test, the total compensation to a mortgage broker, of which a yield spread premium may be a component or the entire amount, must be for goods or facilities provided or services performed. HUD's position is that in order to discern whether a yield spread premium was for goods, facilities or services under the first part of the HUD test, it is necessary to look at each transaction individually, including examining all of the goods or facilities provided or services performed by the broker in the transaction, whether the goods, facilities or services are paid for by the borrower, the lender, or partly by both.[54]

> "…the Department believes that the second part of the test is applied by determining whether a mortgage broker's total compensation is reasonable. Total compensation includes fees paid by a borrower and any yield spread premium paid by a lender, not simply the yield spread premium alone. Yield spread premiums serve to allow the borrower a lower up front cash payment in return for a higher interest rate, while allowing the broker to recoup the total costs of originating the loan. Total compensation to the broker must be reasonably related to the total value of goods or facilities provided or services performed by the broker. Simply delivering a loan with a higher interest rate is not a compensable service. The

---

[49] *Oscar v. Bank One, N.A.*, Civ.A. No. 05-5928, 2006 U.S. Dist. LEXIS 6410 at *9 (E.D.Pa. Feb.17, 2006); In re Bell, 309 B.R. 139, 153 n.9 (Bankr. E.D. Pa. 2004) (citing *Noel v. Fleet Finance, Inc.*, 971 F. Supp. 1102, 1106-07 (E.D. Mich. 1997)).

[50] HUD Policy Statement 1999-1, 64 Fed.Reg. 1080 (March 1, 1999). See, http://www.hud.gov/offices/hsg/sfh/res/resp0222.cfm (Last visited July 20, 2008).

[51] Id.

[52] Id.

[53] Real Estate Settlement Procedures Act Statement of Policy 2001-1: Clarification of Statement of Policy 1999-1 Regarding Lender Payments to Mortgage Brokers, and Guidance Concerning Unearned Fees Under Section 8(b), 66 Fed.Reg. 53,052 (Oct. 18, 2001). See, http://www.thefederalregister.com/d.p/2001-10-18-01-26321 (Last visited July 20, 2008).

[54] Id.

Department affirms the 1999 Statement of Policy's position on this matter for purposes of RESPA enforcement.[55]

Unless the fees and YSP are egregious, this author believes lawsuits based on YSP violations will continue to be difficult to bring, maintain, or win.[56] This is because the test requires a subjective look at the fees associated with each individual loan to ascertain whether they violate RESPA. Considering HOEPA dictates high cost loans to be those with fees exceeding 8% of the loan amount, a borrower claiming YSP was excessive will have an uphill battle if the YSP amounts to 1-2% of the loan amount.

Forced Title Insurance. A seller of real estate property may **not** force the buyer to use a particular title insurance provider as a condition to selling the property.[57] Contrary to many local customs, like those in Central Ohio, the seller may **not** force the buyer use a particular title insurance company. A seller who violates this section is liable to the buyer for three times the amount of *all* charges made for title insurance.[58]

Damages. A seller who requires a buyer use a particular title insurance company is liable to the buyer for three times the amount of *all* charges made for title insurance.[59] The statute of limitations for a violation of this section is 1 year.[60]

Escrow Accounts. At closing, the lender may only collect enough escrow to cover the amount shown on the last bill associated with that cost, plus 1/6 of that amount.[61] During the servicing of the loan, the lender may only collect 1/12 of the annual amount of the estimated escrow, unless the lender determines a deficiency may occur and more escrow is needed.[62] The lender must notify the borrower of any shortages at least one time per year.[63] The lender must provide an escrow statement at closing.[64] A servicer establishing escrow must submit a statement to the borrower during the first 12 months after establishing a servicing account.[65] Thereafter, an annual statement of the escrow account must be given to the borrower.[66]

---

[55] Id.

[56] *Echevarria v. Chicago Title and Trust Co.*, 256 F.3d 623 (7th Cir. 2001); *Willis v. Quality Mortgage USA, Inc.*, 5 F. Supp. 2d 1306 (M.D. Ala. 1998); *Culpepper v. Inland Mortgage Corp.*, 253 F.3d 1324 (11th Cir. 2001); *Heimmermann v. First Union Mortg. Corp.*, 305 F.3d 1257 (11th Cir. 2002).

[57] 12 U.S.C. § 2608(a).

[58] 12 U.S.C. § 2608(b).

[59] 12 U.S.C. § 2608(b).

[60] 12 U.S.C. § 2614.

[61] 12 U.S.C. § 2609(a)(1).

[62] 12 U.S.C. § 2609(a)(2). If a deficiency exists and the homeowner is current on their payments, the servicer is required to pay any deficiency in the escrow account and bill the homeowner over the next 12 months to make up the deficiency. Reg X, 24 C.F.R. § 3500.17(k)(2)

[63] 12 U.S.C. § 2609(b).

[64] 12 U.S.C. § 2609(c)(1)(B).

[65] 12 U.S.C. § 2609(c)(1)(A).

[66] 12 U.S.C. § 2609(c)(2)(A).

The statement must include the amount of the borrower's current monthly payment, the portion of the monthly payment being placed in the escrow account, the total amount paid into the escrow account during the period, the total amount paid out of the escrow account during the period for taxes, insurance premiums, and other charges (as separately identified), and the balance in the escrow account at the conclusion of the period.[67]

Damages. While the section on escrow accounts is detailed, RESPA does not provide for civil liability. Only HUD may assess damages for violations of this section.[68] For purposes of TILA and rescission under 15 U.S.C. § 1635(i), an overcharge here may cause the loan to be rescindable if the overcharge can be established as in excess of $35.[69]

SPOT IT!

Spotting a violation of RESPA is more difficult than spotting violations of other acts or rules, especially because much of the disclosure requirements of the act occur before the loan closings. Many borrowers do not keep all of the pre-closing loan disclosures because it is common for these to be thrown away. The disclosure requirements are not required to be repeated at closing, so the documents will not be with the file most borrowers get at closing. However, discovery can be used to obtain a copy of the mortgage broker's file, which may have a copy of the disclosures, if mailed. Additionally, a mortgage broker that is party to the lawsuit may be deposed during discovery as to whether providing RESPA disclosures was a normal process for that company.

Proving kickbacks were paid may be considerably harder to prove. Many in the industry recognize that kickbacks are illegal, and thus will never admit to taking part in paying them. However, this author is aware of at least one mortgage broker who set up a shell "marketing" company to pay "marketing fees" to real estate agents who referred him loans. The broker thought this was legal if he invoiced the agents for "marketing services" and then paid them with a company check. Unfortunately for the broker and real estate agent, this arrangement is not only illegal, but they managed to document their entire illegal operation.

It would serve the borrower in foreclosure to use discovery to uncover any affiliated businesses of all the parties involved, then to request information related to those businesses to determine if kickbacks were involved. If the borrower is lucky, he or she may uncover a paper trail of checks.

---

[67] 12 U.S.C. § 2609(c)(2)(A). See Regulation X, 24 C.F.R. § 3500.17, generally.
[68] 12 U.S.C. § 2609(d). Most lender appear to be complying with the escrow requirements, although over-escrowing used to be a problem.
[69] 15 U.S.C. § 1635(i).

LIMITATIONS

RESPA does not apply to loans primarily for business, commercial, or agricultural purposes or to government or governmental agencies or instrumentalities.[70] RESPA does not apply to a loan on a property of 25 acres or more,[71] temporary construction financing (if not converted to permanent financing),[72] vacant land,[73] or loan conversions.[74]

RESPA violations alone do not create a right to rescind.[75] In fact, RESPA expressly states violations must not effect the validity or enforceability of any loan, loan agreement, mortgage, or lien made or arising in connection with a federally related mortgage loan.[76] Some RESPA violations have a one year statute of limitation; one violation contains a three year statute of limitation.[77]

RESPA violations do not generate much in damages, limiting most up to $1,000 plus attorneys fees (which could be substantial).

POTENTIAL RECOVERY

This section is merged with the definition section for ease of reading.

In addition to the statutory damages provided for RESPA violations, several courts have found that pain and suffering can be sought for violations of RESPA, when the damages provisions permit the recovery of "actual damages."[78]

STRATEGY

Violations of RESPA may enable the consumer to obtain some damages to offset the liability they may face in foreclosure. RESPA will also enable lawyers' fees to be obtained in a successful RESPA action.

---

[70] 12 U.S.C. § 2606(a)(1),(2).
[71] 24 C.F.R. § 3500.5(b)(1).
[72] 24 C.F.R. § 3500.5(b)(3).
[73] 24 C.F.R. § 3500.5(b)(4).
[74] 24 C.F.R. § 3500.5(b)(6).
[75] 12 U.S.C. § 2615.
[76] Id.
[77] 12 U.S.C. § 2614.
[78] *Johnstone v. Bank of America, N.A.*, 173 F.Supp.2d 809, (N.D.Ill. 2001) (justifies mental anguish by looking at other federal laws, like the FCRA, ECOA, and FHA that permit the same as actual damages); *Hrubec v. Nat'l R.R. Pass. Corp.*, 829 F.Supp. 1502 (N.D.Ill 1993). *But see, Katz v. Dime Sav. Bank, FSB*, 992 F.Supp.250 (W.D.N.Y.1997); *Aiello v. Providian Fin. Corp.*, 239 F.3d 876 (7th Cir. 2001).

For borrowers, the best RESPA defense would be in uncovering fees paid in conjunction with the transaction that were not disclosed as finance charges. In this instance, rescission may be available under TILA. (Violations of TILA are covered in Defense #1.)

A violation of RESPA may trigger the statutory collection of attorneys fees, which would provide an incentive for an attorney to include this defense in the claim. Additionally, it may be used to offset the lender's ability to secure attorneys fees in the case.

APPLICABLE LAW OR CIVIL RULE

The Real Estate Settlement Procedures Act (RESPA), 12 U.S.C. § 2601, et seq., is implemented by Regulation X, which begins at 24 C.F.R. § 3500.

RESPA permits state law to add to the requirements of the act, so long as those requirements are not inconsistent with RESPA.[79]

RESPA complaints against servicers or lenders may be filed with:

> Director, Office of RESPA and Interstate Land Sales
> US Department of Housing and Urban Development
> Room 9154
> 451 7th Street, SW
> Washington, DC 20410

RESPA CHECKLIST

- [ ] Purchase and refinance loans qualify.
- [ ] The lender is remotely connected with a federal agency, or whose loans will be touched by the federal government, or one of its mortgage associates (Freddie Mac, Fannie Mae, FHA, etc.), or who invests in residential real estate loans of $1,000,000 per year.[80]
- [ ] The loan must not be on a business property…. business, commercial, or agricultural purposes or to government or governmental agencies or instrumentalities.[81] The loan is for a 1-4 unit property.
- [ ] The loan must not be for a property of 25 acres or more,[82] temporary construction financing (if not converted to permanent financing),[83] vacant land,[84] or loan conversions.

---

[79] 12 U.S.C. § 2616.
[80] 24 C.F.R. § 3500.2(b)(1)(i).
[81] 12 U.S.C. § 2606(a)(1),(2).
[82] 24 C.F.R. § 3500.5(b)(1).
[83] 24 C.F.R. § 3500.5(b)(3).

- ☐ Good Faith Estimate (GFE).
  - o A GFE was not provided to the consumer at the time of the application, or within 3 days of the loan application.
- ☐ Charm Booklet.
  - o In a mortgage involving a variable rate mortgage, the CHARM booklet was not provided to the consumer. (Very rarely will these ever be delivered by a broker or lender.)
- ☐ Qualified Written Request (QWR).
  - o The request was not acknowledged within 20 days.
  - o A response was not mailed within 60 days.
  - o The statute of limitations has not passed (3 years).[85]
- ☐ Kickbacks and Unearned Fees.
  - o Kickbacks were paid in connection with the loan.
    - ▪ The loan documents will likely not indicate whether kickbacks were paid. Inquiry will be necessary through discovery.
  - o The statute of limitations has not passed (1 year).[86]
- ☐ Forced Title Insurance.
  - o Did the seller required the use of a particular title insurance company as a condition of closing? Look to the purchase contract. (It does not matter that the buyer agreed to use the seller's title company in the contract because having such a requirement is precisely what is unlawful under RESPA.)[87]
  - o The statute of limitations has not passed (1 year).[88]
- ☐ Notice on Servicing.
  - o Each party must provide a notice than contains the following information about servicing:[89]
    - ▪ The effective date of transfer of the servicing described in such paragraph.
    - ▪ The name, address, and toll-free or collect call telephone number of the transferee servicer.
    - ▪ A toll-free or collect call telephone number for (i) an individual employed by the transferor servicer, or (ii) the department of the transferor servicer, that can be contacted by the borrower to answer inquiries relating to the transfer of servicing.

---

[84] 24 C.F.R. § 3500.5(b)(4).

[85] 12 U.S.C. § 2614.

[86] 12 U.S.C. § 2614.

[87] A lawyer once put it this way: "You can have a contract to kill someone, but that does not make it legally binding."

[88] 12 U.S.C. § 2614.

[89] 12 U.S.C. § 2605(b)(3), (c)(3) (direct quote from code).

- The date on which the transferor servicer who is servicing the mortgage loan before the assignment, sale, or transfer will cease to accept payments relating to the loan and the date on which the transferee servicer will begin to accept such payments.
    - Any information concerning the effect the transfer may have, if any, on the terms of or the continued availability of mortgage life or disability insurance or any other type of optional insurance and what action, if any, the borrower must take to maintain coverage.
    - A statement that the assignment, sale, or transfer of the servicing of the mortgage loan does not affect any term or condition of the security instruments other than terms directly related to the servicing of such loan.
  - o The statute of limitations has not passed (3 years).[90]
- □ No fee for preparing HUD-1 or TILA statements.
  - o Was HUD-1 used and provided to the borrower (TILA violation)?
  - o Check if there was a document preparation charge. If so, seek through discovery to determine how much of that charge was for the preparation of the following documents (none may be charged):
    - the HUD-1 settlement statement,
    - escrow account statement, or
    - statements required by TILA.[91]

---

[90] 12 U.S.C. § 2614.
[91] 12 U.S.C. § 2610; 24 C.F.R. § 3500.12.

DEFENSE #7: FAIR DEBT COLLECTION PRACTICES ACT (FDCPA)

Fair Debt Collection Practices Act (FDCPA)

Defined

The Fair Debt Collection Practices Act, 15 U.S.C. § 1692, et seq., (FDCPA) is a law enacted to protect consumers from abusive debt collectors. It provides several layers of protection for consumers, and requires specific disclosures be made within five days of a debt collector making collections attempts.[1] It also requires the debt collector take specific steps when an account is disputed,[2] and stop collection on a debt when instructed by the consumer.[3] However, the borrower must notify the debt collector in writing before it is required to cease communication.[4]

Consumers may bring lawsuits against debt collectors violating the FDCPA, and may obtain damages from the debt collector.

The lender may call a borrower directly to collect on its own debt, if it uses its regular corporate name and is not primarily in the collection business.[5] If the lender or servicer changes after the default, the new lender or servicer must comply with the FDCPA.[6] The law firm representing the lender must comply with the FDCPA.[7]

Spot It!

The FDCPA kicks in after the borrower goes into default and then contact is initiated by a new servicer, lender, or collection agency.

Any communication with the debtor after the debtor informs the debt collector in writing of his or her desire for ceasing communication is a violation of the act.[8] The debtor should keep track of each communication made by the debt collector, and use this as proof of an FDCPA violation.

Additionally, any attorneys fees or other charges imposed by a debt collector that are not expressly authorized in the mortgage violate the FDCPA.[9]

---

[1] 15 U.S.C. § 1692(g).
[2] Id.
[3] 15 U.S.C. § 1692(c)(a).
[4] 15 U.S.C. § 1692(c).
[5] 15 U.S.C. § 1692(a)(6).
[6] Id.
[7] Id. *Miller v. McCalla, Raymer, Padrick, Cobb, Nichols, and Clark, LLC.,* 214 F.3d 872 (7th Cir. 2000). However, if the law firm does not make contact with the borrower other than to file the lawsuit, the Complaint is *not* considered an initial contact. 15 U.S.C. § 1692(g)(d).
[8] 15 U.S.C. § 1692(c)(a).
[9] 15 U.S.C. § 1692(f)(1)

LIMITATIONS

The act does not apply to a lender who owned the loan before default.[10] If the lender did not change, and is foreclosing on its own account, then the FDCPA does not apply to it. However, if the lender changed after the default, then the new lender would need to comply with the act.[11]

POTENTIAL RECOVERY

A debt collector who does not comply with the FDCPA is liable in an amount equal to the sum of:[12]

1. Any actual damage sustained by a violation of the act;
2. Additional damages up to $1,000; and
3. The costs of the action and reasonable attorneys fees.
    a. Note: An action brought in bad faith by the debtor may subject the debtor to the other party's attorneys fees.[13]

APPLICABLE LAW OR CIVIL RULE

The Fair Debt Collection Practices Act begins at 15 U.S.C. § 1692.

ELEMENTS

1. The borrower must be a consumer, meaning any natural person obligated or allegedly obligated to pay any debt (not a LLC or company).
2. The lender must be a debt collector. The technical definition of a debt collector can be pulled directly from the FDCPA in Appendix Q.[14]
3. The debt collector may not engage in an unlawful activity. The FDCPA contains a number of limitations on debt collectors. (See Appendix Q.) This list includes:
    a. ACQUISITION OF LOCATION INFORMATION. Any debt collector communicating with any person other than the consumer for the purpose of acquiring location information about the consumer shall:[15]

---

[10] 15 U.S.C. § 1692(a).
[11] 16 U.S.C. § 1692(a)(6).
[12] 16 U.S.C. § 1692(k)(a)(1), (2)(A).
[13] 16 U.S.C. § 1692(k)(a)(3).
[14] 16 U.S.C. § 1692(a)(6).
[15] 16 U.S.C. § 1692(b).

        i.   identify himself, state that he is confirming or correcting location information concerning the consumer, and, only if expressly requested, identify his employer;

        ii. not state that such consumer owes any debt; and

        iii. not use any language or symbol on any envelope or in the contents of any communication effected by the mails or telegram that indicates that the debt collector is in the debt collection business or that the communication relates to the collection of a debt.

b. CEASING COMMUNICATION. If a consumer notifies a debt collector in writing that the consumer refuses to pay a debt or that the consumer wishes the debt collector to cease further communication with the consumer, the debt collector shall not communicate further with the consumer with respect to such debt, except:[16]

        i.   to advise the consumer that the debt collector's further efforts are being terminated;

        ii. to notify the consumer that the debt collector or creditor may invoke specified remedies which are ordinarily invoked by such debt collector or creditor; or

        iii. where applicable, to notify the consumer that the debt collector or creditor intends to invoke a specified remedy. If such notice from the consumer is made by mail, notification shall be complete upon receipt.

c. HARASSMENT OR ABUSE. A debt collector may not engage in any conduct the natural consequence of which is to harass, oppress, or abuse any person in connection with the collection of a debt.[17]

d. FALSE OR MISLEADING REPRESENTATIONS. A debt collector may not use any false, deceptive, or misleading representation or means in connection with the collection of any debt. Without limiting the general application of the foregoing, the following conduct is a violation of this section:[18]

        i.   The false representation or implication that the debt collector is vouched for, bonded by, or affiliated with the United States or any State, including the use of any badge, uniform, or facsimile thereof.

        ii. The false representation of—

            1. the character, amount, or legal status of any debt; or

---

[16] 16 U.S.C. § 1692(c).
[17] 16 U.S.C. § 1692(d).
[18] 16 U.S.C. § 1692(e).

2. any services rendered or compensation which may be lawfully received by any debt collector for the collection of a debt.

3. The false representation or implication that any individual is an attorney or that any communication is from an attorney.

4. The representation or implication that nonpayment of any debt will result in the arrest or imprisonment of any person or the seizure, garnishment, attachment, or sale of any property or wages of any person unless such action is lawful and the debt collector or creditor intends to take such action.

5. The threat to take any action that cannot legally be taken or that is not intended to be taken.

e. VALIDATION OF DEBT. Within five days after the initial communication with a consumer in connection with the collection of any debt, a debt collector shall, unless the following information is contained in the initial communication or the consumer has paid the debt, send the consumer a written notice containing:[19]

   i. the amount of the debt;

   ii. the name of the creditor to whom the debt is owed;

   iii. a statement that unless the consumer, within thirty days after receipt of the notice, disputes the validity of the debt, or any portion thereof, the debt will be assumed to be valid by the debt collector;

   iv. a statement that if the consumer notifies the debt collector in writing within the thirty-day period that the debt, or any portion thereof, is disputed, the debt collector will obtain verification of the debt or a copy of a judgment against the consumer and a copy of such verification or judgment will be mailed to the consumer by the debt collector; and

   v. a statement that, upon the consumer's written request within the thirty-day period, the debt collector will provide the consumer with the name and address of the original creditor, if different from the current creditor.

---

[19] 15 U.S.C. § 1692g(a)(1)-(5); *Spears v. Brennan*, 745 N.E.2d 862; 2005 LEXIS 33591; 2005 LEXIS 33591; citing, *Walker v. National Recovery, Inc.*, 200 F.3d 500, 501 (7th Cir. 1999). Debt collection notices sent to consumers must not confuse them about the verification rights established by the FDCPA. *Walker*, 200 F.3d at 501; *Marshall-Mosby v. Corporate Receivables, Inc.*, 205 F.3d 323, 326 (7th Cir. 2000) (noting that key consideration is that unsophisticated consumer is to be protected against confusion, whatever form it takes). Indeed, the Act "leaves no room for deviation in the language of the . . . notice." *Jang v. A.M. Miller & Assoc.*, 122 F.3d 480, 482 (7th Cir. 1997).

f. VALIDATION OF DEBT II. If the consumer notifies the debt collector in writing within the thirty-day period described in subsection (a) that the debt, or any portion thereof, is disputed, or that the consumer requests the name and address of the original creditor, the debt collector shall cease collection of the debt, or any disputed portion thereof, until the debt collector obtains verification of the debt or any copy of a judgment, or the name and address of the original creditor, and a copy of such verification or judgment, or name and address of the original creditor, is mailed to the consumer by the debt collector.[20]

    i. Collection activities and communications that do not otherwise violate this title may continue during the 30-day period referred to in subsection (a) unless the consumer has notified the debt collector in writing that the debt, or any portion of the debt, is disputed or that the consumer requests the name and address of the original creditor. Any collection activities and communication during the 30-day period may not overshadow or be inconsistent with the disclosure of the consumer's right to dispute the debt or request the name and address of the original creditor.

g. UNAUTHORIZED FEES. The debt collector may not impose any attorneys fees or other charges unless expressly authorized in the mortgage.[21]

FDCPA CHECKLIST

☐ Verify the lender is a debt collector under the act.[22]

☐ Establish whether the debt collector engaged in an unlawful activity.
- o The lender violated the FDCPA by:_____.
- o The lender did not mail written notice to the consumer when it began collecting the loan after the default.[23]
- o The lender failed to include one of the following in its written notice:[24]
  - o the amount of the debt;
  - o the name of the creditor to whom the debt is owed;
  - o a statement that unless the consumer, within thirty days after receipt of the notice, disputes the validity of the debt, or any

---

[20] 15 U.S.C. § 1692(g)(b).
[21] 15 U.S.C. § 1692(f)(1)
[22] 16 U.S.C. § 1692(a)(6).
[23] 16 U.S.C. § 1692(g).
[24] Id.

portion thereof, the debt will be assumed to be valid by the debt collector;

- o a statement that if the consumer notifies the debt collector in writing within the thirty-day period that the debt, or any portion thereof, is disputed, the debt collector will obtain verification of the debt or a copy of a judgment against the consumer and a copy of such verification or judgment will be mailed to the consumer by the debt collector; and
- o a statement that, upon the consumer's written request within the thirty-day period, the debt collector will provide the consumer with the name and address of the original creditor, if different from the current creditor.
- o Also, check to ensure the attorney for the lender complied with the FDCPA when it took over the loan file for foreclosure. Remember, serving the complaint is *not* an initial communication under the FDCPA (however, other direct communication would trigger the FDCPA notice provisions).[25]
  - o The attorney violated the FDCPA by_____.
  - o The attorney did not mail written notice to the consumer when it began collecting the loan after the default.[26]
  - o The attorney failed to include one of the following in its written notice:[27]
    - o the amount of the debt;
    - o the name of the creditor to whom the debt is owed;
    - o a statement that unless the consumer, within thirty days after receipt of the notice, disputes the validity of the debt, or any portion thereof, the debt will be assumed to be valid by the debt collector;
    - o a statement that if the consumer notifies the debt collector in writing within the thirty-day period that the debt, or any portion thereof, is disputed, the debt collector will obtain verification of the debt or a copy of a judgment against the consumer and a copy of such verification or judgment will be mailed to the consumer by the debt collector; and
    - o a statement that, upon the consumer's written request within the thirty-day period, the debt collector will provide

---

[25] 15 U.S.C. § 1692(g)(d).
[26] 16 U.S.C. § 1692(g).
[27] Id.

the consumer with the name and address of the original creditor, if different from the current creditor.

- o Check to see if any attorneys fees or other charges have been imposed by the debt collector that are not expressly authorized in the mortgage.[28]

DEFENSES

DEFENSES

Use violations of the FDCPA as offset damages against the lender foreclosing. Use counter claims to allege FDCPA violations.

COUNTER CLAIMS

The following is an example of a general FDCPA counter claim with prayer for relief. The violations allege stem from violations of the FDCPA, and common law violations of interference of contract and defamation of character. Note: This example lacks some specifics and details that may need to be added to have a properly plead complaint. For example, it should include what specifically the collection agency did in order to violate each specific section alleged to have been violated.

COUNT ONE – FAIR DEBT COLLECTION PRACTICES ACT

[paragraph no.] Defendant is a consumer, as defined by 15 U.S.C. §§ 1681a(c) and 1692a(3).

[paragraph no.] Plaintiff is a debt collector as defined by 15 U.S.C. § 1692a(3), and a person as defined by 15 U.S.C. § 1681a(b).

[paragraph no.] The account subject to this complaint is a debt, as defined by 15 U.S.C. § 1692a(5).

[paragraph no.] On or before January 1, 2007, without first communicating with Defendant, Plaintiff caused a collection account, number 4567, to be placed on Defendant's TransUnion credit report.

[paragraph no.] On or about June 18, 2007, having received no communication from Plaintiff, Defendant mailed and Plaintiff received a letter disputing the validity of the account, making Plaintiff aware of its obligations under the Fair Debt Collection Practices Act, 15 U.S.C. § 1692, et seq. (FDCPA), and instructing it to immediately remove the account from Defendant's credit report.

---

[28] 15 U.S.C. § 1692(f)(1)

[paragraph no.] On or about August 19, 2007, Defendant mailed Plaintiff a statement seeking payment of a debt in the amount of $200.00, account number 12345, which Plaintiff alleges is the same debt that appears on her credit report.

[paragraph no.] On or about August 30, 2007, Defendant mailed, and Plaintiff received, a letter where she again disputed the validity of the account, thus again making Plaintiff aware of its obligations under the FDCPA; Defendant instructed it to immediately remove the account from Defendant's credit report.

[paragraph no.] Defendant thereafter paid $200.00 to satisfy the amount stated as owed.

[paragraph no.] On October 28, 2007, Plaintiff mailed a letter to Defendant representing account number 12345 was paid in full.

[paragraph no.] On January 3, 2008, Plaintiff mailed a letter to Defendant indicating the "proof of the debt" she had requested was enclosed, and represented the account's balance as $.00.

[paragraph no.] On July 15, 2008, Broker Mortgage Services Inc. obtained Defendant's credit report in connection with a mortgage application that she had submitted.

[paragraph no.] That credit report inaccurately and falsely indicates an outstanding collection account, number 4567, with an unpaid balance of $200.00 naming Plaintiff as the creditor and jeopardizes her ability to obtain financing.

[paragraph no.] Defendant alleges Plaintiff never removed the collection account from Defendant's credit report between January 10, 2007 and July 15, 2008, and the account is still reflected on her credit report as an unpaid collection account

[paragraph no.] Defendant alleges her ability to secure a mortgage loan to purchase a home is compromised by the presence of the inaccurate account on her credit report.

[paragraph no.] Defendant alleges her inability to secure a mortgage loan causes her to continue to rent, when she could be building equity in a home.

[paragraph no.] Defendant alleges the equity she loses each month from not being able to purchase a home amounts to $700 per month.

[paragraph no.] Defendant alleges Plaintiff is in violation of the Fair Debt Collection Practices Act, 15 U.S.C. § 1692, et seq.

COUNT TWO –INTERFERENCE OF CONTRACT

[paragraph no.] Defendant incorporates paragraphs 1 through 17, as if fully rewritten here.

[paragraph no.] Defendant alleges Plaintiff's false reporting of the account to credit bureaus has prevented her from making a contract for a mortgage loan.

COUNT THREE – DEFAMATION OF CHARACTER AND LIBEL

[paragraph no.] Defendant incorporates paragraphs 1 through 19, as if fully rewritten here.

[paragraph no.] Defendant alleges Plaintiff's actions constitute the publication in writing of a false matter maliciously which reflects plaintiff in a defamatory manner and that has caused her damages.

PRAYER FOR RELIEF

WHEREFORE, Defendant prays for the following:

[paragraph no.] Injunctive relief requiring Plaintiff to immediately remove Defendant's account, known to her as number 12345, appearing on her credit report as account number 4567, from any and all credit reporting agencies it reports to, including, but not limited to, TransUnion, Equifax, and Experian;

[paragraph no.] Injunctive relief prohibiting Plaintiff from ever again reporting Defendant's account to any and all credit reporting agencies, including, but not limited to, TransUnion, Equifax, and Experian;

[paragraph no.] Actual damages, pursuant to 15 U.S.C. § 1692k(a)(1), in an amount equal to $700 per month from July 15, 2008, plus $200, which represents the amount of the collection account.

[paragraph no.] Additional damages, pursuant to 15 U.S.C. §§ 1692k(2)(A), in the amount of $1,000;

[paragraph no.] The costs of this action, pursuant to 15 U.S.C. § 1692k(a)(3);

[paragraph no.] Attorney's fees, pursuant to 15 U.S.C. § 1692k(a)(3); and

[paragraph no.] Any other relief this Court deems just and equitable.

THIRD PARTY CLAIMS

Any party subject to the FDCPA may be sued as a third party complainant if they violate the FDCPA, including the lawyer or law firm representing the lender. Any party violating the FDCPA that is not party to the lawsuit may be brought into the lawsuit. Alternatively, a separate lawsuit may be initiated against that party.

FAIR DEBT COLLECTION PRACTICES ACT LETTER TO CEASE COMMUNICATION

Today's Date

Lender Name
Lender Address
City, State, Zip Code

RE: Account Number

To Whom It May Concern:

Pursuant to 15 U.S.C. 1692(c), I hereby notify you of my wishes that your firm ceases further communication with me on the above referenced account. 15 U.S.C. 1692(c) states in part:

> "If a consumer notifies a debt collector in writing that the consumer refuses to pay a debt or that the consumer wishes the debt collector to cease further communication with the consumer, the debt collector shall not communicate further with the consumer with respect to such debt..."

If your firm attempts to communicate with me further in violation of the Fair Debt Collections Practices Act, 15 U.S.C. 1692, *et seq.*, I will file a lawsuit and seek statutory damages pursuant to that Act.

Regards,

Your Name
Your Address
City, State, Zip Code

DEFENSE #8: FAIR CREDIT REPORTING ACT (FCRA)

FAIR CREDIT REPORTING ACT (FCRA)

DEFINED

The Fair Credit Reporting Act (FCRA), 15 U.S.C. § 1681a, et seq., is an act that governs the reporting of consumer information to credit bureaus, as well as information disclosed by bureaus to others. For purposes of foreclosure defense, the credit bureau may be subject to liability if it is improperly reporting the account. Lenders can be held liable under the act, but only by governmental agencies. Falsely reporting the account may subject a bureau to civil liability. Here are some rules associated with credit reporting:

Duties after an adverse action. If the lender takes an adverse action based in part on a credit report, including denying loan modification, the user must provide the consumer with a statement indicating he or she may obtain a free copy of the credit report within 60 days of the denial.[1]

Verify or delete information. The credit bureaus must verify any information the consumer disputes within 30 days of receipt of the dispute, or remove the disputed information from the credit report.[2] However, the bureau does not need to respond to frivolous disputes.[3]

Duty to provide accurate information. It is illegal to report information if the reporting party knows, or reason to believe, the information reported is inaccurate.[4] If the consumer notifies a company that it is reporting inaccurate information, and that information is actually inaccurate, then the company must correct the error.[5]

Notice to Home Loan Applicant. The following notice must have been given to the home loan applicant as part of the application process:[6]

> **Notice To The Home Loan Applicant**
>
> In connection with your application for a home loan, the lender must disclose to you the score that a consumer reporting agency distributed to users and the lender used in connection with your home loan, and the key factors affecting your credit scores.
>
> The credit score is a computer generated summary calculated at the time of the request and based on information that a consumer reporting agency or lender has

---

[1] 15 U.S.C. § 1681m(a).
[2] 15 U.S.C. § 1681i(a)(1)(A).
[3] 15 U.S.C. § 1681i(a)(3).
[4] 15 U.S.C. § 1681s-2(a)(1)(A)
[5] 15 U.S.C. § 1681s-2(a)(1)(B)(i),(II).
[6] 15 U.S.C. § 1681g(g)(1)(D).

on file. The scores are based on data about your credit history and payment patterns. Credit scores are important because they are used to assist the lender in determining whether you will obtain a loan. They may also be used to determine what interest rate you may be offered on the mortgage. Credit scores can change over time, depending on your conduct, how your credit history and payment patterns change, and how credit scoring technologies change.

Because the score is based on information in your credit history, it is very important that you review the credit-related information that is being furnished to make sure it is accurate. Credit records may vary from one company to another.

If you have questions about your credit score or the credit information that is furnished to you, contact the consumer reporting agency at the address and telephone number provided with this notice, or contact the lender, if the lender developed or generated the credit score. The consumer-reporting agency plays no part in the decision to take any action on the loan application and is unable to provide you with specific reasons for the decision on a loan application.

If you have questions concerning the terms of the loan, contact the lender.

The FCRA governs all inaccurate information contained in a credit report, irrespective of any consumer default. That is, if the account is 4 months late, but the bureau is reporting it as 5 months late, then it is reporting inaccurate information. Likewise, if the account is "delinquent," but the bureau indicates the account as being "charged-off," then this is inaccurate reporting.

It may be well worth your effort to obtain a copy of your credit report. Each bureau is required to provide consumers one free copy of their credit report each year. They may be obtained online at www.annualcreditreport.com, by calling 1-877-322-8228, or by completing the Annual Credit Report Request Form[7] and mailing it to: Annual Credit Report Request Service, P.O. Box 105281, Atlanta, GA 30348-5281.

When ordering, be prepared to provide your name, address, Social Security number, and date of birth. To verify your identity when requesting information online and via telephone, additional information that only you would know will need to be provided (like the amount of payment on a car loan).

---

[7] The form is available online at: http://www.ftc.gov/bcp/conline/include/requestformfinal.pdf.

LIMITATIONS

This law offers civil penalties to consumers when the credit bureaus violate the FCRA.[8] However, furnishers of information (creditors) are not subject to civil liability by consumers under the act.[9] Instead, governmental agencies must sue.[10]

POTENTIAL RECOVERY

Civil liability for *willful* noncompliance of the FCRA enables the consumer to recover from the credit bureau 1) actual damages between $100 and $1,000, and 2) costs of the action and attorney's fees.[11]

Civil liability for *negligent* noncompliance of the FCRA enables the consumer to recover 1) any actual damages sustained by the consumer, and 2) costs of the action and attorney's fees.[12]

APPLICABLE LAW OR CIVIL RULE

The Fair Credit Reporting Act (FCRA) begins at 15 U.S.C. § 1681a. There may also be state laws that expand creditors' responsibility for accurate credit reporting.

DEFENSES

An FCRA claim can be used to offset liability in a foreclosure action. The claim would be raised as a third party claim against a credit bureau in the foreclosure lawsuit. FCRA also enables attorneys fees for successful actions, which may be substantial. If the credit bureau is refusing to correctly report a debt, a third party action could be brought against that bureau.

---

[8] 15 U.S.C. § 1681o.
[9] 15 U.S.C. § 1681s-2(c).
[10] 15 U.S.C. § 1681s-2(d).
[11] 15 U.S.C. § 1681n.
[12] 15 U.S.C. § 1681o.

DEFENSE #9: REAL PARTY IN INTEREST

REAL PARTY IN INTEREST

DEFINED

Every foreclosure lawsuit must be brought in the name of the party who has a legal right to foreclose. This is the foundation of being able to file any lawsuit, or to have "standing" to maintain a lawsuit. If the plaintiff is not the party who actually owns the mortgage or note, then it does not have the right to bring or maintain the lawsuit. Arguing that the plaintiff is not the owner of the mortgage challenges its "standing" as the "real party in interest." For example, if you owed your brother Bob $100, your uncle Frank could not bring a lawsuit against you if you did not pay Bob the money. This is because Bob is the party with standing to bring the lawsuit, obviously not Frank. However, if Bob needed the $100 now, he might sell the debt to Frank in exchange for $100, and then Frank would have the right to sue you. Bob can "assign" the debt to Frank. Bob becomes the assignor and Frank the assignee.

Mortgages work the same way. When a borrower closes on a loan, it may be with ABC Mortgage Company. The mortgage and note must be recorded with the proper governmental agency (usually a county recorder), which lets everyone know ABC has an interest in that property. [1]

If another party, XYZ, wants to bring a lawsuit (foreclosure) on a mortgage and note that ABC company owns, then XYZ must obtain an assignment transferring rights to it. Just like Bob assigning his interest to Frank, ABC can make an assignment to XYZ. However, several important procedures must be followed to make that transfer legally effective. Foremost, ABC must sign a written document assigning ABC's interest in the mortgage and note to XYZ. Without a written piece of paper,[2] XYZ cannot prove in court it has standing to bring a foreclosure. There must be a valid assignment, or no standing exists.

Big problems for lenders begin when XYZ forecloses on a borrower's property instead of ABC and XYZ does not bother to get an assignment executed or recorded with the government. This is so common that, chances are, your mortgage foreclosure was brought by a company who did not get an assignment or mortgage executed or recorded before it filed its lawsuit. Unless your state mandates an assignment be recorded before filing a

---

[1] Florida's recording statute is Florida Statute § 701.02(1). Ohio's recording statute is Revised Code § 5301.25. Many states have specific rules that state a mortgage is not valid unless it is recorded, which gives ABC a very big interest in making sure it records its mortgage with the proper authority. Thus, everyone knows by way of recording, that ABC is the holder of the mortgage and/or note. Everyone is also on notice ABC is the party with standing to file any foreclosure lawsuit against you.

[2] Although beyond the scope of this document, failing to have an assignment written violates many states' Statute of Frauds. See Ohio Revised Code § 1335.04.

lawsuit (ensuring the lender executed an assignment),[3] the borrower likely has grounds to move for an immediate dismissal of the foreclosure for lack of standing (if you can prove no assignment exists).

If, on the other hand, the bank has filed an assignment of mortgage, it still likely has not provided an accurate picture as to the correct chain of ownership. That is, even though the assignment indicates XYZ received the mortgage directly from ABC through the assignment, this likely is not what has really happened. In realty, mortgages are bought and sold behind the scenes many, many times before it ends up in the hands of XYZ. This is due to a very complicated way of structuring mortgage debt. Debt structuring enables the mortgage/note to be sold as bonds to Wall Street. Without getting into details, it is very likely that ABC sold the mortgage to DEF, who then sold it to GHI, who then sold it to JKL, and so on, until it ended up in the hands of XYZ. These multiple transfers are the basis of your defense.

CHAIN OF TITLE – WIN THE FORECLOSURE ACTION

The ownership of a mortgage from party to party is commonly referred to as a "chain of title." Just like a chain created by links bound to each other, each transfer of the mortgage is a link that binds the previous owner to the next owner. The importance of the "chain of title" cannot be overemphasized for any person fighting a foreclosure action. It is critical that a proper chain of title exist and be valid from the first assignor to the last assignee. This is the single easiest way to defend the foreclosure because it takes minimal effort and can yield significant results (winning the action outright).

As mentioned, the transfer between ABC and XYZ lenders likely does not represent the true chain of title because there are likely multiple other parties involved between the two. The goal of this defense is to uncover what the true chain of title is, and then attack every single ownership transfer in the chain to ensure it was valid – especially in a written document.

This defense and the discovery listed below will almost surely cause the plaintiff to go into a tail-spin, grinding their case to a halt. This is because big lenders are slow at gathering paperwork and even slower at providing it. Any efforts here are sure to run up against refusals to produce documents. This is due to the very difficult task of producing and verifying a series of ownership documents in existence from numerous sources. It is very likely the lender foreclosing did not bother to secure a chain of title for the borrower's loan before the lender bought it – instead relying upon electronic transfers of information and ownership. This is one of the ways loans have been known to show up in multiple loan

---

[3] This is a matter of how the civil rules are interpreted by each court. Federal rules would require an immediate dismissal for lack of jurisdiction at the time the complaint was filed if no assignment was dated on or before the date of the lawsuit filing - Ohio treats the assignments differently. *Bank of NY v. Stuart*, 9th Dist. No. 06CA008953, 2007-Ohio-1483.

"pools" at the same time – because lenders simply do not take the time to execute written assignments for each loan. Your efforts with this defense will be designed to exploit this sloppiness to, hopefully, win the case.

THE IMPORTANCE OF STANDING

Standing is important because it establishes who the true owner of the mortgage and note is. As much as this defense discusses the procedural reasons behind challenging standings, standing is fundamentally important to every defendant because if the plaintiff is not the true owner, then the true owner could come along and sue the borrower again. That is correct, the same person could face two lawsuits for the same property, one after another, if the correct party with standing is not ascertained. Thus, standing is a critical component of the legal process and one every borrower should work tirelessly to establish.

Some courts take standing very seriously, as evidenced by a District Court judge in Massachusetts imposing sanctions against Ameriquest Mortgage Company in the amount of $250,000, against Wells Fargo in the amount of $250,000, and sanctions against their legal counsel for another $150,000 when they could not show standing.[4]

FEDERAL COURTS RULE ON THIS ISSUE

The Federal District Courts of Ohio have recognized the sloppy filings by mortgage issuers in this state. In dismissing fourteen foreclosure actions late last year for lack of standing, the Northern District Court for Ohio commented, "The [financial] institutions seem to adopt the attitude that since they have been doing this for so long, unchallenged, this practice equates with legal compliance."[5] It continued, "Finally put to the test, their weak legal arguments compel the Court to stop them at the gate."[6] These cases included *thirteen* foreclosures initiated by Deutsche Bank. These dismissals were followed two weeks later by the Southern District Court for Ohio, which acted to dismiss an additional *twenty-seven* foreclosure lawsuits.[7] Thereafter, the Southern District of Ohio dismissed *another fifteen* foreclosures,[8] and the dismissals continue because of lenders' failure to show standing.[9]

---

[4] *Nosek v. Ameriquest*, Case No. 02-46025-JBR, (D.Ma. 2008). You can find a brief article here: http://abajournal.com/news/judge_smacks_law_firms_partner_with_150k_sanctions_but_spares_2_associates
[5] *In re Foreclosure Cases*, (Oct. 31, 2007), N.D. Ohio No. 07-CV-2282, et. al., FN3, slip copy, 2007 WL 3232430, 2007 U.S. Dist. LEXIS 84011
[6] *Id.*
[7] *In re Foreclosure Cases*, (S.D. Ohio 2007), 521 F.Supp.2d 650.
[8] *In re Foreclosure Cases*, (December 27, 2007), S.D. Ohio 2007, No. 07-CV-166, et. al., slip copy 2007 WL 4589765
[9] *Deutsche Bank Nat. Trust Co. v. Steele*, (Jan. 8, 2008), S.D. Ohio No. 07-cv-886, Slip Copy 2008 WL 111227, 2008 U.S. Dist. LEXIS 4937

Spot It!

To spot whether the plaintiff foreclosing has standing, obtain a copy of the original mortgage and note filed with your country recorder or clerk (call either and ask where mortgage documents are recorded in your county). Then, obtain a copy of any subsequently recorded assignments of mortgage or notes from the same county officer.

Next, compare who the last assignee is in the documents (the last bank to show it owns the mortgage/note) with who is foreclosing on the property.

Note: Even if the last assignee *is* the party foreclosing, you **absolutely** want to serve the discovery highlighted below on the plaintiff.

Limitations

If you want to challenge standing using a Motion to Dismiss, then you must do so before filing your answer.[10] After the motion to dismiss is ruled upon (or if none has been filed), a borrower can and should also state lack of standing in their Answer.

Potential Recovery

Successfully attacking standing can cause the foreclosure action to be immediately dismissed (when using a Motion to Dismiss), causing the lender to gather its paperwork before refilling. In the event the lender attempts to lie to cover its tracks, or cannot get its paperwork in order, there is the potential for winning the foreclosure action outright (when the defense is included in the Answer). If the lender's paperwork is very bad and it chooses not to re-file, then a Quiet Title action could be brought to secure the property free and clear of any mortgage or lien.

Strategy

Win on Standing.

If the bank is a national lender, it likely is not the lender on record with the county recorder's office. Loans are bought and sold behind the scenes many times without corresponding assignments being recorded. This litigation strategy uses this fact to attack the sufficiency of the lawsuit, and box the lender into a position it can not back out of later. Here is how it works:

---

[10] See federal rule 12(b), and your state's corresponding rule of civil procedure.

First, file a **motion to dismiss** for lack of standing. (See Appendix C.) If the plaintiff is not the original mortgage holder, and is a big bank, they likely have not spent the time to file a recorded *assignment of mortgage* with the County Recorder. This means that the original mortgage document that is on file with the County does not indicate the owner of the mortgage is the plaintiff. A "Motion to Dismiss" is formulated on this deficiency, if it exists. If the county recorder shows the plaintiff as the current holder, then do not file this motion. Instead, use the discovery outlined below.

The motion (if the author's experience is indicative) will be defended with the bank scrambling to get the "current" holder of mortgage on record (likely the original party) to issue an assignment directly to the plaintiff, signed and dated *currently*. This will possibly defeat the motion to dismiss (in a state case), but will solidify your defense later. In federal court, the federal rules would require an immediate dismissal for lack of jurisdiction at the time the complaint was filed.[11] **After** this motion is ruled on (in the banks favor), file discovery requesting the information outlined below. This discovery is designed to get the bank to produce a chain of title, and to tie it in knots. The bank will have trouble here because it will need to rectify the date and party it tells you in discovery with the assignment it provided to the court in defending the earlier motion.

Mortgages are bought and sold many times behind the scenes without having a recorded assignment. There are blogs on mortgage insiders discussing mortgages even being owned by several "pools" at the same time. At this point in the lawsuit, it will be very difficult for the bank to produce a chain of title. If it does, you can easily pick apart each assignment to ensure it was valid. But, here is the kicker: the bank not only needs to prove chain of title, but that chain needs to include the original party taking back possession of the note before it was transferred to the plaintiff - because this was the assignment asserted in defense of your earlier motion. (Naturally, you will want every one of these assignments in writing and correctly dated.)

The borrower will have a good shot at tying the bank up at this point with lack of standing. The bank with either be unable to proceed with the correct chain of title, or will want to present a chain of title that does not jive with the assignment presented in defense of the earlier motion. If the borrower wanted to step up the pressure, he or she may seek to file a motion to compel or for sanctions when the bank begins to stonewall discovery efforts for fear of producing conflicting assignments.

If the bank attempts to change its story to contradict its earlier chain of title, file a judicial estoppel objection. (Seek the court to force the bank to prove the earlier assignment from the original holder.) Because one of the elements of judicial estoppel is that the court must

---

[11] *In re Foreclosure Cases*, (Oct. 31, 2007), N.D. Ohio No. 07-CV-2282, et. al., FN3, slip copy; *In re Foreclosure Cases*, (S.D. Ohio 2007), 521 F.Supp.2d 650; *In re Foreclosure Cases*, (December 27, 2007), S.D. Ohio 2007, No. 07-CV-166, et. al., slip copy.

be persuaded by the earlier evidence to estop contradictory new evidence from being presented,[12] you'll be able to point to the court's decision denying your motion to dismiss months earlier.

JUDICIAL ESTOPPEL

Judicial estoppel is a common law mechanism (created by the courts) to prevent litigants in court from changing their story half-way into a lawsuit because it is better for them to argue something that is contradictory to what he or she said earlier. Under judicial estoppel, the party making an earlier statement is forced to stick to that story during the lawsuit and in every other lawsuit after the one that the statement was made.

In a foreclosure utilizing this chapter's litigation strategy, this means the lender will need to prove that a chain-of-title that is impossible to prove. (Only one party can own the mortgage at a time.)

GET THE DOCUMENTS SIGNED IN BLUE INK

Expressly request the plaintiff produce for your inspection the original Note and Mortgage (signed in actual ink). In federal court, look to Civil Rule 34(a)(1)(A). See your state's corresponding rule.

APPLICABLE LAW OR CIVIL RULE

Federal Civil Rule 17(a) requires "an action must be prosecuted in the name of the real party in interest." The lender, as plaintiff-assignee, "bears the burden of demonstrating standing and must plead its components with specificity."[13]

In federal court and in Ohio, see Civil Rule 17. In Florida, see Civil Rule 1.210(a).

ELEMENTS

This is a rule based defense, so there are no elements to prove. It is sufficient to raise lack of standing as a defense in the answer to place the lender on notice of this defense. The borrower would be well served to work to obtain documents supporting the notion that the lender is not the real party in interest, but it is the lender's ultimate responsibility to show it

---

[12] *State v. Nunez*, 2nd Dist. No. 21495, 2007-Ohio-1054. Also see, *State v. Burgess*, 2nd Dist. No. 21315, 2006-Ohio-5309; *Zedner v. United States*, 126 S.Ct. 1976. (federal judicial estoppel).

[13] *Valley Forge Christian College v. Americans United for Separation of Church & State, Inc.*, 454 U.S. 464 (1982). *Also see, In re Foreclosure Cases*, (S.D. Ohio 2007), 521 F.Supp.2d 650 (detailing specific reasons why standing is a necessary for the court to have jurisdiction to hear the claim).

has standing. The borrower merely wants to keep poking holes in the lender's position of standing, using evidence obtained in discovery.

STANDING CHECKLIST

- ☐ Does the last owner of the **mortgage**, as recorded by the County, match the lender who filed the foreclosure lawsuit?
  - o Party on record with the County as mortgagee is:_____.
  - o Party foreclosing is: _____.
- ☐ Does the last owner of the **note**, as recorded by the County, match the lender who filed the foreclosure lawsuit?
  - o Party on record with the County as assignee is:_____.
  - o Party foreclosing is: _____.
- ☐ Print copy/obtain copy of the most recent assignment of **mortgage** on record with the County.
- ☐ Does the **mortgage** transfer ownership from the assignor (is the name spelled correctly)?
- ☐ Is the **mortgage** assignment correctly signed by the necessary parties? (I.e., Officer and/or Secretary?)
- ☐ Print copy/obtain copy of the most recent assignment of **note** on record with the County.
- ☐ Does the **note** transfer ownership from the assignor (is the name spelled correctly)?
- ☐ Is the **note** assignment correctly signed by the necessary parties? (I.e., Officer and/or Secretary?)
- ☐ Does the property information on the recorded assignment match the correct property parcel ID on the **mortgage**?
- ☐ Does the property information on the recorded assignment match the correct property parcel ID on the **note**?
- ☐ Does the Assignment reflect a transfer from the original mortgage holder, or does the Assignment reflect some other party acting as "nominee"?

DEFENSES

DEFENSES

First, file a motion to dismiss if the county recorder does not have an assignment of mortgage showing the plaintiff as the "current" owner of the mortgage and note. (See Appendix C.) (Note: filing a motion to dismiss on other grounds, like insufficient process,

must be combined with this motion, so one motion to dismiss contains all those defenses presented by motion before filing an answer.)

Always include the following paragraphs under the defenses section, regardless of whether a motion to dismiss is filed:

[*paragraph no.*] This court lacks subject-matter jurisdiction;

[*paragraph no.*] This plaintiff has failed to state a claim upon which relief can be granted;

You should also consider making a Qualified Written Request to your loan's current servicer to obtain current lender information.

AFFIRMATIVE DEFENSES

The defenses presented here are usually brought as defenses, and not affirmative defenses.[14]

STARTER DISCOVERY

INTERROGATORIES

[*paragraph no.*] State the date the plaintiff became holder of the **Mortgage**.

[*paragraph no.*] Identify Fully the party that sold, transferred, conveyed, or assigned the **Mortgage** to the plaintiff, and state the consideration provided by the plaintiff for such sale, transfer, conveyance, or assignment.

[*paragraph no.*] State the date the plaintiff became holder of the **Note**.

[*paragraph no.*] Identify Fully the party that sold, transferred, conveyed, or assigned the **Note** to the plaintiff, and state the consideration provided by the plaintiff for such sale, transfer, conveyance, or assignment.

[*paragraph no.*] Identify Fully who the "Loan Servicer" of the Mortgage is. If more than one exists, Identify Fully each, as they are known to the Plaintiff.

[*paragraph no.*] Identify Fully who the "Note Purchaser" of the **Mortgage** is, as it is known to the plaintiff. If there is more than one note purchaser, or multiple parties have held this distinction, Fully Identify each, as they are known to the plaintiff (i.e., provide a chain-of-title for the Mortgage).

---

[14] Federal Civil Rule 12(b). See your state's corresponding civil rule.

[*paragraph no.*] Identify Fully who the "Note Purchaser" of the **Note** is, as it is known to the plaintiff. If there is more than one note purchaser, or multiple parties have held this distinction, Fully Identify each, as they are known to the plaintiff (i.e., provide a chain-of-title for the Note).

[*paragraph no.*] Identify Fully each and every holder of the **Mortgage** since *[date of loan's closing – see Settlement Statement]* in chronological order, as this information is known to the plaintiff.

[*paragraph no.*] Identify Fully each and every holder of the **Note** since *[date of loan's closing – see Settlement Statement]* in chronological order, as this information is known to the plaintiff.

[*paragraph no.*] Identify Fully each and every document relied upon by the plaintiff that conferred powers upon the loan servicer to act as agent for the plaintiff in mailing the alleged notice when said notice was mailed.

[*paragraph no.*] Identify Fully the beneficiaries of each and every payment made by the defendant, including a breakdown of which beneficiary received how much of each of defendants payments, as this information is known to the plaintiff.

REQUESTS FOR ADMISSIONS

[*paragraph no.*] Admit the plaintiff did not become holder of the mortgage or note on *[state date appearing on the assignment the bank provided showing transfer to it]*.

[*paragraph no.*] Admit the mortgage broker/ loan originator of this loan was forced to buy-back the loan from the then-owner of the mortgage upon the borrower's alleged default.

REQUESTS FOR THE PRODUCTION OF DOCUMENTS

[*paragraph no.*] Provide each and every document bearing the defendants' name(s) under the control of the plaintiff.

[*paragraph no.*] Provide each and every assignment of mortgage under the plaintiff's control that sells, transfers, conveys, or assigns any or all interest in the **mortgage** subject to this lawsuit from any entity to any other entity.

[*paragraph no.*] Provide each and every assignment of mortgage under the plaintiff's control that sells, transfers, conveys, or assigns any or all interest in the **note** subject to this lawsuit from any entity to any other entity.

DEFENSE #10: UNCONSCIONABILITY

UNCONSCIONABILITY

DEFINED

Unconscionability is the absence of meaningful choice for one of the contracting parties, together with contract terms that are unreasonably favorable to the other party.[1]

In determining reasonableness or fairness, the primary concern is the circumstances that existed at the time the contract was formed.[2]

Unconscionability almost rises to the level of fraud or contractual capacity (unsound mind), but not does not quite get there.

SPOT IT!

To spot unconscionability, one must look at the overall transaction between the parties to determine whether it rises to the level necessary where it becomes evident to the court action must be taken to prevent an injustice from continuing.

LIMITATIONS

Unconscionability is difficult to prove. Generally, courts will not review the adequacy of the consideration or the terms the parties bargained for. Courts will assume the borrower and lender got what each sought from the transaction, so mounting an unconscionability claim is more difficult than merely presenting evidence. It must persuade the court to act.

Additionally, there are numerous regulations that govern the disclosures and procedures for making loans to consumers. Due to the degree of regulation present in the industry, courts will be reluctant to find unconscionability unless something egregious has occurred. Even then, the borrower might be able to obtain relief in federal law versus having to rely on unconscionability to make the case.

As a practical matter, a borrower defending a foreclosure action him/herself should be mindful about including multiple defenses in the transaction if unconscionability is pursued. That is, if the borrower is throwing everything up against the wall in hopes one defense sticks, the chances of unconscionability sticking becomes remote. If the court must dismiss multiple defenses as frivolous, it may assume this one is also frivolous. If a borrower is serious about this defense, he or she may want to seek qualified legal counsel.

---

[1] *Williams v. Walker-Thomas Furniture Co.*, 350 F.2d 445 (D.C. Cir. 1965) (as found in this famous goods transaction).
[2] *Id.*

166

POTENTIAL RECOVERY

A court may find the contract is invalid, the offending terms are invalid, or modification of the contract is warranted.

STRATEGY

The strategy of a borrower arguing unconscionability is to present the absolute worst picture of the situation as possible, listing in detail all of the ways the transaction is wrought with bad conduct.

The borrower should focus on showing 1) there was an absence of meaningful choice when the contract was signed, and 2) the terms are unreasonably favorable to the other party. The borrower should use as many "factors" (listed on the following pages) as possible, with explanations of how they apply here. (These factors are discussed in a memorandum in support/opposition attached to a motion – not as part of the actual motion.) If the borrower has additional reasons why he or she feels the transaction is unconscionable, those factors should also be discussed.

Remember, however, that a detailed recitation of the ways this loan is unconscionable should NOT be included in an answer. The answer only contains a short and plain statement of the defense, like "This note and mortgage are void for unconscionability." A recitation accompanies a motion for/against summary judgment in a memorandum.

APPLICABLE LAW OR CIVIL RULE

Unconscionability is generally a common law defense (not part of a state law), but may be part of statute in your state. For example, Ohio Revised Code § 1345.03 describes what constitutes unconscionable consumer sales acts. However, Ohio's law does not apply to many federal lending institutions,[3] so even a consumer in Ohio might need to rely on common law unconscionability if he or she chooses to pursue it.

Your state attorney general likely has a web page dedicated to informing consumers about your state's consumer protection statutes. Courts may also interpret state statutes, like the Massachusetts Supreme Judicial Court's recent decision that outlines four characteristics of presumptively deceptive and unfair loans. [4]

---

[3] Ohio R.C. § 1345.01(J). Ohio's Consumer Sales Practices Act does provide for unconscionability by mortgage brokers.
[4] Commonwealth v. Fremont Investment & Loan & another, 452 Mass. 733 (2008) (Botsford,J.)   http://www.mass.gov/Cago/docs/press/2008_12_09_sjc_fremont.pdf

ELEMENTS

The elements of unconscionability are generally:[5]

1) The absence of meaningful choice for one of the contracting parties,
2) Together with contract terms that are unreasonably favorable to the other party.
   a. Price alone will not constitute unconscionability.
   b. To establish unconscionability, the court will look to see if both substantive and procedural unconscionability were present at the time the contract was formed.[6]
      i. Substantive Unconscionability deals with unjust or "one-sided" contracts: unfairly oppressive to one of the parties.
      ii. Procedural Unconscionability is concerned with "unfair surprise," like fine print clauses or mistakes or ignorance of important facts.
         1. See the factors section on how to establish each.

FACTORS

Factors are very important in unconscionability defenses because the actions unconscionable actors will take vary from transaction to transaction. Factors are "reasons" why a particular transaction is so bad that it is unconscionable and warrants the court to act. It will be important in any unconscionability claim to paint a picture of bad conduct in such a way that the judge feels she must correct a fundamental wrong.

Most states require both substantive and procedural unconscionability be present, and there are some helpful federal rules that may help establish unconscionability for the borrower. For example, the F.T.C. published unfairness and deception rules that business must abide by, although consumers cannot sue for damages under them. In a foreclosure action, a consumer might not be able to recover damages for violating the rule, but could certainly point to it and say, "look judge, the lender is violating this federal law, which supports my case of unconscionability." The full F.T.C. statements are in the Appendices N and O.

---

[5] An IL court has stated "a contract is unconscionable where it is improvident, oppressive or totally one-sided. Relevant factors include gross disparity in bargaining positions of the parties together with terms unreasonably favorable to the stronger party." *Reuben H. Donnelley v. Krasny Supply Co.*, 592 N.E.2d 8, 12 (Ill.App.Ct 1991).

[6] Some jurisdictions only require either procedural or substantive unconscionability be present, but the majority require both.

GENERAL FACTORS OF UNCONSCIONABILITY

Procedural Unconscionability

Procedural unconscionability is about "unfair surprise." Factors to consider are:

- The age, education, intelligence, business acumen and experience of the borrower.
- The inability of the borrower to understand or read the language of the contract.
- The sales process being conducted in a language other than the language of the contract. (Sale in Spanish, papers are presented in English.)
- The closing conducted in English without an interpreter present.
- The relative bargaining power of the parties.
- Adverse construction of the language of the contract. (Like fine print clauses.)
- Manipulation of the rules.
- The manner in which the contract was formed.
- Whether the terms of the contract were possible.
- Whether the seller or lender knowingly took advantage of the consumer's inability to protect his or her interests.
- Oppressive terms.
- Last minute hikes in the terms.
- Failure to provide accurate initial Good Faith Estimate or disclosures.
- Refinance deception with respect to promising lower payments but actually:
  - New payments do not include taxes or insurance.
  - Number of new payments much larger.
  - Total period of repayment, thus total payments greater (30 years instead of 20).
  - Teaser rates that were false.
- The advertisements run afoul of federal guidelines on deceptive statements.[7]

Substantive Unconscionability

Substantive Unconscionability is about a contract that is too "one-sided." Factors to consider are:

- Relative fairness of the obligations.
- Oppressive terms.
- Overall imbalance of the obligations and rights imposed by the contract.
- Significant price disparities.

---

[7] *F.T.C. Policy Statement of Deception*, 103 F.T.C. 110, 174 (1984). (See Appendices N and O.)

- Inability of the consumer to receive substantial benefits from the transaction. (Like an unnecessary refinance.)
- Gross disparity between other loans on the market that like situated consumers could obtain, versus the one this consumer entered into.
- Not offering to qualify the homeowner for lower mortgage terms at a lower cost instead of going "stated" income.
- The income differences between the application form in the closing documents and the tax returns of the borrower are significant.
  - The broker may have filled out the application, not the borrower.
- Using a No Income No Asset (NINA), Stated Income Stated Asset (SISA), or like program instead of qualifying the borrower at the payment amount he or she could afford.
- Using an adjustable rate product when a fixed rate product was available, especially if used in conjunction with a NINA or SISA program to loan more money. (Remember, brokers are paid on loan sizes, which is an incentive to secure the biggest loan possible).
- The loan has a negative amortization schedule (loan size increases over time).
- The failure of the lender to carefully evaluate the repayment capabilities of the borrower.[8]
- Also, consider the knowledge of sub-prime lenders that their borrowers are prone to credit risks and the incentives present for lenders to conceal those risks. A law review article details the steps lenders take to solve the "lemon" loan problem, including structuring sequential tranches, conservative risk assessments by the rating agencies, diversification, pricing premiums, due diligence (limited), deal provisions, and credit-default swaps.[9]

F.T.C. RULES

The F.T.C. has authority to bring actions against companies that violate its rules on unfairness, as well as its rules on deception[10]. While there is no private right of action prescribed by the law (consumers cannot sue directly under the rules), these statements may prove helpful in supporting a borrower's position that a lender acted unconscionably during the loan process.

---

[8] See the Interagency Guidance on Nontraditional Mortgage Product Risks, 71 FR 58609, in the Appendix.
[9] *Turning a Blind Eye: Wall Street Finance of Predatory Lending*, Kathleen Engel & Patricia McCoy, 75 Fordham L. Rev. 2039, 2006-07
[10] Copies of the rules are included in Appendices N and O.

Unfairness will be determined by: "(1) whether the practice injures consumers; (2) whether it violates established public policy; (3) whether it is unethical or unscrupulous."[11]

Deception will be determined by looking at (1) whether there is a representation, omission, or practice that is likely to mislead the consumer, (2) how a consumer might perceive the practice acting reasonably in the circumstances, and (3) the representation, omission, or practice must be a "material" one. [12] A copy of the F.T.C.'s statements are in Appendices N and O.

UNCONSCIONABILITY CHECKLIST

☐ Was there procedural unconscionability present? Check if any of the following apply:
- o The age, education, intelligence, business acumen and experience of the borrower.
- o The inability of the borrower to understand or read the language of the contract. (Such as Spanish speakers.)
- o The sales process being conducted in a language other than the language of the contract. (Sale in French, papers are presented in English.)
- o The closing conducted in English without an interpreter present.
- o The relative bargaining power of the parties.
- o Adverse construction of the language of the contract. (Like fine print clauses.)
- o Manipulation of the rules.
- o The manner in which the contract was formed.
- o Whether the terms of the contract were possible.
- o Whether the seller or lender knowingly took advantage of the consumer's inability to protect his or her interests.
- o Oppressive terms.
- o Last minute hikes in the terms.
- o Failure to provide accurate initial Good Faith Estimate or disclosures.
- o Refinance deception with respect to promising lower payments but actually:
  - ▪ New payments don't include taxes or insurance.
  - ▪ Number of new payments much larger.

---

[11] F.T.C. Policy Statement on Unfairness, *2-3 (Dec. 17, 1980) (Appended to *International Harvester Co.*, 104 F.T.C. 949, 1070 (1984)). See, *Sperry & Hutchinson*, 405 U.S. 223, 244-45 n.5 (1972). See Appendix O.
[12] F.T.C. Policy Statement on Deception, *1-2 (October 14, 1983) (Appended to *Cliffdale Associates, Inc.*,103 F.T.C. 110, 174 (1984)). See Appendix N.

- Total period of repayment, thus total payments greater (30 years instead of 20).
- Teaser rates that were false.
  - o The advertisements run afoul of federal guidelines on deceptive statements.
- ☐ Can substantive unconscionability be established? Check the following:
  - o Relative fairness of the obligations.
  - o Oppressive terms.
  - o Overall imbalance of the obligations and rights imposed by the contract.
  - o Significant price disparities.
  - o Inability of the consumer to receive substantial benefits from the transaction. (Like an unnecessary refinance.)
  - o Gross disparity between other loan on the market that like situated consumers could obtain, versus the one this consumer entered into.
  - o Not offering to qualify the homeowner for lower mortgage terms at a lower cost instead of going "stated" income.
  - o The income differences between the application form (Document No. 1003) and the tax returns of the borrower are significant.
    - The broker may have filled out the application, not the borrower.
  - o Using a No Income No Asset (NINA), Stated Income Stated Asset (SISA), or like program instead of qualifying the borrower at the payment amount he or she could afford.
  - o Using an adjustable rate product when a fixed rate product was available, especially if used in conjunction with a NINA or SISA program to loan more money. (Remember, brokers are paid on loan sizes, which is an incentive to secure the biggest loan possible).
  - o The loan has a negative amortization schedule (loan size increases over time).
  - o The failure of the lender to carefully evaluate the repayment capabilities of the borrower. See the Interagency Guidance on Nontraditional Mortgage Product Risks, 71 FR 58609, in the Appendix.

DEFENSES

AFFIRMATIVE DEFENSES

Note that in some jurisdictions, the party foreclosing may be immune to an unconscionability defense if it was not involved in the original transaction.[13] If this is the case, you may need to sue the company who took the loan application or acted unconscionably in the consummation of the loan. You can file a third party complain seeking for the original party to indemnify you against any losses suffered in the foreclosure action.

[paragraph no.] Any contract between the parties is void for unconscionability.

STARTER DISCOVERY

INTERROGATORIES

Use interrogatories to uncover rate sheets, internal sales tools, sales manuals, training manuals, and the like that help establish your unconscionability defense. Note: If the plaintiff is not the party that took the loan application, it may not be able to deliver some of this information if it does not have it. You may need to subpoena these types of documents from the broker, or sue the broker using a third party complaint and then conduct discovery.

REQUESTS FOR ADMISSIONS

There could be endless array of requests for admissions, depending on the angle being taken under the umbrella of unconscionability. For example, if the loan was sold in Spanish, but closed in English, you may want to request the following admissions to establish these facts:

[paragraph no.] Admit *[name]* was the mortgage broker involved in brokering Defendant's loan.

[paragraph no.] Admit the loan sales process was conducted primarily in Spanish.

[paragraph no.] Admit the loan closing on *[date]* was conducted in English.

---

[13] See the *Holder in Due Course* doctrine requiring violations be evident on the face of the documents. 15 U.S.C. § 1641(a). But, consider the F.T.C. Holder in Due Course Rule 16 C.F.R. § 433 whereby consumers' claims and defenses against seller survive against holder of contract. With respect to the F.T.C. rule, see, *Brown v LaSalle Northwest National Bank*, 820 F Supp 1078 (ND Ill 1993) (claim against lender survives when lender is a participant ". . . the defendant can be part of a scheme to defraud consumers even if the regulation does not directly apply to lenders.")

REQUESTS FOR THE PRODUCTION OF DOCUMENTS

Request sales related documents, including internal memos, training manuals, and rate sheets to help establish unconscionability. But again, note: if the plaintiff is not the party that took the loan application, it may not be able to deliver some of this information if it does not have it. You may need to subpoena these types of documents from the broker. (See Appendix K).

COUNTER CLAIMS

It may be brought as a counter claim to secure damages for unconscionability if the foreclosing party is the same party as the one that took the loan application. Otherwise, a third party claim will need to be filed to use this as a sword to secure damages. If no foreclosure action is pending, it may be brought as a pre-emptive claim against the lender.

A counterclaim will need to plead the elements of unconscionability, which may look like this:

COUNT ONE

[paragraph no.] Defendant realleges as if set forth in this document paragraphs *[1- all paragraphs]* of the Answer;

[paragraph no.] Defendant alleges the mortgage loan was consummated under the umbrella of unconscionability, in that the Defendant lacked meaningful choice when *[he/she]* consummated the loan.

[paragraph no.] Defendant alleges the mortgage loan was consummated under the umbrella of unconscionability, in that the loan terms were unreasonably favorable to the Plaintiff.

[paragraph no.] Defendant alleges the mortgage loan was substantively unconscionable because *[state the first reason why it was **substantively unconscionable]**.*

[paragraph no.] Defendant alleges the mortgage loan was substantively unconscionable because *[state the second reason why it was **substantively unconscionable,** and repeat the paragraph until you have listed all the ways it was substantively unconscionable, using one paragraph per reason]*.

[paragraph no.] Defendant alleges the mortgage loan was substantively unconscionable because *[state the first reason why it was **procedurally unconscionable]**.*

[paragraph no.] Defendant alleges the mortgage loan was substantively unconscionable because *[state the second reason why it was* **procedurally unconscionable,** *and repeat the paragraph until you have listed all the ways it was procedurally unconscionable, using one paragraph per reason]*.

[paragraph no.] Defendant alleges the mortgage loan upon which this foreclosure is based was consummated under the umbrella of unconscionability, and is void.

[paragraph no.] Defendant alleges the Plaintiff is liable to the defendant for damages due to the mortgage loan's unconscionability.

THIRD PARTY CLAIMS

There is no need to sue third parties if you just seek to rescind the transaction or change the loan terms. However, if you want the mortgage broker to indemnify you for your losses, bring an unconscionability claim against the broker. Remember to allege each of the elements of unconscionability in the third party claim. Use the Counter claim section as a model.

DEFENSE #11: FAILURE TO STATE A CLAIM UPON WHICH RELIEF CAN BE GRANTED

FAILURE TO STATE A CLAIM UPON WHICH RELIEF CAN BE GRANTED

DEFINED

This defense argues the lender's lawsuit paperwork is deficient in some way. For example, if the lender fails to say the loan is in default in the lawsuit paperwork (the complaint), then it has failed to state a claim upon which relief can be granted. There can be no recovery if there is no default.

This defense can also argue the plaintiff cannot recover under the lawsuit, even if all of the facts in the complaint are true. For example, if the legislature decides to require a 180 day cooling-off period before foreclosures can be filed in court, a lender filing before the 180 days will not be entitled to recovery, and will have *failed to state a claim upon which relief can be granted*, even if there is a default.

It is a defense that is used in many different ways, depending on the circumstances of the case.[1]

In foreclosure actions, *failure to state a claim* can be used as an additional way of arguing the plaintiff is not the true owner of the mortgage (when presenting a *standing* defense). If the mortgage has been sold many times behind the scenes, it is possible the plaintiff is not able to recover under the mortgage. That is, although the factual allegations of the complaint are true, the plaintiff cannot foreclosure on the property because it is not the actual owner.[2] Because it is such a broad defense, it can be used in conjunction with just about every defense in this book.

Failure to state a claim is a very common defense used, and in some respects acts as a "catch all" to ensure no defense is waived before trial. It is invoked to ensure the defendant has a way to attack the sufficiency of the lender's case at any time, even if the borrower fails to include a particular defense up front that he or she wants to rely upon later.

Failure to state a claim is an affirmative defense that should be included in the Answer. It may also be used by motion before an answer is filed, or used at trial.[3]

---

[1] For another example, see *Dawson v. Wilheit,* 105 N.M. 734, 737 P.2d 93 (1987). There, the court found that no duty existed between the parties after this defense was raised, thus no recovery was possible, and the lawsuit was dismissed. Even though all the facts of the case were true, the defendant didn't owe the plaintiff a duty – so the plaintiff wasn't allowed to recover from the lawsuit.

[2] Many times the Complaint will not aver the plaintiff is the owner of the mortgage or note – it just assumes a valid sale. Technically, this would also be brought under the affirmative defense, "lack of subject matter jurisdiction."

[3] Civil rule 12(b)(6).

LIMITATIONS

Unless you have something very specific in mind, this defense is a generic tool to ensure you have the opportunity to defend against the lawsuit later, if you forget a particular available defense. However, the lender does have the ability to request the court strike this defense upfront if you are unable to articulate a reason it should be in the Answer. Because it will be rare for the lender to make that kind of request, it's wise to include it just in case.

POTENTIAL RECOVERY

This is another tool in the foreclosure defense toolkit. If the court finds the lender has failed to state a claim upon which relief can be granted, the case will be dismissed. However, expect the court not to rely solely upon this defense if it is used generically, but look towards one of the other defenses listed in this book for its rational.

STRATEGY

Include it as an affirmative defense in every foreclosure lawsuit, as it cannot harm to have it included, and it is a defense that is normally raised.

APPLICABLE LAW OR CIVIL RULE

Federal Civil Rule 12(b) governs this defense in federal court. See your state's corresponding civil rule.

DEFENSES

AFFIRMATIVE DEFENSES

There is nothing fancy to this defense. It is usually stated as follows:

[paragraph no.] Plaintiff has failed to state a claim upon which relief can be granted.

DEFENSE #12: FAILURE TO ESTABLISH CONDITIONS PRECEDENT

FAILURE TO ESTABLISH CONDITIONS PRECEDENT

DEFINED

This defense is very effective in dismissing foreclosure actions immediately, when a condition precedent has not been satisfied. When a condition precedent has not been satisfied, the borrower may immediately file a motion to dismiss before filing an Answer.[1] Alternatively, the borrower may want to raise condition precedent as a defense in the Answer to drag out the proceeding before having it dismissed.[2]

A **condition precedent** is merely something that must occur before a foreclosure action can be started. The most common condition precedent created by every mortgage is found in covenant 21 or 22, whereby the contract requires the lender to mail a *notice of acceleration* to the borrower before starting foreclosure. This covenant also requires the lender wait 30 days after mailing the notice before starting foreclosure. If the lender fails to mail the notice, or fails to wait the 30 days, the lender has failed to meet a condition precedent. If not met, the action *must* be dismissed and the lender must start from scratch (by mailing the notice and waiting 30 days before foreclosing).

SPOT IT!

If the borrower did *not* receive a *notice of acceleration* from the lender, check the mortgage for a covenant (paragraph) requiring a notice be mailed. If a covenant exists, then use this defense.

If the borrower received the notice, but then made a payment that was accepted by the lender, then there may be an argument that the default was temporarily cured, necessitating another notice be mailed and another 30 days pass.

Read the covenant carefully to determine who needs to mail the notice to the borrower. If it states the lender is required to mail the notice, check the mortgage to determine who the lender is.[3]

Check the mortgage for other conditions that may need to occur before foreclosure, which might also be conditions precedent.

---

[1] Civil Rule 12(b)(1), (2), and (6). Failure to perform a condition precedent effectively eliminates the court's jurisdiction to hear the claim.

[2] Civil Rule 9(c). Note that including this in an Answer, but waiting too long, may waive the defense.

[3] Check to see if the mortgage indicates the "lender" will change when the loan is sold to another party. Does the mortgage state the servicer can mail the notice instead of the lender?

If the mortgage is insured by FHA, then specific counseling must be initiated by the lender before foreclosure.[4] If they are not performed, then this failure would be a violation of a conditions precedent. (See Defense #13: FHA.)

LIMITATIONS

Raising *condition precedent* as a defense **requires** the defense be stated with particularity.[5] That means the borrower must specifically state the lender failed to mail the notice of acceleration as required by covenant *[21/22]* of the mortgage. Alternatively, the borrower must specifically state the lender failed to wait 30 days after mailing the notice of acceleration as required by covenant *[21/22]* of the mortgage.

The defense must be raised in the Answer or Motion to Dismiss. Failing to raise this defense may cause the defense to be forever lost (waived). If the Answer has already been filed, you may seek to amend the Answer to include this defense.

POTENTIAL RECOVERY

This defense causes the lender to have to start from scratch in the foreclosure process, first ensuring the condition precedent was met. This means the foreclosure action is dismissed (if a court action). The lender must then cure the condition precedent deficiency before filing a new action in court.

This defense does not obtain damages for the borrower. However, if the lawsuit is dismissed twice, then the dismissal acts as an adjudication of the merits.[6] That is, the lender would be unable to bring a third foreclosure action, effectively enabling the borrower to obtain the home free-and-clear of any mortgage by that lender.[7]

STRATEGY

A borrower may wish to bring up this defense in the Answer, instead of preemptively moving the court in a Motion to Dismiss. This would buy the borrower more time in the home, but caution is noted. Waiting too long in bad faith may waive this defense.

---

[4] 24 C.F.R. § 203.500, et seq.

[5] Civil Rule 9(c).

[6] Civil Rule 41(a)(1)(B). There are some instances where a claim may be dismissed twice and still be brought again, but a borrower is unlikely to experience that event.

[7] If the lender has dismissed the case twice, see an attorney immediately. If the lender files a third time it will be necessary to timely file a proper response. Additionally, an attorney could prepare a *quiet title* action (or motion) with the court to extinguish the mortgage.

APPLICABLE LAW OR CIVIL RULE

The conditions precedent defense in federal court is created by Federal Civil Rule 9(c). See your state's corresponding civil rule.

ELEMENTS

The elements to this defense are straight-forward:

1. Before the foreclosure was started, some condition needed to be met. (Either by the terms of the mortgage, by law, or otherwise.)
2. The lender did not meet that condition.

CONDITIONS PRECEDENT CHECKLIST

☐ Did the borrower receive a *notice of acceleration* from the lender before the lawsuit was started, as required by covenant 21 or 22 of the mortgage?

☐ Did the lender wait 30 days before starting the foreclosure action?

☐ If the borrower received the notice, but then made a payment that was accepted by the lender, was another notice mailed?

☐ Was the notice mailed by the correct party, as stated in the mortgage?

☐ Are there any other conditions precedents created by the mortgage?

DEFENSES

DEFENSES

Note: It may be wise to use this defense in a motion to dismiss for failure to state a claim upon which relief can be granted, instead of including this as a defense in the Answer.

[paragraph no.] The plaintiff has failed to state a claim upon which relief can be granted because the lender failed to meet a condition precedent of the mortgage when it failed to *[mail a notice of acceleration to the defendant]*, as required by covenant *[21/22]* of the mortgage.

AFFIRMATIVE DEFENSES

[*paragraph no.*] The plaintiff has failed to meet a condition precedent created by the mortgage because it failed to mail the notice of acceleration, as required by covenant [*21/22*] of the mortgage.

[*paragraph no.*] The plaintiff has failed to meet a condition precedent created by the mortgage because it failed to wait 30 days after mailing the notice of acceleration before filing this action, as required by covenant [*21/22*] of the mortgage.

STARTER DISCOVERY

INTERROGATORIES

[*paragraph no.*] Identify who the lender of the mortgage was on [*date notice of acceleration was mailed*].

REQUESTS FOR ADMISSIONS

[*paragraph no.*] Admit the notice of acceleration was not mailed to the borrower, as required by covenant [*paragraph number*] of the mortgage.

[*paragraph no.*] Admit the plaintiff was not the holder of either the mortgage or note on [*state the date the notice of acceleration was mailed by the servicer*].[8]

 [*paragraph no.*] Admit the entity that allegedly mailed defendant a notice of acceleration, as required by the mortgage, was not acting in a bona fide legal capacity for the plaintiff on the date said notice was mailed.

[*paragraph no.*] Admit no bona fide legal relationship exists between the plaintiff and the loan servicer.

REQUESTS FOR THE PRODUCTION OF DOCUMENTS

[*paragraph no.*] Provide a copy of the notice of acceleration allegedly mailed to the defendant before filing this lawsuit.

[*paragraph no.*] Provide each and every document relied upon by the plaintiff that conferred powers upon the loan servicer to act as agent for the plaintiff in mailing the alleged notice when said notice was mailed.

---

[8] This request goes to establishing the "lender," as defined in the mortgage, did not mail the notice – but, rather the servicer did so.

[*paragraph no.*] Provide each and every document relied upon by the plaintiff that establishes a bona fide legal relationship between it and the loan servicer.

COUNTER CLAIMS

This is not a counter claim. It is a defense to the foreclosure process.

THIRD PARTY CLAIMS

This defense challenges the lenders ability to foreclose on the mortgage. It is not brought against a non-party.

DEFENSE #13: FAILURE TO COMPLY WITH FHA PRE-FORECLOSURE REQUIREMENTS

FAILURE TO COMPLY WITH FHA PRE-FORECLOSURE REQUIREMENTS

DEFINED

Federal law and the U.S. Department of Housing and Urban Development (HUD) require lenders to take specific loss mitigation steps before filing a foreclosure action on loans insured by HUD.[1] These steps include mailing a publication called *How to Avoid Foreclosure*,[2] and in some instances, arranging a face-to-face meeting with the borrower.[3]

If the lender does not take the minimum steps necessary that comply with the law, then the foreclosure cannot proceed.[4] Failing to comply with FHA pre-foreclosure requirements is treated as a failure to meet a condition precedent.

LIMITATIONS

This defense is limited to loans that are insured by HUD (FHA mortgages). Conventional loans through Fannie Mae or Freddie Mac, as well as sub-prime loans, are not covered by this defense. The VA requires lenders make every effort to help veterans avoid foreclosure.[5]

This defense is limited to the pre-foreclosure steps that the lender must take. Once the lender has satisfied the initial steps (conditions precedent), it may proceed with the foreclosure process, even if loss mitigation or a loan workout is pending.

---

[1] 24 C.F.R. § 203.500, et. seq.; HUD Mortgagee Letter 00-05: Loss Mitigation Program – Comprehensive Clarifications of Policy and Notice of Procedural Changes.

"...in *Federal National Mortgage Association v. Moore*, 609 F.Supp. 194 (N.D.Ill. 1985), a case involving an FHA-insured mortgage, foreclosure was denied because of the mortgagee's failure to give to the mortgagor written notice of default and of intention to foreclose and of the mortgagor's right to apply to HUD for assignment of the mortgage in the form required by HUD regulations. See also, *Mellon Mtge. Co. v. Larios*, 97 C 2330, 1998 WL 292387 (N.D.Ill., May 20, 1998); *Federal Land Bank v. Overboe*, 404 N.W.2d 445 (N.D.1987); *Union Nat'l Bank v. Cobbs*, 567 A.2d 899 (Pa.Super. 1989)." *Federal Land Bank of St. Paul v. Overboe*, 404 N.W.2d 445 (N.D. 1987),

[2] 24 C.F.R. §§ 203.602; HUD Mortgagee Letter 00-05: Loss Mitigation Program – Comprehensive Clarifications of Policy and Notice of Procedural Changes at page 5.

[3] 24 C.F.R. § 203.604(b).

[4] 24 C.F.R. § 203.500. As put by the North Dakota Supreme Court, "...various courts have held that the failure of a lender to follow HUD regulations governing mortgage servicing constitutes a valid defense sufficient to deny the lender the relief it seeks in a foreclosure action. See *Federal National Mortgage Association v. Moore*, 609 F.Supp. 194 (N.D.Ill.1985); *Cross v. Federal National Mortgage Association*, 359 So.2d 464 (Fla.Dist.Ct.App. 1978); *Bankers Life Co. v. Denton*, 120 Ill.App.3d 576, 458 N.E.2d 203 (1983); *Heritage Bank, N.A. v. Ruh*, 191 N.J.Super. 53, 465 A.2d 547 (1983); *Associated East Mortgage Co. v. Young*, 163 N.J.Super. 315, 394 A.2d 899 (1978); *Federal National Mortgage Association v. Ricks*, 83 Misc.2d 814, 372 N.Y.S.2d 485 (1975). But see *Manufacturers Hanover Mortgage Corp. v. Snell*, 142 Mich.App. 548, 370 N.W.2d 401 (1985); *Federal National Mortgage Association v. Prior*, 128 Wis.2d 182, 381 N.W.2d 558 (Ct. App. 1985)." *Federal Land Bank of St. Paul v. Overboe*, 404 N.W.2d 445 (N.D. 1987).

[5] See the 26-94-01 VA Servicing Guide H26-94-1 at http://www.vba.va.gov/ro/south/spete/rlc/Servicer_Handbook.pdf (last visited Aug. 10, 2008.)

POTENTIAL RECOVERY

The failure to provide the necessary disclosures and counseling has been successfully used as an affirmative defense.[6] Additionally, the disclosure requirements create a conditions precedent to foreclosure. That is, foreclosure cannot be filed until all of the pre-foreclosure conditions are satisfied. (See Defense #12: Conditions Precedent.)

APPLICABLE LAW OR CIVIL RULE

The federal law governing FHA lenders' foreclosure duties can be found at 24 C.F.R. § 203.500, et. seq. The guidelines published by HUD that detail FHA lenders' requirements under the law can be found in HUD Mortgagee Letter 2000-05: Loss Mitigation Program – Comprehensive Clarifications of Policy and Notice of Procedural Changes. (Not included in the appendices.)

ELEMENTS

- ☐ The loan must be insured by HUD.
- ☐ There is no statute of limitations, but the borrower must be in default to trigger a lender's responsibility under this section of the law.
- ☐ The lender must mail *How to Avoid Foreclosure* by the end of the second month of any delinquency before foreclosing.[7]
    - o If the loan is reinstated after the pamphlet has been mailed, the lender must mail another copy if the loan again goes delinquent.[8] However, the lender only needs to send one copy every six months.[9]
- ☐ The lender must make a reasonable effort to arrange a face-to-face meeting with the borrower before three monthly installments are due on the mortgage and are unpaid, unless any of the following things apply:[10]
    - o The borrower does not reside in the mortgaged property;
    - o The property is not within 200 miles of the lender, its servicer, of a branch office of either;
    - o The borrower has clearly indicated that he or she will not cooperate in the interview;
    - o A repayment plan in created and the payments become current; or

---

[6] *Federal Land Bank of St. Paul v. Overboe*, 404 N.W.2d 445 (N.D. 1987).
[7] 24 C.F.R. § 203.602; HUD Mortgagee Letter 2000-05: Loss Mitigation Program – Comprehensive Clarifications of Policy and Notice of Procedural Changes at page 5.
[8] 24 C.F.R. § 203.602.
[9] Id.
[10] 24 C.F.R. § 203.604(b).

- o A reasonable effort to arrange a meeting is unsuccessful (consisting or at a minimum of one letter sent and certified as dispatched by the post office, *and* at least one trip to the property).[11]
- □ The lender may not initiate foreclosure until at least three full monthly installments due under the mortgage are unpaid.[12]

DEFENSES

This defense should be raised in a motion to dismiss for failing to perform a condition precedent. (See Defense #12.) Otherwise, a failure to perform duties under this section of the code may be raised as a defense or affirmative defense.

---

[11] 24 C.F.R. § 203.604(c)(5), (d); *Federal Land Bank of St. Paul v. Overboe*, 404 N.W.2d 445 (N.D. 1987); In *Bankers Life Co. v. Denton*, 120 Ill.App.3d 576, 458 N.E.2d 203 (3d Dist. 1983).

[12] 24 C.F.R. § 203.606(a). Section (b) lays out several exceptions to this rule. The lender does not need to wait if it determines the property has been vacant for more than 60 days, the borrower notifies the lender in writing that the default will not be cured, the property is occupied by paying tenants and the money is not being paid to the lender, or if the property is owned by a corporation or partnership. 24 C.F.R. § 203.606(b).

DEFENSE #14: MORTGAGE OR NOTE NOT ATTACHED TO COMPLAINT

Mortgage or Note not Attached to Complaint

Defined

Failing to attach the mortgage and note to a lawsuit is similar to a conditions precedent because it can immediately defeat the lawsuit. This defense is found within the rules of civil procedure, but is not universal to all states. In fact, the federal rules do not include a rule governing attached mortgages. Your state rule may look like Ohio's Civil Rule 10(D)(1), which is as follows:

> "*Account or written instrument.* When any claim or defense is founded on an account or other written instrument, a copy of the account or written instrument must be attached to the pleading. If the account or written instrument is not attached, the reason for the omission must be stated in the pleading.

Failing to attach the mortgage or note is a procedural defect that should be attacked with a motion to dismiss. It can also be included in an answer.

Even when the mortgage and note are attached, they should be accompanied by an affidavit by someone at the plaintiff's office swearing that the documents attached to the complaint are true and accurate copies of the originals, and that the originals are in her possession. Some civil rules may require the plaintiff state it is actually in possession of the original.

It would be very wise to request the plaintiff produce the *original* copies for inspection and coping through discovery. You will likely find that many lenders foreclosing have electronic copies of the documents but do not have the originals in their possession. The originals may be stored in a massive warehouse with millions of other documents, meaning it may be difficult for the lender to produce the actual original.

Get the Document Signed in Blue Ink!

Expressly request the plaintiff produce for your inspection the original Note and Mortgage (signed in actual ink). Civil Rule 34(a)(1)A) provides you this right.[1]

Limitations

There are no limitations on this defense. It requires very little effort on your part, and can be extremely beneficial if it applies in your situation.

---

[1] See, *SMS Financial LLC v Abco Homes, Inc.*, No. 98-50117 (5th Cir. 1999) (one of the elements of a claim on a promissory note is that the plaintiff must prove the existence of the note).

POTENTIAL RECOVERY

If the lender does not attach a copy of the mortgage or note and your civil rules requires it do so, the lawsuit would be subject to a motion to dismiss. If copies of the documents are attached to the complaint, but the originals are lost, you may defeat the entire action.[2]

APPLICABLE LAW OR CIVIL RULE

Each state civil rule will differ. Look for at your state's rules for an applicable civil rule. It might be located within your state's civil rule 10.

NOTE AND MORTGAGE CHECKLIST

- ☐ Does your state have a civil rule requiring a copy of the mortgage and note be attached to the complaint?
- ☐ Has the lender attached a copy of the mortgage and note to the complaint?
- ☐ Has the lender attached an affidavit stating the documents attached to the complaint are true and accurate copies of the original?
- ☐ Has the lender attached an affidavit stating it is in possession of the original mortgage and note?
- ☐ Have you requested through discovery the plaintiff produce the original mortgage and note?

---

[2] *SMS Financial LLC v Abco Homes, Inc.*, No. 98-50117, Feb 18, 1999 (5th Cir.) (one of the elements of a claim on a promissory note is that the plaintiff must prove the existence of the note).

DEFENSE #15: INSUFFICIENCY OF PROCESS

INSUFFICIENCY OF PROCESS

DEFINED

Insufficiency of process means the plaintiff in the lawsuit did not properly give a copy of the Complaint to the defendant. If the defendant did not properly receive a copy of the complaint, then there is insufficient "process" and the lawsuit cannot continue.

This defense is highly dependent on your state, and local rules governing how lawsuits are served on defendants. In federal court, service of process is governed by Rule 4. You will need to consult your state's civil rules of procedure to determine how process is completed and whether or not it was done correctly in this lawsuit.

LIMITATIONS

Many states address what must be done (specifically) to ensure process is completed correctly, so you must review your state's rules on service. Many states require personal service with delivery confirmation that a copy of the lawsuit has been "served" directly on the defendant. In foreclosure actions, this means an individual is dispatched with a copy of the lawsuit in hand to personally deliver it to the borrower. It may be sufficient to deliver the complaint by certified mail, to leave a copy of the lawsuit at the borrowers home, or publish notice of the lawsuit in a local newspaper if the borrower cannot be found.

POTENTIAL RECOVERY

Correct service of process is a matter of constitutional due process. Therefore, it must be done correctly or a lawsuit may not proceed.

DEFENSES

If service of process is defective, then a Motion to Dismiss would be proper.[1] It would also be acceptable to include insufficient process or service of process as a defense in the Answer.[2]

---

[1] Civil Rule 12(b)(4) or (b)(5).
[2] Id.

DEFENSE #16: NATIONAL FLOOD INSURANCE ACT

NATIONAL FLOOD INSURANCE ACT

DEFINED

The National Flood Insurance Act prohibits lenders from making, increasing, extending, or renewing any loan secured by improved real estate or a mobile home located or to be located in an area designated as a flood hazard area without obtaining food insurance coverage.[1] The insurance coverage must be in an amount at least equal to the outstanding principal balance of the loan, or the maximum limit of coverage made available under the Act, with respect to the particular type of property, whichever is less.[2]

The implementing rule requires lenders use a standardized form when disclosing to the home buyer whether or not the property is in a flood zone.[3] It also requires the lender force-place flood insurance if the lender later determines the property is within a flood zone and the consumer fails to obtain his/her own policy.[4]

LIMITATIONS

Failing to provide insurance does not provide the consumer the right to sue the lender under the Act. Instead, the "appropriate federal agency" may impose civil liabilities upon the lender.[5]

POTENTIAL RECOVERY

The homeowner cannot bring a claim directly for a failure to provide the necessary disclosures. Civil monetary penalties for failure to require flood insurance may only be brought by the federal government.

However, a consumer may have a cause of action in foreclosure under tort law if their property is actually damaged in a flood and the lender violated the Act.

Restatement Torts 2d § 286 states the following factors should be considered in determining whether an implied cause of action accrues through negligence under a statute:

> (a) whether the statute is designed to protect a class of persons which includes the one whose interest is invaded;

---

[1] 42 U.S.C. § 4012a(b),
[2] Id.
[3] 12 C.F.R. 339.6(a).
[4] 12 C.F.R. 339.7
[5] 42 U.S.C. § 4012a(f).

(b) to protect the particular interest which is invaded;

(c) to protect that interest against the kind of harm which has resulted; and

(d) to protect that interest against the particular hazard from which the harm results.[6]

APPLICABLE LAW OR CIVIL RULE

National Flood Insurance Act of 1968 begins at 42 U.S.C. 4001 et seq. The regulations requiring lenders use the form (below) is locate at 12 C.F.R. § 339.6 .

STANDARD FORM

APPENDIX A TO 12 C.F.R. 339 —FORM OF NOTICE OF SPECIAL FLOOD HAZARDS AND AVAILABILITY OF FEDERAL DISASTER RELIEF ASSISTANCE

We are giving you this notice to inform you that:

The building or mobile home securing the loan for which you have applied is or will be located in an area with special flood hazards. The area has been identified by the Director of the Federal Emergency Management Agency (FEMA) as a special flood hazard area using FEMA's *Flood Insurance Rate Map* or the *Flood Hazard Boundary Map* for the following community:

__ This area has at least a one percent (1%) chance of a flood equal to or exceeding the base flood elevation (a 100-year flood) in any given year. During the life of a 30-year mortgage loan, the risk of a 100-year flood in a special flood hazard area is 26 percent (26%). Federal law allows a lender and borrower jointly to request the Director of FEMA to review the determination of whether the property securing the loan is located in a special flood hazard area. If you would like to make such a request, please contact us for further information.

__ The community in which the property securing the loan is located participates in the National Flood Insurance Program (NFIP). Federal law will not allow us to make you the loan that you have applied for if you do not purchase flood insurance. The flood insurance must be maintained for the life of the loan. If you fail to purchase or renew flood insurance on the property, Federal law authorizes and requires us to purchase the flood insurance for you at your expense.

---

[6] As stated in Supreme Court case *Wyandotte Transportation Co. v. United States*, 389 U.S. 191, 88 S.Ct. 379, 19 L.Ed.2d 407 (1967).

___ Flood insurance coverage under the NFIP may be purchased through an insurance agent who will obtain the policy either directly through the NFIP or through an insurance company that participates in the NFIP. Flood insurance also may be available from private insurers that do not participate in the NFIP.

___ At a minimum, flood insurance purchased must cover *the lesser of:*

(1) the outstanding principal balance of the loan; *or*

(2) the maximum amount of coverage allowed for the type of property under the NFIP. Flood insurance coverage under the NFIP is limited to the overall value of the property securing the loan minus the value of the land on which the property is located.

___ Federal disaster relief assistance (usually in the form of a low-interest loan) may be available for damages incurred in excess of your flood insurance if your community's participation in the NFIP is in accordance with NFIP requirements.

___ Flood insurance coverage under the NFIP is not available for the property securing the loan because the community in which the property is located does not participate in the NFIP. In addition, if the nonparticipating community has been identified for at least one year as containing a special flood hazard area, properties located in the community will not be eligible for Federal disaster relief assistance in the event of a Federally-declared flood disaster.

DEFENSE #17: BANKRUPTCY

BANKRUPTCY

DEFINED

Filing for bankruptcy immediately stops all efforts to collect or recover against a debtor on debts that arose before the commencement of the bankruptcy case.[1] This means any foreclosure action must be stopped and no further action can be taken to recover the property until the bankruptcy court has an opportunity to review the issue. An "automatic stay" is created by the bankruptcy filing that stops the lender's foreclosure.

"The purpose of the automatic stay is twofold. First, it provides the bankrupt Debtor 'with relief from the pressure and harassment of Creditors seeking to collect their claims,' and second, it protects Creditors by 'preventing dismemberment of a Debtor's assets by individual Creditors levying on the property.'"[2] After discharge, the stay may become a permanent injunction.[3]

Bankruptcy is filed in federal bankruptcy court, which means it will almost certainly be in a different court than the foreclosure action. Thus, once bankruptcy is filed, the homeowner should immediately inform the foreclosure court of the bankruptcy filing. This will cause that court to halt its proceeding until you, or the lender, obtain an order from the bankruptcy judge reinstating the foreclosure.

Filing bankruptcy is well outside the scope of this book. However, it offers several benefits to someone facing foreclosure.

Foremost, it immediately stops the foreclosure process, even if the bankruptcy is filed the morning that the property is scheduled to be sold. It then "stays" the sale until the bankruptcy court can determine whether you are able to repay the loan. If you are unable to pay the mortgage, the loan will be discharged and you will have no further obligation on it. The foreclosure process will resume and you will be required to leave the property upon the finalization of the foreclosure process.

Second, the bankruptcy court has the power to order changes in the payment schedule if you are able to make the regular mortgage payments but cannot afford the arrearage. It also allows you to establish a payment plan with your creditors.

Bankruptcy will also wipe out your unsecured debt, like credit cards, so you can better manage your mortgage payment. Not having to pay unsecured debt each month lowers

---

[1] 11 U.S.C. § 362(a)(6); *Singly v. Am. Gen. Fin.*, 233 B.R. 170, 1999 Bankr. LEXIS 514 (S.D. Ga. 1999).; 41 Collier Bankr. Cas. 2d (p. 362-13 to 14 (15th ed. 1997).

[2] *Singly v. Am. Gen. Fin.*, 233 B.R. 170, citing, *Singly*, 41 Collier Bankr. Cas. 2d (p. 362-13 to 14 (15th ed. 1997).

[3] 11 U.S.C. § 524.

your expenses and makes the mortgage payment more manageable. Bankruptcy also may enable you to have any second or third mortgages "stripped off" of the home, making those debts disappear.

LIMITATIONS

One of the biggest perceived limitations to individuals filing bankruptcy is the fear of damaged credit. This fear is generally misplaced. Most people filing for bankruptcy have mountains of debt, very few assets, and limited income. In the vast majority of cases this author has encountered, the amount of time necessary to pay off all of a debtor's debt is measured in the tens of years (15-30 years). Sometimes, the amount of debt and interest accumulating on the debt can never be paid off.

Compare the amount of time it will take to pay off all of your debt to the amount of time bankruptcy will be on your credit report: 7 – 10 years. Also consider that most people can qualify to buy a home four years out of foreclosure, and sometimes 2 years out of bankruptcy. Additionally, many people see their credit scores *improve* 12 months out of bankruptcy. This occurs when the debtor begins making on time payments post-bankruptcy and the "bad payment history" becomes older than the new, "good history."

This author recommends talking to a bankruptcy attorney if you think you will lose your home to foreclosure, especially if you will be facing a deficiency judgment (owing the lender money even after the home is sold). Bankruptcy clears away mountains of debt and can be very beneficial. Bankruptcy is designed to be a "fresh start" for debtors on hard times, so do not let credit scoring scare you way. Bankruptcy is designed to help people in your situation.

APPLICABLE LAW OR CIVIL RULE

The bankruptcy code is contained in Title 11 of the United States Code.

DEFENSES

Bankruptcy defenses only kick-in after a bankruptcy petition is filed with federal bankruptcy court. See a bankruptcy attorney if you seek to use bankruptcy to defend your foreclosure action. If you file, you must notify the foreclosure court of the bankruptcy to stop those proceedings.

DEFENSE #18: MORTGAGE ELECTRONIC REGISTRATION SYSTEMS, INC. (MERS)

MORTGAGE ELECTRONIC REGISTRATION SYSTEMS, INC. (MERS)

DEFINED

MERS stands for Mortgage Electronic Registration Systems, Inc. It is an organization established by the mortgage industry to make the transfer of mortgage documents between corporations less cumbersome.

MERS states its purpose is to act as the "nominee" for the lender to make the sale of loans to other entities seamless. MERS permits the lender to sell its interest in the loan to another lender without having to record its interest with the local recorder. Instead of costly recording, MERS keeps track of these internal transfers in its database so no outside disclosure is necessary. This enables the transfer of loan rights/ownership to a series of different entities through electronic means, without ever having to record an assignment with the local governmental office. MERS remains the mortgagee of record (holder of the mortgage), while other entities buy and sell the rights associated with the loans.

MERS regularly disclaims ownership interest in mortgage loans, seeking only to act as "nominee" for the true mortgage lender/holder. Yet, it also regularly states it is the "mortgagee" within loan documents, holding "ownership" for purposes of ease of transfer for its clients. It also claims to be the party in interest in order to perform a variety of actions against homeowners.[1] In other words, it apparently disclaims ownership of mortgage loans in some situations, while simultaneously claiming ownership in other situations.

MERS is an ideal corporate fiction for the mortgage industry. It serves as the owner of mortgages (mortgagee) so lenders do not have to record assignments with the county recorders' offices, but does not act as owner of mortgages for the purposes of securitization. That is, MERS can claim to be mortgagee to effect trading between banks, while the banks (and bond holders) can place the mortgages on their balance sheets.[2]

Further, MERS provides an easy mechanism to affect rapid foreclosures. When the lender seeks to foreclose, it merely "transfers" that right to MERS or "directs" MERS to foreclose on its behalf. This would appear to make MERS an owner, a non-owner, agent, and non-agent at the same time.

---

[1] In one class action case, a federal district judge threw out a lawsuit against MERS, finding it *was* the party in interest in a number of lawsuits. "What MERS did is obtain a legal interest in a note from third-party lenders (becoming the holder of the note so that it could lawfully foreclose) and then proceeded to foreclosure." *Trent et al v. Mortgage Electronic Registration Systems, Inc.*, 3:2006cv00374, April 25, 2006 (MD Fla) But see, *In re: Mortgage Electronic Registration Systems, Inc. (MERS)* Case No, 05-001295CI-11, et seq., slip op. (Pinellas Cty Cir. Ct Aug. 2005) (MERS could not prove standing).

[2] MERS maintains it sues in a representative capacity for the corporation who holds the note, but in some situations, MERS has no idea who the actual owner might be. *In re: Mortgage Electronic Registration Systems, Inc. (MERS)* Case No, 05-001295CI-11, et seq., slip op. (Pinellas Cty Cir. Ct Aug. 2005)

The following case before the Nebraska Supreme Court illustrates this divergence of MERS ownership claims. MERS appealed the Nebraska Department of Banking and Finance's (Department) ruling that it did "acquire" mortgage loans under the Mortgage Bankers Registration and Licensing Act (Act), Neb. Rev. Stat. § 45-701, et seq. The Department found MERS was a mortgage banker under the Act because it acquired loans. The district court agreed with the Department, but the Nebraska Supreme Court overturned this decision. The supreme court found MERS does not "acquire" mortgage loans and was not subject to the act. The findings are informative, but raise important questions about what MERS actually does.

The Nebraska Supreme Court found this to be an accurate description of MERS:[3]

> "The MERS system was created to facilitate the transfer of ownership interests and servicing rights in mortgage loans. Under the System, MERS serves as mortgagee of record for participating members through assignment of the members' interests to MERS. Mortgage lenders participate in the MERS System as members upon completion of a membership application.

The court included the Nebraska Department of Banking description of MERS functions as follows:[4]

> "Mortgage lenders hire MERS to act as their nominee for mortgages, which allows the lenders to trade the mortgage note and servicing rights on the market without recording subsequent trades with the various register of deeds throughout Nebraska.

> "To execute a MERS Mortgage, the borrower **conveys the mortgage to MERS**, who is acting as a contractual nominee. **MERS becomes the recorded grantee**, however, the lender retains the note and servicing right. The lender can then sell that note and servicing rights on the market and MERS records each transaction electronically on its files. When the mortgage loan is repaid, MERS, as agent grantor, **conveys the property to the borrower**. MERS represents that this system saves the lender and the consumer the transaction costs that would be associated with manually recording every transaction. (emphasis added.)

The court summarized MERS position as follows:

> "MERS argues that it does not acquire mortgage loans and is therefore not a mortgage banker under § 45-702(6) because it only holds legal title to members'

---

[3] Mortgage Elec. Reg. Sys. v. Nebraska Dept. of Banking, 270 Neb. 529 October 21, 2005. No. S-04-786, at http://caselaw.lp.findlaw.com/scripts/getcase.pl?court=ne&vol=sc/oct21/s04-786&invol=1 (last visited July 23, 200*)
[4] Id.

mortgages in a nominee capacity and is contractually prohibited from exercising any rights with respect to the mortgages (i.e., foreclosure) without the authorization of the members. Further, MERS argues that it does not own the promissory notes secured by the mortgages and has no right to payments made on the notes. MERS explains that it merely "immobilizes the mortgage lien while transfers of the promissory notes and servicing rights continue to occur." Brief for appellant at 12.

The Nebraska Supreme Court concludes MERS does not acquire mortgage loans because "MERS itself has not extended any credit and none of the mortgage debtors owe MERS any money."[5]

This is a very interesting ruling. While the issue before the court was whether MERS needed to register with the state banking department, its ruling implies MERS is *not* the holder of any mortgage loan (mortgage loan is defined under the Act as any extension of credit secured by a lien on real property). If the court finds MERS is not the holder of a mortgage, then MERS cannot act in a "holder" capacity for individual lenders. That is, lenders would not be able to rely on MERS as a holding entity because MERS cannot be an actual holder of the mortgage. This ruling would appear to prevent MERS from ever claiming rights under the mortgage or note, and calls into question ownership rights of lenders relying on MERS as a transfer vehicle. While the decision apparently upholds MERS "nominee" status, it strips from MERS any ability to claim it is a valid "mortgagee." After all, what is the point of calling an entity a "mortgagee" if its rights are so restricted it has little power to act as such?

The Nebraska Supreme Court's decision is as follows:

> "Although we agree with the district court's characterization of the services provided by MERS and its contractual relationship with its members, we conclude that such services are not equivalent to acquiring mortgage loans, as defined by the Act. In other words, through its services to its members as characterized by the district court, MERS does not acquire "any loan or extension of credit secured by a lien on real property." MERS does not itself extend credit or acquire rights to receive payments on mortgage loans. Rather, the lenders retain the promissory notes and servicing rights to the mortgage, while MERS acquires legal title to the mortgage for recordation purposes.[6]

> "MERS serves as legal title holder in a nominee capacity, permitting lenders to sell their interests in the notes and servicing rights to investors without recording each transaction. But, simply stated, MERS has no independent right to collect on any debt because MERS itself has not extended credit, and none of the mortgage

---

[5] Id.
[6] Court does not define "acquires."

debtors owe MERS any money. Based on the foregoing, we conclude that MERS does not acquire mortgage loans, as defined in § 45-702(8), and therefore, MERS is not subject to the requirements of the Act.

MERS apparently seeks to be the mortgagee on one hand, yet seeks to be just a transcriptionist on the other.[7] This ruling limits MERS standing to that of a transcriptionist without any power beyond keeping track of lender's transfers. If that is the case, then MERS has no real ability to effect transfers of rights of loans, and its legal ability to act as a mortgagee is questionable.[8] Additionally, MERS ability to claim it is a party with standing in a foreclosure action is also questionable. If MERS cannot act as a mortgagee, then transfers involving MERS between lenders pose significant questions about who is the real party in interest. A lender, when hard pressed, may have problems proving a valid assignment from an entity that, as a matter of law, cannot be holder of a loan.

In this authors mind, the "standing" problems created by MERS are significant. While the recording laws generally require an assignee of a mortgage debt record its interest before a homeowner is liable at law for an action on the debt, MERS throws a wrench in this process. If MERS does not *own* the mortgage or note, and because the mortgage and note have been traded multiple times behind the scenes, it may be unclear as to who is the true owner of the mortgage. Which of the mortgage pools actually claims ownership to the mortgage and note? Who is the true party in interest to file the foreclosure action? Traditionally, this would be whoever is listed as the owner of record with the county recorder, but with MERS, the true owner could be any number of corporations or entities.

LIMITATIONS

Check your jurisdiction's rulings on MERS to determine whether attacking MERS has been successful thus far. Local law librarians can assist with this task. In this author's opinion, the more defendants that attack MERS' standing, the more likely it is for the courts to take notice.

POTENTIAL RECOVERY

Attacking MERS using standing as a defense could cause MERS to lose the action altogether. However, this result is unlikely by just attacking MERS. It may be more helpful to attack each assignment of mortgage to ensure their validity, in addition to MERS.

---

[7] MERS maintains it never holds the mortgage or note.
[8] The Nebraska Supreme Court implicitly grants MERS this right in Nebraska, but the court's ruling should raise serious questions outside Nebraska.

APPLICABLE LAW OR CIVIL RULE

The law of the state will dictate how MERS is perceived, as will the court depending on the issue before it. In the case of foreclosure actions, MERS will likely assert it is the holder of the mortgage, or it will assert itself as an agent of the owner. Based on the Nebraska decision, MERS appears not to acquire any mortgage loans, yet MERS apparently has standing to bring the action. Until there is additional litigation on MERS, it will be somewhat unclear what MERS can and cannot do.

DEFENSES

MERS puts the homeowner in an extremely dangerous position if it makes a mistake with a loan file. For example, if MERS assigns interest in the loan to two different lenders (insiders admit seeing loans in two mortgage pools at the same time, but not necessarily when MERS is a party), the homeowner could be subject to multiple lawsuits to collect on the same defaulted loan. This is why "standing" is such an important issue to address in each foreclosure action. It is also the point of having recording laws to begin with.

As a mortgage defense, it is extremely effective to pick apart a plaintiff's standing to bring the lawsuit. If MERS is involved, it would be wise to obtain as much information from it as possible in discovery, especially look for each transfer it recorded, and the parties involved. You should certainly ask it to produce all allonges and assignments it has for the loan in question to attack the plaintiff's standing.

If your loan documents and foreclosure complaint do not reference MERS, it is a good idea to still check MERS system to see if the loan ever was managed by MERS. If it was, the plaintiff has instant "real party in interest/standing" problems. (See Defense #9.) If you can show another party had interest in the loan at some time, a genuine issue of material fact exists with respect to standing. Check MERS website to see if your loan was ever managed by it. (See www.mers-servicerid.org (last visited July 15, 2008).)

DEFENSE #19: PREDATORY LENDING

PREDATORY LENDING

DEFINED

Predatory lending is a term that encompasses many different types of abusive actions by loan originators to secure loans. There are no set elements to a predatory lending claim. Instead, many individual factors come together to paint a picture of lending abuse. Each individual component may be legal, but taken together as a whole, the loan is predatory.

The Office of the Comptroller of the Currency (OCC) issued a rule in 2003 cautioning banks under its purview to be cautious about accepting loans originated by brokers that may be predatory.[1] The OCC warned banks that they may be subject to liability for disregarding banking controls. The advisory opinion is Appendix P.

The OCC described the heart of predatory lending as "a disregard of basic principles of loan underwriting," indicating a variety of other marketing practices may make a loan predatory, such as:[2]

- Loan "flipping" – frequent refinancings that result in little or no economic benefit to the borrower and are undertaken with the primary or sole objective of generating additional loan fees, prepayment penalties, and fees from the financing of credit-related products;
- Refinancings of special subsidized mortgages that result in the loss of beneficial loan terms;
- "Packing" of excessive and sometimes "hidden" fees in the amount financed;
- Using loan terms or structures – such as negative amortization – to make it more difficult or impossible for borrowers to reduce or repay their indebtedness;
- Using balloon payments to conceal the true burden of the financing and to force borrowers into costly refinancing transactions or foreclosures;
- Targeting inappropriate or excessively expensive credit products to older borrowers,[3] to persons who are not financially sophisticated or who may be otherwise vulnerable to abusive practices, and to persons who could qualify for mainstream credit products and terms;
- Inadequate disclosure of the true costs, risks and, where necessary, appropriateness to the borrower of loan transactions;
- The offering of single premium credit life insurance; and
- The use of mandatory arbitration clauses.

---

[1] OCC Advisory Letter AL 2003-2. See Appendix P.
[2] Id. (List quoted from advisory opinion.)
[3] See AARP "Subprime Mortgage Lending and Older Americans," (March 2001) (predatory lending practices often are targeted at older homeowners), available at http://www.research.aarp.org/consume/dd57_lending.html.

The OCC also directed banks to consider creating policies to identify whether loans made involve features associated with predatory lending, including:[4]

- Frequent, sequential refinancings;
- Rates higher than what the borrower qualifies for.
- Refinancings of special subsidized mortgages that contain terms favorable to the borrower;
- Single-premium credit life insurance or similar products;
- Negative amortization;
- Balloon payments in short-term transactions;
- Prepayment penalties that are not limited to the early years of a loan;
- Financing points, fees, penalties, and other charges;
- Interest rate increases upon default;
- Mandatory arbitration clauses; and
- Making loans subject to HOEPA.[5]

In addition to this list, if your loan contains violations of other defenses stated in this book, it would help establish the loan is predatory. Each minor and major violation of federal law begins to paint a picture of abuse. If several different violations of the law are present, then it may be wise to include predatory lending as a defense.

LIMITATIONS

The OCC opinion is directed at national banks under the purview of the OCC. However, the opinion could certainly be used as per-se evidence of predatory lending if the loan runs afoul of several of the items outlined by the opinion.

Predatory lending does not have its own set of elements, so proving a loan is predatory will require an individual review of the circumstances surrounding that particular loan. You may also wish to review the chapter on unconscionability, as these defenses are similar. (See Defense #10.)

POTENTIAL RECOVERY

A predatory lending defense is one of equity (fairness), so the court would have great leeway in deciding how a loan would be modified if predatory lending is found. It could cancel the debt, modify the offending terms, or take any other action it deems appropriate.

---

[4] Id. (List quoted from advisory opinion.)
[5] See Defense #4: HOEPA.

APPLICABLE LAW OR CIVIL RULE

There are no federal laws that specifically state elements of predatory lending. However, your state may have statutes that protect consumers and are referred to as "predatory lending laws." These would include consumer protection laws and broker registration laws.

A copy of the O.C.C. Advisory Letter on Predatory Lending is Appendix P.

DEFENSE #20: FAILURE TO VERIFY INCOME OR ASSETS

FAILURE TO VERIFY INCOME OR ASSETS

DEFINED

"Stated Income Stated Asset" (SISA) and "No Income No Asset" (NINA) loans are loans whereby the income or assets are not verified by the lender (or verification is minimal). As the names imply, "stated" income means the borrower states his or her income to the bank and the bank believes him. These loans were originally designed to help tipped workers and self-employed individuals qualify for mortgages without using tax returns or other customary financial verification methods. However, the loans became a source of abuse when originators began using SISA and NINA to approve borrowers with little actual ability to substantiate their income. Additionally, when borrowers want bigger homes, SISA and NINA could be used to secure loan approvals for loans otherwise turned-down. SISA loans usually have an employer stated on the application and an income amount stated. Assets in SISA loans are also stated, whether or not the assets actually exist. (In practice, assets are usually verified, even if income is not).

Whereas SISA loans required the employer and income be stated on the application, NINA loans were left blank. The employer, income, and asset sections contained no information during the underwriting process.

SISA and NINA loans were very common in the mortgage industry between about 2000-2007. These loans are not per-se illegal, but the federal government issued a "final guidance" letter on October 4, 2006 outlining actions bank holding companies and insured financial institutions should take to ensure borrower income and assets were properly reviewed.[1] The letter was jointly issued by the Department of Treasury Office of the Comptroller of the Currency (OCC), Federal Reserve System (FRS), Federal Deposit Insurance Corporation (FDIC), Department of the Treasury Office of Thrift Supervision (OTS), and the National Credit Union Administration (NCUA).

The revisions to TILA that passed in July, 2008 eliminate sub-prime lenders ability to use SISA and NINA loan programs. TILA now requires all loans that have an interest rate over 1.5% of the prime rate index (effectively all sub-prime loans) have verified income and assets.[2]

---

[1] Interagency Guidance on Nontraditional Mortgage Product Risks, 71 FR 58609. Also, see the *Statement on Subprime Mortgage Lending*, 72 F.R. 37569-01. On June 7, 2006 the Conference of State Bank Supervisors (CSBS) and the American Association of Residential Mortgage Regulators (AARMR) announced their intent to develop parallel guidelines. Available at http://www.dllr.state.md.us/finance/nontradmortgage.htm.
[2] 12 C.F.R. § 226.34(a)(4)

SPOT IT!

Look to see whether the loan was SISA or NINA if the borrower defaulted within six months of the loan closing. This may indicate the borrower never had an ability to repay the loan and the loan application was significantly inflated. Also look to see if the loan was a refinance with cash-out if the borrower defaulted quickly. The cash-out may have been the actual funds used to make the mortgage payment.

While it is helpful to start by asking the borrower if he or she provided income or asset documentation to the mortgage originator, the borrower may *not* know whether the loan actually ended up being SISA or NINA. If the originator was a broker, the broker may have shopped the loan to several different lenders, choosing the lender with the best options (or highest yield spread premium). If the broker was having difficulty with a lender in verifying income or assets, the broker may have opted just to place it with another lender who did not require verification. Thus, the borrower may have provided income documentation to the broker, but it was never used in the loan underwriting.

In discovery, you should ask the plaintiff directly whether the loan was SISA or NINA. The plaintiff will likely know because this information would be used for pricing and risk analysis. Additionally, the loan may also be a combination of SISA or NINA. For example, the loan may be "Stated Income No Assets" or "SINA." Conversely, the loan may be "No Income Stated Assets", or "NISA." Thus, the income and the asset portion of the loan must be scrutinized individually.

Some of the following things on the application (form 1003) may tip you off to whether the loan is SISA, NINA, or a combination of both:

Income:

☐ The income is a round, whole number. For example, the monthly income is exactly $10,000. Usually, income calculated from W2's or paystubs will not be whole numbers. If the income was verified, the originator will want to get every penny out of the income, so a borrower making $46,156 last year will likely see $3,846 as the monthly income on the application ($46,156 / 12). If the income is a round number, it is worth checking into.

☐ The job title is glorified. If the borrower is a "janitor," but the form says he is a "sanitation engineer," you can bet the loan is stated income. Many lenders will compare the title stated on the application against a reference source that lists incomes for each job title. The better the broker can make the job sound, the more income the underwriter will be able to justify. It is worth noting that the underwriter working for the lender, the broker, and everyone else that touches these loans pretty much sees right through applications like these, knowing full-well the income is inflated.

- ☐ The number of years on the job is inflated. This may not indicate stated income, but like the glorification of job title, more years in one line of work mean more money is made. Thus, if a broker can indicate a person has been on the job for 20 years instead of 2, more income can be justified in a stated income program.
- ☐ The income seems a little high for the job indicated. If the job is accurately portrayed, but the income seems a little high, this may be an indication the loan is stated.
- ☐ There is not at least 2 years of job history shown on the application. Almost all lenders who verify income require 2 years of job history, unless the borrower has just finished school. If there is less than 2 years, this may be a stated loan.
- ☐ There is no job shown on the application. If there is no job shown and no income shown, the loan is a "No Income" loan.

Assets:

- ☐ The bank account balances are round, whole number. For example, the bank account indicates exactly $40,000. Like stated income, whole numbers may indicate no verification occurred.
- ☐ The bank account number or address is missing from the application. Sometimes this is not required by the lender, so it may *not* be indicative of a stated product. More inquiry is needed.
- ☐ If there are no assets stated on the application, it may be a "No Asset" loan, but it may *not* be a sub-prime stated asset loan. This will vary from loan to loan. For example, many borrowers who qualify for "prime" mortgages do not need to show assets. This is due to Fannie Mae and Freddie Mac automating their underwriting process. Beginning in the late 1990's, loans could be underwritten immediately via the internet, indicating instantly whether assets needed to be verified. If assets were not needed, the broker would not waste the borrowers time compiling them. Thus, the loan may be "no income," but be harmless.
- ☐ If retirement or IRA accounts are shown, it is likely *not* a stated asset loan. This is a matter of practicality. If the broker can just inflate a bank account balance, what is the point in including a retirement account on the application?
- ☐ If the application has bank accounts not attributed to the borrower, the loan may be stated income or asset. It may also mean fraud is involved.

LIMITATIONS

SISA and NINA loans are not per-se illegal. While the interagency guidance letter lays an important foundation for verifying borrowers' ability to repay the loan for bank holding companies and insured financial institutions, it is not dispositive of a lending violation.

However, if the loan indicates income or assets clearly outside the realm or normalcy, or the borrower has absolutely no ability to repay its terms, the guidance letter will provide significant support to the borrowers' defense.

If the borrower has been able to repay the loan for at least a year or two, the ability to use SISA or NINA as a defense is diminished. Paying on the mortgage for 12-24 months may establish the lender correctly underwrote the loan (although a contrary argument can always be made). Remember that TILA was revised in July, 2008 to pretty much outlaw these types of loans. [3]

POTENTIAL RECOVERY

If the borrower clearly had no way of paying back a loan and the loan was SISA or NINA, look to the following defenses: fraud, unconscionability, misrepresentation, and negligence. Additionally, SISA and NINA loans that adversely affected the borrower would be factors in a predatory lending defense. The guidance letter will support the borrower's defense.

APPLICABLE LAW OR CIVIL RULE

The Interagency Guidance on Nontraditional Mortgage Product Risks, 71 FR 58609, is the guidance letter that applies to bank holding companies and insured financial institutions. This includes loans originated by third parties, but underwritten and purchased by banks and insured financial institutions.[4] The letter is included as Appendix M.

The changes to TILA outlawing SISA and NINA loans in subprime lending is located in 12 C.F.R. § 226.34.

ELEMENTS

There are no elements for this defense. Instead, look to factors for support.

---

[3] 12 C.F.R. § 226.34(a)(4)

[4] Interagency Guidance on Nontraditional Mortgage Product Risks, 71 FR 58609. See section titled "Third Party Originations."

FACTORS

If a sub-prime loan closed after October 4, 2006 and the original lender is a bank or insured financial institution, the letter recommends the following things be done by the lender:

1. For negative amortization and interest-only loans: the borrower should be qualified at the fully indexed rate at the total principal amount (not qualified on just in introductory teaser rate).
2. The lender should perform a credible analysis of the borrowers willingness and ability to repay the loan that is consistent with prudent lending practices.
3. The lender should exercise appropriate due diligence prior to entering into third party relationships (with brokers) and provide effective oversight and control.
4. The lender has a responsibility to ensure consumers have sufficient information to clearly understand the loan terms *before* the TILA disclosures are due to be provided.

For all non-traditional mortgage loan products, a lender's evaluation "should include an evaluation of their ability to repay the debt by final maturity at the fully indexed rate, assuming a fully amortizing repayment schedule."[5]

The letter requires lenders develop a range of reasonable tolerances for payment shock when qualifying borrowers, especially for borrowers with high loan-to-value (LTV) ratios,[6] high debt-to-income (DTI) ratios,[7] and low credit scores.[8] These tolerances should be based on prudent and appropriate underwriting standards.[9] The following are additional recommended practices:[10]

1. Communications with Consumers--When promoting or describing nontraditional mortgage products, institutions should provide consumers with information that is designed to help them make informed decisions when selecting and using these products. Meeting this objective requires appropriate attention to the timing, content, and clarity of information presented to consumers.
2. Promotional Materials and Product Descriptions. Promotional materials and other product descriptions should provide information about the costs, terms, features, and risks of nontraditional mortgages that can assist consumers in their product selection decisions, including information about the matters discussed below.
   a. Payment Shock
   b. Negative Amortization

---

[5] Interagency Guidance on Nontraditional Mortgage Product Risks, 71 FR 58609.
[6] A $90,000 loan for a property costing $100,000 would yield a 90% LTV.
[7] A borrower whose pays $5,000 per month while earning $10,000 per month has a 50% DTI.
[8] Interagency Guidance on Nontraditional Mortgage Product Risks, 71 FR 58609.
[9] Id.
[10] Id.

     c.   Prepayment Penalties

     d.   Cost of Reduced Documentation Loans

3. Monthly Statements on Payment Option ARMs. Monthly statements that are provided to consumers on payment option ARMs should provide information that enables consumers to make informed payment choices, including an explanation of each payment option available and the impact of that choice on loan balances.

4. Practices to Avoid. Institutions also should avoid practices that obscure significant risks to the consumer.

5. Control Systems--Institutions should develop and use strong control systems to monitor whether actual practices are consistent with their policies and procedures relating to nontraditional mortgage products. Institutions should design control systems to address compliance and consumer information concerns as well as the safety and soundness considerations discussed in this guidance.

STATED INCOME CHECKLIST

Each loan will differ with respect to SISA and NINA. Use this chapter to identify:

- ☐ Is the income amount stated in the loan remotely accurate?
- ☐ Is the employer stated, but incorrect?
- ☐ Is the asset information stated in the loan, but not remotely accurate?
- ☐ Is the income or asset information blank?
- ☐ If the loan is SISA or NINA, did the borrower default on the loan within a very short period of time, indicating his/her repayment ability was severely diminished?
- ☐ Does the interagency memo provide any support to the defense?

DEFENSES

DEFENSES

The author would consider this defense akin to *illegality*, which is an affirmative defense.[11]

AFFIRMATIVE DEFENSES

This defense is best used in conjunction with fraud, unconscionability, or another common law defense. This defense may also be used to beef up a case of predatory lending. A possible defense may look something like this:

---

[11] Fed. C. R. 8(c).

[paragraph no.] The lender failed to *[state each of the failures in a separate line, like failure to provide disclosures or failure to perform a payment shock calculation].*

[paragraph no.] The loan is void for failure to comply with Interagency Guidance on Nontraditional Mortgage Product Risks, 71 FR 58609.

STARTER DISCOVERY

Please note that the discovery listed should be directed to the party who is able to address the request. For example, if the plaintiff is a trust and was not the lender, then questions about the lender's practices might be better served on the lender. However, the trust may have parameters established with respect to what types of loans it holds. These may provide assistance in determining the lender's standard of review.

INTERROGATORIES

[paragraph no.] (For negative amortization and interest-only loans:) state how the lender qualified the borrower at the fully indexed rate at the total principal amount.

[paragraph no.] State how the lender performed a credible analysis of the borrower's willingness and ability to repay the loan that is consistent with prudent lending practices.

[paragraph no.] State what due diligence was performed with respect to third parties prior to entering into third party relationships.

[paragraph no.] State what procedures were in place that provided effective oversight and control of originating third parties the lender maintained relationships.

[paragraph no.] State the payment shock calculations performed on this loan as part of the loan underwriting process conducted by the lender.

REQUESTS FOR ADMISSIONS

[paragraph no.] (For negative amortization and interest-only loans:) admit the borrower was not qualified at the fully indexed rate at the total principal amount (not qualified on just in introductory teaser rate).

[paragraph no.] Admit the lender did not perform a credible analysis of the borrower's willingness and ability to repay the loan that is consistent with prudent lending practices.

[paragraph no.] Admit the lender did not exercise appropriate due diligence prior to entering into third party relationships and did not have procedures to provide effective oversight and control.

[paragraph no.] Admit the lender did not provide information/disclosures directly to the consumer about the loan terms and conditions before disclosures were required by TILA.

[paragraph no.] Admit the lender did not perform payment shock calculations on this loan as part of the loan underwriting process conducted by the lender.

REQUESTS FOR THE PRODUCTION OF DOCUMENTS

[paragraph no.] (For negative amortization and interest-only loans:) provide a copy of the manuals or formulas relied upon in qualifying the borrower at the fully indexed rate at the total principal amount.

[paragraph no.] Produce the documents that describe the lender's process in analyzing the borrower's willingness and ability to repay the loan that is consistent with prudent lending practices.

[paragraph no.] Produce those documents that describe the lenders exercise of due diligence prior to entering into third party relationships (with brokers) and provide effective oversight and control.

[paragraph no.] (To broker:) Provide a copy of all advertising materials distributed to the public between *[date range from before origination through loan closing]* by you, including all print, radio, T.V., and internet material.

> (The letter requires compliance with TILA advertising. TILA advertising violations do not by themselves provide a private right of action.)

[paragraph no.] Produce a copy of all disclosures provided directly to the consumer about the loan terms and conditions.

[paragraph no.] Produce a copy of all documents that describe how the lender conducts it payment shock calculations.

[paragraph no.] Produce a copy of all documents provided to the borrower that disclose:

    a. Payment Shock;
    b. Negative Amortization;
    c. Prepayment Penalties; and
    d. Cost of Reduced Documentation Loans.

COUNTER CLAIMS

This defense would not be used as a counter claim.

THIRD PARTY CLAIMS

A claim could easily be made against the original lender for it failing to ensure the borrower's ability to repay the loan. The claim would seek the lender to indemnify (cover the losses) the borrower from any money the borrower may be required to pay the plaintiff. It would probably be a claim best asserted against the lender (versus broker), but could be raised against the broker nevertheless. Most brokers are required to maintain surety bonds with the states they are licensed to do business in, which could be sought to pay for a successful suit against a broker. Surety bonds usually survive the closing of a mortgage company for two years or more.

DEFENSE #21: DEFECTIVE MORTGAGE OR NOTE

DEFECTIVE MORTGAGE OR NOTE

DEFINED

The mortgage and note may be defective in a number of ways. The terms might not match, the terms in one of the riders do not match the mortgage or note, or the note may be defective if the terms stated are impossible. (For example, the loan may state the rate will adjust in 5 years, but the adjustment date is only 2 years from the date of closing.)

The loan might have been accidently released (filed with the recorder as paid off), or the loan could have been modified without the signatures of all necessary borrowers. The notary could have made a mistake if the stamp is incorrect (or her license was expired). There are a number of ways a note and mortgage may be defective, and reading each document carefully will help identify inconsistencies. Follow the checklist in this chapter for assistance in determining whether a defense is present for a defective mortgage or note.

POTENTIAL RECOVERY

The recovery will vary greatly, depending on the terms that are invalid. If several material terms are materially defective, then the court may rule the entire loan void. However, if one or two immaterial terms are incorrect, then the court may just modify the offending terms.

If the defective terms are actually a miscalculation of payments or interest amounts, then there are likely serious problems with the Truth in Lending statement. Review the loan terms carefully to ensure their accuracy.

APPLICABLE LAW OR CIVIL RULE

Errors in the Mortgage or Note would certainly fall under the realm of common law, which is law created by the courts over time. These laws may change from state to state.

The errors in the mortgage or note may violate state laws that dictate what can and cannot be in a note or mortgage. Look to your state's mortgage laws for direction. Most *law* libraries have state law books and a librarian should be able to direct you to that section.

If the offending terms violate TILA, then look to TILA for damages. See Defenses #1 through #4.

DEFECTIVE MORTGAGE OR NOTE CHECKLIST

- ☐ Do the terms in the Mortgage and Note match each other?
- ☐ Do the terms in any riders match the terms in the mortgage and note?
- ☐ Are the terms possible (i.e., the adjustment date is correct)?
- ☐ Is the amortization correct for the mortgage and note?
- ☐ Are there potential TILA violations that arise from any errors?
- ☐ If there is an allonge or assignment with the documents, is that properly endorsed?
- ☐ If either is blank, does the form match with what the lender attached to the complaint?
- ☐ Do the mortgage and note match the document attached to the complaint?
- ☐ Are the copies attached to the complaint signed by the borrower?
- ☐ Are there multiple parties in the transaction, but not all of them signed the mortgage or note?
- ☐ Does the interest rate trigger HOEPA?
- ☐ If the borrower is married, did the spouse waive dower or sign the note/mortgage, if necessary?
- ☐ Did all the joint tenants sign, if necessary?
- ☐ Was the mortgage released by accident?
- ☐ Is the notary stamp statutorily deficient or expired? (Look to state laws.)
- ☐ Was the mortgage or note re-filed with the recorder with some term added, or without an additional signature?
- ☐ If the loan was modified, is the modification agreement signed by each party?
- ☐ If the loan was modified, who is the lender that signed the agreement? Is it the same lender that is foreclosing? Is there a chain-of-title that includes the lender that signed the modification agreement? (Real party in interest defense, Defense #9.)

DEFENSE #22: EQUAL CREDIT OPPORTUNITY ACT (ECOA)

EQUAL CREDIT OPPORTUNITY ACT (ECOA)

DEFINED

The Equal Credit Opportunity Act (ECOA), 15 U.S.C. § 1691, et seq., prohibits discrimination in lending based on race, color, religion, national origin, sex or marital status. [1] It does not provide minimum civil damages for violations of the act, but a creditor may be liable for a borrower's actual damages, punitive damages up to $10,000, and attorneys fees.[2] The statute of limitation for an ECOA claim is two years. A violation of the ECOA may also be a violation of the Fair Housing Act, 42 U.S.C. 3601, et seq.[3]

The Home Mortgage Disclosure Act (HMDA),[4] requires financial institutions publish EEOC related information that is available to the public. The HMDA reports, that are available online, are extremely helpful sources for anyone who thinks their lender is engaged in discriminatory lending.[5] The reports break down by zip code or Metropolitan Statistical Area (MSA), how many applications for loans were taken by each lender per racial characteristic, and include the interest rate offered to each group.

For example, the following information represents Countrywide Home Loan's lending characteristics for the Columbus, Ohio MSA in 2006:[6]

Census Tract Characteristics; Racial/Ethnic Composition	Number of loans without pricing data reported	Number of loans that pricing was available	The average interest rate above the treasury rate (only including loans with APR above the threshold)
Less than 10% Minority	840	97	4.97%
10-19% Minority	328	44	5.78%
20-49% Minority	172	57	5.83%
50-79% Minority	11	25	6.06%
80-100% Minority	14	11	6.43%

The ECOA prohibits red-lining and reverse red-lining, when different credit terms are offered (or not offered) to areas defined by racial characteristics.[7]

---

[1] 15 U.S.C. § 1691(a).

[2] 15 U.S.C. § 1691e.

[3] http://www.hud.gov/offices/fheo/FHLaws/yourrights.cfm (last visited June 27, 2008)

[4] 12 U.S.C. § 2801, et seq.

[5] http://www.ffiec.gov/hmda/online_rpts.htm (last visited July 27, 2008).

[6] Disclosure Table 11-3: Pricing Information for conventional home-purchase loans, first lien, 1-4 family owner occupied dwelling (excludes manufactured homes), by borrower or census tract characteristics, 2006 for MSA/MD: 18140 – Columbus, OH for institution: 0001644643 – 2 Countrywide Home Loans (report last viewed June 1, 2006).

230

LIMITATIONS

ECOA lawsuits may be very difficult for a pro-se litigant to maintain. If you firmly believe the lender has violated the ECOA for your loan, seeking an qualified attorney would be the wisest course of action.

POTENTIAL RECOVERY

The ECOA does not provide minimum civil damages for violations of the act in lending, but a creditor may be liable a borrower's actual damages, punitive damages up to $10,000, and attorneys fees.[8] A lawyer who specializes in ECOA claims should be sought to evaluate your claim. If a valid claim is present, the attorney may agree to represent you without out-of-pocket costs because the law provides for statutory attorneys fees.

APPLICABLE LAW OR CIVIL RULE

The Equal Credit Opportunity Act is located at 15 U.S.C. §1691, et seq. ("ECOA"), and its implementing regulations located at 12 CFR § 202 ("Regulation B").

---

[7] The amicus curiae brief of the United States in *Hargraves v. Capital City Mortgage Corp.*, Civ. Action No. 98-1021 (D.D.C. 2000) succinctly discusses the case law on redlining as follows:

> "As used by Congress and district courts, "reverse redlining" refers to "the practice of targeting residents in certain geographic areas for credit on unfair terms." Newton v. United Companies Fin. Corp., 24 F. Supp.2d 444, 455 (E.D. Pa. 1998); accord Williams v. Gelt Fin. Corp., 237 B.R. 590, 594 (E.D. Penn. 1999) ("reverse redlining" is the practice of "targeting of persons for 'credit on unfair terms' based on their income, race, or ethnicity") (quoting S. Rep. No. 103-169, at 21 (1993)). In contrast to "redlining," which "is the practice of denying the extension of credit to specific geographic areas due to the income, race, or ethnicity of its residents," "[r]everse redlining is the practice of extending credit on unfair terms to those same communities." United Companies Lending Corp. v. Sargeant, 20 F. Supp.2d 192, 203 n.5 (D. Mass. 1998) (citing S. Rep. No. 103-169, at 21 (1993)).

The brief is available at: http://www.usdoj.gov/crt/housing/documents/hargraves1.htm (last visited June 26, 2008)

[8] 15 U.S.C. § 1691e.

DEFENSE #23: SERVICING ABUSE

SERVICING ABUSE

DEFINED

Servicing abuse occurs when the company servicing a mortgage loan takes actions or imposes fees that are not permitted by law or that are abusive. There are numerous ways a servicer may abuse a borrower, with one prominent bankruptcy attorney identifying fifty different servicing abuses.[1]

Servicing abuse can cost homeowners a range of fees, from a few dollars to forcing the homeowner into default. Servicing abuses include actions like not crediting a payment on time, creating false late fees, or charging for services not rendered.

False late fees can cause the servicer to impose additional fees, like inspection or appraisal fees, in preparation for potential default. Then, if these fees are not paid, more fees are added onto the mortgage to be paid the following month, and the cycle can continue until the fees are so great that default occurs.

Up until TILA was revised in July, 2008, some states permitted the "pyramiding" of fees, whereby one late payment would accumulate late fees for months afterward.[2] Now, TILA outlaws this practice.[3] Additionally, the revisions of TILA require all payments be credited to a consumers account the day they are received.[4]

Unauthorized charges have also been a problem for borrowers. This includes charging for fees that are not authorized in the mortgage, or charging for services not actually rendered. Use the Qualified Written Request (QWR) located in Appendix G to obtain copies of any property reports or other documents that the servicer indicates was charged for to verify the charges validity.

Another area of vast abuse is in the realm of forced placed homeowners insurance. While the servicer usually has the right (under the mortgage) to buy an insurance policy on the property if the borrower lets his policy lapse, these policies are usually outrageously expensive. The policies that are "forced placed" by the servicers are usually several times more expensive than a policy available on the market to a homeowner and generate profits for servicers.

In one case, this author reviewed documents of a homeowner in default because the servicer forced placed insurance on a property that already had sufficient insurance. The servicer did not recognize the policy as valid because the policy only covered the dwelling

---

[1] See O. Max Gardner III's Nifty Fifty Mortgage Servicing Abuses.
[2] Other states have prohibited this act for some time.
[3] 12 C.F.R. § 226.36(c)(1)(ii).
[4] 12 C.F.R. § 226.36(c)(1)(i).

(and not the land), although the policy was adequate under the mortgage. The homeowner worked for months to convince the servicer that the policy was sufficient, and even had her national insurance carrier call to talk to the servicer, with no results. The insurance policy forced placed by the servicer was *thousands* of dollars more than her policy, causing her ultimately to default on the mortgage. As part of her defense, she claimed breach of contract and violations of her state's insurance code because of the servicer's actions.

POTENTIAL RECOVERY

Servicing abuse can be used to offset some of the damages the homeowner will need to pay the bank in the foreclosure action. If the abuses are bad enough, the borrower may have an entire defense to the foreclosure action, as was the case in the above example.

APPLICABLE LAW OR CIVIL RULE

Regulation Z of TILA provides statutory language for some prohibited actions.[5] Your state's laws might provide additional support to a claim.

For example, some state laws provide support when a servicer force places insurance. Florida Statutes § 626.9551(a) provides that no person may:

> (a) Require, as a condition precedent or condition subsequent to the lending of money or extension of credit or any renewal thereof, that the person to whom such money or credit is extended, or whose obligation the creditor is to acquire or finance, negotiate any policy or contract of insurance through a particular insurer or group of insurers or agent or broker or group of agents or brokers.

California Civil Code 2955.5(a) provides:

> (a) No lender shall require a borrower, as a condition of receiving or maintaining a loan secured by real property, to provide hazard insurance coverage against risks to the improvements on that real property in an amount exceeding the replacement value of the improvements on the property.

---

[5] 12 C.F.R. § 226.36.

DEFENSES

Servicing abuse may be used as affirmative defenses to the lawsuit, or maybe alleged as counterclaims. The following is an example of a counterclaim used to sue the lender for the servicer's violations of the Florida insurance laws.[6]

COUNT ONE

1. …
2. Plaintiff forced placed home owners hazard insurance on Defendant's property on [date] through [date], although that policy was superfluous to Defendant's insurance policy through Company ABC;
3. Defendant alleges Plaintiff unreasonably disapproved the insurance policy provided by her through Company ABC for the protection of the property securing the note and mortgage when it forced placed said insurance policy;
4. Defendant alleges her insurance policy through Company ABC was adequate under the mortgage;
5. Defendant alleges Plaintiff's refusal to accept her insurance coverage through Company ABC was not based on reasonable standards;[7]
6. Defendant alleges Plaintiff discriminated against Company ABC without cause;
7. Defendant alleges Plaintiff did not act fairly or honestly towards the Defendant and acted without regard for her interests in force placing said insurance;
8. Defendant alleges Plaintiff failed to promptly correct its error, even after repeated efforts by the Defendant to communicate Plaintiff's error to it; and
9. Defendant alleges Plaintiff violated Florida anti-coercion insurance statute, Florida Statutes § 626.9551.

---

[6] The lender can be held responsible for the servicer's actions under the doctrine of respondeat superior. (The master is responsible for the actions of his agents.)

[7] These are elements of a Florida state insurance claim.

30+ OTHER DEFENSES TO FORECLOSURE

1. Racketeer influences and corrupt organizations act (RICO), Federal and state.[1]
2. Aiding and abetting.
3. Gramm, Leach, Bliley Act (Disclosure of personal information & notice requirements).
4. Fraud.
5. Constructive Fraud
6. Fraudulent Misrepresentation.
7. Fruits of the fraud.
8. Unjust enrichment.
9. Negligent misrepresentation.
10. Intentional misrepresentation.
11. Negligent infliction of emotional distress.
12. Intentional infliction of emotional distress.
13. Breach of duty to act in good faith and fair dealing.
14. Home Equity Loan Consumer Protection Act Violations (for HELOC second mortgages).
15. Breach of Fiduciary Duty.[2]
16. Defective Deed when the deed is conveyed to an non-incorporated entity.
17. Immaterial Breach.[3]
18. Assignee not registered with the Secretary of State.
19. Unfair and deceptive practices.
20. Licensing violations of state laws (mortgage broker, lender, servicer, etc.).
21. Federal False Claims Act, where false insurance claim is submitted to FHA.
22. Attack Plaintiff's affidavits as hearsay or incompetent.[4]
23. Incorrect ARM adjustments.[5]
24. Payment of the mortgage; payment recorded incorrectly.
25. Failing to join all necessary parties.
26. Civil Conspiracy.[6]

---

[1] See, 42 U.S.C. §§ 1981 and 1982.

[2] *Arnold v. United Companies Lending Corp.*, 511 S.E.2d 854, 864-65 (W.Va. 1998).

[3] *Sahadi v. Continental Illinois Nat'l Bank & Trust Co.*, 706 F.2d 193 (7th Cir. 1983).

[4] *New England Savings Bank v. Bedford Realty Corp.*, 238 Conn. 745, 680 A.2d 301, 208-09 (1996), then later opinion, 246 Conn. 584 (1998).

[5] To calculate, go to: http://www.loantech.com

[6] Use the "Pooling and Servicing Agreement" or correspondent agreements as evidence of a joint venture. *Short v. Wells Fargo*, 401 F. Supp 2d 549, 563-65 (S.D.W. Va. 2005). Also use failure of lender to adhere to the rules as constructive knowledge of fraud. Review *England v. MG Investments*, 93 F Supp. 2d 718, 723 (S.D.W. Va. 2000). Some jurisdictions do not recognize it. See: *Farmland Indus. V. Frazier-Parrott Commodities, Inc.*, 871 D.2d 1402, 1409 (8th Cir. 1989) (Missouri does not recognize a separate cause of action for civil conspiracy); Shope v. Boyer, 268 N.C. 401, 150 S.E.2d 771, (S.Ct. NC. 1966) (North Carolina does not

27. Pain and Suffering.[7]
28. Special defenses may be present for individuals currently in the military.[8]
29. Attorneys Fees Void as a Matter of Public Policy.[9]
30. Miscalculation of the adjustable rate or mis-adjustment of the rate.
    a. Check to see if the correct index was used, as well as the correct value.
31. False Advertising.
32. Concealment.
33. Defective Notary Stamp/ Expired.
34. Notary Malfeasence.

---

recognize civil conspiracy), *But See*, *DesLauries v. Shea*, 300 Mass. 30, 12 N.E.2d 932 (S. Ct. Mass 1938) (recognizing conspiracy as a cause of action in Massachusetts).

[7] Several courts have found that pain and suffering can be sought for violations of federal laws when the damages provisions of those laws permit the recovery of "actual damages." *Johnstone v. Bank of America, N.A.*, 173 F.Supp.2d 809, (N.D.Ill. 2001) (justifies mental anguish in a RESPA claim by looking at other federal laws, like the FCRA, ECOA, and FHA that permit the same as actual damages); *Hrubec v. Nat'l R.R. Pass. Corp.*, 829 F.Supp. 1502 (N.D.Ill 1993). *But see, Katz v. Dime Sav. Bank, FSB*, 992 F.Supp.250 (W.D.N.Y.1997); *Aiello v. Providian Fin. Corp.*, 239 F.3d 876 (7th Cir. 2001).

[8] 24 C.F.R. §§ 203.610; Soldiers and Sailors Civil Relief Act of 1940.

[9] See schedule of approved attorneys fees published by HUD, Freddie and Fannie. Also, HUD mortgage Letter 05-30 and Fannie and Freddie Mac servicing guides; Freddie Mac Single-Family Seller/Servicer Guide, vol. 2b, exh. 57a (Oct 6 2006); Fannie Mae Single Family Servicer Guidelines, Part III § 303; State common law.

APPENDICES

APPENDIX A

RESCISSION NOTICE TO LENDER

Your Name
Your Address
City, State & Zip

Today's Date

Mortgage Servicer Name
(Also send copies to the lender, if known.)
Address
City, State & Zip

RE: Account No.: XXX

VIA CERTIFIED MAIL

Dear Mortgage Servicer:

Pursuant to TILA, 15 U.S.C. § 1635 and Regulation Z, 12 C.F.R. § 226.23, I hereby exercise my right to rescind the mortgage transaction that is identified by the above referenced account number. The primary basis of the rescission is that *[I was not provided with a completed copy of the notice of my right to rescind the consumer credit transaction, in violation of 15 U.S.C. § 1635(a) and Regulation Z, 12 C.F.R. §§ 226.17 and 226.23].*

Pursuant to TILA and Regulation Z, you have twenty days after receipt of this Notice of Rescission to return all monies paid and to take action necessary and appropriate to terminate the security interest. Please be advised that the mortgage is automatically voided by operation of law upon rescission under 15 U.S.C. § 1635(b). Therefore, any attempt to report this mortgage to a credit agency is a willful violation of TILA and the Fair Credit Reporting Act, 15 U.S.C. § 1681a, et seq.

Please contact me at *[phone number]* to arrange the delivery to me of all monies paid under the mortgage, including all closing costs, principal, and interest. Additionally, please mail me confirmation the mortgage has been voided and no negative information will be reported to the credit bureaus with respect to this loan.

Regards,

Your Name

APPENDIX B

MOTION TO EXTEND TIME

IN THE COURT OF COMMON PLEAS
_____ COUNTY, STATE
(Use the heading format provided on the Complaint.)

XYZ LENDER, INC.,	:	
Plaintiffs,	:	Case No. 08 CVE 01-1110
v.	:	Judge: JONES
JOHN SMITH,	:	
Defendant	:	

DEFENDANT JOHN SMITH'S
MOTION TO EXTEND TIME TO FILE RESPONSIVE PLEADING

Defendant John Smith moves this Court for an order allowing him an additional 28 days to prepare and file his responsive pleading in the above captioned case, *[and so he/she may confer with counsel on how to proceed]*.

> *[Sign every motion and pleading!]*
> John Smith
> 123 Any Street
> Anytown, OH 43215
> (614) 111-3456
> Defendant, *Pro Se*

[You must fill out the" certificate of service" and mail this motion to every party in the lawsuit. Remember that the court may require multiple copies, so call the clerk of court to find out how many copies are required.]

CERTIFICATE OF SERVICE

The undersigned certifies that a copy of the foregoing was served upon the following parties by regular USPS mail, postage prepaid, on this ___ day of _____, 20____ :

Jane Doe
Big Law Firm
Address
Address
Attorney for Plaintiff

Rick Jones
Defendant #2
Address
Address

Other Defendant #1
…

_____
John Smith

APPENDIX C

MOTION TO DISMISS

IN THE COURT OF COMMON PLEAS
_____ COUNTY, STATE
(Use the heading format provided on the Complaint.)

XYZ LENDER, INC.,   :

    Plaintiffs,   :   Case No. 08 CVE 01-1110

    v.   :   Judge: JONES

JOHN SMITH,   :

    Defendant   :

DEFENDANT JOHN SMITH'S
MOTION TO DISMISS

Defendant John Smith, moves this Court, pursuant to *[Civil Rule 12(B)(1)]* and *[12(B)(6)]*, to dismiss the complaint for lack of subject-matter jurisdiction, and for the plaintiff's failure to state a claim upon which relief can be granted.

As demonstrated on the attached Mortgage and Note, identified as Exhibits *[A and B]*, recorded with the *[County Recorder]*, *[ABC Mortgage Co.]* is the current holder of the Mortgage and Note *[or: ABC Mortgage Co. was the owner at the time the complaint was filed]*. Therefore the plaintiff, *[XYZ Lender, Inc.]*, *[is/was]* not the real party in interest, and *[does not/did not]* have standing to bring or maintain this claim. The attached affidavit, identified as Exhibit *[C]* states the defendant has researched the matter and there are no assignments on record with the *[Franklin County Recorder]* indicating the plaintiff *[ever/belatedly]* became successor-in-interest to the mortgage or note.

[Add any other Motion to Dismiss items here. For example, if the borrower is contesting a conditions precedent was met. (See Defense #12).]

Respectfully Submitted,

John Smith
123 Any Street
Anytown, OH 43215
(614) 111-3456
Defendant, *Pro Se*

CERTIFICATE OF SERVICE

The undersigned certifies that a copy of the foregoing Motion was served upon the following parties by regular USPS mail, postage prepaid, on this ___ day of _____, _____:

Jane Doe
Big Law Firm
Address
Address
Attorney for Plaintiff

Rick Jones
Defendant #2
Address
Address

Other Defendant #1
…

_____
John Smith

[Attach copies of the mortgage and any assignments obtained by the county recorder to this motion, and attach an affidavit to the effect there are no other assignments known to the borrower. Affidavits are specific to each state, so searching online is necessary to obtain a correct version. An example is in Appendix F.]

APPENDIX D

ANSWER

IN THE CIRCUIT COURT OF THE _____ DISTRICT

JUDICIAL CIRCUIT IN AND FOR _____
COUNTY FLORIDA

CASE NO. <u>2007 -12345678-CA-6</u>

LENDER NAME HERE

     Plaintiff,

v.

JANE SMITH; *et al,*

     Defendant.

_____ /

DEFENDANT JANE SMITH'S
ANSWER AND COUNTERCLAIMS

Defendant, Jane Smith, states she:

1. Admits the allegations in paragraph 1 of the complaint;

2. Admits the allegations in paragraph 2 of the complaint that Jane Smith executed and delivered a promissory note which was recorded October 3, 2005 in O.R. Book 12345, Page 12345, Public Records of Dade County, Florida, and mortgaged the property described in the mortgage, owned by and in possession of the mortgagor, and that true and correct copies of the note and mortgage are attached to the Complaint, and denies the remainder;

3. Is without knowledge or information sufficient to form a belief regarding the allegations in paragraphs 3, 6, 7, 9, 10, 11, 12, 13, 14, and 15 of the complaint, and therefore denies the same;

4. Admits the allegations in paragraph 4 that Jane Smith is the present record title owner of said property and is in possession of same, and denies the remainder;

5. Admits the allegations in paragraph 5 of the complaint, except that she denies the allegation in paragraph 5 that she is in default under the note and mortgage; and

6. Denies the allegations in paragraph 8 of the complaint.

DEFENSES

Defendant, Jane Smith states the following defenses to each claim asserted by the Plaintiff:

7. Defendant incorporates paragraphs 1-6 of this document as if rewritten here;

8. Plaintiff's prayer for attorney's fees is against the public policy of this state; and

9. Those covenants of the mortgage that provide attorneys fees to the plaintiff upon breach are against the public policy of this state.

AFFIRMATIVE DEFENSES

Defendant, Jane Smith stated the following affirmative defenses to each claim asserted by Plaintiff:

10. Defendant incorporates paragraphs 1-9 of this document as if rewritten here;

11. Plaintiff has failed to state a cause of action;

12. This court lacks jurisdiction over the subject matter;

13. Plaintiff lacks standing to maintain this action;

14. Plaintiff lacked standing at the time this action was filed;

15. Plaintiff's assignment from MERS is without legal effect;

16. Plaintiff has failed to plead the performance or occurrence of conditions precedent, that the proper and valid agent of the mortgagee mailed Defendant a proper notice of acceleration as required in covenant 22 of the Mortgage;

17. Plaintiff has failed to comply with the post-closing loan disclosure requirements of 12 C.F.R. § 226.9, et seq.;

18. Plaintiff breached its contract with Defendant when it forced placed home owner's insurance upon Defendant in an amount in excess of that required under the contract, increasing Defendant's required monthly payments substantially, actually and proximately causing Defendant to no longer meet her obligation under the contract, and excusing her performance under the contract;

19. Defendant's performance under the contract is excused;

20. Upon reason and belief, the mortgage transaction is void for fraud due to the original mortgage assignees', Fremont Investment & Loan Corporation ("Fremont"), and Mortgage Electronic Registration Systems, Inc., ("MERS"), violations of the Real Estate Settlement and Procedures Act ("RESPA"), 12 U.S.C. § 2601, et seq., in paying kickbacks and/or unearned fees to Mortgage Broker, 12345 South Dixie Highway, Miami, Florida 33156, ("Broker"), the mortgage broker involved in this transaction;

21. The loan documents relied upon by Plaintiff are void for lack of compliance with RESPA, 12 U.S.C. § 2601, et seq.;

22. The loan documents relied upon by Plaintiff are void for lack of compliance with Regulation Z of the Truth in Lending Act, 12 C.F.R. § 226.1, et seq.;

23. The mortgage transaction is void for common law fraud due to Broker's, as agent for Fremont and MERS, presentation of a substantially lower interest rate during its sales presentation (5.99%, thirty year fixed mortgage) than Defendant ultimately received (8.75%, 10.844% APR, 2 year ARM), that Defendant relied upon Broker's misrepresentation of said better terms, that Defendant was induced into a real estate contract with the property's seller due to Broker's misrepresentations, and that Defendant

was forced to accept the worse terms to avoid breaching her contract with the property's seller;

24. The alleged mortgagee, MERS, was not licensed to conduct business in Florida at the time the loan was made as a federally chartered bank, state-chartered commercial bank, credit union, savings association, nondeposit trust company, international banking office, consumer finance company, mortgage broker businesses, mortgage broker individual, retail installment seller, or sales finance company; and

25. The mortgage is void for want of MERS registering with Florida's Division of Financial Institutions or Florida's Division of Finance.

COUNTERCLAIMS

COUNT ONE

1. Defendant realleges as if set forth in this document paragraphs 1-25 of the Answer;

2. Defendant alleges a mortgage contract exists between the parties;

3. Defendant alleges Plaintiff forced placed hazard, wind, fire, and/or flood insurance upon Defendant about July, 2006 and again in February, 2007, requiring Defendant to pay the premium for said insurance;

4. Defendant alleges said forced placed insurance was substantially more expensive than similar insurance available on the market;

5. Defendant alleges said forced placed insurance was unnecessary because Defendant had sufficient insurance in place.

6. Defendant alleges she repeatedly communicated with Plaintiff about the said forced placed insurance, specifically demonstrating her insurance was sufficient under the terms of the parties' contract.

7. Defendant alleges Plaintiff breached its contract with Defendant when it forced placed said insurance upon Defendant in an amount in excess of that required under the contract's "Hazard Insurance Authorization & Requirements";

8. Defendant alleges Plaintiff's actions caused Defendant to no longer be able to make her payments under the contract;

9. Defendant alleges her inability to make the payments under the contract actually and proximately caused the present action in foreclosure, damaging Defendant's credit, causing her to incur late fees, compounded interest, attorney's fees, and other damages arising from the breach; and

10. Defendant alleges Plaintiff was unjustly enriched by force placing said unnecessary insurance and is liable to Defendant for damages.

COUNT TWO

11. Defendant realleges as if set forth in this document paragraphs 1-10 of this counterclaim;

12. Defendant alleges Plaintiff unreasonably disapproved the insurance policy provided by her for the protection of the property securing the note and mortgage when it forced placed said insurance policy;

13. Defendant alleges Plaintiff's refusal to accept her insurance coverage was not based on reasonable standards;

14. Defendant alleges Plaintiff discriminated against her insurance carrier without cause;

15. Defendant alleges Plaintiff did not act fairly or honestly towards the Defendant and acted without regard for her interests in force placing said insurance;

16. Defendant alleges Plaintiff failed to promptly correct its error, even after repeated efforts by the Defendant to communicate Plaintiff's error to it; and

17. Defendant alleges Plaintiff violated Florida anti-coercion insurance statute, Florida Statutes § 626.9551.

WHEREFORE, Defendant prays this court:

A. Grant her relief in the form of contract reformation, reforming her mortgage contract to reflect those terms she was originally promised by the mortgage broker, Broker: a thirty year amortized mortgage with a fixed interest rate of 5.99%, effective September 16, 2005;

B. Credit her payments in excess of the amortized amount after reformation to the loan's principle balance;

C. Permit any interest or costs accrued since Plaintiff's breach of contract be awarded as damages to Defendant;

D. Order Plaintiff to immediately discontinue its forced placed home owner's hazard, wind, flood, and/or fire insurance;

E. Order Plaintiff to accept hazard insurance coverage in an amount equal to the replacement value of improvements on the property to be sufficient, as stated in the parties contract addendum titled "Hazard Insurance Authorization & Requirements";

F. Order Plaintiff to update Defendant's credit report, removing any negative coding arising from the issues presented in this action, including foreclosure;

G. Reduction of the interest rate;

H. Extension of the loan repayment period;

I. Reamortization with capitalization of arrears;

J. Reduction of the principal balance;

K. Injunctive relief in the form of…;

L. Declaratory relief in the form of…..;

M. Grant Defendant reasonable attorneys fees;

N. Deny Plaintiff's requested relief; and

O. Grant Defendant any and all other relief this Court deems equitable.

I HEREBY CERTIFY that a copy of the foregoing has been furnished by regular, prepaid, U.S. Mail this _____ day of _____, 2008, to:

LAW FIRM FOR PLAINTIFF
Name of Lawyer
12345 U.S. Highway 19 North
Clearwater, Florida 33764
Counsel for Plaintiff

OTHER DEFENDANTS
Their Addresses

Respectfully Submitted,

Jane Smith
123 Any Street
Anytown, OH 43215
(614) 111-3456
Defendant, *Pro Se*

APPENDIX E

AMENDED ANSWER

[Copy the heading format used in the Complaint - instead of copying how this form looks.]

IN THE CIRCUIT COURT OF THE _____ DISTRICT
JUDICIAL CIRCUIT IN AND FOR _____
COUNTY FLORIDA

CASE NO. <u>2008 – 12345 -CA-1</u>

LENDER NAME HERE

      Plaintiff,

v.

JOHN SMITH; *et al,*

      Defendant.

_____/

DEFENDANT JOHN SMITH'S
MOTION FOR LEAVE TO FILE AMENDED ANSWER AND COUNTERCLAIMS

Defendant, John Smith, respectfully requests leave to file the attached Amended Answer and Counterclaims pursuant to *[Civil Rule 15, or in Florida, Fla. R. Civ. P. 1.190(a) and (e)].* The defendant states that as a pro-se litigant, it has taken him additional time to become familiar with his legal defenses, and is only now aware of his legal defenses and counterclaims, and now wishes to assert the same.

Leave to amend should be liberally granted; it should not be denied unless the privilege has been abused, there is prejudice to the opposing party, or amendment would be futile. <u>Torrey v. Leesburg Reg'l Med. Ctr.</u>, 769 So.2d 1040 (2000), *quoting* <u>North Am. Specialty Ins. Co. v. Bergeron Land Dev., Inc.</u>,745 So. 2d 359, 362 (Fla. 4th DCA 1999) ("Florida Rule of Civil Procedure 1.190(a) provides that leave to amend shall be liberally granted... As a general rule, '[l]eave to amend should not be denied unless the privilege has been abused, there is prejudice to the opposing party, or amendment would be futile.'")

Here, the defendant respectfully submits he has not abused this privilege, becoming aware of his defenses and counterclaims only upon new legal research, the plaintiff would not be unduly prejudiced by the amendment, and the amendment would provide defendant substantive defenses, and therefore not be futile. Additionally, as stated in his attached affidavit, defendant states *[tell a brief story about why defending this case is in the best interest of justice – woo the court in a paragraph. For example: he used nearly his entire life savings, $82,000, as a down payment to purchase the property subject to this action, and losing it without an opportunity to fully defend his position would be devastating]*. Although the Amended Answer is late coming, Defendant respectfully submits permitting the Amended Answer would help facilitate justice, and ensure a family's life savings does not evaporate without defense.

WHEREFORE, Defendant respectfully requests leave from this Court to file his Amended Answer and Counterclaims.

Respectfully Submitted,

John Smith
123 Any Street
Anytown, OH 43215
(614) 111-3456
Defendant, *Pro Se*

[Remember to attach a certificate of service to every document filed with the court.]

[Copy the heading format used in the Complaint - instead of copying how this form looks.]

IN THE CIRCUIT COURT OF THE _____ DISTRICT
JUDICIAL CIRCUIT IN AND FOR _____
COUNTY FLORIDA

CASE NO. <u>2008 – 12345 -CA-1</u>

LENDER NAME HERE

     Plaintiff,

v.

JOHN SMITH; *et al,*

     Defendant.

_____/

DEFENDANT JOHN SMITH'S
AMENDED ANSWER AND COUNTERCLAIMS

[When a motion to amend the answer if filed, most jurisdictions require that you file a copy of the actual amended answer to the complaint. This form uses the exact format as the Answer, just the title is called "Amended Answer" instead of just "Answer." Complete this form using the proper form for the Answer, just change the heading. Also sign the Amended Answer, and include a Certificate of Service, just like the Answer.]

                      Respectfully Submitted,

                      John Smith
                      123 Any Street
                      Anytown, OH 43215
                      (614) 111-3456
                      Defendant, *Pro Se*

[Don't forget to add a Certificate of Service.]

APPENDIX F

AFFIDAVIT

AFFIDAVIT OF *[JOHN SMITH]*

State of Florida
County of Dade

BEFORE ME, the undersigned Notary, _____, on this _____ day of April 2008, personally appeared *[JOHN SMITH]* known to me to be a credible person and of lawful age, who being by me first duly sworn, on his oath, deposes and says:

_____

_____

_____

_____

_____

_____

[JOHN SMITH]
ADDRESS HERE

State of Florida
County of Dade

Sworn to (or affirmed) and subscribed before me this _____ day of April, 2008, by *[JOHN SMITH]*.

_____

Notary Public

Personally Known _____ OR Produced Identification _____

Type of Identification Produced _____

APPENDIX G

QUALIFIED WRITTEN REQUEST (QWR)

Your Name
Your Address
City, State & Zip

Today's Date

Mortgage Servicer Name
Address
City, State & Zip

RE: Account No.: [Account No. Here]

To Whom It May Concern:
I hereby request information about the fees, costs, and escrow accounting of my loan. This letter is a qualified written request (QWR), pursuant to the Real Estate Settlement and Procedures Act (RESPA), 12 U.S.C. § 2605(e).

The information I request as part of this QWR is as follows:

1) The current interest rate on this account.
2) The adjustment dates of each interest rate adjustment on this account, with the corresponding adjustment amount.
3) Who the current holder of the mortgage/deed of trust is, and their mailing address for process of service, along with a current telephone number.
4) Who the current holder of the note is, and their mailing address for process of service, along with a current telephone number.
5) The date that the current holder acquired this mortgage and from whom it was acquired from.
6) The date your firm began servicing the loan.
7) The previous servicer of the loan.
8) The monthly principal and interest payments, and monthly escrow payments received from the date of the loan's closing to the date of this QWR;
9) A complete payment history of how those payments were applied, including the amounts applied to principal, interest, escrow, and other charges;
10) The total amount due of any unpaid principal, interest, escrow charges, and other charges due as of the date of this letter. Please separately and identify each amount due;
11) The total amount of principal paid on the account up to the date of this letter;
12) The payment dates, purposes of payment and recipient of any and all foreclosure fees and costs that have been charged to my account;
13) A breakdown of the current escrow charges showing how it is calculated and the reasons for any increase within the last 24 months;

14) A breakdown of any shortage, deficiency or surplus in our escrow account over the past three years.

15) A breakdown of all charges accrued on the account since the date of closing, that includes but is not limited by, late charges, appraisal fees, property inspection fees, forced placed insurance charges, legal fees, and recoverable corporate advances.

16) A statement indicating which covenants of the mortgage and/or note authorize each charge.

17) Please provide a copy of all appraisals, property inspections, and risk assessments completed for this account.

18) Please provide a copy of all trust agreements pertaining to this account.

19) Please provide a copy of all servicing agreements (master, sub-servicing, contingency, specialty, and back-up) pertaining to this account.

20) Please provide a copy of all written loss-mitigation rules and work-out procedures for this account.

21) Please provide a copy of all manuals pertaining to the servicing of this account.

22) Please provide a copy of the LSAMS Transaction History Report for this account, and include a description of all fee codes.

23) If this account is registered with MERS, state its MIN number.

24) A statement indicating the amount to pay this loan off in full as [pick date about 30 days after this letter is dated].

I hereby dispute all late fees, charges, inspection fees, property appraisal fees, forced placed insurance charges, legal fees, and corporate advances charged to this account. Additionally, I believe my account is in error for the following reasons: [state reasons here].[1] Pursuant to 12 U.S.C. § 2605(e), you are hereby notified that placing any negative coding on my credit report before responding to this letter is a violation of RESPA and the FCRA. Your organization will be subject to civil liability if negative coding appears for this account before a response to this QWR is issued to me.

Please provide me confirmation that you have received this QWR within 20 days, as required under 12 U.S.C. § 2605(e). Thereafter, please respond to these questions within 60 days of receipt of this letter, also as required under 12 U.S.C. § 2605(e).

Regards,

Your Name

---

[1] *[Not necessary, but you may indicate reasons here.]*

APPENDIX H

REQUESTS FOR ADMISSIONS

John Smith
123 Any Street
Anytown, OH 43215
(614) 111-3456
Defendant, *Pro Se*

IN THE COURT OF COMMON PLEAS
_____ COUNTY, STATE
(Use the heading format provided on the Complaint.)

XYZ LENDER, INC.,	:	
Plaintiffs,	:	Case No. 08 CVE 01-1110
v.	:	Judge: JONES
JOHN SMITH,	:	
Defendant	:	

**DEFENDANT JOHN SMITH'S
FIRST REQUESTS FOR ADMISSIONS
TO PLAINTIFF *[LENDER NAME HERE]***

Defendant John Smith requests, pursuant to *[Civil Rule 36]*, with delivery to the Defendant's address above, that the plaintiff respond under oath within 30 days of service to the following requests for admissions. A failure to do so will deem each admitted.

For purposes of responding to these requests, "plaintiff" means employees, agents, attorneys, investigators, etc. of Plaintiff(s) in this action).

For purposes of responding to these requests, the term "Mortgage" is the document attached to the complaint and titled "Mortgage" or "Deed of Trust". The term "Note" is the document attached to the complaint and titled "Fixed/Adjustable Rate Note" and all riders.

Each of these requests is addressed to the personal and continuing knowledge of plaintiff and plaintiff's counsel. If plaintiff cannot respond to any request due to lack of information available to it, defendant requests the plaintiff respond to those portions of the request it is able to answer and specifically state that portion of the request it cannot answer due to lack of information, and provide a reason why it believes it lacks sufficient information to respond. If any of these requests cannot now be answered because of lack of information or documentation and such information or documentation subsequently comes to the knowledge of Plaintiff or Plaintiff's counsel, Defendant requests Plaintiff to serve supplemental documentation on Defendant within a reasonable time after such information or documentation is acquired.

1. Admit the notice of acceleration described by the Mortgage, covenant numbered as "22" on page 13, was not provided to the defendant directly by the "Lender", which is defined in the Mortgage.

[Generally, you will be required to serve an electronic copy upon the other party, either by diskette or via email. Call the attorney for the lender to find out the way it prefers.]

2. Admit the notice of acceleration described by the Mortgage/Deed of Trust, covenant numbered as "22," was not provided to the defendant directly by *[Name of Lender in the Mortgage/Deed of Trust]*, or the plaintiff in this action.

3. Admit the *[Servicer Name, i.e., Countrywide Home Loans, Inc.]* is not the "Lender" as defined by the Mortgage/Deed of Trust.

[This question attempts to establish the Mortgage requires the "Lender," as specifically defined in the Mortgage document did not provide the requisite notice of acceleration to the defendant. Failing to do so is argued as failing to meet a condition precedent.]

4. Admit the Plaintiff did not provide the Defendant all of the disclosures required by law for closed-ended mortgage transactions.

5. Admit that it is known to the plaintiff that *[The second mortgage company, EMC Mortgage Corporation]* holds a valid lien against the property known as *[state the property address]*.

6. Admit the Plaintiff did not provide the Defendant a booklet titled "Consumer Handbook on Adjustable Rate Mortgages" at the time the mortgage application form was provided to the Defendant.

7. Admit the Plaintiff did not provide the Defendant an explanation of how the Defendant may calculate the payments for the loan amount at the time the mortgage application form was provided to the Defendant.

[As required by TILA. Seek admittance of any TILA deficiencies.]

8. *[Add in requests suggested in chapters used in defense. There may be limit as to how many requests can be served. See your local court rules first, then your state's rules of civil procedure to determine what that limit is.]*

Date: *[Today's Date]*

_____
John Smith, Defendant Pro Se

[You must fill out the certificate of service; the verification portion is for the other party to fill out. Remember to send a copy to every party plus mail two copies to the Clerk of Courts. (Call the clerk of courts to find out how many copies are required – the judge may or may not get a copy in your jurisdiction.]

CERTIFICATE OF SERVICE

The undersigned certifies that a copy of the foregoing Requests for Admissions were served upon the following parties by regular USPS mail, postage prepaid, on this ___ day of _____, _____:

Jane Doe
Big Law Firm
Address
Address
Attorney for Plaintiff

Rick Jones
Defendant #2
Address
Address

Other Defendants
…

_____
John Smith

VERIFICATION

I, _____, hereby certify that to the best of my knowledge and belief, the responses stated in the foregoing responses to requests for admissions are true, correct, and based on my personal knowledge.

_____

Sworn and subscribed before me this _____ day of _____, 20_____.
Notary Public
My Commission Expires: _____
(seal)

APPENDIX I

REQUESTS FOR THE PRODUCTION OF DOCUMENTS

You may want to use this discovery method to request the following documents, in addition to those listed in the model form:

Pooling and Servicing Agreement

Underwriting standards

Rate sheets: include section on how to read them??

Agreements between parties (broker/lender, lender/assignee, lender/trustee)

Payment history

Articles of incorporation

Annual report

Entire creditor file (if creditor is a party to the lawsuit)

Entire broker file (if broker is a party to the lawsuit)

Complaints to lender and assignee about problems similar to borrower's complaints.

Employee training manuals

Other loans with same parties

Consider using PACER to access federal lawsuits against the same lender. Some state libraries offer access to PACER for free. PACER provides you access to all the federal lawsuits files in the United States. Call local *state* library for info.

John Smith
123 Any Street
Anytown, OH 43215
(614) 111-3456
Defendant, *Pro Se*

IN THE COURT OF COMMON PLEAS
_____ COUNTY, STATE
(Use the heading format provided on the Complaint.)

XYZ LENDER, INC.,	:	
Plaintiffs,	:	Case No. 08 CVE 01-1110
v.	:	Judge: JONES
JOHN SMITH,	:	
Defendant	:	

DEFENDANT JOHN SMITH'S
FIRST REQUEST FOR PRODUCTION OF DOCUMENTS
TO PLAINTIFF *[LENDER NAME HERE]*

Defendant John Smith requests, pursuant to *[Civil Rule 34]*, with delivery to the Defendant's address above, that the plaintiff respond under oath within 30 days of service to the following requests for production of documents.

For purposes of responding to these requests, the term "identify" shall mean providing the full name, aliases, title, work address, and work telephone numbers, work email address of the person or entity. "Plaintiff" means employees, agents, attorneys, investigators, etc. of Plaintiff(s) in this action):

For purposes of responding to these requests, the term "document" shall mean all written or printed matter of any kind, including originals and all non-identical copies, whether different from the originals by reason of any notation made on such copies or otherwise, including, without limitation, correspondence, e-mail, memoranda, notes, diaries, statistics, letters, telegraphs, minutes, addenda, expense accounts, contracts, reports, studies, checks, statements, receipts, returns, summaries, pamphlets, books,, inter-office and intra-office communications, notations of any sort of any conversations, including telephone conversations or meetings, bulletins, computer print-outs, teletypes, telefaxes, invoices, worksheets, any drafts, alterations, modifications, changes, and amendments of any of the foregoing.

For purposes of responding to these requests, the term "document" also includes, but is not limited to, all graphic or manual records, or representations of any kind (including, but not limited to, photographs, charts, graphs, microfilms, microfiche, videotapes, records, and motion pictures), and all electronic, mechanical, or electric records or representations of any kind including, but not limited to, audio tapes, cassettes, discs, and recordings.

For purposes of responding to these requests, the term "Mortgage" is the document attached to the complaint and titled "Mortgage" or "Deed of Trust". The term "Note" is the document attached to the complaint and titled "Fixed/Adjustable Rate Note" and all riders.

Each of these requests is addressed to the personal and continuing knowledge of plaintiff and plaintiff's counsel. If plaintiff cannot respond to any request due to lack of information available to it, defendant requests the plaintiff respond to those portions of the request it is able to answer and specifically state that portion of the request it cannot answer due to lack of information, and provide a reason why it believes it lacks sufficient information to respond. If any of these requests cannot now be answered because of lack of information or documentation and such information or documentation subsequently comes to the knowledge of Plaintiff or Plaintiff's counsel, Defendant requests Plaintiff to serve supplemental documentation on Defendant within a reasonable time after such information or documentation is acquired.

The items to produce are:

1.   A copy of all documents which create the trustee relationship by, between, or otherwise relating to Deutsche Bank National Trust, IMH Assets Corp, Mortgage Electronic Registration Systems, Inc, Southstar Funding, LLC and/or Countrywide Home Loans.

[Use if the plaintiff is a trustee for someone else – which will be indicated by the name of the plaintiff on the Complaint. Substitute the parties named in the Complaint for the parties indicated here.]

2.   Produce the original Mortgage/Deed of Trust and Note for inspection and copying at _____(location), at (date) and (time).

3.   A copy of all documents which create the successor relationship by, between, or otherwise relating to Deutsche Bank National Trust, IMH Assets Corp, Mortgage Electronic Registration Systems, Inc, Southstar Funding, LLC and/or Countrywide Home Loans that demonstrate the Plaintiff has standing to bring this Complaint in Foreclosure.

4. A copy of all documents which create the nominee relationship by, between, or otherwise relating to Deutsche Bank National Trust, IMH Assets Corp, Mortgage Electronic Registration Systems, Inc, Southstar Funding, LLC and/or Countrywide Home Loans that demonstrate the Plaintiff has standing to bring this Complaint in Foreclosure.

5. A copy of the documents that are relied upon by the Plaintiff to demonstrate who is defined as the "Lender" by the Mortgage.

6. If the "Lender" is no longer Southstar Funding, LLC, a copy of the documents demonstrating who is now the "Lender."

7. A copy of the document(s) that reference the Defendant or his account and *[any second mortgage holder, i.e., EMC Mortgage Corporation]* which are directly or indirectly in control of the Plaintiff and that are not protected by attorney-client privilege.

8. A copy of all document(s) referencing the Defendant or his account under the control of the Plaintiff that are not protected by attorney-client privilege.

9. A copy of all document(s) that are relied upon by the Plaintiff to demonstrate the Plaintiff has standing to bring and maintain this lawsuit.

10. A copy of all documents that are relied upon by the Plaintiff to demonstrate Countrywide Home Loans is an agent of the Plaintiff in respect to the Mortgage and Note.

11. A copy of any and all documents the Plaintiff intends to rely upon at trial that have not already been provided to the Defendant.

12. Any document referred to by the Plaintiff in preparation to respond to Defendant's posed interrogatories.

13. A copy of documents provided to the Defendant at the time of application through closing, including all TILA and RESPA disclosures.

14. Provide any assignments or conveyances of mortgage/deed of trust and transferring the mortgage and note from immediate predecessor-in-interest of the Mortgage/Deed of Trust and Note to the plaintiff.

15. Provide any assignments or conveyances of the note transferring the mortgage and note from immediate predecessor-in-interest of the Mortgage/Deed of Trust and Note to the plaintiff.

16. Provide copies of all allonges to note under Plaintiff's control for the mortgage and note subject to this lawsuit.

17. Provide copies of all assignments or conveyances of mortgage under Plaintiff's control for the mortgage and note subject to this lawsuit.

18. Provide copies of all assignments or conveyances of deeds-of-trust under Plaintiff's control for the mortgage and note subject to this lawsuit.

19. If the chain of title does not provide the entire ownership of the note and mortgage uninterrupted, provide the documents which demonstrate the uninterrupted ownership of the note and mortgage from closing until today.

20. Provide the **documents**, as defined above, in the possession of the Plaintiff which reference the defendant or his account.

21. Provide the **documents** that include memos, notes, and correspondence in the possession of Mortgage Electronic Registration Systems, Inc. which reference the defendant or his account which have not been provided as of yet.

9. *[Add in requests suggested in chapters used in defense. There may be limit as to how many requests can be served. See your local court rules first, then your state's rules of civil procedure to determine what that limit is.]*

Date: *[Today's Date]*

_____
John Smith, Defendant Pro Se

[You must fill out the certificate of service; the verification portion is for the other party to fill out. Remember to send a copy to every party plus mail two copies to the Clerk of Courts. (Call the clerk of courts to find out how many copies are required – the judge may or may not get a copy in your jurisdiction.]

CERTIFICATE OF SERVICE

The undersigned certifies that a copy of the foregoing Requests for Admissions were served upon the following parties by regular USPS mail, postage prepaid, on this ____ day of _____, _____:

Jane Doe
Big Law Firm
Address
Address
Attorney for Plaintiff

Other Defendants

…

_____
John Smith

VERIFICATION

I, _____, hereby certify that to the best of my knowledge and belief, the responses stated in the foregoing responses to requests for admissions are true, correct, and based on my personal knowledge.

_____

Sworn and subscribed before me this _____ day of _____, 20_____.
Notary Public
My Commission Expires: _____
(seal)

APPENDIX J

REQUEST FOR INTERROGATORY RESPONSES

John Smith
123 Any Street
Anytown, OH 43215
(614) 111-3456
Defendant, *Pro Se*

IN THE COURT OF COMMON PLEAS
_____ COUNTY, STATE
(Use the heading format provided on the Complaint.)

XYZ LENDER, INC.,	:	
Plaintiffs,	:	Case No. 08 CVE 01-1110
v.	:	Judge: JONES
JOHN SMITH,	:	
Defendant	:	

**DEFENDANT JOHN SMITH'S
FIRST REQUEST FOR ANSWERS TO INTERROGATORIES
TO PLAINTIFF [LENDER NAME HERE]**

Defendant John Smith requests, pursuant to *[Civil Rule 33]*, with delivery to the Defendant's address above, that the plaintiff respond under oath within 28 days of service to the following interrogatories.

For purposes of responding to these requests, the term "identify" shall mean providing the full name, aliases, title, work address, and work telephone numbers, work email address of the person or entity. "Plaintiff" means employees, agents, attorneys, investigators, etc. of Plaintiff(s) in this action):

For purposes of responding to these requests, the term "document" shall mean all written or printed matter of any kind, including originals and all non-identical copies, whether different from the originals by reason of any notation made on such copies or otherwise, including, without limitation, correspondence, e-mail, memoranda, notes, diaries, statistics, letters, telegraphs, minutes, addenda, expense accounts, contracts, reports, studies, checks, statements, receipts, returns, summaries, pamphlets, books,, inter-office and intra-office communications, notations of any sort of any conversations, including telephone conversations or meetings, bulletins, computer print-outs, teletypes, telefaxes, invoices, worksheets, any drafts, alterations, modifications, changes, and amendments of any of the foregoing.

For purposes of responding to these requests, the term "document" also includes, but is not limited to, all graphic or manual records, or representations of any kind (including, but not limited to, photographs, charts, graphs, microfilms, microfiche, videotapes, records, and motion pictures), and all electronic, mechanical, or electric records or representations of any kind including, but not limited to, audio tapes, cassettes, discs, and recordings.

For purposes of responding to these requests, the term "Mortgage" is the document attached to the complaint and titled "Mortgage" or "Deed of Trust." The term "Note" is the document attached to the complaint and titled "Fixed/Adjustable Rate Note".

Each of these requests is addressed to the personal and continuing knowledge of plaintiff and plaintiff's counsel. If plaintiff cannot respond to any request due to lack of information available to it, defendant requests the plaintiff respond to those portions of the request it is able to answer and specifically state that portion of the request it cannot answer due to lack of information, and provide a reason why it believes it lacks sufficient information to respond. If any of these requests cannot now be answered because of lack of information or documentation and such information or documentation subsequently comes to the knowledge of Plaintiff or Plaintiff's counsel, Defendant requests Plaintiff to serve supplemental documentation on Defendant within a reasonable time after such information or documentation is acquired.

1.   Identify the person(s) who have answered these interrogatories.
ANSWER:

[Most courts require 4-5 spaces between each question so the other party has room to fill in an answer. Generally, you will be required to serve an electronic copy upon the other party, either by diskette or via email. Call the attorney for the lender to find out the way it prefers.]

2.   Identify each and every person Plaintiff may call as a witness in this case.
ANSWER:

3.   Identify each and every document Plaintiff may introduce into evidence in this case.
ANSWER:

4.   State the complete payment history of this account from the date of closing to the present, including dates of payments received and the amount received.
ANSWER:

5.   Identify fully who the "Lender" is, as described in the Mortgage/Deed of Trust. If more than one exists, state each.
ANSWER:

6. Identify fully who the "Loan Servicer" of the Mortgage/ Deed of Trust is. If more than one exists, state each.
ANSWER:

7. Identify fully who the "Note Purchaser" of the Mortgage/ Deed of Trust is. If there are more than one, or multiple parties have held this distinction, state each.
ANSWER:

8. What document(s) do the Plaintiff rely upon which confer powers to the *[servicer name here, i.e., Countrywide Home Loans]* to provide notice of acceleration to the defendant in the event of default?
ANSWER:

9. State where in the Mortgage that the "Lender" will change when the Note or Mortgage/ Deed of Trust is sold.
ANSWER:

10. State the total dollar amount paid, and the entity it was paid to, when the Plaintiff gained control over the Mortgage and/or Note.
ANSWER:

11. State the date on which these payments were made and state the principle balance of the mortgage loan at that time.
ANSWER:

12. Identify fully the individual who took the original mortgage application.
ANSWER:

13. State whether the Plaintiff maintained any affiliated businesses that provided services to the Defendant prior to or at closing.
ANSWER:

14. Identify fully the owner of the Mortgage/ Deed of Trust.
ANSWER:

15. Identify fully the owner of the Note.
ANSWER:

16. Identify fully the person(s) who have answered these questions.
ANSWER:

17. Identify fully each and every witness that you intend to call at the trial, or other disposition of this matter, and provide a brief description of what you anticipate that witness's testimony to be.
ANSWER:

18. State which entity (corporation, company, person, etc.) was the beneficiary of each payment the defendant made on the Mortgage/ Deed of Trust and Note.
ANSWER:

19. State the date that *[full plaintiff name]* became the holder (owner) of the Mortgage/ Deed of Trust and Note. *****THIS INTERROGATORY IS A KILLER*****
ANSWER:

20. State the party from whom *[full plaintiff name]* directly obtained the Mortgage/ Deed of Trust and note from (i.e., the party that conveyed/assigned the Mortgage to the plaintiff).
ANSWER:

21. State the consideration plaintiff paid to the party identified in the immediately preceeding interrogatory for said assignment/conveyance.
ANSWER:

22. State the number of allonges referencing this Note that plaintiff has reason to know are in existence.
ANSWER:

23. State the number of assignments of mortgage or assignments of deed-of-trust that plaintiff has reason to know are in existence.
ANSWER:

24. *[Add in suggested interrogatories as suggested in those chapters used in defense. Remember, there is generally a limit as to how many interrogatories can be requested. See your state's rules of civil procedure to determine what that limit is. Some localities also impose limitations; see any local court rules for these.]*
ANSWER:

Date: *[Today's Date]*

_____
John Smith, Defendant Pro Se

[You must fill out the certificate of service; the verification portion is for the other party to fill out. Remember to send a copy to every party plus mail two copies to the Clerk of Courts. (Call the clerk of courts to find out how many copies are required – the judge may or may not get a copy in your jurisdiction.]

CERTIFICATE OF SERVICE

The undersigned certifies that a copy of the foregoing was served upon the following parties by regular USPS mail, postage prepaid, on this ____ day of _____, _____:

Jane Doe
Big Law Firm
Address
Address
Attorney for Plaintiff

Rick Jones
Defendant #2
Address
Address

Other Defendants
…

_____
John Smith

VERIFICATION

I, _____, hereby certify that to the best of my knowledge and belief, the responses stated in the foregoing responses to interrogatories are true, correct, and based on my personal knowledge.

_____

Sworn and subscribed before me this _____ day of _____, 20_____.
Notary Public
My Commission Expires: _____
(seal)

APPENDIX K

SUBPOENA

A subpoena compels a person to appear in court, at a hearing, or at a particular place and time. It can be used to force a party to bring with them documents or other tangible property that may be in their possession. A copy of the subpoena form published by the California Court system to force a party to appear and produce business records is in this appendix as an example.

You will need to contact your local court for their approved subpoena forms and process for serving a subpoena.

SUBP-010

ATTORNEY OR PARTY WITHOUT ATTORNEY *(Name, State Bar number, and address)*:	FOR COURT USE ONLY
TELEPHONE NO.: FAX NO. *(Optional)*: E-MAIL ADDRESS *(Optional)*: ATTORNEY FOR *(Name)*:	

SUPERIOR COURT OF CALIFORNIA, COUNTY OF
STREET ADDRESS:
MAILING ADDRESS:
CITY AND ZIP CODE:
BRANCH NAME:

PLAINTIFF/PETITIONER:
DEFENDANT/RESPONDENT:

DEPOSITION SUBPOENA FOR PRODUCTION OF BUSINESS RECORDS	CASE NUMBER:

THE PEOPLE OF THE STATE OF CALIFORNIA, TO *(name, address, and telephone number of deponent, if known)*:

1. YOU ARE ORDERED TO PRODUCE THE BUSINESS RECORDS described in item 3, as follows:

> To *(name of deposition officer)*:
> On *(date)*: At *(time)*:
> Location *(address)*:
>
> Do not release the requested records to the deposition officer prior to the date and time stated above.

   a. ☐ by delivering a true, legible, and durable copy of the business records described in item 3, enclosed in a sealed inner wrapper with the title and number of the action, name of witness, and date of subpoena clearly written on it. The inner wrapper shall then be enclosed in an outer envelope or wrapper, sealed, and mailed to the deposition officer at the address in item 1.

   b. ☐ by delivering a true, legible, and durable copy of the business records described in item 3 to the deposition officer at the witness's address, on receipt of payment in cash or by check of the reasonable costs of preparing the copy, as determined under Evidence Code section 1563(b).

   c. ☐ by making the original business records described in item 3 available for inspection at your business address by the attorney's representative and permitting copying at your business address under reasonable conditions during normal business hours.

2. *The records are to be produced by the date and time shown in item 1 (but not sooner than 20 days after the issuance of the deposition subpoena, or 15 days after service, whichever date is later). Reasonable costs of locating records, making them available or copying them, and postage, if any, are recoverable as set forth in Evidence Code section 1563(b). The records shall be accompanied by an affidavit of the custodian or other qualified witness pursuant to Evidence Code section 1561.*

3. The records to be produced are described as follows:

   ☐ Continued on Attachment 3.

4. IF YOU HAVE BEEN SERVED WITH THIS SUBPOENA AS A CUSTODIAN OF CONSUMER OR EMPLOYEE RECORDS UNDER CODE OF CIVIL PROCEDURE SECTION 1985.3 OR 1985.6 AND A MOTION TO QUASH OR AN OBJECTION HAS BEEN SERVED ON YOU, A COURT ORDER OR AGREEMENT OF THE PARTIES, WITNESSES, *AND* CONSUMER OR EMPLOYEE AFFECTED MUST BE OBTAINED BEFORE YOU ARE REQUIRED TO PRODUCE CONSUMER OR EMPLOYEE RECORDS.

> DISOBEDIENCE OF THIS SUBPOENA MAY BE PUNISHED AS CONTEMPT BY THIS COURT. YOU WILL ALSO BE LIABLE FOR THE SUM OF FIVE HUNDRED DOLLARS AND ALL DAMAGES RESULTING FROM YOUR FAILURE TO OBEY.

Date issued:

▶

_____ _____
(TYPE OR PRINT NAME) (SIGNATURE OF PERSON ISSUING SUBPOENA)

(Proof of service on reverse) (TITLE) Page 1 of 2

Form Adopted for Mandatory Use Judicial Council of California SUBP-010 [Rev. January 1, 2007]	DEPOSITION SUBPOENA FOR PRODUCTION OF BUSINESS RECORDS	Code of Civil Procedure, §§ 2020.410–2020.440; Civil Code, § 15(a)(e); Government Code § 68097.1 www.courtinfo.ca.gov

SUBP-010

PLAINTIFF/PETITIONER:	CASE NUMBER:
DEFENDANT/RESPONDENT:	

PROOF OF SERVICE OF DEPOSITION SUBPOENA FOR PRODUCTION OF BUSINESS RECORDS

1. I served this *Deposition Subpoena for Production of Business Records* by personally delivering a copy to the person served as follows:

    a. Person served *(name)*:

    b. Address where served:

    c. Date of delivery:

    d. Time of delivery:

    e. (1) ☐ Witness fees were paid.
          Amount: . . . . $ _____
      (2) ☐ Copying fees were paid.
          Amount: . . . . $ _____

    f. Fee for service: . . . . $ _____

2. I received this subpoena for service on *(date)*:

3. Person serving:
    a. ☐ Not a registered California process server.
    b. ☐ California sheriff or marshal.
    c. ☐ Registered California process server.
    d. ☐ Employee or independent contractor of a registered California process server.
    e. ☐ Exempt from registration under Business and Professions Code section 22350(b).
    f. ☐ Registered professional photocopier.
    g. ☐ Exempt from registration under Business and Professions Code section 22451.
    h. Name, address, telephone number, and, if applicable, county of registration and number:

I declare under penalty of perjury under the laws of the State of California that the foregoing is true and correct.

Date:

▶ _____
         (SIGNATURE)

(For California sheriff or marshal use only)
I certify that the foregoing is true and correct.

Date:

▶ _____
         (SIGNATURE)

SUBP-010 [Rev. January 1, 2007]   **PROOF OF SERVICE OF DEPOSITION SUBPOENA FOR PRODUCTION OF BUSINESS RECORDS**   Page 2 of 2

APPENDIX L

FEDERAL RULES OF CIVIL PROCEDURE

FEDERAL RULES OF CIVIL PROCEDURE (JUNE, 2008) **(WITHOUT FORMS)**

Rule 1. Scope and Purpose

These rules govern the procedure in all civil actions and proceedings in the United States district courts, except as stated in Rule 81. They should be construed and administered to secure the just, speedy, and inexpensive determination of every action and proceeding.

Rule 2. One Form of Action

There is one form of action--the civil action.

Rule 3. Commencing an Action

A civil action is commenced by filing a complaint with the court.

Rule 4. Summons

(a) Contents; Amendments.

   (1) *Contents.* A summons must:

     (A) name the court and the parties;

     (B) be directed to the defendant;

     (C) state the name and address of the plaintiff's attorney or--if unrepresented--of the plaintiff;

     (D) state the time within which the defendant must appear and defend;

     (E) notify the defendant that a failure to appear and defend will result in a default judgment against the defendant for the relief demanded in the complaint;

     (F) be signed by the clerk; and

     (G) bear the court's seal.

   (2) *Amendments.* The court may permit a summons to be amended.

 (b) Issuance. On or after filing the complaint, the plaintiff may present a summons to the clerk for signature and seal. If the summons is properly completed, the clerk must sign, seal, and issue it to the plaintiff for service on the defendant. A summons--or a copy of a summons that is addressed to multiple defendants--must be issued for each defendant to be served.

(c) Service.

   (1) *In General.* A summons must be served with a copy of the complaint. The plaintiff is responsible for having the summons and complaint served within the time allowed by Rule 4(m) and must furnish the necessary copies to the person who makes service.

   (2) *By Whom.* Any person who is at least 18 years old and not a party may serve a summons and complaint.

   (3) *By a Marshal or Someone Specially Appointed.* At the plaintiff's request, the court may order that service be made by a United States marshal or deputy marshal or by a person specially appointed by the court. The court must so order if the plaintiff is authorized to proceed in forma pauperis under 28 U.S.C. § 1915 or as a seaman under 28 U.S.C. § 1916.

 (d) Waiving Service.

   (1) *Requesting a Waiver.* An individual, corporation, or association that is subject to service under Rule 4(e), (f), or (h) has a duty to avoid unnecessary expenses of serving the summons. The plaintiff may notify such a defendant that an action has been commenced and request that the defendant waive service of a summons. The notice and request must:

     (A) be in writing and be addressed:

(i) to the individual defendant; or

(ii) for a defendant subject to service under Rule 4(h), to an officer, a managing or general agent, or any other agent authorized by appointment or by law to receive service of process;

(B) name the court where the complaint was filed;

(C) be accompanied by a copy of the complaint, two copies of a waiver form, and a prepaid means for returning the form;

(D) inform the defendant, using text prescribed in Form 5, of the consequences of waiving and not waiving service;

(E) state the date when the request is sent;

(F) give the defendant a reasonable time of at least 30 days after the request was sent--or at least 60 days if sent to the defendant outside any judicial district of the United States--to return the waiver; and

(G) be sent by first-class mail or other reliable means.

(2) *Failure to Waive.* If a defendant located within the United States fails, without good cause, to sign and return a waiver requested by a plaintiff located within the United States, the court must impose on the defendant:

(A) the expenses later incurred in making service; and

(B) the reasonable expenses, including attorney's fees, of any motion required to collect those service expenses.

(3) *Time to Answer After a Waiver.* A defendant who, before being served with process, timely returns a waiver need not serve an answer to the complaint until 60 days after the request was sent--or until 90 days after it was sent to the defendant outside any judicial district of the United States.

(4) *Results of Filing a Waiver.* When the plaintiff files a waiver, proof of service is not required and these rules apply as if a summons and complaint had been served at the time of filing the waiver.

(5) *Jurisdiction and Venue Not Waived.* Waiving service of a summons does not waive any objection to personal jurisdiction or to venue.

(e) Serving an Individual Within a Judicial District of the United States. Unless federal law provides otherwise, an individual--other than a minor, an incompetent person, or a person whose waiver has been filed--may be served in a judicial district of the United States by:

(1) following state law for serving a summons in an action brought in courts of general jurisdiction in the state where the district court is located or where service is made; or

(2) doing any of the following:

(A) delivering a copy of the summons and of the complaint to the individual personally;

(B) leaving a copy of each at the individual's dwelling or usual place of abode with someone of suitable age and discretion who resides there; or

(C) delivering a copy of each to an agent authorized by appointment or by law to receive service of process.

(f) Serving an Individual in a Foreign Country. Unless federal law provides otherwise, an individual--other than a minor, an incompetent person, or a person whose waiver has been filed--may be served at a place not within any judicial district of the United States:

(1) by any internationally agreed means of service that is reasonably calculated to give notice, such as those authorized by the Hague Convention on the Service Abroad of Judicial and Extrajudicial Documents;

(2) if there is no internationally agreed means, or if an international agreement allows but does not specify other means, by a method that is reasonably calculated to give notice:

(A) as prescribed by the foreign country's law for service in that country in an action in its courts of general jurisdiction;

(B) as the foreign authority directs in response to a letter rogatory or letter of request; or

(C) unless prohibited by the foreign country's law, by:

(i) delivering a copy of the summons and of the complaint to the individual personally; or

(ii) using any form of mail that the clerk addresses and sends to the individual and that requires a signed receipt; or

(3) by other means not prohibited by international agreement, as the court orders.

(g) Serving a Minor or an Incompetent Person. A minor or an incompetent person in a judicial district of the United States must be served by following state law for serving a summons or like process on such a defendant in an action brought in the courts of general jurisdiction of the state where service is made. A minor or an incompetent person who is not within any judicial district of the United States must be served in the manner prescribed by Rule 4(f)(2)(A), (f)(2)(B), or (f)(3).

(h) Serving a Corporation, Partnership, or Association. Unless federal law provides otherwise or the defendant's waiver has been filed, a domestic or foreign corporation, or a partnership or other unincorporated association that is subject to suit under a common name, must be served:

(1) in a judicial district of the United States:

(A) in the manner prescribed by Rule 4(e)(1) for serving an individual; or

(B) by delivering a copy of the summons and of the complaint to an officer, a managing or general agent, or any other agent authorized by appointment or by law to receive service of process and--if the agent is one authorized by statute and the statute so requires--by also mailing a copy of each to the defendant; or

(2) at a place not within any judicial district of the United States, in any manner prescribed by Rule 4(f) for serving an individual, except personal delivery under (f)(2)(C)(i).

(i) Serving the United States and Its Agencies, Corporations, Officers, or Employees.

(1) *United States.* To serve the United States, a party must:

(A)

(i) deliver a copy of the summons and of the complaint to the United States attorney for the district where the action is brought--or to an assistant United States attorney or clerical employee whom the United States attorney designates in a writing filed with the court clerk--or

(ii) send a copy of each by registered or certified mail to the civil-process clerk at the United States attorney's office;

(B) send a copy of each by registered or certified mail to the Attorney General of the United States at Washington, D.C.; and

(C) if the action challenges an order of a nonparty agency or officer of the United States, send a copy of each by registered or certified mail to the agency or officer.

(2) *Agency; Corporation; Officer or Employee Sued in an Official Capacity.* To serve a United States agency or corporation, or a United States officer or employee sued only in an official capacity, a party must serve the United States and also send a copy of the summons and of the complaint by registered or certified mail to the agency, corporation, officer, or employee.

(3) *Officer or Employee Sued Individually.* To serve a United States officer or employee sued in an individual capacity for an act or omission occurring in connection with duties performed on the United States' behalf (whether or not the officer or employee is also sued in an official capacity), a party must serve the United States and also serve the officer or employee under Rule 4(e), (f), or (g).

(4) *Extending Time.* The court must allow a party a reasonable time to cure its failure to:

(A) serve a person required to be served under Rule 4(i)(2), if the party has served either the United States attorney or the Attorney General of the United States; or

(B) serve the United States under Rule 4(i)(3), if the party has served the United States officer or employee.

(j) Serving a Foreign, State, or Local Government.

(1) *Foreign State.* A foreign state or its political subdivision, agency, or instrumentality must be served in accordance with 28 U.S.C. § 1608.

(2) *State or Local Government.* A state, a municipal corporation, or any other state-created governmental organization that is subject to suit must be served by:

(A) delivering a copy of the summons and of the complaint to its chief executive officer; or

(B) serving a copy of each in the manner prescribed by that state's law for serving a summons or like process on such a defendant.

(k) Territorial Limits of Effective Service.

(1) *In General.* Serving a summons or filing a waiver of service establishes personal jurisdiction over a defendant:

(A) who is subject to the jurisdiction of a court of general jurisdiction in the state where the district court is located;

(B) who is a party joined under Rule 14 or 19 and is served within a judicial district of the United States and not more than 100 miles from where the summons was issued; or

(C) when authorized by a federal statute.

(2) *Federal Claim Outside State-Court Jurisdiction.* For a claim that arises under federal law, serving a summons or filing a waiver of service establishes personal jurisdiction over a defendant if:

(A) the defendant is not subject to jurisdiction in any state's courts of general jurisdiction; and

(B) exercising jurisdiction is consistent with the United States Constitution and laws.

(l) Proving Service.

(1) *Affidavit Required.* Unless service is waived, proof of service must be made to the court. Except for service by a United States marshal or deputy marshal, proof must be by the server's affidavit.

(2) *Service Outside the United States.* Service not within any judicial district of the United States must be proved as follows:

(A) if made under Rule 4(f)(1), as provided in the applicable treaty or convention; or

(B) if made under Rule 4(f)(2) or (f)(3), by a receipt signed by the addressee, or by other evidence satisfying the court that the summons and complaint were delivered to the addressee.

(3) *Validity of Service; Amending Proof.* Failure to prove service does not affect the validity of service. The court may permit proof of service to be amended.

(m) Time Limit for Service. If a defendant is not served within 120 days after the complaint is filed, the court--on motion or on its own after notice to the plaintiff--must dismiss the action without prejudice against that defendant or order that service be made within a specified time. But if the plaintiff shows good cause for the failure, the court must extend the time for service for an appropriate period. This subdivision (m) does not apply to service in a foreign country under Rule 4(f) or 4(j)(1).

(n) Asserting Jurisdiction over Property or Assets.

(1) *Federal Law.* The court may assert jurisdiction over property if authorized by a federal statute. Notice to claimants of the property must be given as provided in the statute or by serving a summons under this rule.

(2) *State Law.* On a showing that personal jurisdiction over a defendant cannot be obtained in the district where the action is brought by reasonable efforts to serve a summons under this rule, the court may assert jurisdiction over the defendant's assets found in the district. Jurisdiction is acquired by seizing the assets under the circumstances and in the manner provided by state law in that district.

Rule 4.1. Serving Other Process

(a) In General. Process--other than a summons under Rule 4 or a subpoena under Rule 45--must be served by a United States marshal or deputy marshal or by a person specially appointed for that purpose. It may be served anywhere within the territorial limits of the state where the district court is located and, if authorized by a federal statute, beyond those limits. Proof of service must be made under Rule 4(l).

(b) Enforcing Orders: Committing for Civil Contempt. An order committing a person for civil contempt of a decree or injunction issued to enforce federal law may be served and enforced in any district. Any other order in a civil-contempt proceeding may be served only in the state where the issuing court is located or elsewhere in the United States within 100 miles from where the order was issued.

RULE 5. SERVING AND FILING PLEADINGS AND OTHER PAPERS

(a) Service: When Required.

(1) *In General.* Unless these rules provide otherwise, each of the following papers must be served on every party:

(A) an order stating that service is required;

(B) a pleading filed after the original complaint, unless the court orders otherwise under Rule 5(c) because there are numerous defendants;

(C) a discovery paper required to be served on a party, unless the court orders otherwise;

(D) a written motion, except one that may be heard ex parte; and

(E) a written notice, appearance, demand, or offer of judgment, or any similar paper.

(2) *If a Party Fails to Appear.* No service is required on a party who is in default for failing to appear. But a pleading that asserts a new claim for relief against such a party must be served on that party under Rule 4.

(3) *Seizing Property.* If an action is begun by seizing property and no person is or need be named as a defendant, any service required before the filing of an appearance, answer, or claim must be made on the person who had custody or possession of the property when it was seized.

(b) Service: How Made.

(1) *Serving an Attorney.* If a party is represented by an attorney, service under this rule must be made on the attorney unless the court orders service on the party.

(2) *Service in General.* A paper is served under this rule by:

(A) handing it to the person;

(B) leaving it:

(i) at the person's office with a clerk or other person in charge or, if no one is in charge, in a conspicuous place in the office; or

(ii) if the person has no office or the office is closed, at the person's dwelling or usual place of abode with someone of suitable age and discretion who resides there;

(C) mailing it to the person's last known address--in which event service is complete upon mailing;

(D) leaving it with the court clerk if the person has no known address;

(E) sending it by electronic means if the person consented in writing--in which event service is complete upon transmission, but is not effective if the serving party learns that it did not reach the person to be served; or

(F) delivering it by any other means that the person consented to in writing--in which event service is complete when the person making service delivers it to the agency designated to make delivery.

(3) *Using Court Facilities.* If a local rule so authorizes, a party may use the court's transmission facilities to make service under Rule 5(b)(2)(E).

(c) Serving Numerous Defendants.

(1) *In General.* If an action involves an unusually large number of defendants, the court may, on motion or on its own, order that:

(A) defendants' pleadings and replies to them need not be served on other defendants;

(B) any crossclaim, counterclaim, avoidance, or affirmative defense in those pleadings and replies to them will be treated as denied or avoided by all other parties; and

(C) filing any such pleading and serving it on the plaintiff constitutes notice of the pleading to all parties.

(2) *Notifying Parties.* A copy of every such order must be served on the parties as the court directs.

(d) Filing.

(1) *Required Filings; Certificate of Service.* Any paper after the complaint that is required to be served--together with a certificate of service--must be filed within a reasonable time after service. But disclosures under Rule 26(a)(1) or (2) and the following discovery requests and responses must not be filed until they are used in the proceeding or the court orders filing: depositions, interrogatories, requests for documents or tangible things or to permit entry onto land, and requests for admission.

(2) *How Filing Is Made--In General.* A paper is filed by delivering it:

(A) to the clerk; or

(B) to a judge who agrees to accept it for filing, and who must then note the filing date on the paper and promptly send it to the clerk.

(3) *Electronic Filing, Signing, or Verification.* A court may, by local rule, allow papers to be filed, signed, or verified by electronic means that are consistent with any technical standards established by the Judicial Conference of the United States. A local rule may require electronic filing only if reasonable exceptions are allowed. A paper filed electronically in compliance with a local rule is a written paper for purposes of these rules.

(4) *Acceptance by the Clerk.* The clerk must not refuse to file a paper solely because it is not in the form prescribed by these rules or by a local rule or practice.

RULE 6. COMPUTING AND EXTENDING TIME; TIME FOR MOTION PAPERS

(a) Computing Time. The following rules apply in computing any time period specified in these rules or in any local rule, court order, or statute:

(1) *Day of the Event Excluded.* Exclude the day of the act, event, or default that begins the period.

(2) *Exclusions from Brief Periods.* Exclude intermediate Saturdays, Sundays, and legal holidays when the period is less than 11 days.

(3) *Last Day.* Include the last day of the period unless it is a Saturday, Sunday, legal holiday, or--if the act to be done is filing a paper in court--a day on which weather or other conditions make the clerk's office inaccessible. When the last day is excluded, the period runs until the end of the next day that is not a Saturday, Sunday, legal holiday, or day when the clerk's office is inaccessible.

(4) *"Legal Holiday" Defined.* As used in these rules, "legal holiday" means:

(A) the day set aside by statute for observing New Year's Day, Martin Luther King Jr.'s Birthday, Washington's Birthday, Memorial Day, Independence Day, Labor Day, Columbus Day, Veterans' Day, Thanksgiving Day, or Christmas Day; and

(B) any other day declared a holiday by the President, Congress, or the state where the district court is located.

(b) Extending Time.

(1) *In General.* When an act may or must be done within a specified time, the court may, for good cause,

extend the time:

(A) with or without motion or notice if the court acts, or if a request is made, before the original time or its extension expires; or

(B) on motion made after the time has expired if the party failed to act because of excusable neglect.

(2) *Exceptions.* A court must not extend the time to act under Rules 50(b) and (d), 52(b), 59(b), (d), and (e), and 60(b), except as those rules allow.

(c) Motions, Notices of Hearing, and Affidavits.

(1) *In General.* A written motion and notice of the hearing must be served at least 5 days before the time specified for the hearing, with the following exceptions:

(A) when the motion may be heard ex parte;

(B) when these rules set a different time; or

(C) when a court order--which a party may, for good cause, apply for ex parte--sets a different time.

(2) *Supporting Affidavit.* Any affidavit supporting a motion must be served with the motion. Except as Rule 59(c) provides otherwise, any opposing affidavit must be served at least 1 day before the hearing, unless the court permits service at another time.

(d) Additional Time After Certain Kinds of Service. When a party may or must act within a specified time after service and service is made under Rule 5(b)(2)(C), (D), (E), or (F), 3 days are added after the period would otherwise expire under Rule 6(a).

RULE 7. PLEADINGS ALLOWED; FORM OF MOTIONS & OTHER PAPERS

(a) Pleadings. Only these pleadings are allowed:

(1) a complaint;

(2) an answer to a complaint;

(3) an answer to a counterclaim designated as a counterclaim;

(4) an answer to a crossclaim;

(5) a third-party complaint;

(6) an answer to a third-party complaint; and

(7) if the court orders one, a reply to an answer.

(b) Motions and Other Papers.

(1) *In General.* A request for a court order must be made by motion. The motion must:

(A) be in writing unless made during a hearing or trial;

(B) state with particularity the grounds for seeking the order; and

(C) state the relief sought.

(2) *Form.* The rules governing captions and other matters of form in pleadings apply to motions and other papers.

Rule 7.1. Disclosure Statement

(a) Who Must File; Contents. A nongovernmental corporate party must file two copies of a disclosure statement that:

(1) identifies any parent corporation and any publicly held corporation owning 10% or more of its stock; or

(2) states that there is no such corporation.

(b) Time to File; Supplemental Filing. A party must:

(1) file the disclosure statement with its first appearance, pleading, petition, motion, response, or other

request addressed to the court; and

(2) promptly file a supplemental statement if any required information changes.

Rule 8. General Rules of Pleading

(a) Claim for Relief. A pleading that states a claim for relief must contain:

(1) a short and plain statement of the grounds for the court's jurisdiction, unless the court already has jurisdiction and the claim needs no new jurisdictional support;

(2) a short and plain statement of the claim showing that the pleader is entitled to relief; and

(3) a demand for the relief sought, which may include relief in the alternative or different types of relief.

(b) Defenses; Admissions and Denials.

(1) *In General.* In responding to a pleading, a party must:

(A) state in short and plain terms its defenses to each claim asserted against it; and

(B) admit or deny the allegations asserted against it by an opposing party.

(2) *Denials--Responding to the Substance.* A denial must fairly respond to the substance of the allegation.

(3) *General and Specific Denials.* A party that intends in good faith to deny all the allegations of a pleading--including the jurisdictional grounds--may do so by a general denial. A party that does not intend to deny all the allegations must either specifically deny designated allegations or generally deny all except those specifically admitted.

(4) *Denying Part of an Allegation.* A party that intends in good faith to deny only part of an allegation must admit the part that is true and deny the rest.

(5) *Lacking Knowledge or Information.* A party that lacks knowledge or information sufficient to form a belief about the truth of an allegation must so state, and the statement has the effect of a denial.

(6) *Effect of Failing to Deny.* An allegation--other than one relating to the amount of damages--is admitted if a responsive pleading is required and the allegation is not denied. If a responsive pleading is not required, an allegation is considered denied or avoided.

(c) Affirmative Defenses.

(1) *In General.* In responding to a pleading, a party must affirmatively state any avoidance or affirmative defense, including:

. accord and satisfaction;

. arbitration and award;

. assumption of risk;

. contributory negligence;

. discharge in bankruptcy;

. duress;

. estoppel;

. failure of consideration;

. fraud;

. illegality;

. injury by fellow servant;

. laches;

. license;

. payment;

. release;

. res judicata;

. statute of frauds;

. statute of limitations; and

. waiver.

(2) *Mistaken Designation.* If a party mistakenly designates a defense as a counterclaim, or a counterclaim as a defense, the court must, if justice requires, treat the pleading as though it were correctly designated, and may impose terms for doing so.

(d) Pleading to Be Concise and Direct; Alternative Statements; Inconsistency.

(1) *In General.* Each allegation must be simple, concise, and direct. No technical form is required.

(2) *Alternative Statements of a Claim or Defense.* A party may set out two or more statements of a claim or defense alternatively or hypothetically, either in a single count or defense or in separate ones. If a party makes alternative statements, the pleading is sufficient if any one of them is sufficient.

(3) *Inconsistent Claims or Defenses.* A party may state as many separate claims or defenses as it has, regardless of consistency.

(d) Construing Pleadings. Pleadings must be construed so as to do justice.

RULE 9. PLEADING SPECIAL MATTERS

(a) Capacity or Authority to Sue; Legal Existence.

(1) *In General.* Except when required to show that the court has jurisdiction, a pleading need not allege:

(A) a party's capacity to sue or be sued;

(B) a party's authority to sue or be sued in a representative capacity; or

(C) the legal existence of an organized association of persons that is made a party.

(2) *Raising Those Issues.* To raise any of those issues, a party must do so by a specific denial, which must state any supporting facts that are peculiarly within the party's knowledge.

(b) Fraud or Mistake; Conditions of Mind. In alleging fraud or mistake, a party must state with particularity the circumstances constituting fraud or mistake. Malice, intent, knowledge, and other conditions of a person's mind may be alleged generally.

(c) Conditions Precedent. In pleading conditions precedent, it suffices to allege generally that all conditions precedent have occurred or been performed. But when denying that a condition precedent has occurred or been performed, a party must do so with particularity.

(d) Official Document or Act. In pleading an official document or official act, it suffices to allege that the document was legally issued or the act legally done.

(e) Judgment. In pleading a judgment or decision of a domestic or foreign court, a judicial or quasi-judicial tribunal, or a board or officer, it suffices to plead the judgment or decision without showing jurisdiction to render it.

(f) Time and Place. An allegation of time or place is material when testing the sufficiency of a pleading.

(g) Special Damages. If an item of special damage is claimed, it must be specifically stated.

(h) Admiralty or Maritime Claim.

(1) *How Designated.* If a claim for relief is within the admiralty or maritime jurisdiction and also within the court's subject-matter jurisdiction on some other ground, the pleading may designate the claim as an admiralty or maritime claim for purposes of Rules 14(c), 38(e), and 82 and the Supplemental Rules for Admiralty or Maritime Claims and Asset Forfeiture Actions. A claim cognizable only in the admiralty or maritime jurisdiction is an admiralty or maritime claim for those purposes, whether or not so designated.

(2) *Designation for Appeal.* A case that includes an admiralty or maritime claim within this subdivision (h) is an admiralty case within 28 U.S.C. § 1292(a)(3).

RULE 10. FORM OF PLEADINGS

(a) Caption; Names of Parties. Every pleading must have a caption with the court's name, a title, a file number, and a Rule 7(a) designation. The title of the complaint must name all the parties; the title of other pleadings, after naming the first party on each side, may refer generally to other parties.

 (b) Paragraphs; Separate Statements. A party must state its claims or defenses in numbered paragraphs, each limited as far as practicable to a single set of circumstances. A later pleading may refer by number to a paragraph in an earlier pleading. If doing so would promote clarity, each claim founded on a separate transaction or occurrence--and each defense other than a denial--must be stated in a separate count or defense.

 (c) Adoption by Reference; Exhibits. A statement in a pleading may be adopted by reference elsewhere in the same pleading or in any other pleading or motion. A copy of a written instrument that is an exhibit to a pleading is a part of the pleading for all purposes.

RULE 11. SIGNING PLEADINGS, MOTIONS, & OTHER PAPERS; REPRESENTATIONS TO THE COURT; SANCTIONS

(a) Signature. Every pleading, written motion, and other paper must be signed by at least one attorney of record in the attorney's name--or by a party personally if the party is unrepresented. The paper must state the signer's address, e-mail address, and telephone number. Unless a rule or statute specifically states otherwise, a pleading need not be verified or accompanied by an affidavit. The court must strike an unsigned paper unless the omission is promptly corrected after being called to the attorney's or party's attention.

 (b) Representations to the Court. By presenting to the court a pleading, written motion, or other paper--whether by signing, filing, submitting, or later advocating it--an attorney or unrepresented party certifies that to the best of the person's knowledge, information, and belief, formed after an inquiry reasonable under the circumstances:

   (1) it is not being presented for any improper purpose, such as to harass, cause unnecessary delay, or needlessly increase the cost of litigation;

   (2) the claims, defenses, and other legal contentions are warranted by existing law or by a nonfrivolous argument for extending, modifying, or reversing existing law or for establishing new law;

   (3) the factual contentions have evidentiary support or, if specifically so identified, will likely have evidentiary support after a reasonable opportunity for further investigation or discovery; and

   (4) the denials of factual contentions are warranted on the evidence or, if specifically so identified, are reasonably based on belief or a lack of information.

 (c) Sanctions.

   (1) *In General.* If, after notice and a reasonable opportunity to respond, the court determines that Rule 11(b) has been violated, the court may impose an appropriate sanction on any attorney, law firm, or party that violated the rule or is responsible for the violation. Absent exceptional circumstances, a law firm must be held jointly responsible for a violation committed by its partner, associate, or employee.

   (2) *Motion for Sanctions.* A motion for sanctions must be made separately from any other motion and must describe the specific conduct that allegedly violates Rule 11(b). The motion must be served under Rule 5, but it must not be filed or be presented to the court if the challenged paper, claim, defense, contention, or denial is withdrawn or appropriately corrected within 21 days after service or within another time the court sets. If warranted, the court may award to the prevailing party the reasonable expenses, including attorney's fees, incurred for the motion.

   (3) *On the Court's Initiative.* On its own, the court may order an attorney, law firm, or party to show cause why conduct specifically described in the order has not violated Rule 11(b).

(4) *Nature of a Sanction.* A sanction imposed under this rule must be limited to what suffices to deter repetition of the conduct or comparable conduct by others similarly situated. The sanction may include nonmonetary directives; an order to pay a penalty into court; or, if imposed on motion and warranted for effective deterrence, an order directing payment to the movant of part or all of the reasonable attorney's fees and other expenses directly resulting from the violation.

(5) *Limitations on Monetary Sanctions.* The court must not impose a monetary sanction:

(A) against a represented party for violating Rule 11(b)(2); or

(B) on its own, unless it issued the show-cause order under Rule 11(c)(3) before voluntary dismissal or settlement of the claims made by or against the party that is, or whose attorneys are, to be sanctioned.

(6) *Requirements for an Order.* An order imposing a sanction must describe the sanctioned conduct and explain the basis for the sanction.

(d) Inapplicability to Discovery. This rule does not apply to disclosures and discovery requests, responses, objections, and motions under Rules 26 through 37.

RULE 12. DEFENSES AND OBJECTIONS: WHEN AND HOW PRESENTED; MOTION FOR JUDGMENT ON THE PLEADINGS; CONSOLIDATING MOTIONS; WAIVING DEFENSES; PRETRIAL HEARING

(a) Time to Serve a Responsive Pleading.

(1) *In General.* Unless another time is specified by this rule or a federal statute, the time for serving a responsive pleading is as follows:

(A) A defendant must serve an answer:

(i) within 20 days after being served with the summons and complaint; or

(ii) if it has timely waived service under Rule 4(d), within 60 days after the request for a waiver was sent, or within 90 days after it was sent to the defendant outside any judicial district of the United States.

(B) A party must serve an answer to a counterclaim or crossclaim within 20 days after being served with the pleading that states the counterclaim or crossclaim.

(C) A party must serve a reply to an answer within 20 days after being served with an order to reply, unless the order specifies a different time.

(2) *United States and Its Agencies, Officers, or Employees Sued in an Official Capacity.* The United States, a United States agency, or a United States officer or employee sued only in an official capacity must serve an answer to a complaint, counterclaim, or crossclaim within 60 days after service on the United States attorney.

(3) *United States Officers or Employees Sued in an Individual Capacity.* A United States officer or employee sued in an individual capacity for an act or omission occurring in connection with duties performed on the United States' behalf must serve an answer to a complaint, counterclaim, or crossclaim within 60 days after service on the officer or employee or service on the United States attorney, whichever is later.

(4) *Effect of a Motion.* Unless the court sets a different time, serving a motion under this rule alters these periods as follows:

(A) if the court denies the motion or postpones its disposition until trial, the responsive pleading must be served within 10 days after notice of the court's action; or

(B) if the court grants a motion for a more definite statement, the responsive pleading must be served within 10 days after the more definite statement is served.

(b) How to Present Defenses. Every defense to a claim for relief in any pleading must be asserted in the responsive pleading if one is required. But a party may assert the following defenses by motion:

(1) lack of subject-matter jurisdiction;

(2) lack of personal jurisdiction;

(3) improper venue;

(4) insufficient process;

(5) insufficient service of process;

(6) failure to state a claim upon which relief can be granted; and

(7) failure to join a party under Rule 19.

A motion asserting any of these defenses must be made before pleading if a responsive pleading is allowed. If a pleading sets out a claim for relief that does not require a responsive pleading, an opposing party may assert at trial any defense to that claim. No defense or objection is waived by joining it with one or more other defenses or objections in a responsive pleading or in a motion.

(c) Motion for Judgment on the Pleadings. After the pleadings are closed--but early enough not to delay trial--a party may move for judgment on the pleadings.

(d) Result of Presenting Matters Outside the Pleadings. If, on a motion under Rule 12(b)(6) or 12(c), matters outside the pleadings are presented to and not excluded by the court, the motion must be treated as one for summary judgment under Rule 56. All parties must be given a reasonable opportunity to present all the material that is pertinent to the motion.

(e) Motion for a More Definite Statement. A party may move for a more definite statement of a pleading to which a responsive pleading is allowed but which is so vague or ambiguous that the party cannot reasonably prepare a response. The motion must be made before filing a responsive pleading and must point out the defects complained of and the details desired. If the court orders a more definite statement and the order is not obeyed within 10 days after notice of the order or within the time the court sets, the court may strike the pleading or issue any other appropriate order.

(f) Motion to Strike. The court may strike from a pleading an insufficient defense or any redundant, immaterial, impertinent, or scandalous matter. The court may act:

(1) on its own; or

(2) on motion made by a party either before responding to the pleading or, if a response is not allowed, within 20 days after being served with the pleading.

(g) Joining Motions.

(1) *Right to Join.* A motion under this rule may be joined with any other motion allowed by this rule.

(2) *Limitation on Further Motions.* Except as provided in Rule 12(h)(2) or (3), a party that makes a motion under this rule must not make another motion under this rule raising a defense or objection that was available to the party but omitted from its earlier motion.

(h) Waiving and Preserving Certain Defenses.

(1) *When Some Are Waived.* A party waives any defense listed in Rule 12(b)(2)-(5) by:

(A) omitting it from a motion in the circumstances described in Rule 12(g)(2); or

(B) failing to either:

(i) make it by motion under this rule; or

(ii) include it in a responsive pleading or in an amendment allowed by Rule 15(a)(1) as a matter of course.

(2) *When to Raise Others.* Failure to state a claim upon which relief can be granted, to join a person required by Rule 19(b), or to state a legal defense to a claim may be raised:

(A) in any pleading allowed or ordered under Rule 7(a);

(B) by a motion under Rule 12(c); or

(C) at trial.

(3) *Lack of Subject-Matter Jurisdiction.* If the court determines at any time that it lacks subject-matter

jurisdiction, the court must dismiss the action.

(i) Hearing Before Trial. If a party so moves, any defense listed in Rule 12(b)(1)-(7)--whether made in a pleading or by motion--and a motion under Rule 12(c) must be heard and decided before trial unless the court orders a deferral until trial.

RULE 13. COUNTERCLAIM AND CROSS CLAIM

(a) Compulsory Counterclaim.

(1) *In General.* A pleading must state as a counterclaim any claim that--at the time of its service--the pleader has against an opposing party if the claim:

(A) arises out of the transaction or occurrence that is the subject matter of the opposing party's claim; and

(B) does not require adding another party over whom the court cannot acquire jurisdiction.

(2) *Exceptions.* The pleader need not state the claim if:

(A) when the action was commenced, the claim was the subject of another pending action; or

(B) the opposing party sued on its claim by attachment or other process that did not establish personal jurisdiction over the pleader on that claim, and the pleader does not assert any counterclaim under this rule.

(b) Permissive Counterclaim. A pleading may state as a counterclaim against an opposing party any claim that is not compulsory.

(c) Relief Sought in a Counterclaim. A counterclaim need not diminish or defeat the recovery sought by the opposing party. It may request relief that exceeds in amount or differs in kind from the relief sought by the opposing party.

(d) Counterclaim Against the United States. These rules do not expand the right to assert a counterclaim--or to claim a credit--against the United States or a United States officer or agency.

(e) Counterclaim Maturing or Acquired After Pleading. The court may permit a party to file a supplemental pleading asserting a counterclaim that matured or was acquired by the party after serving an earlier pleading.

(f) Omitted Counterclaim. The court may permit a party to amend a pleading to add a counterclaim if it was omitted through oversight, inadvertence, or excusable neglect or if justice so requires.

(g) Crossclaim Against a Coparty. A pleading may state as a crossclaim any claim by one party against a coparty if the claim arises out of the transaction or occurrence that is the subject matter of the original action or of a counterclaim, or if the claim relates to any property that is the subject matter of the original action. The crossclaim may include a claim that the coparty is or may be liable to the crossclaimant for all or part of a claim asserted in the action against the crossclaimant.

(h) Joining Additional Parties. Rules 19 and 20 govern the addition of a person as a party to a counterclaim or crossclaim.

(i) Separate Trials; Separate Judgments. If the court orders separate trials under Rule 42(b), it may enter judgment on a counterclaim or crossclaim under Rule 54(b) when it has jurisdiction to do so, even if the opposing party's claims have been dismissed or otherwise resolved.

RULE 14. THIRD-PARTY PRACTICE

(a) When a Defending Party May Bring in a Third Party.

(1) *Timing of the Summons and Complaint.* A defending party may, as third-party plaintiff, serve a summons and complaint on a nonparty who is or may be liable to it for all or part of the claim against it. But the third-party plaintiff must, by motion, obtain the court's leave if it files the third-party complaint more than 10 days after serving its original answer.

(2) *Third-Party Defendant's Claims and Defenses.* The person served with the summons and third-party

complaint--the "third-party defendant":

(A) must assert any defense against the third-party plaintiff's claim under Rule 12;

(B) must assert any counterclaim against the third-party plaintiff under Rule 13(a), and may assert any counterclaim against the third-party plaintiff under Rule 13(b) or any crossclaim against another third-party defendant under Rule 13(g);

(C) may assert against the plaintiff any defense that the third-party plaintiff has to the plaintiff's claim; and

(D) may also assert against the plaintiff any claim arising out of the transaction or occurrence that is the subject matter of the plaintiff's claim against the third-party plaintiff.

(3) *Plaintiff's Claims Against a Third-Party Defendant.* The plaintiff may assert against the third-party defendant any claim arising out of the transaction or occurrence that is the subject matter of the plaintiff's claim against the third-party plaintiff. The third-party defendant must then assert any defense under Rule 12 and any counterclaim under Rule 13(a), and may assert any counterclaim under Rule 13(b) or any crossclaim under Rule 13(g).

(4) *Motion to Strike, Sever, or Try Separately.* Any party may move to strike the third-party claim, to sever it, or to try it separately.

(5) *Third-Party Defendant's Claim Against a Nonparty.* A third-party defendant may proceed under this rule against a nonparty who is or may be liable to the thirdparty defendant for all or part of any claim against it.

(6) *Third-Party Complaint In Rem.* If it is within the admiralty or maritime jurisdiction, a third-party complaint may be in rem. In that event, a reference in this rule to the "summons" includes the warrant of arrest, and a reference to the defendant or third-party plaintiff includes, when appropriate, a person who asserts a right under Supplemental Rule C(6)(a)(i) in the property arrested.

 (b) When a Plaintiff May Bring in a Third Party. When a claim is asserted against a plaintiff, the plaintiff may bring in a third party if this rule would allow a defendant to do so.

 (c) Admiralty or Maritime Claim.

(1) *Scope of Impleader.* If a plaintiff asserts an admiralty or maritime claim under Rule 9(h), the defendant or a person who asserts a right under Supplemental Rule C(6)(a)(i) may, as a third-party plaintiff, bring in a third-party defendant who may be wholly or partly liable--either to the plaintiff or to the third-party plaintiff-- for remedy over, contribution, or otherwise on account of the same transaction, occurrence, or series of transactions or occurrences.

(2) *Defending Against a Demand for Judgment for the Plaintiff.* The third-party plaintiff may demand judgment in the plaintiff's favor against the third-party defendant. In that event, the third-party defendant must defend under Rule 12 against the plaintiff's claim as well as the third-party plaintiff's claim; and the action proceeds as if the plaintiff had sued both the third-party defendant and the third-party plaintiff.

RULE 15. AMENDED AND SUPPLEMENTAL PLEADINGS

(a) Amendments Before Trial.

(1) *Amending as a Matter of Course.* A party may amend its pleading once as a matter of course:

(A) before being served with a responsive pleading; or

(B) within 20 days after serving the pleading if a responsive pleading is not allowed and the action is not yet on the trial calendar.

(2) *Other Amendments.* In all other cases, a party may amend its pleading only with the opposing party's written consent or the court's leave. The court should freely give leave when justice so requires.

(3) *Time to Respond.* Unless the court orders otherwise, any required response to an amended pleading must

be made within the time remaining to respond to the original pleading or within 10 days after service of the amended pleading, whichever is later.

(b) Amendments During and After Trial.

(1) *Based on an Objection at Trial.* If, at trial, a party objects that evidence is not within the issues raised in the pleadings, the court may permit the pleadings to be amended. The court should freely permit an amendment when doing so will aid in presenting the merits and the objecting party fails to satisfy the court that the evidence would prejudice that party's action or defense on the merits. The court may grant a continuance to enable the objecting party to meet the evidence.

(2) *For Issues Tried by Consent.* When an issue not raised by the pleadings is tried by the parties' express or implied consent, it must be treated in all respects as if raised in the pleadings. A party may move--at any time, even after judgment--to amend the pleadings to conform them to the evidence and to raise an unpleaded issue. But failure to amend does not affect the result of the trial of that issue.

(c) Relation Back of Amendments.

(1) *When an Amendment Relates Back.* An amendment to a pleading relates back to the date of the original pleading when:

(A) the law that provides the applicable statute of limitations allows relation back;

(B) the amendment asserts a claim or defense that arose out of the conduct, transaction, or occurrence set out--or attempted to be set out--in the original pleading; or

(C) the amendment changes the party or the naming of the party against whom a claim is asserted, if Rule 15(c)(1)(B) is satisfied and if, within the period provided by Rule 4(m) for serving the summons and complaint, the party to be brought in by amendment:

(i) received such notice of the action that it will not be prejudiced in defending on the merits; and

(ii) knew or should have known that the action would have been brought against it, but for a mistake concerning the proper party's identity.

(2) *Notice to the United States.* When the United States or a United States officer or agency is added as a defendant by amendment, the notice requirements of Rule 15(c)(1)(C)(i) and (ii) are satisfied if, during the stated period, process was delivered or mailed to the United States attorney or the United States attorney's designee, to the Attorney General of the United States, or to the officer or agency.

(d) Supplemental Pleadings. On motion and reasonable notice, the court may, on just terms, permit a party to serve a supplemental pleading setting out any transaction, occurrence, or event that happened after the date of the pleading to be supplemented. The court may permit supplementation even though the original pleading is defective in stating a claim or defense. The court may order that the opposing party plead to the supplemental pleading within a specified time.

RULE 16. PRETRIAL CONFERENCES; SCHEDULING; MANAGEMENT

(a) Purposes of a Pretrial Conference. In any action, the court may order the attorneys and any unrepresented parties to appear for one or more pretrial conferences for such purposes as:

(1) expediting disposition of the action;

(2) establishing early and continuing control so that the case will not be protracted because of lack of management;

(3) discouraging wasteful pretrial activities;

(4) improving the quality of the trial through more thorough preparation; and

(5) facilitating settlement.

(b) Scheduling.

(1) *Scheduling Order.* Except in categories of actions exempted by local rule, the district judge--or a magistrate judge when authorized by local rule--must issue a scheduling order:

(A) after receiving the parties' report under Rule 26(f); or

(B) after consulting with the parties' attorneys and any unrepresented parties at a scheduling conference or by telephone, mail, or other means.

(2) *Time to Issue.* The judge must issue the scheduling order as soon as practicable, but in any event within the earlier of 120 days after any defendant has been served with the complaint or 90 days after any defendant has appeared.

(3) *Contents of the Order.*

(A) Required Contents. The scheduling order must limit the time to join other parties, amend the pleadings, complete discovery, and file motions.

(B) Permitted Contents. The scheduling order may:

(i) modify the timing of disclosures under Rules 26(a) and 26(e)(1);

(ii) modify the extent of discovery;

(iii) provide for disclosure or discovery of electronically stored information;

(iv) include any agreements the parties reach for asserting claims of privilege or of protection as trial-preparation material after information is produced;

(v) set dates for pretrial conferences and for trial; and

(vi) include other appropriate matters.

(4) *Modifying a Schedule.* A schedule may be modified only for good cause and with the judge's consent.

(c) Attendance and Matters for Consideration at a Pretrial Conference.

(1) *Attendance.* A represented party must authorize at least one of its attorneys to make stipulations and admissions about all matters that can reasonably be anticipated for discussion at a pretrial conference. If appropriate, the court may require that a party or its representative be present or reasonably available by other means to consider possible settlement.

(2) *Matters for Consideration.* At any pretrial conference, the court may consider and take appropriate action on the following matters:

(A) formulating and simplifying the issues, and eliminating frivolous claims or defenses;

(B) amending the pleadings if necessary or desirable;

(C) obtaining admissions and stipulations about facts and documents to avoid unnecessary proof, and ruling in advance on the admissibility of evidence;

(D) avoiding unnecessary proof and cumulative evidence, and limiting the use of testimony under Federal Rule of Evidence 702;

(E) determining the appropriateness and timing of summary adjudication under Rule 56;

(F) controlling and scheduling discovery, including orders affecting disclosures and discovery under Rule 26 and Rules 29 through 37;

(G) identifying witnesses and documents, scheduling the filing and exchange of any pretrial briefs, and setting dates for further conferences and for trial;

(H) referring matters to a magistrate judge or a master;

(I) settling the case and using special procedures to assist in resolving the dispute when authorized by statute or local rule;

(J) determining the form and content of the pretrial order;

(K) disposing of pending motions;

(L) adopting special procedures for managing potentially difficult or protracted actions that may involve complex issues, multiple parties, difficult legal questions, or unusual proof problems;

(M) ordering a separate trial under Rule 42(b) of a claim, counterclaim, crossclaim, third-party claim, or particular issue;

(N) ordering the presentation of evidence early in the trial on a manageable issue that might, on the evidence, be the basis for a judgment as a matter of law under Rule 50(a) or a judgment on partial findings under Rule 52(c);

(O) establishing a reasonable limit on the time allowed to present evidence; and

(P) facilitating in other ways the just, speedy, and inexpensive disposition of the action.

(d) Pretrial Orders. After any conference under this rule, the court should issue an order reciting the action taken. This order controls the course of the action unless the court modifies it.

(e) Final Pretrial Conference and Orders. The court may hold a final pretrial conference to formulate a trial plan, including a plan to facilitate the admission of evidence. The conference must be held as close to the start of trial as is reasonable, and must be attended by at least one attorney who will conduct the trial for each party and by any unrepresented party. The court may modify an order issued after a final pretrial conference only to prevent manifest injustice.

(f) Sanctions.

(1) *In General.* On motion or on its own, the court may issue any just orders, including those authorized by Rule 37(b)(2)(A)(ii)-(vii), if a party or its attorney:

(A) fails to appear at a scheduling or other pretrial conference;

(B) is substantially unprepared to participate--or does not participate in good faith--in the conference; or

(C) fails to obey a scheduling or other pretrial order.

(2) *Imposing Fees and Costs.* Instead of or in addition to any other sanction, the court must order the party, its attorney, or both to pay the reasonable expenses--including attorney's fees--incurred because of any noncompliance with this rule, unless the noncompliance was substantially justified or other circumstances make an award of expenses unjust.

Rule 17. Plaintiff and Defendant; Capacity; Public Officers

(a) Real Party in Interest.

(1) *Designation in General.* An action must be prosecuted in the name of the real party in interest. The following may sue in their own names without joining the person for whose benefit the action is brought:

(A) an executor;

(B) an administrator;

(C) a guardian;

(D) a bailee;

(E) a trustee of an express trust;

(F) a party with whom or in whose name a contract has been made for another's benefit; and

(G) a party authorized by statute.

(2) *Action in the Name of the United States for Another's Use or Benefit.* When a federal statute so provides, an action for another's use or benefit must be brought in the name of the United States.

(3) *Joinder of the Real Party in Interest.* The court may not dismiss an action for failure to prosecute in the name of the real party in interest until, after an objection, a reasonable time has been allowed for the real party in interest to ratify, join, or be substituted into the action. After ratification, joinder, or substitution, the action proceeds as if it had been originally commenced by the real party in interest.

(b) Capacity to Sue or Be Sued. Capacity to sue or be sued is determined as follows:

(1) for an individual who is not acting in a representative capacity, by the law of the individual's domicile;

(2) for a corporation, by the law under which it was organized; and

(3) for all other parties, by the law of the state where the court is located, except that:

(A) a partnership or other unincorporated association with no such capacity under that state's law may sue or be sued in its common name to enforce a substantive right existing under the United States Constitution or laws; and

(B) 28 U.S.C. §§ 754 and 959(a) govern the capacity of a receiver appointed by a United States court to sue or be sued in a United States court.

(c) Minor or Incompetent Person.

(1) *With a Representative.* The following representatives may sue or defend on behalf of a minor or an incompetent person:

(A) a general guardian;

(B) a committee;

(C) a conservator; or

(D) a like fiduciary.

(2) *Without a Representative.* A minor or an incompetent person who does not have a duly appointed representative may sue by a next friend or by a guardian ad litem. The court must appoint a guardian ad litem--or issue another appropriate order--to protect a minor or incompetent person who is unrepresented in an action.

(d) Public Officer's Title and Name. A public officer who sues or is sued in an official capacity may be designated by official title rather than by name, but the court may order that the officer's name be added.

Rule 18. Joinder of Claims

(a) In General. A party asserting a claim, counterclaim, crossclaim, or third-party claim may join, as independent or alternative claims, as many claims as it has against an opposing party.

(b) Joinder of Contingent Claims. A party may join two claims even though one of them is contingent on the disposition of the other; but the court may grant relief only in accordance with the parties' relative substantive rights. In particular, a plaintiff may state a claim for money and a claim to set aside a conveyance that is fraudulent as to that plaintiff, without first obtaining a judgment for the money.

RULE 19. REQUIRED JOINDER OF PARTIES

(a) Persons Required to Be Joined if Feasible.

(1) *Required Party.* A person who is subject to service of process and whose joinder will not deprive the court of subject-matter jurisdiction must be joined as a party if:

(A) in that person's absence, the court cannot accord complete relief among existing parties; or

(B) that person claims an interest relating to the subject of the action and is so situated that disposing of the action in the person's absence may:

(i) as a practical matter impair or impede the person's ability to protect the interest; or

(ii) leave an existing party subject to a substantial risk of incurring double, multiple, or otherwise inconsistent obligations because of the interest.

(2) *Joinder by Court Order.* If a person has not been joined as required, the court must order that the person be made a party. A person who refuses to join as a plaintiff may be made either a defendant or, in a proper case, an involuntary plaintiff.

(3) *Venue.* If a joined party objects to venue and the joinder would make venue improper, the court must dismiss that party.

(b) When Joinder Is Not Feasible. If a person who is required to be joined if feasible cannot be joined, the court must determine whether, in equity and good conscience, the action should proceed among the existing parties or should be dismissed. The factors for the court to consider include:

(1) the extent to which a judgment rendered in the person's absence might prejudice that person or the existing parties;

(2) the extent to which any prejudice could be lessened or avoided by:

(A) protective provisions in the judgment;

(B) shaping the relief; or

(C) other measures;

(3) whether a judgment rendered in the person's absence would be adequate; and

(4) whether the plaintiff would have an adequate remedy if the action were dismissed for nonjoinder.

(c) Pleading the Reasons for Nonjoinder. When asserting a claim for relief, a party must state:

(1) the name, if known, of any person who is required to be joined if feasible but is not joined; and

(2) the reasons for not joining that person.

(d) Exception for Class Actions. This rule is subject to Rule 23.

RULE 20. PERMISSIVE JOINDER OF PARTIES

(a) Persons Who May Join or Be Joined.

(1) *Plaintiffs.* Persons may join in one action as plaintiffs if:

(A) they assert any right to relief jointly, severally, or in the alternative with respect to or arising out of the same transaction, occurrence, or series of transactions or occurrences; and

(B) any question of law or fact common to all plaintiffs will arise in the action.

(2) *Defendants.* Persons--as well as a vessel, cargo, or other property subject to admiralty process in rem-- may be joined in one action as defendants if:

(A) any right to relief is asserted against them jointly, severally, or in the alternative with respect to or arising out of the same transaction, occurrence, or series of transactions or occurrences; and

(B) any question of law or fact common to all defendants will arise in the action.

(3) *Extent of Relief.* Neither a plaintiff nor a defendant need be interested in obtaining or defending against all the relief demanded. The court may grant judgment to one or more plaintiffs according to their rights, and against one or more defendants according to their liabilities.

(b) Protective Measures. The court may issue orders--including an order for separate trials--to protect a party against embarrassment, delay, expense, or other prejudice that arises from including a person against whom the party asserts no claim and who asserts no claim against the party.

RULE 21. MISJOINDER AND NONJOINDER OF PARTIES

Misjoinder of parties is not a ground for dismissing an action. On motion or on its own, the court may at any time, on just terms, add or drop a party. The court may also sever any claim against a party.

RULE 22. INTERPLEADER

(a) Grounds.

(1) *By a Plaintiff.* Persons with claims that may expose a plaintiff to double or multiple liability may be joined as defendants and required to interplead. Joinder for interpleader is proper even though:

(A) the claims of the several claimants, or the titles on which their claims depend, lack a common origin or are adverse and independent rather than identical; or

(B) the plaintiff denies liability in whole or in part to any or all of the claimants.

(2) *By a Defendant.* A defendant exposed to similar liability may seek interpleader through a crossclaim or counterclaim.

(b) Relation to Other Rules and Statutes. This rule supplements--and does not limit--the joinder of parties allowed by Rule 20. The remedy it provides is in addition to--and does not supersede or limit--the remedy provided by 28 U.S.C. §§ 1335, 1397, and 2361. An action under those statutes must be conducted under these rules.

RULE 23. CLASS ACTIONS

(a) Prerequisites. One or more members of a class may sue or be sued as representative parties on behalf of all members only if:

(1) the class is so numerous that joinder of all members is impracticable;

(2) there are questions of law or fact common to the class;

(3) the claims or defenses of the representative parties are typical of the claims or defenses of the class; and

(4) the representative parties will fairly and adequately protect the interests of the class.

(b) Types of Class Actions. A class action may be maintained if Rule 23(a) is satisfied and if:

(1) prosecuting separate actions by or against individual class members would create a risk of:

(A) inconsistent or varying adjudications with respect to individual class members that would establish incompatible standards of conduct for the party opposing the class; or

(B) adjudications with respect to individual class members that, as a practical matter, would be dispositive of the interests of the other members not parties to the individual adjudications or would substantially impair or impede their ability to protect their interests;

(2) the party opposing the class has acted or refused to act on grounds that apply generally to the class, so that final injunctive relief or corresponding declaratory relief is appropriate respecting the class as a whole; or

(3) the court finds that the questions of law or fact common to class members predominate over any questions affecting only individual members, and that a class action is superior to other available methods for fairly and efficiently adjudicating the controversy. The matters pertinent to these findings include:

(A) the class members' interests in individually controlling the prosecution or defense of separate actions;

(B) the extent and nature of any litigation concerning the controversy already begun by or against class members;

(C) the desirability or undesirability of concentrating the litigation of the claims in the particular forum; and

(D) the likely difficulties in managing a class action.

(c) Certification Order; Notice to Class Members; Judgment; Issues Classes; Subclasses.

(1) *Certification Order.*

(A) Time to Issue. At an early practicable time after a person sues or is sued as a class representative, the court must determine by order whether to certify the action as a class action.

(B) Defining the Class; Appointing Class Counsel. An order that certifies a class action must define the class and the class claims, issues, or defenses, and must appoint class counsel under Rule 23(g).

(C) Altering or Amending the Order. An order that grants or denies class certification may be altered or amended before final judgment.

(2) *Notice.*

(A) For (b)(1) or (b)(2) Classes. For any class certified under Rule 23(b)(1) or (b)(2), the court may direct appropriate notice to the class.

(B) For (b)(3) Classes. For any class certified under Rule 23(b)(3), the court must direct to class members the best notice that is practicable under the circumstances, including individual notice to all members who can be identified through reasonable effort. The notice must clearly and concisely state in plain, easily understood language:

    (i) the nature of the action;

    (ii) the definition of the class certified;

    (iii) the class claims, issues, or defenses;

    (iv) that a class member may enter an appearance through an attorney if the member so desires;

    (v) that the court will exclude from the class any member who requests exclusion;

    (vi) the time and manner for requesting exclusion; and

    (vii) the binding effect of a class judgment on members under Rule 23(c)(3).

(3) *Judgment.* Whether or not favorable to the class, the judgment in a class action must:

  (A) for any class certified under Rule 23(b)(1) or (b)(2), include and describe those whom the court finds to be class members; and

  (B) for any class certified under Rule 23(b)(3), include and specify or describe those to whom the Rule 23(c)(2) notice was directed, who have not requested exclusion, and whom the court finds to be class members.

(4) *Particular Issues.* When appropriate, an action may be maintained as a class action with respect to particular issues.

(5) *Subclasses.* When appropriate, a class may be divided into subclasses that are each treated as a class under this rule.

(d) Conducting the Action.

(1) *In General.* In conducting an action under this rule, the court may issue orders that:

  (A) determine the course of proceedings or prescribe measures to prevent undue repetition or complication in presenting evidence or argument;

  (B) require--to protect class members and fairly conduct the action--giving appropriate notice to some or all class members of:

    (i) any step in the action;

    (ii) the proposed extent of the judgment; or

    (iii) the members' opportunity to signify whether they consider the representation fair and adequate, to intervene and present claims or defenses, or to otherwise come into the action;

  (C) impose conditions on the representative parties or on intervenors;

  (D) require that the pleadings be amended to eliminate allegations about representation of absent persons and that the action proceed accordingly; or

  (E) deal with similar procedural matters.

(2) *Combining and Amending Orders.* An order under Rule 23(d)(1) may be altered or amended from time to time and may be combined with an order under Rule 16.

(e) Settlement, Voluntary Dismissal, or Compromise. The claims, issues, or defenses of a certified class may be settled, voluntarily dismissed, or compromised only with the court's approval. The following procedures apply to a proposed settlement, voluntary dismissal, or compromise:

(1) The court must direct notice in a reasonable manner to all class members who would be bound by the proposal.

(2) If the proposal would bind class members, the court may approve it only after a hearing and on finding that it is fair, reasonable, and adequate.

(3) The parties seeking approval must file a statement identifying any agreement made in connection with

the proposal.

(4) If the class action was previously certified under Rule 23(b)(3), the court may refuse to approve a settlement unless it affords a new opportunity to request exclusion to individual class members who had an earlier opportunity to request exclusion but did not do so.

(5) Any class member may object to the proposal if it requires court approval under this subdivision (e); the objection may be withdrawn only with the court's approval.

(f) Appeals. A court of appeals may permit an appeal from an order granting or denying class-action certification under this rule if a petition for permission to appeal is filed with the circuit clerk within 10 days after the order is entered. An appeal does not stay proceedings in the district court unless the district judge or the court of appeals so orders.

(g) Class Counsel.

(1) *Appointing Class Counsel.* Unless a statute provides otherwise, a court that certifies a class must appoint class counsel. In appointing class counsel, the court:

(A) must consider:

(i) the work counsel has done in identifying or investigating potential claims in the action;

(ii) counsel's experience in handling class actions, other complex litigation, and the types of claims asserted in the action;

(iii) counsel's knowledge of the applicable law; and

(iv) the resources that counsel will commit to representing the class;

(B) may consider any other matter pertinent to counsel's ability to fairly and adequately represent the interests of the class;

(C) may order potential class counsel to provide information on any subject pertinent to the appointment and to propose terms for attorney's fees and nontaxable costs;

(D) may include in the appointing order provisions about the award of attorney's fees or nontaxable costs under Rule 23(h); and

(E) may make further orders in connection with the appointment.

(2) *Standard for Appointing Class Counsel.* When one applicant seeks appointment as class counsel, the court may appoint that applicant only if the applicant is adequate under Rule 23(g)(1) and (4). If more than one adequate applicant seeks appointment, the court must appoint the applicant best able to represent the interests of the class.

(3) *Interim Counsel.* The court may designate interim counsel to act on behalf of a putative class before determining whether to certify the action as a class action.

(4) *Duty of Class Counsel.* Class counsel must fairly and adequately represent the interests of the class.

(h) Attorney's Fees and Nontaxable Costs. In a certified class action, the court may award reasonable attorney's fees and nontaxable costs that are authorized by law or by the parties' agreement. The following procedures apply:

(1) A claim for an award must be made by motion under Rule 54(d)(2), subject to the provisions of this subdivision (h), at a time the court sets. Notice of the motion must be served on all parties and, for motions by class counsel, directed to class members in a reasonable manner.

(2) A class member, or a party from whom payment is sought, may object to the motion.

(3) The court may hold a hearing and must find the facts and state its legal conclusions under Rule 52(a).

(4) The court may refer issues related to the amount of the award to a special master or a magistrate judge, as provided in Rule 54(d)(2)(D).

RULE 23.1. DERIVATIVE ACTIONS

(a) Prerequisites. This rule applies when one or more shareholders or members of a corporation or an unincorporated association bring a derivative action to enforce a right that the corporation or association may properly assert but has failed to enforce. The derivative action may not be maintained if it appears that the plaintiff does not fairly and adequately represent the interests of shareholders or members who are similarly situated in enforcing the right of the corporation or association.

 (b) Pleading Requirements. The complaint must be verified and must:

   (1) allege that the plaintiff was a shareholder or member at the time of the transaction complained of, or that the plaintiff's share or membership later devolved on it by operation of law;

   (2) allege that the action is not a collusive one to confer jurisdiction that the court would otherwise lack; and

   (3) state with particularity:

     (A) any effort by the plaintiff to obtain the desired action from the directors or comparable authority and, if necessary, from the shareholders or members; and

     (B) the reasons for not obtaining the action or not making the effort.

 (b) Settlement, Dismissal, and Compromise. A derivative action may be settled, voluntarily dismissed, or compromised only with the court's approval. Notice of a proposed settlement, voluntary dismissal, or compromise must be given to shareholders or members in the manner that the court orders.

RULE 23.2. ACTIONS RELATING TO UNINCORPORATED ASSOCIATIONS

This rule applies to an action brought by or against the members of an unincorporated association as a class by naming certain members as representative parties. The action may be maintained only if it appears that those parties will fairly and adequately protect the interests of the association and its members. In conducting the action, the court may issue any appropriate orders corresponding with those in Rule 23(d), and the procedure for settlement, voluntary dismissal, or compromise must correspond with the procedure in Rule 23(e).

RULE 24. INTERVENTION

(a) Intervention of Right. On timely motion, the court must permit anyone to intervene who:

   (1) is given an unconditional right to intervene by a federal statute; or

   (2) claims an interest relating to the property or transaction that is the subject of the action, and is so situated that disposing of the action may as a practical matter impair or impede the movant's ability to protect its interest, unless existing parties adequately represent that interest.

(b) Permissive Intervention.

   (1) *In General.* On timely motion, the court may permit anyone to intervene who:

     (A) is given a conditional right to intervene by a federal statute; or

     (B) has a claim or defense that shares with the main action a common question of law or fact.

   (2) *By a Government Officer or Agency.* On timely motion, the court may permit a federal or state governmental officer or agency to intervene if a party's claim or defense is based on:

     (A) a statute or executive order administered by the officer or agency; or

     (B) any regulation, order, requirement, or agreement issued or made under the statute or executive order.

   (3) *Delay or Prejudice.* In exercising its discretion, the court must consider whether the intervention will unduly delay or prejudice the adjudication of the original parties' rights.

 (c) Notice and Pleading Required. A motion to intervene must be served on the parties as provided in Rule 5.

The motion must state the grounds for intervention and be accompanied by a pleading that sets out the claim or defense for which intervention is sought.

RULE 25. SUBSTITUTION OF PARTIES

(a) Death.

(1) *Substitution if the Claim Is Not Extinguished.* If a party dies and the claim is not extinguished, the court may order substitution of the proper party. A motion for substitution may be made by any party or by the decedent's successor or representative. If the motion is not made within 90 days after service of a statement noting the death, the action by or against the decedent must be dismissed.

(2) *Continuation Among the Remaining Parties.* After a party's death, if the right sought to be enforced survives only to or against the remaining parties, the action does not abate, but proceeds in favor of or against the remaining parties. The death should be noted on the record.

(3) *Service.* A motion to substitute, together with a notice of hearing, must be served on the parties as provided in Rule 5 and on nonparties as provided in Rule 4. A statement noting death must be served in the same manner. Service may be made in any judicial district.

(b) Incompetency. If a party becomes incompetent, the court may, on motion, permit the action to be continued by or against the party's representative. The motion must be served as provided in Rule 25(a)(3).

(c) Transfer of Interest. If an interest is transferred, the action may be continued by or against the original party unless the court, on motion, orders the transferee to be substituted in the action or joined with the original party. The motion must be served as provided in Rule 25(a)(3).

(d) Public Officers; Death or Separation from Office. An action does not abate when a public officer who is a party in an official capacity dies, resigns, or otherwise ceases to hold office while the action is pending. The officer's successor is automatically substituted as a party. Later proceedings should be in the substituted party's name, but any misnomer not affecting the parties' substantial rights must be disregarded. The court may order substitution at any time, but the absence of such an order does not affect the substitution.

RULE 26. DUTY TO DISCLOSE; GENERAL PROVISIONS GOVERNING DISCOVERY

(a) Required Disclosures.

(1) *Initial Disclosure.*

(A) In General. Except as exempted by Rule 26(a)(1)(B) or as otherwise stipulated or ordered by the court, a party must, without awaiting a discovery request, provide to the other parties:

(i) the name and, if known, the address and telephone number of each individual likely to have discoverable information--along with the subjects of that information--that the disclosing party may use to support its claims or defenses, unless the use would be solely for impeachment;

(ii) a copy--or a description by category and location--of all documents, electrically stored information, and tangible things that the disclosing party has in its possession, custody, or control and may use to support its claims or defenses, unless the use would be solely for impeachment;

(iii) a computation of each category of damages claimed by the disclosing party--who must also make available for inspection and copying as under Rule 34 the documents or other evidentiary material, unless privileged or protected from disclosure, on which each computation is based, including materials bearing on the nature and extent of injuries suffered; and

(iv) for inspection and copying as under Rule 34, any insurance agreement under which an insurance business may be liable to satisfy all or part of a possible judgment in the action or to indemnify or reimburse for payments made to satisfy the judgment.

(B) Proceedings Exempt from Initial Disclosure. The following proceedings are exempt from initial disclosure:

(i) an action for review on an administrative record;

(ii) a forfeiture action in rem arising from a federal statute;

(iii) a petition for habeas corpus or any other proceeding to challenge a criminal conviction or sentence;

(iv) an action brought without an attorney by a person in the custody of the United States, a state, or a state subdivision;

(v) an action to enforce or quash an administrative summons or subpoena;

(vi) an action by the United States to recover benefit payments;

(vii) an action by the United States to collect on a student loan guaranteed by the United States;

(viii) a proceeding ancillary to a proceeding in another court; and

(ix) an action to enforce an arbitration award.

(C) Time for Initial Disclosures--In General. A party must make the initial disclosures at or within 14 days after the parties' Rule 26(f) conference unless a different time is set by stipulation or court order, or unless a party objects during the conference that initial disclosures are not appropriate in this action and states the objection in the proposed discovery plan. In ruling on the objection, the court must determine what disclosures, if any, are to be made and must set the time for disclosure.

(D) Time for Initial Disclosures--For Parties Served or Joined Later. A party that is first served or otherwise joined after the Rule 26(f) conference must make the initial disclosures within 30 days after being served or joined, unless a different time is set by stipulation or court order.

(E) Basis for Initial Disclosure; Unacceptable Excuses. A party must make its initial disclosures based on the information then reasonably available to it. A party is not excused from making its disclosures because it has not fully investigated the case or because it challenges the sufficiency of another party's disclosures or because another party has not made its disclosures.

(2) *Disclosure of Expert Testimony.*

(A) In General. In addition to the disclosures required by Rule 26(a)(1), a party must disclose to the other parties the identity of any witness it may use at trial to present evidence under Federal Rule of Evidence 702, 703, or 705.

(B) Written Report. Unless otherwise stipulated or ordered by the court, this disclosure must be accompanied by a written report--prepared and signed by the witness--if the witness is one retained or specially employed to provide expert testimony in the case or one whose duties as the party's employee regularly involve giving expert testimony. The report must contain:

(i) a complete statement of all opinions the witness will express and the basis and reasons for them;

(ii) the data or other information considered by the witness in forming them;

(iii) any exhibits that will be used to summarize or support them;

(iv) the witness's qualifications, including a list of all publications authored in the previous ten years;

(v) a list of all other cases in which, during the previous four years, the witness testified as an expert at trial or by deposition; and

(vi) a statement of the compensation to be paid for the study and testimony in the case.

(C) Time to Disclose Expert Testimony. A party must make these disclosures at the times and in the sequence that the court orders. Absent a stipulation or a court order, the disclosures must be made:

(i) at least 90 days before the date set for trial or for the case to be ready for trial; or

(ii) if the evidence is intended solely to contradict or rebut evidence on the same subject matter identified by another party under Rule 26(a)(2)(B), within 30 days after the other party's disclosure.

(D) Supplementing the Disclosure. The parties must supplement these disclosures when required under

Rule 26(e).

(3) *Pretrial Disclosures.*

(A) In General. In addition to the disclosures required by Rule 26(a)(1) and (2), a party must provide to the other parties and promptly file the following information about the evidence that it may present at trial other than solely for impeachment:

(i) the name and, if not previously provided, the address and telephone number of each witness-- separately identifying those the party expects to present and those it may call if the need arises;

(ii) the designation of those witnesses whose testimony the party expects to present by deposition and, if not taken stenographically, a transcript of the pertinent parts of the deposition; and

(iii) an identification of each document or other exhibit, including summaries of other evidence-- separately identifying those items the party expects to offer and those it may offer if the need arises.

(B) Time for Pretrial Disclosures; Objections. Unless the court orders otherwise, these disclosures must be made at least 30 days before trial. Within 14 days after they are made, unless the court sets a different time, a party may serve and promptly file a list of the following objections: any objections to the use under Rule 32(a) of a deposition designated by another party under Rule 26(a)(3)(A)(ii); and any objection, together with the grounds for it, that may be made to the admissibility of materials identified under Rule 26(a)(3)(A)(iii). An objection not so made--except for one under Federal Rule of Evidence 402 or 403--is waived unless excused by the court for good cause.

(4) *Form of Disclosures.* Unless the court orders otherwise, all disclosures under Rule 26(a) must be in writing, signed, and served.

(b) Discovery Scope and Limits.

(1) *Scope in General.* Unless otherwise limited by court order, the scope of discovery is as follows: Parties may obtain discovery regarding any nonprivileged matter that is relevant to any party's claim or defense-- including the existence, description, nature, custody, condition, and location of any documents or other tangible things and the identity and location of persons who know of any discoverable matter. For good cause, the court may order discovery of any matter relevant to the subject matter involved in the action. Relevant information need not be admissible at the trial if the discovery appears reasonably calculated to lead to the discovery of admissible evidence. All discovery is subject to the limitations imposed by Rule 26(b)(2)(C).

(2) *Limitations on Frequency and Extent.*

(A) When Permitted. By order, the court may alter the limits in these rules on the number of depositions and interrogatories or on the length of depositions under Rule 30. By order or local rule, the court may also limit the number of requests under Rule 36.

(B) Specific Limitations on Electronically Stored Information. A party need not provide discovery of electronically stored information from sources that the party identifies as not reasonably accessible because of undue burden or cost. On motion to compel discovery or for a protective order, the party from whom discovery is sought must show that the information is not reasonably accessible because of undue burden or cost. If that showing is made, the court may nonetheless order discovery from such sources if the requesting party shows good cause, considering the limitations of Rule 26(b)(2)(C). The court may specify conditions for the discovery.

(C) When Required. On motion or on its own, the court must limit the frequency or extent of discovery otherwise allowed by these rules or by local rule if it determines that:

(i) the discovery sought is unreasonably cumulative or duplicative, or can be obtained from some other source that is more convenient, less burdensome, or less expensive;

(ii) the party seeking discovery has had ample opportunity to obtain the information by discovery in the action; or

(iii) the burden or expense of the proposed discovery outweighs its likely benefit, considering the needs of the case, the amount in controversy, the parties' resources, the importance of the issues at stake in the action, and the importance of the discovery in resolving the issues.

(3) *Trial Preparation: Materials.*

(A) Documents and Tangible Things. Ordinarily, a party may not discover documents and tangible things that are prepared in anticipation of litigation or for trial by or for another party or its representative (including the other party's attorney, consultant, surety, indemnitor, insurer, or agent). But, subject to Rule 26(b)(4), those materials may be discovered if:

(i) they are otherwise discoverable under Rule 26(b)(1); and

(ii) the party shows that it has substantial need for the materials to prepare its case and cannot, without undue hardship, obtain their substantial equivalent by other means.

(B) Protection Against Disclosure. If the court orders discovery of those materials, it must protect against disclosure of the mental impressions, conclusions, opinions, or legal theories of a party's attorney or other representative concerning the litigation.

(C) Previous Statement. Any party or other person may, on request and without the required showing, obtain the person's own previous statement about the action or its subject matter. If the request is refused, the person may move for a court order, and Rule 37(a)(5) applies to the award of expenses. A previous statement is either:

(i) a written statement that the person has signed or otherwise adopted or approved; or

(ii) a contemporaneous stenographic, mechanical, electrical, or other recording--or a transcription of it-- that recites substantially verbatim the person's oral statement.

(4) *Trial Preparation: Experts.*

(A) Expert Who May Testify. A party may depose any person who has been identified as an expert whose opinions may be presented at trial. If Rule 26(a)(2)(B) requires a report from the expert, the deposition may be conducted only after the report is provided.

(B) Expert Employed Only for Trial Preparation. Ordinarily, a party may not, by interrogatories or deposition, discover facts known or opinions held by an expert who has been retained or specially employed by another party in anticipation of litigation or to prepare for trial and who is not expected to be called as a witness at trial. But a party may do so only:

(i) as provided in Rule 35(b); or

(ii) on showing exceptional circumstances under which it is impracticable for the party to obtain facts or opinions on the same subject by other means.

(C) Payment. Unless manifest injustice would result, the court must require that the party seeking discovery:

(i) pay the expert a reasonable fee for time spent in responding to discovery under Rule 26(b)(4)(A) or (B); and

(ii) for discovery under (B), also pay the other party a fair portion of the fees and expenses it reasonably incurred in obtaining the expert's facts and opinions.

(5) *Claiming Privilege or Protecting Trial-Preparation Materials.*

(A) Information Withheld. When a party withholds information otherwise discoverable by claiming that the information is privileged or subject to protection as trial-preparation material, the party must:

(i) expressly make the claim; and

(ii) describe the nature of the documents, communications, or tangible things not produced or disclosed- -and do so in a manner that, without revealing information itself privileged or protected, will enable other parties to assess the claim.

(B) Information Produced. If information produced in discovery is subject to a claim of privilege or of protection as trial-preparation material, the party making the claim may notify any party that received the information of the claim and the basis for it. After being notified, a party must promptly return, sequester, or destroy the specified information and any copies it has; must not use or disclose the information until the claim is resolved; must take reasonable steps to retrieve the information if the party disclosed it before being notified; and may promptly present the information to the court under seal for a determination of the claim. The producing party must preserve the information until the claim is resolved.

(c) Protective Orders.

(1) *In General.* A party or any person from whom discovery is sought may move for a protective order in the court where the action is pending--or as an alternative on matters relating to a deposition, in the court for the district where the deposition will be taken. The motion must include a certification that the movant has in good faith conferred or attempted to confer with other affected parties in an effort to resolve the dispute without court action. The court may, for good cause, issue an order to protect a party or person from annoyance, embarrassment, oppression, or undue burden or expense, including one or more of the following:

(A) forbidding the disclosure or discovery;

(B) specifying terms, including time and place, for the disclosure or discovery;

(C) prescribing a discovery method other than the one selected by the party seeking discovery;

(D) forbidding inquiry into certain matters, or limiting the scope of disclosure or discovery to certain matters;

(E) designating the persons who may be present while the discovery is conducted;

(F) requiring that a deposition be sealed and opened only on court order;

(G) requiring that a trade secret or other confidential research, development, or commercial information not be revealed or be revealed only in a specified way; and

(H) requiring that the parties simultaneously file specified documents or information in sealed envelopes, to be opened as the court directs.

(2) *Ordering Discovery.* If a motion for a protective order is wholly or partly denied, the court may, on just terms, order that any party or person provide or permit discovery.

(3) *Awarding Expenses.* Rule 37(a)(5) applies to the award of expenses.

(d) Timing and Sequence of Discovery.

(1) *Timing.* A party may not seek discovery from any source before the parties have conferred as required by Rule 26(f), except in a proceeding exempted from initial disclosure under Rule 26(a)(1)(B), or when authorized by these rules, by stipulation, or by court order.

(2) *Sequence.* Unless, on motion, the court orders otherwise for the parties' and witnesses' convenience and in the interests of justice:

(A) methods of discovery may be used in any sequence; and

(B) discovery by one party does not require any other party to delay its discovery.

(e) Supplementing Disclosures and Responses.

(1) *In General.* A party who has made a disclosure under Rule 26(a)--or who has responded to an interrogatory, request for production, or request for admission--must supplement or correct its disclosure or response:

(A) in a timely manner if the party learns that in some material respect the disclosure or response is incomplete or incorrect, and if the additional or corrective information has not otherwise been made known to the other parties during the discovery process or in writing; or

(B) as ordered by the court.

(2) *Expert Witness.* For an expert whose report must be disclosed under Rule 26(a)(2)(B), the party's duty to supplement extends both to information included in the report and to information given during the expert's deposition. Any additions or changes to this information must be disclosed by the time the party's pretrial disclosures under Rule 26(a)(3) are due.

(f) Conference of the Parties; Planning for Discovery.

(1) *Conference Timing.* Except in a proceeding exempted from initial disclosure under Rule 26(a)(1)(B) or when the court orders otherwise, the parties must confer as soon as practicable--and in any event at least 21 days before a scheduling conference is held or a scheduling order is due under Rule 16(b).

(2) *Conference Content; Parties' Responsibilities.* In conferring, the parties must consider the nature and basis of their claims and defenses and the possibilities for promptly settling or resolving the case; make or arrange for the disclosures required by Rule 26(a)(1); discuss any issues about preserving discoverable information; and develop a proposed discovery plan. The attorneys of record and all unrepresented parties that have appeared in the case are jointly responsible for arranging the conference, for attempting in good faith to agree on the proposed discovery plan, and for submitting to the court within 14 days after the conference a written report outlining the plan. The court may order the parties or attorneys to attend the conference in person.

(3) *Discovery Plan.* A discovery plan must state the parties' views and proposals on:

(A) what changes should be made in the timing, form, or requirement for disclosures under Rule 26(a), including a statement of when initial disclosures were made or will be made;

(B) the subjects on which discovery may be needed, when discovery should be completed, and whether discovery should be conducted in phases or be limited to or focused on particular issues;

(C) any issues about disclosure or discovery of electronically stored information, including the form or forms in which it should be produced;

(D) any issues about claims of privilege or of protection as trial-preparation materials, including--if the parties agree on a procedure to assert these claims after production--whether to ask the court to include their agreement in an order;

(E) what changes should be made in the limitations on discovery imposed under these rules or by local rule, and what other limitations should be imposed; and

(F) any other orders that the court should issue under Rule 26(c) or under Rule 16(b) and (c).

(4) *Expedited Schedule.* If necessary to comply with its expedited schedule for Rule 16(b) conferences, a court may by local rule:

(A) require the parties' conference to occur less than 21 days before the scheduling conference is held or a scheduling order is due under Rule 16(b); and

(B) require the written report outlining the discovery plan to be filed less than 14 days after the parties' conference, or excuse the parties from submitting a written report and permit them to report orally on their discovery plan at the Rule 16(b) conference.

(g) Signing Disclosures and Discovery Requests, Responses, and Objections.

(1) *Signature Required; Effect of Signature.* Every disclosure under Rule 26(a)(1) or (a)(3) and every discovery request, response, or objection must be signed by at least one attorney of record in the attorney's own name--or by the party personally, if unrepresented--and must state the signer's address, e-mail address, and telephone number. By signing, an attorney or party certifies that to the best of the person's knowledge, information, and belief formed after a reasonable inquiry:

(A) with respect to a disclosure, it is complete and correct as of the time it is made; and

(B) with respect to a discovery request, response, or objection, it is:

(i) consistent with these rules and warranted by existing law or by a nonfrivolous argument for extending, modifying, or reversing existing law, or for establishing new law;

(ii) not interposed for any improper purpose, such as to harass, cause unnecessary delay, or needlessly increase the cost of litigation; and

(iii) neither unreasonable nor unduly burdensome or expensive, considering the needs of the case, prior discovery in the case, the amount in controversy, and the importance of the issues at stake in the action.

(2) *Failure to Sign.* Other parties have no duty to act on an unsigned disclosure, request, response, or objection until it is signed, and the court must strike it unless a signature is promptly supplied after the omission is called to the attorney's or party's attention.

(3) *Sanction for Improper Certification.* If a certification violates this rule without substantial justification, the court, on motion or on its own, must impose an appropriate sanction on the signer, the party on whose behalf the signer was acting, or both. The sanction may include an order to pay the reasonable expenses, including attorney's fees, caused by the violation.

RULE 27. DEPOSITIONS TO PERPETUATE TESTIMONY

(a) Before an Action Is Filed.

(1) *Petition.* A person who wants to perpetuate testimony about any matter cognizable in a United States court may file a verified petition in the district court for the district where any expected adverse party resides. The petition must ask for an order authorizing the petitioner to depose the named persons in order to perpetuate their testimony. The petition must be titled in the petitioner's name and must show:

(A) that the petitioner expects to be a party to an action cognizable in a United States court but cannot presently bring it or cause it to be brought;

(B) the subject matter of the expected action and the petitioner's interest;

(C) the facts that the petitioner wants to establish by the proposed testimony and the reasons to perpetuate it;

(D) the names or a description of the persons whom the petitioner expects to be adverse parties and their addresses, so far as known; and

(E) the name, address, and expected substance of the testimony of each deponent.

(2) *Notice and Service.* At least 20 days before the hearing date, the petitioner must serve each expected adverse party with a copy of the petition and a notice stating the time and place of the hearing. The notice may be served either inside or outside the district or state in the manner provided in Rule 4. If that service cannot be made with reasonable diligence on an expected adverse party, the court may order service by publication or otherwise. The court must appoint an attorney to represent persons not served in the manner provided in Rule 4 and to cross-examine the deponent if an unserved person is not otherwise represented. If any expected adverse party is a minor or is incompetent, Rule 17(c) applies.

(3) *Order and Examination.* If satisfied that perpetuating the testimony may prevent a failure or delay of justice, the court must issue an order that designates or describes the persons whose depositions may be taken, specifies the subject matter of the examinations, and states whether the depositions will be taken orally or by written interrogatories. The depositions may then be taken under these rules, and the court may issue orders like those authorized by Rules 34 and 35. A reference in these rules to the court where an action is pending means, for purposes of this rule, the court where the petition for the deposition was filed.

(4) *Using the Deposition.* A deposition to perpetuate testimony may be used under Rule 32(a) in any later-filed district-court action involving the same subject matter if the deposition either was taken under these rules or, although not so taken, would be admissible in evidence in the courts of the state where it was taken.

(b) Pending Appeal.

(1) *In General.* The court where a judgment has been rendered may, if an appeal has been taken or may still be taken, permit a party to depose witnesses to perpetuate their testimony for use in the event of further proceedings in that court.

(2) *Motion.* The party who wants to perpetuate testimony may move for leave to take the depositions, on the same notice and service as if the action were pending in the district court. The motion must show:

(A) the name, address, and expected substance of the testimony of each deponent; and

(B) the reasons for perpetuating the testimony.

(3) *Court Order.* If the court finds that perpetuating the testimony may prevent a failure or delay of justice, the court may permit the depositions to be taken and may issue orders like those authorized by Rules 34 and 35. The depositions may be taken and used as any other deposition taken in a pending district-court action.

(c) Perpetuation by an Action. This rule does not limit a court's power to entertain an action to perpetuate testimony.

RULE 28. PERSONS BEFORE WHOM DEPOSITIONS MAY BE TAKEN

(a) Within the United States.

(1) *In General.* Within the United States or a territory or insular possession subject to United States jurisdiction, a deposition must be taken before:

(A) an officer authorized to administer oaths either by federal law or by the law in the place of examination; or

(B) a person appointed by the court where the action is pending to administer oaths and take testimony.

(2) *Definition of "Officer."* The term "officer" in Rules 30, 31, and 32 includes a person appointed by the court under this rule or designated by the parties under Rule 29(a).

(b) In a Foreign Country.

(1) *In General.* A deposition may be taken in a foreign country:

(A) under an applicable treaty or convention;

(B) under a letter of request, whether or not captioned a "letter interrogatory";

(C) on notice, before a person authorized to administer oaths either by federal law or by the law in the place of examination; or

(D) before a person commissioned by the court to administer any necessary oath and take testimony.

(2) *Issuing a Letter of Request or a Commission.* A letter of request, a commission, or both may be issued:

(A) on appropriate terms after an application and notice of it; and

(B) without a showing that taking the deposition in another manner is impracticable or inconvenient.

(3) *Form of a Request, Notice, or Commission.* When a letter of request or any other device is used according to a treaty or convention, it must be captioned in the form prescribed by that treaty or convention. A letter of request may be addressed "To the Appropriate Authority in [name of country]." A deposition notice or a commission must designate by name or descriptive title the person before whom the deposition is to be taken.

(4) *Letter of Request--Admitting Evidence.* Evidence obtained in response to a letter of request need not be excluded merely because it is not a verbatim transcript, because the testimony was not taken under oath, or because of any similar departure from the requirements for depositions taken within the United States.

(c) Disqualification. A deposition must not be taken before a person who is any party's relative, employee, or attorney; who is related to or employed by any party's attorney; or who is financially interested in the action.

RULE 29. STIPULATIONS ABOUT DISCOVERY PROCEDURE

Unless the court orders otherwise, the parties may stipulate that:

 (a) a deposition may be taken before any person, at any time or place, on any notice, and in the manner specified--in which event it may be used in the same way as any other deposition; and

 (b) other procedures governing or limiting discovery be modified--but a stipulation extending the time for any form of discovery must have court approval if it would interfere with the time set for completing discovery, for hearing a motion, or for trial.

RULE 30. DEPOSITIONS BY ORAL EXAMINATION

(a) When a Deposition May Be Taken.

   (1) *Without Leave.* A party may, by oral questions, depose any person, including a party, without leave of court except as provided in Rule 30(a)(2). The deponent's attendance may be compelled by subpoena under Rule 45.

   (2) *With Leave.* A party must obtain leave of court, and the court must grant leave to the extent consistent with Rule 26(b)(2):

      (A) if the parties have not stipulated to the deposition and:

         (i) the deposition would result in more than 10 depositions being taken under this rule or Rule 31 by the plaintiffs, or by the defendants, or by the third-party defendants;

         (ii) the deponent has already been deposed in the case; or

         (iii) the party seeks to take the deposition before the time specified in Rule 26(d), unless the party certifies in the notice, with supporting facts, that the deponent is expected to leave the United States and be unavailable for examination in this country after that time; or

      (B) if the deponent is confined in prison.

 (b) Notice of the Deposition; Other Formal Requirements.

   (1) *Notice in General.* A party who wants to depose a person by oral questions must give reasonable written notice to every other party. The notice must state the time and place of the deposition and, if known, the deponent's name and address. If the name is unknown, the notice must provide a general description sufficient to identify the person or the particular class or group to which the person belongs.

   (2) *Producing Documents.* If a subpoena duces tecum is to be served on the deponent, the materials designated for production, as set out in the subpoena, must be listed in the notice or in an attachment. The notice to a party deponent may be accompanied by a request complying with Rule 34 to produce documents and tangible things at the deposition.

   (3) *Method of Recording.*

      (A) Method Stated in the Notice. The party who notices the deposition must state in the notice the method for recording the testimony. Unless the court orders otherwise, testimony may be recorded by audio, audiovisual, or stenographic means. The noticing party bears the recording costs. Any party may arrange to transcribe a deposition.

      (B) Additional Method. With prior notice to the deponent and other parties, any party may designate another method for recording the testimony in addition to that specified in the original notice. That party bears the expense of the additional record or transcript unless the court orders otherwise.

   (4) *By Remote Means.* The parties may stipulate--or the court may on motion order--that a deposition be taken by telephone or other remote means. For the purpose of this rule and Rules 28(a), 37(a)(2), and 37(b)(1), the deposition takes place where the deponent answers the questions.

   (5) *Officer's Duties.*

      (A) Before the Deposition. Unless the parties stipulate otherwise, a deposition must be conducted before an officer appointed or designated under Rule 28. The officer must begin the deposition with an on-the-record statement that includes:

> (i) the officer's name and business address;
>
> (ii) the date, time, and place of the deposition;
>
> (iii) the deponent's name;
>
> (iv) the officer's administration of the oath or affirmation to the deponent; and
>
> (v) the identity of all persons present.

(B) *Conducting the Deposition; Avoiding Distortion.* If the deposition is recorded nonstenographically, the officer must repeat the items in Rule 30(b)(5)(A)(i)-(iii) at the beginning of each unit of the recording medium. The deponent's and attorneys' appearance or demeanor must not be distorted through recording techniques.

(C) *After the Deposition.* At the end of a deposition, the officer must state on the record that the deposition is complete and must set out any stipulations made by the attorneys about custody of the transcript or recording and of the exhibits, or about any other pertinent matters.

(6) *Notice or Subpoena Directed to an Organization.* In its notice or subpoena, a party may name as the deponent a public or private corporation, a partnership, an association, a governmental agency, or other entity and must describe with reasonable particularity the matters for examination. The named organization must then designate one or more officers, directors, or managing agents, or designate other persons who consent to testify on its behalf; and it may set out the matters on which each person designated will testify. A subpoena must advise a nonparty organization of its duty to make this designation. The persons designated must testify about information known or reasonably available to the organization. This paragraph (6) does not preclude a deposition by any other procedure allowed by these rules.

(c) Examination and Cross-Examination; Record of the Examination; Objections; Written Questions.

(1) *Examination and Cross-Examination.* The examination and cross-examination of a deponent proceed as they would at trial under the Federal Rules of Evidence, except Rules 103 and 615. After putting the deponent under oath or affirmation, the officer must record the testimony by the method designated under Rule 30(b)(3)(A). The testimony must be recorded by the officer personally or by a person acting in the presence and under the direction of the officer.

(2) *Objections.* An objection at the time of the examination--whether to evidence, to a party's conduct, to the officer's qualifications, to the manner of taking the deposition, or to any other aspect of the deposition-- must be noted on the record, but the examination still proceeds; the testimony is taken subject to any objection. An objection must be stated concisely in a nonargumentative and nonsuggestive manner. A person may instruct a deponent not to answer only when necessary to preserve a privilege, to enforce a limitation ordered by the court, or to present a motion under Rule 30(d)(3).

(3) *Participating Through Written Questions.* Instead of participating in the oral examination, a party may serve written questions in a sealed envelope on the party noticing the deposition, who must deliver them to the officer. The officer must ask the deponent those questions and record the answers verbatim.

(d) Duration; Sanction; Motion to Terminate or Limit.

(1) *Duration.* Unless otherwise stipulated or ordered by the court, a deposition is limited to 1 day of 7 hours. The court must allow additional time consistent with Rule 26(b)(2) if needed to fairly examine the deponent or if the deponent, another person, or any other circumstance impedes or delays the examination.

(2) *Sanction.* The court may impose an appropriate sanction--including the reasonable expenses and attorney's fees incurred by any party--on a person who impedes, delays, or frustrates the fair examination of the deponent.

(3) *Motion to Terminate or Limit.*

(A) Grounds. At any time during a deposition, the deponent or a party may move to terminate or limit it on the ground that it is being conducted in bad faith or in a manner that unreasonably annoys, embarrasses, or oppresses the deponent or party. The motion may be filed in the court where the action is pending or the deposition is being taken. If the objecting deponent or party so demands, the deposition must be suspended for the time necessary to obtain an order.

(B) Order. The court may order that the deposition be terminated or may limit its scope and manner as provided in Rule 26(c). If terminated, the deposition may be resumed only by order of the court where the action is pending.

(C) Award of Expenses. Rule 37(a)(5) applies to the award of expenses.

(e) Review by the Witness; Changes.

(1) *Review; Statement of Changes.* On request by the deponent or a party before the deposition is completed, the deponent must be allowed 30 days after being notified by the officer that the transcript or recording is available in which:

(A) to review the transcript or recording; and

(B) if there are changes in form or substance, to sign a statement listing the changes and the reasons for making them.

(2) *Changes Indicated in the Officer's Certificate.* The officer must note in the certificate prescribed by Rule 30(f)(1) whether a review was requested and, if so, must attach any changes the deponent makes during the 30-day period.

(f) Certification and Delivery; Exhibits; Copies of the Transcript or Recording; Filing.

(1) *Certification and Delivery.* The officer must certify in writing that the witness was duly sworn and that the deposition accurately records the witness's testimony. The certificate must accompany the record of the deposition. Unless the court orders otherwise, the officer must seal the deposition in an envelope or package bearing the title of the action and marked "Deposition of [witness's name]" and must promptly send it to the attorney who arranged for the transcript or recording. The attorney must store it under conditions that will protect it against loss, destruction, tampering, or deterioration.

(2) *Documents and Tangible Things.*

(A) Originals and Copies. Documents and tangible things produced for inspection during a deposition must, on a party's request, be marked for identification and attached to the deposition. Any party may inspect and copy them. But if the person who produced them wants to keep the originals, the person may:

(i) offer copies to be marked, attached to the deposition, and then used as originals--after giving all parties a fair opportunity to verify the copies by comparing them with the originals; or

(ii) give all parties a fair opportunity to inspect and copy the originals after they are marked--in which event the originals may be used as if attached to the deposition.

(B) Order Regarding the Originals. Any party may move for an order that the originals be attached to the deposition pending final disposition of the case.

(3) *Copies of the Transcript or Recording.* Unless otherwise stipulated or ordered by the court, the officer must retain the stenographic notes of a deposition taken stenographically or a copy of the recording of a deposition taken by another method. When paid reasonable charges, the officer must furnish a copy of the transcript or recording to any party or the deponent.

(4) *Notice of Filing.* A party who files the deposition must promptly notify all other parties of the filing.

(g) Failure to Attend a Deposition or Serve a Subpoena; Expenses. A party who, expecting a deposition to be taken, attends in person or by an attorney may recover reasonable expenses for attending, including attorney's fees, if the noticing party failed to:

(1) attend and proceed with the deposition; or

(2) serve a subpoena on a nonparty deponent, who consequently did not attend.

RULE 31. DEPOSITIONS BY WRITTEN QUESTIONS

(a) When a Deposition May Be Taken.

(1) *Without Leave.* A party may, by written questions, depose any person, including a party, without leave of court except as provided in Rule 31(a)(2). The deponent's attendance may be compelled by subpoena under Rule 45.

(2) *With Leave.* A party must obtain leave of court, and the court must grant leave to the extent consistent with Rule 26(b)(2):

  (A) if the parties have not stipulated to the deposition and:

   (i) the deposition would result in more than 10 depositions being taken under this rule or Rule 30 by the plaintiffs, or by the defendants, or by the third-party defendants;

   (ii) the deponent has already been deposed in the case; or

   (iii) the party seeks to take a deposition before the time specified in Rule 26(d); or

  (B) if the deponent is confined in prison.

(3) *Service; Required Notice.* A party who wants to depose a person by written questions must serve them on every other party, with a notice stating, if known, the deponent's name and address. If the name is unknown, the notice must provide a general description sufficient to identify the person or the particular class or group to which the person belongs. The notice must also state the name or descriptive title and the address of the officer before whom the deposition will be taken.

(4) *Questions Directed to an Organization.* A public or private corporation, a partnership, an association, or a governmental agency may be deposed by written questions in accordance with Rule 30(b)(6).

(5) *Questions from Other Parties.* Any questions to the deponent from other parties must be served on all parties as follows: cross-questions, within 14 days after being served with the notice and direct questions; redirect questions, within 7 days after being served with cross-questions; and recross-questions, within 7 days after being served with redirect questions. The court may, for good cause, extend or shorten these times.

(b) Delivery to the Officer; Officer's Duties. The party who noticed the deposition must deliver to the officer a copy of all the questions served and of the notice. The officer must promptly proceed in the manner provided in Rule 30(c), (e), and (f) to:

  (1) take the deponent's testimony in response to the questions;

  (2) prepare and certify the deposition; and

  (3) send it to the party, attaching a copy of the questions and of the notice.

(c) Notice of Completion or Filing.

  (1) *Completion.* The party who noticed the deposition must notify all other parties when it is completed.

  (2) *Filing.* A party who files the deposition must promptly notify all other parties of the filing.

RULE 32. USING DEPOSITIONS IN COURT PROCEEDINGS

(a) Using Depositions.

(1) *In General.* At a hearing or trial, all or part of a deposition may be used against a party on these conditions:

  (A) the party was present or represented at the taking of the deposition or had reasonable notice of it;

  (B) it is used to the extent it would be admissible under the Federal Rules of Evidence if the deponent were present and testifying; and

(C) the use is allowed by Rule 32(a)(2) through (8).

(2) *Impeachment and Other Uses.* Any party may use a deposition to contradict or impeach the testimony given by the deponent as a witness, or for any other purpose allowed by the Federal Rules of Evidence.

(3) *Deposition of Party, Agent, or Designee.* An adverse party may use for any purpose the deposition of a party or anyone who, when deposed, was the party's officer, director, managing agent, or designee under Rule 30(b)(6) or 31(a)(4).

(4) *Unavailable Witness.* A party may use for any purpose the deposition of a witness, whether or not a party, if the court finds:

(A) that the witness is dead;

(B) that the witness is more than 100 miles from the place of hearing or trial or is outside the United States, unless it appears that the witness's absence was procured by the party offering the deposition;

(C) that the witness cannot attend or testify because of age, illness, infirmity, or imprisonment;

(D) that the party offering the deposition could not procure the witness's attendance by subpoena; or

(E) on motion and notice, that exceptional circumstances make it desirable--in the interest of justice and with due regard to the importance of live testimony in open court--to permit the deposition to be used.

(5) *Limitations on Use.*

(A) Deposition Taken on Short Notice. A deposition must not be used against a party who, having received less than 11 days' notice of the deposition, promptly moved for a protective order under Rule 26(c)(1)(B) requesting that it not be taken or be taken at a different time or place--and this motion was still pending when the deposition was taken.

(B) Unavailable Deponent; Party Could Not Obtain an Attorney. A deposition taken without leave of court under the unavailability provision of Rule 30(a)(2)(A)(iii) must not be used against a party who shows that, when served with the notice, it could not, despite diligent efforts, obtain an attorney to represent it at the deposition.

(6) *Using Part of a Deposition.* If a party offers in evidence only part of a deposition, an adverse party may require the offeror to introduce other parts that in fairness should be considered with the part introduced, and any party may itself introduce any other parts.

(7) *Substituting a Party.* Substituting a party under Rule 25 does not affect the right to use a deposition previously taken.

(8) *Deposition Taken in an Earlier Action.* A deposition lawfully taken and, if required, filed in any federal- or state-court action may be used in a later action involving the same subject matter between the same parties, or their representatives or successors in interest, to the same extent as if taken in the later action. A deposition previously taken may also be used as allowed by the Federal Rules of Evidence.

(b) Objections to Admissibility. Subject to Rules 28(b) and 32(d)(3), an objection may be made at a hearing or trial to the admission of any deposition testimony that would be inadmissible if the witness were present and testifying.

(c) Form of Presentation. Unless the court orders otherwise, a party must provide a transcript of any deposition testimony the party offers, but may provide the court with the testimony in nontranscript form as well. On any party's request, deposition testimony offered in a jury trial for any purpose other than impeachment must be presented in nontranscript form, if available, unless the court for good cause orders otherwise.

(d) Waiver of Objections.

(1) *To the Notice.* An objection to an error or irregularity in a deposition notice is waived unless promptly served in writing on the party giving the notice.

(2) *To the Officer's Qualification.* An objection based on disqualification of the officer before whom a

deposition is to be taken is waived if not made:

(A) before the deposition begins; or

(B) promptly after the basis for disqualification becomes known or, with reasonable diligence, could have been known.

(3) *To the Taking of the Deposition.*

(A) Objection to Competence, Relevance, or Materiality. An objection to a deponent's competence--or to the competence, relevance, or materiality of testimony--is not waived by a failure to make the objection before or during the deposition, unless the ground for it might have been corrected at that time.

(B) Objection to an Error or Irregularity. An objection to an error or irregularity at an oral examination is waived if:

(i) it relates to the manner of taking the deposition, the form of a question or answer, the oath or affirmation, a party's conduct, or other matters that might have been corrected at that time; and

(ii) it is not timely made during the deposition.

(C) *Objection to a Written Question.* An objection to the form of a written question under Rule 31 is waived if not served in writing on the party submitting the question within the time for serving responsive questions or, if the question is a recross-question, within 5 days after being served with it.

(4) *To Completing and Returning the Deposition.* An objection to how the officer transcribed the testimony--or prepared, signed, certified, sealed, endorsed, sent, or otherwise dealt with the deposition--is waived unless a motion to suppress is made promptly after the error or irregularity becomes known or, with reasonable diligence, could have been known.

RULE 33. INTERROGATORIES TO PARTIES

(a) In General.

(1) *Number.* Unless otherwise stipulated or ordered by the court, a party may serve on any other party no more than 25 written interrogatories, including all discrete subparts. Leave to serve additional interrogatories may be granted to the extent consistent with Rule 26(b)(2).

(2) *Scope.* An interrogatory may relate to any matter that may be inquired into under Rule 26(b). An interrogatory is not objectionable merely because it asks for an opinion or contention that relates to fact or the application of law to fact, but the court may order that the interrogatory need not be answered until designated discovery is complete, or until a pretrial conference or some other time.

(b) Answers and Objections.

(1) *Responding Party.* The interrogatories must be answered:

(A) by the party to whom they are directed; or

(B) if that party is a public or private corporation, a partnership, an association, or a governmental agency, by any officer or agent, who must furnish the information available to the party.

(2) *Time to Respond.* The responding party must serve its answers and any objections within 30 days after being served with the interrogatories. A shorter or longer time may be stipulated to under Rule 29 or be ordered by the court.

(3) *Answering Each Interrogatory.* Each interrogatory must, to the extent it is not objected to, be answered separately and fully in writing under oath.

(4) *Objections.* The grounds for objecting to an interrogatory must be stated with specificity. Any ground not stated in a timely objection is waived unless the court, for good cause, excuses the failure.

(5) *Signature.* The person who makes the answers must sign them, and the attorney who objects must sign any objections.

(c) Use. An answer to an interrogatory may be used to the extent allowed by the Federal Rules of Evidence.

(d) Option to Produce Business Records. If the answer to an interrogatory may be determined by examining, auditing, compiling, abstracting, or summarizing a party's business records (including electronically stored information), and if the burden of deriving or ascertaining the answer will be substantially the same for either party, the responding party may answer by:

(1) specifying the records that must be reviewed, in sufficient detail to enable the interrogating party to locate and identify them as readily as the responding party could; and

(2) giving the interrogating party a reasonable opportunity to examine and audit the records and to make copies, compilations, abstracts, or summaries.

RULE 34. PRODUCING DOCUMENTS, ELECTRONICALLY STORED INFORMATION, AND TANGIBLE THINGS, OR ENTERING ONTO LAND, FOR INSPECTION AND OTHER PURPOSES

(a) In General. A party may serve on any other party a request within the scope of Rule 26(b):

(1) to produce and permit the requesting party or its representative to inspect, copy, test, or sample the following items in the responding party's possession, custody, or control:

(A) any designated documents or electronically stored information--including writings, drawings, graphs, charts, photographs, sound recordings, images, and other data or data compilations--stored in any medium from which information can be obtained either directly or, if necessary, after translation by the responding party into a reasonably usable form; or

(B) any designated tangible things; or

(2) to permit entry onto designated land or other property possessed or controlled by the responding party, so that the requesting party may inspect, measure, survey, photograph, test, or sample the property or any designated object or operation on it.

(b) Procedure.

(1) *Contents of the Request.* The request:

(A) must describe with reasonable particularity each item or category of items to be inspected;

(B) must specify a reasonable time, place, and manner for the inspection and for performing the related acts; and

(C) may specify the form or forms in which electronically stored information is to be produced.

(2) *Responses and Objections.*

(A) Time to Respond. The party to whom the request is directed must respond in writing within 30 days after being served. A shorter or longer time may be stipulated to under Rule 29 or be ordered by the court.

(B) Responding to Each Item. For each item or category, the response must either state that inspection and related activities will be permitted as requested or state an objection to the request, including the reasons.

(C) Objections. An objection to part of a request must specify the part and permit inspection of the rest.

(D) Responding to a Request for Production of Electronically Stored Information. The response may state an objection to a requested form for producing electronically stored information. If the responding party objects to a requested form--or if no form was specified in the request--the party must state the form or forms it intends to use.

(E) Producing the Documents or Electronically Stored Information. Unless otherwise stipulated or ordered by the court, these procedures apply to producing documents or electronically stored information:

(i) A party must produce documents as they are kept in the usual course of business or must organize and label them to correspond to the categories in the request;

(ii) If a request does not specify a form for producing electronically stored information, a party must produce it in a form or forms in which it is ordinarily maintained or in a reasonably usable form or forms; and

(iii) A party need not produce the same electronically stored information in more than one form.

(c) Nonparties. As provided in Rule 45, a nonparty may be compelled to produce documents and tangible things or to permit an inspection.

RULE 35. PHYSICAL AND MENTAL EXAMINATIONS

(a) Order for an Examination.

(1) *In General.* The court where the action is pending may order a party whose mental or physical condition--including blood group--is in controversy to submit to a physical or mental examination by a suitably licensed or certified examiner. The court has the same authority to order a party to produce for examination a person who is in its custody or under its legal control.

(2) *Motion and Notice; Contents of the Order.* The order:

(A) may be made only on motion for good cause and on notice to all parties and the person to be examined; and

(B) must specify the time, place, manner, conditions, and scope of the examination, as well as the person or persons who will perform it.

(b) Examiner's Report.

(1) *Request by the Party or Person Examined.* The party who moved for the examination must, on request, deliver to the requester a copy of the examiner's report, together with like reports of all earlier examinations of the same condition. The request may be made by the party against whom the examination order was issued or by the person examined.

(2) *Contents.* The examiner's report must be in writing and must set out in detail the examiner's findings, including diagnoses, conclusions, and the results of any tests.

(3) *Request by the Moving Party.* After delivering the reports, the party who moved for the examination may request--and is entitled to receive--from the party against whom the examination order was issued like reports of all earlier or later examinations of the same condition. But those reports need not be delivered by the party with custody or control of the person examined if the party shows that it could not obtain them.

(4) *Waiver of Privilege.* By requesting and obtaining the examiner's report, or by deposing the examiner, the party examined waives any privilege it may have--in that action or any other action involving the same controversy--concerning testimony about all examinations of the same condition.

(5) *Failure to Deliver a Report.* The court on motion may order--on just terms--that a party deliver the report of an examination. If the report is not provided, the court may exclude the examiner's testimony at trial.

(6) *Scope.* This subdivision (b) applies also to an examination made by the parties' agreement, unless the agreement states otherwise. This subdivision does not preclude obtaining an examiner's report or deposing an examiner under other rules.

RULE 36. REQUESTS FOR ADMISSION

(a) Scope and Procedure.

(1) *Scope.* A party may serve on any other party a written request to admit, for purposes of the pending action only, the truth of any matters within the scope of Rule 26(b)(1) relating to:

(A) facts, the application of law to fact, or opinions about either; and

(B) the genuineness of any described documents.

(2) *Form; Copy of a Document.* Each matter must be separately stated. A request to admit the genuineness of a document must be accompanied by a copy of the document unless it is, or has been, otherwise furnished

or made available for inspection and copying.

(3) *Time to Respond; Effect of Not Responding.* A matter is admitted unless, within 30 days after being served, the party to whom the request is directed serves on the requesting party a written answer or objection addressed to the matter and signed by the party or its attorney. A shorter or longer time for responding may be stipulated to under Rule 29 or be ordered by the court.

(4) *Answer.* If a matter is not admitted, the answer must specifically deny it or state in detail why the answering party cannot truthfully admit or deny it. A denial must fairly respond to the substance of the matter; and when good faith requires that a party qualify an answer or deny only a part of a matter, the answer must specify the part admitted and qualify or deny the rest. The answering party may assert lack of knowledge or information as a reason for failing to admit or deny only if the party states that it has made reasonable inquiry and that the information it knows or can readily obtain is insufficient to enable it to admit or deny.

(5) *Objections.* The grounds for objecting to a request must be stated. A party must not object solely on the ground that it presents a genuine issue for trial.

(6) *Motion Regarding the Sufficiency of an Answer or Objection.* The requesting party may move to determine the sufficiency of an answer or objection. Unless the court finds an objection justified, it must order that an answer be served. On finding that an answer does not comply with this rule, the court may order either that the matter is admitted or that an amended answer be served. The court may defer its final decision until a pretrial conference or a specified time before trial. Rule 37(a)(5) applies to an award of expenses.

(b) Effect of an Admission; Withdrawing or Amending It. A matter admitted under this rule is conclusively established unless the court, on motion, permits the admission to be withdrawn or amended. Subject to Rule 16(e), the court may permit withdrawal or amendment if it would promote the presentation of the merits of the action and if the court is not persuaded that it would prejudice the requesting party in maintaining or defending the action on the merits. An admission under this rule is not an admission for any other purpose and cannot be used against the party in any other proceeding.

RULE 37. FAILURE TO MAKE DISCLOSURES OR TO COOPERATE IN DISCOVERY; SANCTIONS

(a) Motion for an Order Compelling Disclosure or Discovery.

(1) *In General.* On notice to other parties and all affected persons, a party may move for an order compelling disclosure or discovery. The motion must include a certification that the movant has in good faith conferred or attempted to confer with the person or party failing to make disclosure or discovery in an effort to obtain it without court action.

(2) *Appropriate Court.* A motion for an order to a party must be made in the court where the action is pending. A motion for an order to a nonparty must be made in the court where the discovery is or will be taken.

(3) *Specific Motions.*

(A) To Compel Disclosure. If a party fails to make a disclosure required by Rule 26(a), any other party may move to compel disclosure and for appropriate sanctions.

(B) To Compel a Discovery Response. A party seeking discovery may move for an order compelling an answer, designation, production, or inspection. This motion may be made if:

(i) a deponent fails to answer a question asked under Rule 30 or 31;

(ii) a corporation or other entity fails to make a designation under Rule 30(b)(6) or 31(a)(4);

(iii) a party fails to answer an interrogatory submitted under Rule 33; or

(iv) a party fails to respond that inspection will be permitted--or fails to permit inspection--as requested under Rule 34.

(C) Related to a Deposition. When taking an oral deposition, the party asking a question may complete or adjourn the examination before moving for an order.

(4) *Evasive or Incomplete Disclosure, Answer, or Response.* For purposes of this subdivision (a), an evasive or incomplete disclosure, answer, or response must be treated as a failure to disclose, answer, or respond.

(5) *Payment of Expenses; Protective Orders.*

(A) If the Motion Is Granted (or Disclosure or Discovery Is Provided After Filing). If the motion is granted--or if the disclosure or requested discovery is provided after the motion was filed--the court must, after giving an opportunity to be heard, require the party or deponent whose conduct necessitated the motion, the party or attorney advising that conduct, or both to pay the movant's reasonable expenses incurred in making the motion, including attorney's fees. But the court must not order this payment if:

(i) the movant filed the motion before attempting in good faith to obtain the disclosure or discovery without court action;

(ii) the opposing party's nondisclosure, response, or objection was substantially justified; or

(iii) other circumstances make an award of expenses unjust.

(B) If the Motion Is Denied. If the motion is denied, the court may issue any protective order authorized under Rule 26(c) and must, after giving an opportunity to be heard, require the movant, the attorney filing the motion, or both to pay the party or deponent who opposed the motion its reasonable expenses incurred in opposing the motion, including attorney's fees. But the court must not order this payment if the motion was substantially justified or other circumstances make an award of expenses unjust.

(C) If the Motion Is Granted in Part and Denied in Part. If the motion is granted in part and denied in part, the court may issue any protective order authorized under Rule 26(c) and may, after giving an opportunity to be heard, apportion the reasonable expenses for the motion.

(b) Failure to Comply with a Court Order.

(1) *Sanctions in the District Where the Deposition Is Taken.* If the court where the discovery is taken orders a deponent to be sworn or to answer a question and the deponent fails to obey, the failure may be treated as contempt of court.

(2) *Sanctions in the District Where the Action Is Pending.*

(A) For Not Obeying a Discovery Order. If a party or a party's officer, director, or managing agent--or a witness designated under Rule 30(b)(6) or 31(a)(4)--fails to obey an order to provide or permit discovery, including an order under Rule 26(f), 35, or 37(a), the court where the action is pending may issue further just orders. They may include the following:

(i) directing that the matters embraced in the order or other designated facts be taken as established for purposes of the action, as the prevailing party claims;

(ii) prohibiting the disobedient party from supporting or opposing designated claims or defenses, or from introducing designated matters in evidence;

(iii) striking pleadings in whole or in part;

(iv) staying further proceedings until the order is obeyed;

(v) dismissing the action or proceeding in whole or in part;

(vi) rendering a default judgment against the disobedient party; or

(vii) treating as contempt of court the failure to obey any order except an order to submit to a physical or mental examination.

(B) For Not Producing a Person for Examination. If a party fails to comply with an order under Rule 35(a) requiring it to produce another person for examination, the court may issue any of the orders listed in Rule 37(b)(2)(A)(i)-(vi), unless the disobedient party shows that it cannot produce the other person.

(C) Payment of Expenses. Instead of or in addition to the orders above, the court must order the disobedient party, the attorney advising that party, or both to pay the reasonable expenses, including attorney's fees, caused by the failure, unless the failure was substantially justified or other circumstances make an award of expenses unjust.

(c) Failure to Disclose, to Supplement an Earlier Response, or to Admit.

(1) *Failure to Disclose or Supplement.* If a party fails to provide information or identify a witness as required by Rule 26(a) or (e), the party is not allowed to use that information or witness to supply evidence on a motion, at a hearing, or at a trial, unless the failure was substantially justified or is harmless. In addition to or instead of this sanction, the court, on motion and after giving an opportunity to be heard:

(A) may order payment of the reasonable expenses, including attorney's fees, caused by the failure;

(B) may inform the jury of the party's failure; and

(C) may impose other appropriate sanctions, including any of the orders listed in Rule 37(b)(2)(A)(i)-(vi).

(2) *Failure to Admit.* If a party fails to admit what is requested under Rule 36 and if the requesting party later proves a document to be genuine or the matter true, the requesting party may move that the party who failed to admit pay the reasonable expenses, including attorney's fees, incurred in making that proof. The court must so order unless:

(A) the request was held objectionable under Rule 36(a);

(B) the admission sought was of no substantial importance;

(C) the party failing to admit had a reasonable ground to believe that it might prevail on the matter; or

(D) there was other good reason for the failure to admit.

(d) Party's Failure to Attend Its Own Deposition, Serve Answers to Interrogatories, or Respond to a Request for Inspection.

(1) *In General.*

(A) Motion; Grounds for Sanctions. The court where the action is pending may, on motion, order sanctions if:

(i) a party or a party's officer, director, or managing agent--or a person designated under Rule 30(b)(6) or 31(a)(4)--fails, after being served with proper notice, to appear for that person's deposition; or

(ii) a party, after being properly served with interrogatories under Rule 33 or a request for inspection under Rule 34, fails to serve its answers, objections, or written response.

(B) Certification. A motion for sanctions for failing to answer or respond must include a certification that the movant has in good faith conferred or attempted to confer with the party failing to act in an effort to obtain the answer or response without court action.

(2) *Unacceptable Excuse for Failing to Act.* A failure described in Rule 37(d)(1)(A) is not excused on the ground that the discovery sought was objectionable, unless the party failing to act has a pending motion for a protective order under Rule 26(c).

(3) *Types of Sanctions.* Sanctions may include any of the orders listed in Rule 37(b)(2)(A)(i)-(vi). Instead of or in addition to these sanctions, the court must require the party failing to act, the attorney advising that party, or both to pay the reasonable expenses, including attorney's fees, caused by the failure, unless the failure was substantially justified or other circumstances make an award of expenses unjust.

(e) Failure to Provide Electronically Stored Information. Absent exceptional circumstances, a court may not impose sanctions under these rules on a party for failing to provide electronically stored information lost as a result of the routine, good-faith operation of an electronic information system.

(f) Failure to Participate in Framing a Discovery Plan. If a party or its attorney fails to participate in good faith in developing and submitting a proposed discovery plan as required by Rule 26(f), the court may, after giving an opportunity to be heard, require that party or attorney to pay to any other party the reasonable expenses, including attorney's fees, caused by the failure.

RULE 38. RIGHT TO A JURY TRIAL; DEMAND

(a) Right Preserved. The right of trial by jury as declared by the Seventh Amendment to the Constitution--or as provided by a federal statute--is preserved to the parties inviolate.

 (b) Demand. On any issue triable of right by a jury, a party may demand a jury trial by:

 (1) serving the other parties with a written demand--which may be included in a pleading--no later than 10 days after the last pleading directed to the issue is served; and

 (2) filing the demand in accordance with Rule 5(d).

 (c) Specifying Issues. In its demand, a party may specify the issues that it wishes to have tried by a jury; otherwise, it is considered to have demanded a jury trial on all the issues so triable. If the party has demanded a jury trial on only some issues, any other party may--within 10 days after being served with the demand or within a shorter time ordered by the court--serve a demand for a jury trial on any other or all factual issues triable by jury.

 (d) Waiver; Withdrawal. A party waives a jury trial unless its demand is properly served and filed. A proper demand may be withdrawn only if the parties consent.

(e) Admiralty and Maritime Claims. These rules do not create a right to a jury trial on issues in a claim designated as an admiralty or maritime claim under Rule 9(h).

RULE 39. TRIAL BY JURY OR BY THE COURT

(a) When a Demand Is Made. When a jury trial has been demanded under Rule 38, the action must be designated on the docket as a jury action. The trial on all issues so demanded must be by jury unless:

 (1) the parties or their attorneys file a stipulation to a nonjury trial or so stipulate on the record; or

 (2) the court, on motion or on its own, finds that on some or all of those issues there is no federal right to a jury trial.

 (b) When No Demand Is Made. Issues on which a jury trial is not properly demanded are to be tried by the court. But the court may, on motion, order a jury trial on any issue for which a jury might have been demanded.

 (c) Advisory Jury; Jury Trial by Consent. In an action not triable of right by a jury, the court, on motion or on its own:

 (1) may try any issue with an advisory jury; or

 (2) may, with the parties' consent, try any issue by a jury whose verdict has the same effect as if a jury trial had been a matter of right, unless the action is against the United States and a federal statute provides for a nonjury trial.

RULE 40. SCHEDULING CASES FOR TRIAL

Each court must provide by rule for scheduling trials. The court must give priority to actions entitled to priority by a federal statute.

RULE 41. DISMISSAL OF ACTIONS

(a) Voluntary Dismissal.

 (1) By the Plaintiff.

(A) Without a Court Order. Subject to Rules 23(e), 23.1(c), 23.2, and 66 and any applicable federal statute, the plaintiff may dismiss an action without a court order by filing:

(i) a notice of dismissal before the opposing party serves either an answer or a motion for summary judgment; or

(ii) a stipulation of dismissal signed by all parties who have appeared.

(B) Effect. Unless the notice or stipulation states otherwise, the dismissal is without prejudice. But if the plaintiff previously dismissed any federal- or state-court action based on or including the same claim, a notice of dismissal operates as an adjudication on the merits.

(2) *By Court Order; Effect.* Except as provided in Rule 41(a)(1), an action may be dismissed at the plaintiff's request only by court order, on terms that the court considers proper. If a defendant has pleaded a counterclaim before being served with the plaintiff's motion to dismiss, the action may be dismissed over the defendant's objection only if the counterclaim can remain pending for independent adjudication. Unless the order states otherwise, a dismissal under this paragraph (2) is without prejudice.

(b) Involuntary Dismissal; Effect. If the plaintiff fails to prosecute or to comply with these rules or a court order, a defendant may move to dismiss the action or any claim against it. Unless the dismissal order states otherwise, a dismissal under this subdivision (b) and any dismissal not under this rule--except one for lack of jurisdiction, improper venue, or failure to join a party under Rule 19--operates as an adjudication on the merits.

(c) Dismissing a Counterclaim, Crossclaim, or Third-Party Claim. This rule applies to a dismissal of any counterclaim, crossclaim, or third-party claim. A claimant's voluntary dismissal under Rule 41(a)(1)(A)(i) must be made:

(1) before a responsive pleading is served; or

(2) if there is no responsive pleading, before evidence is introduced at a hearing or trial.

(d) Costs of a Previously Dismissed Action. If a plaintiff who previously dismissed an action in any court files an action based on or including the same claim against the same defendant, the court:

(1) may order the plaintiff to pay all or part of the costs of that previous action; and

(2) may stay the proceedings until the plaintiff has complied.

RULE 42. CONSOLIDATION; SEPARATE TRIALS

(a) Consolidation. If actions before the court involve a common question of law or fact, the court may:

(1) join for hearing or trial any or all matters at issue in the actions;

(2) consolidate the actions; or

(3) issue any other orders to avoid unnecessary cost or delay.

(b) Separate Trials. For convenience, to avoid prejudice, or to expedite and economize, the court may order a separate trial of one or more separate issues, claims, crossclaims, counterclaims, or third-party claims. When ordering a separate trial, the court must preserve any federal right to a jury trial.

RULE 43. TAKING TESTIMONY

(a) In Open Court. At trial, the witnesses' testimony must be taken in open court unless a federal statute, the Federal Rules of Evidence, these rules, or other rules adopted by the Supreme Court provide otherwise. For good cause in compelling circumstances and with appropriate safeguards, the court may permit testimony in open court by contemporaneous transmission from a different location.

(b) Affirmation Instead of an Oath. When these rules require an oath, a solemn affirmation suffices.

(c) Evidence on a Motion. When a motion relies on facts outside the record, the court may hear the matter on affidavits or may hear it wholly or partly on oral testimony or on depositions.

(d) Interpreter. The court may appoint an interpreter of its choosing; fix reasonable compensation to be paid from funds provided by law or by one or more parties; and tax the compensation as costs.

RULE 44. PROVING AN OFFICIAL RECORD

(a) Means of Proving.

(1) *Domestic Record.* Each of the following evidences an official record--or an entry in it--that is otherwise admissible and is kept within the United States, any state, district, or commonwealth, or any territory subject to the administrative or judicial jurisdiction of the United States:

(A) an official publication of the record; or

(B) a copy attested by the officer with legal custody of the record--or by the officer's deputy--and accompanied by a certificate that the officer has custody. The certificate must be made under seal:

(i) by a judge of a court of record in the district or political subdivision where the record is kept; or

(ii) by any public officer with a seal of office and with official duties in the district or political subdivision where the record is kept.

(2) *Foreign Record.*

(A) In General. Each of the following evidences a foreign official record--or an entry in it--that is otherwise admissible:

(i) an official publication of the record; or

(ii) the record--or a copy--that is attested by an authorized person and is accompanied either by a final certification of genuineness or by a certification under a treaty or convention to which the United States and the country where the record is located are parties.

(B) Final Certification of Genuineness. A final certification must certify the genuineness of the signature and official position of the attester or of any foreign official whose certificate of genuineness relates to the attestation or is in a chain of certificates of genuineness relating to the attestation. A final certification may be made by a secretary of a United States embassy or legation; by a consul general, vice consul, or consular agent of the United States; or by a diplomatic or consular official of the foreign country assigned or accredited to the United States.

(C) Other Means of Proof. If all parties have had a reasonable opportunity to investigate a foreign record's authenticity and accuracy, the court may, for good cause, either:

(i) admit an attested copy without final certification; or

(ii) permit the record to be evidenced by an attested summary with or without a final certification.

(b) Lack of a Record. A written statement that a diligent search of designated records revealed no record or entry of a specified tenor is admissible as evidence that the records contain no such record or entry. For domestic records, the statement must be authenticated under Rule 44(a)(1). For foreign records, the statement must comply with (a)(2)(C)(ii).

(c) Other Proof. A party may prove an official record--or an entry or lack of an entry in it--by any other method authorized by law.

Rule 44.1. Determining Foreign Law

A party who intends to raise an issue about a foreign country's law must give notice by a pleading or other writing. In determining foreign law, the court may consider any relevant material or source, including testimony, whether or not submitted by a party or admissible under the Federal Rules of Evidence. The court's determination must be treated as a ruling on a question of law.

RULE 45. SUBPOENA

(a) In General.

(1) *Form and Contents.*

(A) Requirements--In General. Every subpoena must:

(i) state the court from which it issued;

(ii) state the title of the action, the court in which it is pending, and its civil-action number;

(iii) command each person to whom it is directed to do the following at a specified time and place: attend and testify; produce designated documents, electronically stored information, or tangible things in that person's possession, custody, or control; or permit the inspection of premises; and

(iv) set out the text of Rule 45(c) and (d).

(B) Command to Attend a Deposition--Notice of the Recording Method. A subpoena commanding attendance at a deposition must state the method for recording the testimony.

(C) Combining or Separating a Command to Produce or to Permit Inspection; Specifying the Form for Electronically Stored Information. A command to produce documents, electronically stored information, or tangible things or to permit the inspection of premises may be included in a subpoena commanding attendance at a deposition, hearing, or trial, or may be set out in a separate subpoena. A subpoena may specify the form or forms in which electronically stored information is to be produced.

(D) Command to Produce; Included Obligations. A command in a subpoena to produce documents, electronically stored information, or tangible things requires the responding party to permit inspection, copying, testing, or sampling of the materials.

(2) *Issued from Which Court.* A subpoena must issue as follows:

(A) for attendance at a hearing or trial, from the court for the district where the hearing or trial is to be held;

(B) for attendance at a deposition, from the court for the district where the deposition is to be taken; and

(C) for production or inspection, if separate from a subpoena commanding a person's attendance, from the court for the district where the production or inspection is to be made.

(3) *Issued by Whom.* The clerk must issue a subpoena, signed but otherwise in blank, to a party who requests it. That party must complete it before service. An attorney also may issue and sign a subpoena as an officer of:

(A) a court in which the attorney is authorized to practice; or

(B) a court for a district where a deposition is to be taken or production is to be made, if the attorney is authorized to practice in the court where the action is pending.

(b) Service.

(1) *By Whom; Tendering Fees; Serving a Copy of Certain Subpoenas.* Any person who is at least 18 years old and not a party may serve a subpoena. Serving a subpoena requires delivering a copy to the named person and, if the subpoena requires that person's attendance, tendering the fees for 1 day's attendance and the mileage allowed by law. Fees and mileage need not be tendered when the subpoena issues on behalf of the United States or any of its officers or agencies. If the subpoena commands the production of documents, electronically stored information, or tangible things or the inspection of premises before trial, then before it is served, a notice must be served on each party.

(2) *Service in the United States.* Subject to Rule 45(c)(3)(A)(ii), a subpoena may be served at any place:

(A) within the district of the issuing court;

(B) outside that district but within 100 miles of the place specified for the deposition, hearing, trial, production, or inspection;

(C) within the state of the issuing court if a state statute or court rule allows service at that place of a subpoena issued by a state court of general jurisdiction sitting in the place specified for the deposition, hearing, trial, production, or inspection; or

(D) that the court authorizes on motion and for good cause, if a federal statute so provides.

(3) *Service in a Foreign Country.* 28 U.S.C. § 1783 governs issuing and serving a subpoena directed to a United States national or resident who is in a foreign country.

(4) *Proof of Service.* Proving service, when necessary, requires filing with the issuing court a statement showing the date and manner of service and the names of the persons served. The statement must be certified by the server.

(c) Protecting a Person Subject to a Subpoena.

(1) *Avoiding Undue Burden or Expense; Sanctions.* A party or attorney responsible for issuing and serving a subpoena must take reasonable steps to avoid imposing undue burden or expense on a person subject to the subpoena. The issuing court must enforce this duty and impose an appropriate sanction--which may include lost earnings and reasonable attorney's fees--on a party or attorney who fails to comply.

(2) *Command to Produce Materials or Permit Inspection.*

(A) Appearance Not Required. A person commanded to produce documents, electronically stored information, or tangible things, or to permit the inspection of premises, need not appear in person at the place of production or inspection unless also commanded to appear for a deposition, hearing, or trial.

(B) Objections. A person commanded to produce documents or tangible things or to permit inspection may serve on the party or attorney designated in the subpoena a written objection to inspecting, copying, testing or sampling any or all of the materials or to inspecting the premises--or to producing electronically stored information in the form or forms requested. The objection must be served before the earlier of the time specified for compliance or 14 days after the subpoena is served. If an objection is made, the following rules apply:

(i) At any time, on notice to the commanded person, the serving party may move the issuing court for an order compelling production or inspection.

(ii) These acts may be required only as directed in the order, and the order must protect a person who is neither a party nor a party's officer from significant expense resulting from compliance.

(3) *Quashing or Modifying a Subpoena.*

(A) When Required. On timely motion, the issuing court must quash or modify a subpoena that:

(i) fails to allow a reasonable time to comply;

(ii) requires a person who is neither a party nor a party's officer to travel more than 100 miles from where that person resides, is employed, or regularly transacts business in person--except that, subject to Rule 45(c)(3)(B)(iii), the person may be commanded to attend a trial by traveling from any such place within the state where the trial is held;

(iii) requires disclosure of privileged or other protected matter, if no exception or waiver applies; or

(iv) subjects a person to undue burden.

(B) When Permitted. To protect a person subject to or affected by a subpoena, the issuing court may, on motion, quash or modify the subpoena if it requires:

(i) disclosing a trade secret or other confidential research, development, or commercial information;

(ii) disclosing an unretained expert's opinion or information that does not describe specific occurrences in dispute and results from the expert's study that was not requested by a party; or

(iii) a person who is neither a party nor a party's officer to incur substantial expense to travel more than 100 miles to attend trial.

(C) Specifying Conditions as an Alternative. In the circumstances described in Rule 45(c)(3)(B), the court may, instead of quashing or modifying a subpoena, order appearance or production under specified conditions if the serving party:

(i) shows a substantial need for the testimony or material that cannot be otherwise met without undue hardship; and

(ii) ensures that the subpoenaed person will be reasonably compensated.

(d) Duties in Responding to a Subpoena.

(1) *Producing Documents or Electronically Stored Information.* These procedures apply to producing documents or electronically stored information:

(A) Documents. A person responding to a subpoena to produce documents must produce them as they are kept in the ordinary course of business or must organize and label them to correspond to the categories in the demand.

(B) Form for Producing Electronically Stored Information Not Specified. If a subpoena does not specify a form for producing electronically stored information, the person responding must produce it in a form or forms in which it is ordinarily maintained or in a reasonably usable form or forms.

(C) Electronically Stored Information Produced in Only One Form. The person responding need not produce the same electronically stored information in more than one form.

(D) Inaccessible Electronically Stored Information. The person responding need not provide discovery of electronically stored information form sources that the person identifies as not reasonably accessible because of undue burden or cost. On motion to compel discovery or for a protective order, the person responding must show that the information is not reasonably accessible because of undue burden or cost. If that showing is made, the court may nonetheless order discovery from such sources if the requesting party shows good cause, considering the limitations of Rule 26(b)(2)(C). The court may specify conditions for the discovery.

(2) *Claiming Privilege or Protection.*

(A) Information Withheld. A person withholding subpoenaed information under a claim that it is privileged or subject to protection as trial-preparation material must:

(i) expressly make the claim; and

(ii) describe the nature of the withheld documents, communications, or tangible things in a manner that, without revealing information itself privileged or protected, will enable the parties to assess the claim.

(B) Information Produced. If information produced in response to a subpoena is subject to a claim of privilege or of protection as trial-preparation material, the person making the claim may notify any party that received the information of the claim and the basis for it. After being notified, a party must promptly return, sequester, or destroy the specified information and any copies it has; must not use or disclose the information until the claim is resolved; must take reasonable steps to retrieve the information if the party disclosed it before being notified; and may promptly present the information to the court under seal for a determination of the claim. The person who produced the information must preserve the information until the claim is resolved.

(e) Contempt. The issuing court may hold in contempt a person who, having been served, fails without adequate excuse to obey the subpoena. A nonparty's failure to obey must be excused if the subpoena purports to require the nonparty to attend or produce at a place outside the limits of Rule 45(c)(3)(A)(ii).

RULE 46.   OBJECTING TO A RULING OR ORDER

A formal exception to a ruling or order is unnecessary. When the ruling or order is requested or made, a party need only state the action that it wants the court to take or objects to, along with the grounds for the request or objection. Failing to object does not prejudice a party who had no opportunity to do so when the ruling or order was made.

RULE 47. SELECTING JURORS

(a) Examining Jurors. The court may permit the parties or their attorneys to examine prospective jurors or may itself do so. If the court examines the jurors, it must permit the parties or their attorneys to make any further inquiry it considers proper, or must itself ask any of their additional questions it considers proper.

 (b) Peremptory Challenges. The court must allow the number of peremptory challenges provided by 28 U.S.C. § 1870.

 (c) Excusing a Juror. During trial or deliberation, the court may excuse a juror for good cause.

RULE 48. NUMBER OF JURORS; VERDICT

A jury must initially have at least 6 and no more than 12 members, and each juror must participate in the verdict unless excused under Rule 47(c). Unless the parties stipulate otherwise, the verdict must be unanimous and be returned by a jury of at least 6 members.

RULE 49. SPECIAL VERDICT; GENERAL VERDICT AND QUESTIONS

(a) Special Verdict.

 (1) *In General.* The court may require a jury to return only a special verdict in the form of a special written finding on each issue of fact. The court may do so by:

   (A) submitting written questions susceptible of a categorical or other brief answer;

   (B) submitting written forms of the special findings that might properly be made under the pleadings and evidence; or

   (C) using any other method that the court considers appropriate.

 (2) *Instructions.* The court must give the instructions and explanations necessary to enable the jury to make its findings on each submitted issue.

 (3) *Issues Not Submitted.* A party waives the right to a jury trial on any issue of fact raised by the pleadings or evidence but not submitted to the jury unless, before the jury retires, the party demands its submission to the jury. If the party does not demand submission, the court may make a finding on the issue. If the court makes no finding, it is considered to have made a finding consistent with its judgment on the special verdict.

 (b) General Verdict with Answers to Written Questions.

 (1) *In General.* The court may submit to the jury forms for a general verdict, together with written questions on one or more issues of fact that the jury must decide. The court must give the instructions and explanations necessary to enable the jury to render a general verdict and answer the questions in writing, and must direct the jury to do both.

 (2) *Verdict and Answers Consistent.* When the general verdict and the answers are consistent, the court must approve, for entry under Rule 58, an appropriate judgment on the verdict and answers.

 (3) *Answers Inconsistent with the Verdict.* When the answers are consistent with each other but one or more is inconsistent with the general verdict, the court may:

   (A) approve, for entry under Rule 58, an appropriate judgment according to the answers, notwithstanding the general verdict;

   (B) direct the jury to further consider its answers and verdict; or

   (C) order a new trial.

 (4) *Answers Inconsistent with Each Other and the Verdict.* When the answers are inconsistent with each

other and one or more is also inconsistent with the general verdict, judgment must not be entered; instead, the court must direct the jury to further consider its answers and verdict, or must order a new trial.

RULE 50. JUDGMENT AS A MATTER OF LAW IN A JURY TRIAL; RELATED MOTION FOR A NEW TRIAL; CONDITIONAL RULING

(a) Judgment as a Matter of Law.

(1) *In General.* If a party has been fully heard on an issue during a jury trial and the court finds that a reasonable jury would not have a legally sufficient evidentiary basis to find for the party on that issue, the court may:

(A) resolve the issue against the party; and

(B) grant a motion for judgment as a matter of law against the party on a claim or defense that, under the controlling law, can be maintained or defeated only with a favorable finding on that issue.

(2) *Motion.* A motion for judgment as a matter of law may be made at any time before the case is submitted to the jury. The motion must specify the judgment sought and the law and facts that entitle the movant to the judgment.

(b) Renewing the Motion After Trial; Alternative Motion for a New Trial. If the court does not grant a motion for judgment as a matter of law made under Rule 50(a), the court is considered to have submitted the action to the jury subject to the court's later deciding the legal questions raised by the motion. No later than 10 days after the entry of judgment--or if the motion addresses a jury issue not decided by a verdict, no later than 10 days after the jury was discharged--the movant may file a renewed motion for judgment as a matter of law and may include an alternative or joint request for a new trial under Rule 59. In ruling on the renewed motion, the court may:

(1) allow judgment on the verdict, if the jury returned a verdict;

(2) order a new trial; or

(3) direct the entry of judgment as a matter of law.

(c) Granting the Renewed Motion; Conditional Ruling on a Motion for a New Trial.

(1) *In General.* If the court grants a renewed motion for judgment as a matter of law, it must also conditionally rule on any motion for a new trial by determining whether a new trial should be granted if the judgment is later vacated or reversed. The court must state the grounds for conditionally granting or denying the motion for a new trial.

(2) *Effect of a Conditional Ruling.* Conditionally granting the motion for a new trial does not affect the judgment's finality; if the judgment is reversed, the new trial must proceed unless the appellate court orders otherwise. If the motion for a new trial is conditionally denied, the appellee may assert error in that denial; if the judgment is reversed, the case must proceed as the appellate court orders.

(d) Time for a Losing Party's New-Trial Motion. Any motion for a new trial under Rule 59 by a party against whom judgment as a matter of law is rendered must be filed no later than 10 days after the entry of the judgment.

(e) Denying the Motion for Judgment as a Matter of Law; Reversal on Appeal. If the court denies the motion for judgment as a matter of law, the prevailing party may, as appellee, assert grounds entitling it to a new trial should the appellate court conclude that the trial court erred in denying the motion. If the appellate court reverses the judgment, it may order a new trial, direct the trial court to determine whether a new trial should be granted, or direct the entry of judgment.

RULE 51. INSTRUCTIONS TO THE JURY; OBJECTIONS; PRESERVING A CLAIM OF ERROR

(a) Requests.

(1) *Before or at the Close of the Evidence.* At the close of the evidence or at any earlier reasonable time that the court orders, a party may file and furnish to every other party written requests for the jury instructions it wants the court to give.

(2) *After the Close of the Evidence.* After the close of the evidence, a party may:

(A) file requests for instructions on issues that could not reasonably have been anticipated by an earlier time that the court set for requests; and

(B) with the court's permission, file untimely requests for instructions on any issue.

(b) Instructions. The court:

(1) must inform the parties of its proposed instructions and proposed action on the requests before instructing the jury and before final jury arguments;

(2) must give the parties an opportunity to object on the record and out of the jury's hearing before the instructions and arguments are delivered; and

(3) may instruct the jury at any time before the jury is discharged.

(c) Objections.

(1) *How to Make.* A party who objects to an instruction or the failure to give an instruction must do so on the record, stating distinctly the matter objected to and the grounds for the objection.

(2) *When to Make.* An objection is timely if:

(A) a party objects at the opportunity provided under Rule 51(b)(2); or

(B) a party was not informed of an instruction or action on a request before that opportunity to object, and the party objects promptly after learning that the instruction or request will be, or has been, given or refused.

(d) Assigning Error; Plain Error.

(1) *Assigning Error.* A party may assign as error:

(A) an error in an instruction actually given, if that party properly objected; or

(B) a failure to give an instruction, if that party properly requested it and--unless the court rejected the request in a definitive ruling on the record--also properly objected.

(2) *Plain Error.* A court may consider a plain error in the instructions that has not been preserved as required by Rule 51(d)(1) if the error affects substantial rights.

RULE 52. FINDINGS AND CONCLUSIONS BY THE COURT; JUDGMENT ON PARTIAL FINDINGS

(a) Findings and Conclusions.

(1) *In General.* In an action tried on the facts without a jury or with an advisory jury, the court must find the facts specially and state its conclusions of law separately. The findings and conclusions may be stated on the record after the close of the evidence or may appear in an opinion or a memorandum of decision filed by the court. Judgment must be entered under Rule 58.

(2) *For an Interlocutory Injunction.* In granting or refusing an interlocutory injunction, the court must similarly state the findings and conclusions that support its action.

(3) *For a Motion.* The court is not required to state findings or conclusions when ruling on a motion under Rule 12 or 56 or, unless these rules provide otherwise, on any other motion.

(4) *Effect of a Master's Findings.* A master's findings, to the extent adopted by the court, must be considered the court's findings.

(5) *Questioning the Evidentiary Support.* A party may later question the sufficiency of the evidence supporting the findings, whether or not the party requested findings, objected to them, moved to amend them,

or moved for partial findings.

(6) *Setting Aside the Findings.* Findings of fact, whether based on oral or other evidence, must not be set aside unless clearly erroneous, and the reviewing court must give due regard to the trial court's opportunity to judge the witnesses' credibility.

(b) Amended or Additional Findings. On a party's motion filed no later than 10 days after the entry of judgment, the court may amend its findings--or make additional findings--and may amend the judgment accordingly. The motion may accompany a motion for a new trial under Rule 59.

(c) Judgment on Partial Findings. If a party has been fully heard on an issue during a nonjury trial and the court finds against the party on that issue, the court may enter judgment against the party on a claim or defense that, under the controlling law, can be maintained or defeated only with a favorable finding on that issue. The court may, however, decline to render any judgment until the close of the evidence. A judgment on partial findings must be supported by findings of fact and conclusions of law as required by Rule 52(a).

RULE 53. MASTERS

(a) Appointment.

(1) *Scope.* Unless a statute provides otherwise, a court may appoint a master only to:

(A) perform duties consented to by the parties;

(B) hold trial proceedings and make or recommend findings of fact on issues to be decided without a jury if appointment is warranted by:

(i) some exceptional condition; or

(ii) the need to perform an accounting or resolve a difficult computation of damages; or

(C) address pretrial and posttrial matters that cannot be effectively and timely addressed by an available district judge or magistrate judge of the district.

(2) *Disqualification.* A master must not have a relationship to the parties, attorneys, action, or court that would require disqualification of a judge under 28 U.S.C. § 455, unless the parties, with the court's approval, consent to the appointment after the master discloses any potential grounds for disqualification.

(3) *Possible Expense or Delay.* In appointing a master, the court must consider the fairness of imposing the likely expenses on the parties and must protect against unreasonable expense or delay.

(b) Order Appointing a Master.

(1) *Notice.* Before appointing a master, the court must give the parties notice and an opportunity to be heard. Any party may suggest candidates for appointment.

(2) *Contents.* The appointing order must direct the master to proceed with all reasonable diligence and must state:

(A) the master's duties, including any investigation or enforcement duties, and any limits on the master's authority under Rule 53(c);

(B) the circumstances, if any, in which the master may communicate ex parte with the court or a party;

(C) the nature of the materials to be preserved and filed as the record of the master's activities;

(D) the time limits, method of filing the record, other procedures, and standards for reviewing the master's orders, findings, and recommendations; and

(E) the basis, terms, and procedure for fixing the master's compensation under Rule 53(g).

(3) *Issuing.* The court may issue the order only after:

(A) the master files an affidavit disclosing whether there is any ground for disqualification under 28 U.S.C. § 455; and

(B) if a ground is disclosed, the parties, with the court's approval, waive the disqualification.

(4) *Amending.* The order may be amended at any time after notice to the parties and an opportunity to be heard.

(c) Master's Authority.

(1) *In General.* Unless the appointing order directs otherwise, a master may:

(A) regulate all proceedings;

(B) take all appropriate measures to perform the assigned duties fairly and efficiently; and

(C) if conducting an evidentiary hearing, exercise the appointing court's power to compel, take, and record evidence.

(2) *Sanctions.* The master may by order impose on a party any noncontempt sanction provided by Rule 37 or 45, and may recommend a contempt sanction against a party and sanctions against a nonparty.

(d) Master's Orders. A master who issues an order must file it and promptly serve a copy on each party. The clerk must enter the order on the docket.

(e) Master's Reports. A master must report to the court as required by the appointing order. The master must file the report and promptly serve a copy on each party, unless the court orders otherwise.

(f) Action on the Master's Order, Report, or Recommendations.

(1) *Opportunity for a Hearing; Action in General.* In acting on a master's order, report, or recommendations, the court must give the parties notice and an opportunity to be heard; may receive evidence; and may adopt or affirm, modify, wholly or partly reject or reverse, or resubmit to the master with instructions.

(2) *Time to Object or Move to Adopt or Modify.* A party may file objections to--or a motion to adopt or modify--the master's order, report, or recommendations no later than 20 days after a copy is served, unless the court sets a different time.

(3) *Reviewing Factual Findings.* The court must decide de novo all objections to findings of fact made or recommended by a master, unless the parties, with the court's approval, stipulate that:

(A) the findings will be reviewed for clear error; or

(B) the findings of a master appointed under Rule 53(a)(1)(A) or (C) will be final.

(4) *Reviewing Legal Conclusions.* The court must decide de novo all objections to conclusions of law made or recommended by a master.

(5) *Reviewing Procedural Matters.* Unless the appointing order establishes a different standard of review, the court may set aside a master's ruling on a procedural matter only for an abuse of discretion.

(g) Compensation.

(1) *Fixing Compensation.* Before or after judgment, the court must fix the master's compensation on the basis and terms stated in the appointing order, but the court may set a new basis and terms after giving notice and an opportunity to be heard.

(2) *Payment.* The compensation must be paid either:

(A) by a party or parties; or

(B) from a fund or subject matter of the action within the court's control.

(3) *Allocating Payment.* The court must allocate payment among the parties after considering the nature and amount of the controversy, the parties' means, and the extent to which any party is more responsible than other parties for the reference to a master. An interim allocation may be amended to reflect a decision on the merits.

(h) Appointing a Magistrate Judge. A magistrate judge is subject to this rule only when the order referring a matter to the magistrate judge states that the reference is made under this rule.

RULE 54. JUDGMENTS; COSTS

(a) Definition; Form. "Judgment" as used in these rules includes a decree and any order from which an appeal lies. A judgment must not include recitals of pleadings, a master's report, or a record of prior proceedings.

(b) Judgment on Multiple Claims or Involving Multiple Parties. When an action presents more than one claim for relief--whether as a claim, counterclaim, crossclaim, or third-party claim--or when multiple parties are involved, the court may direct entry of a final judgment as to one or more, but fewer than all, claims or parties only if the court expressly determines that there is no just reason for delay. Otherwise, any order or other decision, however designated, that adjudicates fewer than all the claims or the rights and liabilities of fewer than all the parties does not end the action as to any of the claims or parties and may be revised at any time before the entry of a judgment adjudicating all the claims and all the parties' rights and liabilities.

(c) Demand for Judgment; Relief to Be Granted. A default judgment must not differ in kind from, or exceed in amount, what is demanded in the pleadings. Every other final judgment should grant the relief to which each party is entitled, even if the party has not demanded that relief in its pleadings.

(d) Costs; Attorney's Fees.

(1) *Costs Other Than Attorney's Fees.* Unless a federal statute, these rules, or a court order provides otherwise, costs--other than attorney's fees--should be allowed to the prevailing party. But costs against the United States, its officers, and its agencies may be imposed only to the extent allowed by law. The clerk may tax costs on 1 day's notice. On motion served within the next 5 days, the court may review the clerk's action.

(2) *Attorney's Fees.*

(A) Claim to Be by Motion. A claim for attorney's fees and related nontaxable expenses must be made by motion unless the substantive law requires those fees to be proved at trial as an element of damages.

(B) Timing and Contents of the Motion. Unless a statute or a court order provides otherwise, the motion must:

(i) be filed no later than 14 days after the entry of judgment;

(ii) specify the judgment and the statute, rule, or other grounds entitling the movant to the award;

(iii) state the amount sought or provide a fair estimate of it; and

(iv) disclose, if the court so orders, the terms of any agreement about fees for the services for which the claim is made.

(C) Proceedings. Subject to Rule 23(h), the court must, on a party's request, give an opportunity for adversary submissions on the motion in accordance with Rule 43(c) or 78. The court may decide issues of liability for fees before receiving submissions on the value of services. The court must find the facts and state its conclusions of law as provided in Rule 52(a).

(D) Special Procedures by Local Rule; Reference to a Master or a Magistrate Judge. By local rule, the court may establish special procedures to resolve fee-related issues without extensive evidentiary hearings. Also, the court may refer issues concerning the value of services to a special master under Rule 53 without regard to the limitations of Rule 53(a)(1), and may refer a motion for attorney's fees to a magistrate judge under Rule 72(b) as if it were a dispositive pretrial matter.

(E) Exceptions. Subparagraphs (A)-(D) do not apply to claims for fees and expenses as sanctions for violating these rules or as sanctions under 28 U.S.C. § 1927.

RULE 55. DEFAULT; DEFAULT JUDGMENT

(a) Entering a Default. When a party against whom a judgment for affirmative relief is sought has failed to plead or otherwise defend, and that failure is shown by affidavit or otherwise, the clerk must enter the party's default.

(b) Entering a Default Judgment.

(1) *By the Clerk.* If the plaintiff's claim is for a sum certain or a sum that can be made certain by computation, the clerk--on the plaintiff's request, with an affidavit showing the amount due--must enter judgment for that amount and costs against a defendant who has been defaulted for not appearing and who is neither a minor nor an incompetent person.

(2) *By the Court.* In all other cases, the party must apply for a default judgment. A default judgment may be entered against a minor or incompetent person only if represented by a general guardian, conservator, or other like fiduciary who has appeared. If the party against whom a default judgment is sought has appeared personally or by a representative, that party or its representative must be served with written notice of the application at least 3 days before the hearing. The court may conduct hearings or make referrals--preserving any federal statutory right to a jury trial--when, to enter or effectuate judgment, it needs to:

(A) conduct an accounting;

(B) determine the amount of damages;

(C) establish the truth of any allegation by evidence; or

(D) investigate any other matter.

(c) Setting Aside a Default or a Default Judgment. The court may set aside an entry of default for good cause, and it may set aside a default judgment under Rule 60(b).

(d) Judgment Against the United States. A default judgment may be entered against the United States, its officers, or its agencies only if the claimant establishes a claim or right to relief by evidence that satisfies the court.

RULE 56. SUMMARY JUDGMENT

(a) By a Claiming Party. A party claiming relief may move, with or without supporting affidavits, for summary judgment on all or part of the claim. The motion may be filed at any time after:

(1) 20 days have passed from commencement of the action; or

(2) the opposing party serves a motion for summary judgment.

(b) By a Defending Party. A party against whom relief is sought may move at any time, with or without supporting affidavits, for summary judgment on all or part of the claim.

(c) Serving the Motion; Proceedings. The motion must be served at least 10 days before the day set for the hearing. An opposing party may serve opposing affidavits before the hearing day. The judgment sought should be rendered if the pleadings, the discovery and disclosure materials on file, and any affidavits show that there is no genuine issue as to any material fact and that the movant is entitled to judgment as a matter of law.

(d) Case Not Fully Adjudicated on the Motion.

(1) *Establishing Facts.* If summary judgment is not rendered on the whole action, the court should, to the extent practicable, determine what material facts are not genuinely at issue. The court should so determine by examining the pleadings and evidence before it and by interrogating the attorneys. It should then issue an order specifying what facts--including items of damages or other relief--are not genuinely at issue. The facts so specified must be treated as established in the action.

(2) *Establishing Liability.* An interlocutory summary judgment may be rendered on liability alone, even if there is a genuine issue on the amount of damages.

(e) Affidavits; Further Testimony.

(1) *In General.* A supporting or opposing affidavit must be made on personal knowledge, set out facts that would be admissible in evidence, and show that the affiant is competent to testify on the matters stated. If a

paper or part of a paper is referred to in an affidavit, a sworn or certified copy must be attached to or served with the affidavit. The court may permit an affidavit to be supplemented or opposed by depositions, answers to interrogatories, or additional affidavits.

(2) *Opposing Party's Obligation to Respond.* When a motion for summary judgment is properly made and supported, an opposing party may not rely merely on allegations or denials in its own pleading; rather, its response must--by affidavits or as otherwise provided in this rule--set out specific facts showing a genuine issue for trial. If the opposing party does not so respond, summary judgment should, if appropriate, be entered against that party.

(f) When Affidavits Are Unavailable. If a party opposing the motion shows by affidavit that, for specified reasons, it cannot present facts essential to justify its opposition, the court may:

(1) deny the motion;

(2) order a continuance to enable affidavits to be obtained, depositions to be taken, or other discovery to be undertaken; or

(3) issue any other just order.

(g) Affidavit Submitted in Bad Faith. If satisfied that an affidavit under this rule is submitted in bad faith or solely for delay, the court must order the submitting party to pay the other party the reasonable expenses, including attorney's fees, it incurred as a result. An offending party or attorney may also be held in contempt.

RULE 57. DECLARATORY JUDGMENT

These rules govern the procedure for obtaining a declaratory judgment under 28 U.S.C. § 2201. Rules 38 and 39 govern a demand for a jury trial. The existence of another adequate remedy does not preclude a declaratory judgment that is otherwise appropriate. The court may order a speedy hearing of a declaratory-judgment action.

RULE 58. ENTERING JUDGMENT

(a) Separate Document. Every judgment and amended judgment must be set out in a separate document, but a separate document is not required for an order disposing of a motion:

(1) for judgment under Rule 50(b);

(2) to amend or make additional findings of fact under Rule 52(b);

(3) for attorney's fees under Rule 54;

(4) for a new trial, or to alter or amend the judgment, under Rule 59; or

(5) for relief under Rule 60.

(b) Entering Judgment.

(1) *Without the Court's Direction.* Subject to Rule 54(b) and unless the court orders otherwise, the clerk must, without awaiting the court's direction, promptly prepare, sign, and enter the judgment when:

(A) the jury returns a general verdict;

(B) the court awards only costs or a sum certain; or

(C) the court denies all relief.

(2) *Court's Approval Required.* Subject to Rule 54(b), the court must promptly approve the form of the judgment, which the clerk must promptly enter, when:

(A) the jury returns a special verdict or a general verdict with answers to written questions; or

(B) the court grants other relief not described in this subdivision (b).

(c) Time of Entry. For purposes of these rules, judgment is entered at the following times:

(1) if a separate document is not required, when the judgment is entered in the civil docket under Rule

79(a); or

    (2) if a separate document is required, when the judgment is entered in the civil docket under Rule 79(a) and the earlier of these events occurs:

      (A) it is set out in a separate document; or

      (B) 150 days have run from the entry in the civil docket.

 (d) Request for Entry. A party may request that judgment be set out in a separate document as required by Rule 58(a).

 (e) Cost or Fee Awards. Ordinarily, the entry of judgment may not be delayed, nor the time for appeal extended, in order to tax costs or award fees. But if a timely motion for attorney's fees is made under Rule 54(d)(2), the court may act before a notice of appeal has been filed and become effective to order that the motion have the same effect under Federal Rule of Appellate Procedure 4(a)(4) as a timely motion under Rule 59.

RULE 59. NEW TRIAL; ALTERING OR AMENDING A JUDGMENT

(a) In General.

    (1) *Grounds for New Trial.* The court may, on motion, grant a new trial on all or some of the issues--and to any party--as follows:

      (A) after a jury trial, for any reason for which a new trial has heretofore been granted in an action at law in federal court; or

      (B) after a nonjury trial, for any reason for which a rehearing has heretofore been granted in a suit in equity in federal court.

    (2) *Further Action After a Nonjury Trial.* After a nonjury trial, the court may, on motion for a new trial, open the judgment if one has been entered, take additional testimony, amend findings of fact and conclusions of law or make new ones, and direct the entry of a new judgment.

 (b) Time to File a Motion for a New Trial. A motion for a new trial must be filed no later than 10 days after the entry of judgment.

 (c) Time to Serve Affidavits. When a motion for a new trial is based on affidavits, they must be filed with the motion. The opposing party has 10 days after being served to file opposing affidavits; but that period may be extended for up to 20 days, either by the court for good cause or by the parties' stipulation. The court may permit reply affidavits.

 (d) New Trial on the Court's Initiative or for Reasons Not in the Motion. No later than 10 days after the entry of judgment, the court, on its own, may order a new trial for any reason that would justify granting one on a party's motion. After giving the parties notice and an opportunity to be heard, the court may grant a timely motion for a new trial for a reason not stated in the motion. In either event, the court must specify the reasons in its order.

 (e) Motion to Alter or Amend a Judgment. A motion to alter or amend a judgment must be filed no later than 10 days after the entry of the judgment.

RULE 60. RELIEF FROM A JUDGMENT OR ORDER

(a) Corrections Based on Clerical Mistakes; Oversights and Omissions. The court may correct a clerical mistake or a mistake arising from oversight or omission whenever one is found in a judgment, order, or other part of the record. The court may do so on motion or on its own, with or without notice. But after an appeal has been docketed in the appellate court and while it is pending, such a mistake may be corrected only with the appellate court's leave.

(b) Grounds for Relief from a Final Judgment, Order, or Proceeding. On motion and just terms, the court may relieve a party or its legal representative from a final judgment, order, or proceeding for the following reasons:

(1) mistake, inadvertence, surprise, or excusable neglect;

(2) newly discovered evidence that, with reasonable diligence, could not have been discovered in time to move for a new trial under Rule 59(b);

(3) fraud (whether previously called intrinsic or extrinsic), misrepresentation, or misconduct by an opposing party;

(4) the judgment is void;

(5) the judgment has been satisfied, released, or discharged; it is based on an earlier judgment that has been reversed or vacated; or applying it prospectively is no longer equitable; or

(6) any other reason that justifies relief.

(c) Timing and Effect of the Motion.

(1) *Timing*. A motion under Rule 60(b) must be made within a reasonable time--and for reasons (1), (2), and (3) no more than a year after the entry of the judgment or order or the date of the proceeding.

(2) *Effect on Finality*. The motion does not affect the judgment's finality or suspend its operation.

(d) Other Powers to Grant Relief. This rule does not limit a court's power to:

(1) entertain an independent action to relieve a party from a judgment, order, or proceeding;

(2) grant relief under 28 U.S.C. § 1655 to a defendant who was not personally notified of the action; or

(3) set aside a judgment for fraud on the court.

(e) Bills and Writs Abolished. The following are abolished: bills of review, bills in the nature of bills of review, and writs of coram nobis, coram vobis, and audita querela.

RULE 61. HARMLESS ERROR

Unless justice requires otherwise, no error in admitting or excluding evidence--or any other error by the court or a party--is ground for granting a new trial, for setting aside a verdict, or for vacating, modifying, or otherwise disturbing a judgment or order. At every stage of the proceeding, the court must disregard all errors and defects that do not affect any party's substantial rights.

RULE 62. STAY OF PROCEEDINGS TO ENFORCE A JUDGMENT

(a) Automatic Stay; Exceptions for Injunctions, Receiverships, and Patent Accountings. Except as stated in this rule, no execution may issue on a judgment, nor may proceedings be taken to enforce it, until 10 days have passed after its entry. But unless the court orders otherwise, the following are not stayed after being entered, even if an appeal is taken:

(1) an interlocutory or final judgment in an action for an injunction or a receivership; or

(2) a judgment or order that directs an accounting in an action for patent infringement.

(b) Stay Pending the Disposition of a Motion. On appropriate terms for the opposing party's security, the court may stay the execution of a judgment--or any proceedings to enforce it--pending disposition of any of the following motions:

(1) under Rule 50, for judgment as a matter of law;

(2) under Rule 52(b), to amend the findings or for additional findings;

(3) under Rule 59, for a new trial or to alter or amend a judgment; or

(4) under Rule 60, for relief from a judgment or order.

(c) Injunction Pending an Appeal. While an appeal is pending from an interlocutory order or final judgment that grants, dissolves, or denies an injunction, the court may suspend, modify, restore, or grant an injunction on terms for bond or other terms that secure the opposing party's rights. If the judgment appealed from is rendered by a statutory three-judge district court, the order must be made either:

   (1) by that court sitting in open session; or

   (2) by the assent of all its judges, as evidenced by their signatures.

(d) Stay with Bond on Appeal. If an appeal is taken, the appellant may obtain a stay by supersedeas bond, except in an action described in Rule 62(a)(1) or (2). The bond may be given upon or after filing the notice of appeal or after obtaining the order allowing the appeal. The stay takes effect when the court approves the bond.

(e) Stay Without Bond on an Appeal by the United States, Its Officers, or Its Agencies. The court must not require a bond, obligation, or other security from the appellant when granting a stay on an appeal by the United States, its officers, or its agencies or on an appeal directed by a department of the federal government.

(f) Stay in Favor of a Judgment Debtor Under State Law. If a judgment is a lien on the judgment debtor's property under the law of the state where the court is located, the judgment debtor is entitled to the same stay of execution the state court would give.

(g) Appellate Court's Power Not Limited. This rule does not limit the power of the appellate court or one of its judges or justices:

   (1) to stay proceedings--or suspend, modify, restore, or grant an injunction--while an appeal is pending; or

   (2) to issue an order to preserve the status quo or the effectiveness of the judgment to be entered.

(h) Stay with Multiple Claims or Parties. A court may stay the enforcement of a final judgment entered under Rule 54(b) until it enters a later judgment or judgments, and may prescribe terms necessary to secure the benefit of the stayed judgment for the party in whose favor it was entered.

RULE 63. JUDGE'S INABILITY TO PROCEED

If a judge conducting a hearing or trial is unable to proceed, any other judge may proceed upon certifying familiarity with the record and determining that the case may be completed without prejudice to the parties. In a hearing or a nonjury trial, the successor judge must, at a party's request, recall any witness whose testimony is material and disputed and who is available to testify again without undue burden. The successor judge may also recall any other witness.

RULE 64. SEIZING A PERSON OR PROPERTY

(a) Remedies Under State Law--In General. At the commencement of and throughout an action, every remedy is available that, under the law of the state where the court is located, provides for seizing a person or property to secure satisfaction of the potential judgment. But a federal statute governs to the extent it applies.

(b) Specific Kinds of Remedies. The remedies available under this rule include the following--however designated and regardless of whether state procedure requires an independent action:

- arrest;
- attachment;
- garnishment;
- replevin;
- sequestration; and
- other corresponding or equivalent remedies.

RULE 65.   INJUNCTIONS AND RESTRAINING ORDERS

(a) Preliminary Injunction.

(1) *Notice.* The court may issue a preliminary injunction only on notice to the adverse party.

(2) *Consolidating the Hearing with the Trial on the Merits.* Before or after beginning a hearing on a motion for a preliminary injunction, the court may advance the trial on the merits and consolidate it with the hearing. Even when consolidation is not ordered, evidence that is received on the motion and that would be admissible at trial becomes part of the trial record and need not be repeated at trial. But the court must preserve any party's right to a jury trial.

(b) Temporary Restraining Order.

(1) *Issuing Without Notice.* The court may issue a temporary restraining order without written or oral notice to the adverse party or its attorney only if:

(A) specific facts in an affidavit or a verified complaint clearly show that immediate and irreparable injury, loss, or damage will result to the movant before the adverse party can be heard in opposition; and

(B) the movant's attorney certifies in writing any efforts made to give notice and the reasons why it should not be required.

(2) *Contents; Expiration.* Every temporary restraining order issued without notice must state the date and hour it was issued; describe the injury and state why it is irreparable; state why the order was issued without notice; and be promptly filed in the clerk's office and entered in the record. The order expires at the time after entry--not to exceed 10 days--that the court sets, unless before that time the court, for good cause, extends it for a like period or the adverse party consents to a longer extension. The reasons for an extension must be entered in the record.

(3) *Expediting the Preliminary-Injunction Hearing.* If the order is issued without notice, the motion for a preliminary injunction must be set for hearing at the earliest possible time, taking precedence over all other matters except hearings on older matters of the same character. At the hearing, the party who obtained the order must proceed with the motion; if the party does not, the court must dissolve the order.

(4) *Motion to Dissolve.* On 2 days' notice to the party who obtained the order without notice--or on shorter notice set by the court--the adverse party may appear and move to dissolve or modify the order. The court must then hear and decide the motion as promptly as justice requires.

(c) Security. The court may issue a preliminary injunction or a temporary restraining order only if the movant gives security in an amount that the court considers proper to pay the costs and damages sustained by any party found to have been wrongfully enjoined or restrained. The United States, its officers, and its agencies are not required to give security.

(d) Contents and Scope of Every Injunction and Restraining Order.

(1) *Contents.* Every order granting an injunction and every restraining order must:

(A) state the reasons why it issued;

(B) state its terms specifically; and

(C) describe in reasonable detail--and not by referring to the complaint or other document--the act or acts restrained or required.

(2) *Persons Bound.* The order binds only the following who receive actual notice of it by personal service or otherwise:

(A) the parties;

(B) the parties' officers, agents, servants, employees, and attorneys; and

(C) other persons who are in active concert or participation with anyone described in Rule 65(d)(2)(A) or (B).

(e) Other Laws Not Modified. These rules do not modify the following:

(1) any federal statute relating to temporary restraining orders or preliminary injunctions in actions affecting employer and employee;

(2) 28 U.S.C. § 2361, which relates to preliminary injunctions in actions of interpleader or in the nature of interpleader; or

(3) 28 U.S.C. § 2284, which relates to actions that must be heard and decided by a three-judge district court.

(f) Copyright Impoundment. This rule applies to copyright-impoundment proceedings.

RULE 66. RECEIVERS

These rules govern an action in which the appointment of a receiver is sought or a receiver sues or is sued. But the practice in administering an estate by a receiver or a similar court-appointed officer must accord with the historical practice in federal courts or with a local rule. An action in which a receiver has been appointed may be dismissed only by court order.

RULE 67. DEPOSIT INTO COURT

(a) Depositing Property. If any part of the relief sought is a money judgment or the disposition of a sum of money or some other deliverable thing, a party--on notice to every other party and by leave of court--may deposit with the court all or part of the money or thing, whether or not that party claims any of it. The depositing party must deliver to the clerk a copy of the order permitting deposit.

(b) Investing and Withdrawing Funds. Money paid into court under this rule must be deposited and withdrawn in accordance with 28 U.S.C. §§ 2041 and 2042 and any like statute. The money must be deposited in an interest-bearing account or invested in a court-approved, interest-bearing instrument.

RULE 68. OFFER OF JUDGMENT

(a) Making an Offer; Judgment on an Accepted Offer. More than 10 days before the trial begins, a party defending against a claim may serve on an opposing party an offer to allow judgment on specified terms, with the costs then accrued. If, within 10 days after being served, the opposing party serves written notice accepting the offer, either party may then file the offer and notice of acceptance, plus proof of service. The clerk must then enter judgment.

(b) Unaccepted Offer. An unaccepted offer is considered withdrawn, but it does not preclude a later offer. Evidence of an unaccepted offer is not admissible except in a proceeding to determine costs.

(c) Offer After Liability Is Determined. When one party's liability to another has been determined but the extent of liability remains to be determined by further proceedings, the party held liable may make an offer of judgment. It must be served within a reasonable time--but at least 10 days--before a hearing to determine the extent of liability.

(d) Paying Costs After an Unaccepted Offer. If the judgment that the offeree finally obtains is not more favorable than the unaccepted offer, the offeree must pay the costs incurred after the offer was made.

RULE 69. EXECUTION

(a) In General.

(1) *Money Judgment; Applicable Procedure.* A money judgment is enforced by a writ of execution, unless the court directs otherwise. The procedure on execution--and in proceedings supplementary to and in aid of judgment or execution--must accord with the procedure of the state where the court is located, but a federal statute governs to the extent it applies.

(2) *Obtaining Discovery.* In aid of the judgment or execution, the judgment creditor or a successor in interest whose interest appears of record may obtain discovery from any person--including the judgment debtor--as provided in these rules or by the procedure of the state where the court is located.

(b) Against Certain Public Officers. When a judgment has been entered against a revenue officer in the circumstances stated in 28 U.S.C. § 2006, or against an officer of Congress in the circumstances stated in 2 U.S.C. § 118, the judgment must be satisfied as those statutes provide.

RULE 70. ENFORCING A JUDGMENT FOR A SPECIFIC ACT

(a) Party's Failure to Act; Ordering Another to Act. If a judgment requires a party to convey land, to deliver a deed or other document, or to perform any other specific act and the party fails to comply within the time specified, the court may order the act to be done--at the disobedient party's expense--by another person appointed by the court. When done, the act has the same effect as if done by the party.

(b) Vesting Title. If the real or personal property is within the district, the court--instead of ordering a conveyance--may enter a judgment divesting any party's title and vesting it in others. That judgment has the effect of a legally executed conveyance.

(c) Obtaining a Writ of Attachment or Sequestration. On application by a party entitled to performance of an act, the clerk must issue a writ of attachment or sequestration against the disobedient party's property to compel obedience.

(d) Obtaining a Writ of Execution or Assistance. On application by a party who obtains a judgment or order for possession, the clerk must issue a writ of execution or assistance.

(e) Holding in Contempt. The court may also hold the disobedient party in contempt.

RULE 71. ENFORCING RELIEF FOR OR AGAINST A NONPARTY

When an order grants relief for a nonparty or may be enforced against a nonparty, the procedure for enforcing the order is the same as for a party.

RULE 71.1. CONDEMNING REAL OR PERSONAL PROPERTY

(a) Applicability of Other Rules. These rules govern proceedings to condemn real and personal property by eminent domain, except as this rule provides otherwise.

(b) Joinder of Properties. The plaintiff may join separate pieces of property in a single action, no matter whether they are owned by the same persons or sought for the same use.

(c) Complaint.

(1) *Caption.* The complaint must contain a caption as provided in Rule 10(a). The plaintiff must, however, name as defendants both the property--designated generally by kind, quantity, and location--and at least one owner of some part of or interest in the property.

(2) *Contents.* The complaint must contain a short and plain statement of the following:

(A) the authority for the taking;

(B) the uses for which the property is to be taken;

(C) a description sufficient to identify the property;

(D) the interests to be acquired; and

(E) for each piece of property, a designation of each defendant who has been joined as an owner or owner of an interest in it.

(3) *Parties.* When the action commences, the plaintiff need join as defendants only those persons who have or claim an interest in the property and whose names are then known. But before any hearing on

compensation, the plaintiff must add as defendants all those persons who have or claim an interest and whose names have become known or can be found by a reasonably diligent search of the records, considering both the property's character and value and the interests to be acquired. All others may be made defendants under the designation "Unknown Owners."

(4) *Procedure.* Notice must be served on all defendants as provided in Rule 71.1(d), whether they were named as defendants when the action commenced or were added later. A defendant may answer as provided in Rule 71.1(e). The court, meanwhile, may order any distribution of a deposit that the facts warrant.

(5) *Filing; Additional Copies.* In addition to filing the complaint, the plaintiff must give the clerk at least one copy for the defendants' use and additional copies at the request of the clerk or a defendant.

(d) Process.

(1) *Delivering Notice to the Clerk.* On filing a complaint, the plaintiff must promptly deliver to the clerk joint or several notices directed to the named defendants. When adding defendants, the plaintiff must deliver to the clerk additional notices directed to the new defendants.

(2) *Contents of the Notice.*

(A) Main Contents. Each notice must name the court, the title of the action, and the defendant to whom it is directed. It must describe the property sufficiently to identify it, but need not describe any property other than that to be taken from the named defendant. The notice must also state:

(i) that the action is to condemn property;

(ii) the interest to be taken;

(iii) the authority for the taking;

(iv) the uses for which the property is to be taken;

(v) that the defendant may serve an answer on the plaintiff's attorney within 20 days after being served with the notice;

(vi) that the failure to so serve an answer constitutes consent to the taking and to the court's authority to proceed with the action and fix the compensation; and

(vii) that a defendant who does not serve an answer may file a notice of appearance.

(B) Conclusion. The notice must conclude with the name, telephone number, and e-mail address of the plaintiff's attorney and an address within the district in which the action is brought where the attorney may be served.

(3) *Serving the Notice.*

(A) Personal Service. When a defendant whose address is known resides within the United States or a territory subject to the administrative or judicial jurisdiction of the United States, personal service of the notice (without a copy of the complaint) must be made in accordance with Rule 4.

(B) Service by Publication.

(i) A defendant may be served by publication only when the plaintiff's attorney files a certificate stating that the attorney believes the defendant cannot be personally served, because after diligent inquiry within the state where the complaint is filed, the defendant's place of residence is still unknown or, if known, that it is beyond the territorial limits of personal service. Service is then made by publishing the notice--once a week for at least three successive weeks--in a newspaper published in the county where the property is located or, if there is no such newspaper, in a newspaper with general circulation where the property is located. Before the last publication, a copy of the notice must also be mailed to every defendant who cannot be personally served but whose place of residence is then known. Unknown owners may be served by publication in the same manner by a notice addressed to "Unknown Owners."

(ii) Service by publication is complete on the date of the last publication. The plaintiff's attorney must prove publication and mailing by a certificate, attach a printed copy of the published notice, and mark on the copy the newspaper's name and the dates of publication.

(4) *Effect of Delivery and Service.* Delivering the notice to the clerk and serving it have the same effect as serving a summons under Rule 4.

(5) *Proof of Service; Amending the Proof or Notice.* Rule 4(l) governs proof of service. The court may permit the proof or the notice to be amended.

(e) Appearance or Answer.

(1) *Notice of Appearance.* A defendant that has no objection or defense to the taking of its property may serve a notice of appearance designating the property in which it claims an interest. The defendant must then be given notice of all later proceedings affecting the defendant.

(2) *Answer.* A defendant that has an objection or defense to the taking must serve an answer within 20 days after being served with the notice. The answer must:

   (A) identify the property in which the defendant claims an interest;

   (B) state the nature and extent of the interest; and

   (C) state all the defendant's objections and defenses to the taking.

(3) *Waiver of Other Objections and Defenses; Evidence on Compensation.* A defendant waives all objections and defenses not stated in its answer. No other pleading or motion asserting an additional objection or defense is allowed. But at the trial on compensation, a defendant--whether or not it has previously appeared or answered--may present evidence on the amount of compensation to be paid and may share in the award.

(f) Amending Pleadings. Without leave of court, the plaintiff may--as often as it wants--amend the complaint at any time before the trial on compensation. But no amendment may be made if it would result in a dismissal inconsistent with Rule 71.1(i)(1) or (2). The plaintiff need not serve a copy of an amendment, but must serve notice of the filing, as provided in Rule 5(b), on every affected party who has appeared and, as provided in Rule 71.1(d), on every affected party who has not appeared. In addition, the plaintiff must give the clerk at least one copy of each amendment for the defendants' use, and additional copies at the request of the clerk or a defendant. A defendant may appear or answer in the time and manner and with the same effect as provided in Rule 71.1(e).

(g) Substituting Parties. If a defendant dies, becomes incompetent, or transfers an interest after being joined, the court may, on motion and notice of hearing, order that the proper party be substituted. Service of the motion and notice on a nonparty must be made as provided in Rule 71.1(d)(3).

(h) Trial of the Issues.

(1) *Issues Other Than Compensation; Compensation.* In an action involving eminent domain under federal law, the court tries all issues, including compensation, except when compensation must be determined:

   (A) by any tribunal specially constituted by a federal statute to determine compensation; or

   (B) if there is no such tribunal, by a jury when a party demands one within the time to answer or within any additional time the court sets, unless the court appoints a commission.

(2) *Appointing a Commission; Commission's Powers and Report.*

   (A) Reasons for Appointing. If a party has demanded a jury, the court may instead appoint a three-person commission to determine compensation because of the character, location, or quantity of the property to be condemned or for other just reasons.

   (B) Alternate Commissioners. The court may appoint up to two additional persons to serve as alternate commissioners to hear the case and replace commissioners who, before a decision is filed, the court finds unable or disqualified to perform their duties. Once the commission renders its final decision, the court must discharge any alternate who has not replaced a commissioner.

   (C) Examining the Prospective Commissioners. Before making its appointments, the court must advise the parties of the identity and qualifications of each prospective commissioner and alternate, and may permit the parties to examine them. The parties may not suggest appointees, but for good cause may object to a prospective commissioner or alternate.

(D) Commission's Powers and Report. A commission has the powers of a master under Rule 53(c). Its action and report are determined by a majority. Rule 53(d), (e), and (f) apply to its action and report.

(i) Dismissal of the Action or a Defendant.

(1) *Dismissing the Action.*

(A) By the Plaintiff. If no compensation hearing on a piece of property has begun, and if the plaintiff has not acquired title or a lesser interest or taken possession, the plaintiff may, without a court order, dismiss the action as to that property by filing a notice of dismissal briefly describing the property.

(B) By Stipulation. Before a judgment is entered vesting the plaintiff with title or a lesser interest in or possession of property, the plaintiff and affected defendants may, without a court order, dismiss the action in whole or in part by filing a stipulation of dismissal. And if the parties so stipulate, the court may vacate a judgment already entered.

(C) By Court Order. At any time before compensation has been determined and paid, the court may, after a motion and hearing, dismiss the action as to a piece of property. But if the plaintiff has already taken title, a lesser interest, or possession as to any part of it, the court must award compensation for the title, lesser interest, or possession taken.

(2) *Dismissing a Defendant.* The court may at any time dismiss a defendant who was unnecessarily or improperly joined.

(3) *Effect.* A dismissal is without prejudice unless otherwise stated in the notice, stipulation, or court order.

(j) Deposit and Its Distribution.

(1) *Deposit.* The plaintiff must deposit with the court any money required by law as a condition to the exercise of eminent domain and may make a deposit when allowed by statute.

(2) *Distribution; Adjusting Distribution.* After a deposit, the court and attorneys must expedite the proceedings so as to distribute the deposit and to determine and pay compensation. If the compensation finally awarded to a defendant exceeds the amount distributed to that defendant, the court must enter judgment against the plaintiff for the deficiency. If the compensation awarded to a defendant is less than the amount distributed to that defendant, the court must enter judgment against that defendant for the overpayment.

(k) Condemnation Under a State's Power of Eminent Domain. This rule governs an action involving eminent domain under state law. But if state law provides for trying an issue by jury--or for trying the issue of compensation by jury or commission or both--that law governs.

(l) Costs. Costs are not subject to Rule 54(d).

RULE 72. MAGISTRATE JUDGES: PRETRIAL ORDER

(a) Nondispositive Matters. When a pretrial matter not dispositive of a party's claim or defense is referred to a magistrate judge to hear and decide, the magistrate judge must promptly conduct the required proceedings and, when appropriate, issue a written order stating the decision. A party may serve and file objections to the order within 10 days after being served with a copy. A party may not assign as error a defect in the order not timely objected to. The district judge in the case must consider timely objections and modify or set aside any part of the order that is clearly erroneous or is contrary to law.

(b) Dispositive Motions and Prisoner Petitions.

(1) *Findings and Recommendations.* A magistrate judge must promptly conduct the required proceedings

when assigned, without the parties' consent, to hear a pretrial matter dispositive of a claim or defense or a prisoner petition challenging the conditions of confinement. A record must be made of all evidentiary proceedings and may, at the magistrate judge's discretion, be made of any other proceedings. The magistrate judge must enter a recommended disposition, including, if appropriate, proposed findings of fact. The clerk must promptly mail a copy to each party.

(2) *Objections.* Within 10 days after being served with a copy of the recommended disposition, a party may serve and file specific written objections to the proposed findings and recommendations. A party may respond to another party's objections within 10 days after being served with a copy. Unless the district judge orders otherwise, the objecting party must promptly arrange for transcribing the record, or whatever portions of it the parties agree to or the magistrate judge considers sufficient.

(3) *Resolving Objections.* The district judge must determine de novo any part of the magistrate judge's disposition that has been properly objected to. The district judge may accept, reject, or modify the recommended disposition; receive further evidence; or return the matter to the magistrate judge with instructions.

RULE 73. MAGISTRATE JUDGES: TRIAL BY CONSENT; APPEAL

(a) Trial by Consent. When authorized under 28 U.S.C. § 636(c), a magistrate judge may, if all parties consent, conduct a civil action or proceeding, including a jury or nonjury trial. A record must be made in accordance with 28 U.S.C. § 636(c)(5).

(b) Consent Procedure.

(1) *In General.* When a magistrate judge has been designated to conduct civil actions or proceedings, the clerk must give the parties written notice of their opportunity to consent under 28 U.S.C. § 636(c). To signify their consent, the parties must jointly or separately file a statement consenting to the referral. A district judge or magistrate judge may be informed of a party's response to the clerk's notice only if all parties have consented to the referral.

(2) *Reminding the Parties About Consenting.* A district judge, magistrate judge, or other court official may remind the parties of the magistrate judge's availability, but must also advise them that they are free to withhold consent without adverse substantive consequences.

(3) *Vacating a Referral.* On its own for good cause--or when a party shows extraordinary circumstances-- the district judge may vacate a referral to a magistrate judge under this rule.

(c) Appealing a Judgment. In accordance with 28 U.S.C. § 636(c)(3), an appeal from a judgment entered at a magistrate judge's direction may be taken to the court of appeals as would any other appeal from a district-court judgment.

RULE 77. CONDUCTING BUSINESS; CLERK'S AUTHORITY; NOTICE OF AN ORDER OR JUDGMENT

(a) When Court Is Open. Every district court is considered always open for filing any paper, issuing and returning process, making a motion, or entering an order.

(b) Place for Trial and Other Proceedings. Every trial on the merits must be conducted in open court and, so far as convenient, in a regular courtroom. Any other act or proceeding may be done or conducted by a judge in chambers, without the attendance of the clerk or other court official, and anywhere inside or outside the district. But no hearing--other than one ex parte--may be conducted outside the district unless all the affected parties consent.

(c) Clerk's Office Hours; Clerk's Orders.

(1) *Hours.* The clerk's office--with a clerk or deputy on duty--must be open during business hours every day

except Saturdays, Sundays, and legal holidays. But a court may, by local rule or order, require that the office be open for specified hours on Saturday or a particular legal holiday other than one listed in Rule 6(a)(4)(A).

(2) *Orders.* Subject to the court's power to suspend, alter, or rescind the clerk's action for good cause, the clerk may:

(A) issue process;

(B) enter a default;

(C) enter a default judgment under Rule 55(b)(1); and

(D) act on any other matter that does not require the court's action.

(d) Serving Notice of an Order or Judgment.

(1) *Service.* Immediately after entering an order or judgment, the clerk must serve notice of the entry, as provided in Rule 5(b), on each party who is not in default for failing to appear. The clerk must record the service on the docket. A party also may serve notice of the entry as provided in Rule 5(b).

(2) *Time to Appeal Not Affected by Lack of Notice.* Lack of notice of the entry does not affect the time for appeal or relieve--or authorize the court to relieve--a party for failing to appeal within the time allowed, except as allowed by Federal Rule of Appellate Procedure (4)(a).

RULE 78. HEARING MOTIONS; SUBMISSION ON BRIEFS

(a) Providing a Regular Schedule for Oral Hearings. A court may establish regular times and places for oral hearings on motions.

(b) Providing for Submission on Briefs. By rule or order, the court may provide for submitting and determining motions on briefs, without oral hearings.

RULE 79. RECORDS KEPT BY THE CLERK

(a) Civil Docket.

(1) *In General.* The clerk must keep a record known as the "civil docket" in the form and manner prescribed by the Director of the Administrative Office of the United States Courts with the approval of the Judicial Conference of the United States. The clerk must enter each civil action in the docket. Actions must be assigned consecutive file numbers, which must be noted in the docket where the first entry of the action is made.

(2) *Items to be Entered.* The following items must be marked with the file number and entered chronologically in the docket:

(A) papers filed with the clerk;

(B) process issued, and proofs of service or other returns showing execution; and

(C) appearances, orders, verdicts, and judgments.

(3) *Contents of Entries; Jury Trial Demanded.* Each entry must briefly show the nature of the paper filed or writ issued, the substance of each proof of service or other return, and the substance and date of entry of each order and judgment. When a jury trial has been properly demanded or ordered, the clerk must enter the word "jury" in the docket.

(b) Civil Judgments and Orders. The clerk must keep a copy of every final judgment and appealable order; of every order affecting title to or a lien on real or personal property; and of any other order that the court directs to be kept. The clerk must keep these in the form and manner prescribed by the Director of the Administrative Office of the United States Courts with the approval of the Judicial Conference of the United States.

(c) Indexes; Calendars. Under the court's direction, the clerk must:

(1) keep indexes of the docket and of the judgments and orders described in Rule 79(b); and

(2) prepare calendars of all actions ready for trial, distinguishing jury trials from nonjury trials.

(d) Other Records. The clerk must keep any other records required by the Director of the Administrative Office of the United States Courts with the approval of the Judicial Conference of the United States.

RULE 80. STENOGRAPHIC TRANSCRIPT AS EVIDENCE

If stenographically reported testimony at a hearing or trial is admissible in evidence at a later trial, the testimony may be proved by a transcript certified by the person who recorded it.

RULE 81. APPLICABILITY OF THE RULES IN GENERAL; REMOVED ACTIONS

(a) Applicability to Particular Proceedings.

(1) *Prize Proceedings.* These rules do not apply to prize proceedings in admiralty governed by 10 U.S.C. §§ 7651-7681.

(2) *Bankruptcy.* These rules apply to bankruptcy proceedings to the extent provided by the Federal Rules of Bankruptcy Procedure.

(3) *Citizenship.* These rules apply to proceedings for admission to citizenship to the extent that the practice in those proceedings is not specified in federal statutes and has previously conformed to the practice in civil actions. The provisions of 8 U.S.C. § 1451 for service by publication and for answer apply in proceedings to cancel citizenship certificates.

(4) *Special Writs.* These rules apply to proceedings for habeas corpus and for quo warranto to the extent that the practice in those proceedings:

(A) is not specified in a federal statute, the Rules Governing Section 2254 Cases, or the Rules Governing Section 2255 Cases; and

(B) has previously conformed to the practice in civil actions.

(5) *Proceedings Involving a Subpoena.* These rules apply to proceedings to compel testimony or the production of documents through a subpoena issued by a United States officer or agency under a federal statute, except as otherwise provided by statute, by local rule, or by court order in the proceedings.

(6) *Other Proceedings.* These rules, to the extent applicable, govern proceedings under the following laws, except as these laws provide other procedures:

(A) 7 U.S.C. §§ 292, 499g(c), for reviewing an order of the Secretary of Agriculture;

(B) 9 U.S.C., relating to arbitration;

(C) 15 U.S.C. § 522, for reviewing an order of the Secretary of the Interior;

(D) 15 U.S.C. § 715d(c), for reviewing an order denying a certificate of clearance;

(E) 29 U.S.C. §§ 159, 160, for enforcing an order of the National Labor Relations Board;

(F) 33 U.S.C. §§ 918, 921, for enforcing or reviewing a compensation order under the Longshore and Harbor Workers' Compensation Act; and

(G) 45 U.S.C. § 159, for reviewing an arbitration award in a railway-labor dispute.

(b) Scire Facias and Mandamus. The writs of scire facias and mandamus are abolished. Relief previously available through them may be obtained by appropriate action or motion under these rules.

(c) Removed Actions.

(1) *Applicability.* These rules apply to a civil action after it is removed from a state court.

(2) *Further Pleading.* After removal, repleading is unnecessary unless the court orders it. A defendant who did not answer before removal must answer or present other defenses or objections under these rules within the longest of these periods:

(A) 20 days after receiving--through service or otherwise--a copy of the initial pleading stating the claim for relief;

(B) 20 days after being served with the summons for an initial pleading on file at the time of service; or

(C) 5 days after the notice of removal is filed.

(3) *Demand for a Jury Trial.*

(A) *As Affected by State Law.* A party who, before removal, expressly demanded a jury trial in accordance with state law need not renew the demand after removal. If the state law did not require an express demand for a jury trial, a party need not make one after removal unless the court orders the parties to do so within a specified time. The court must so order at a party's request and may so order on its own. A party who fails to make a demand when so ordered waives a jury trial.

(B) *Under Rule 38.* If all necessary pleadings have been served at the time of removal, a party entitled to a jury trial under Rule 38 must be given one if the party serves a demand within 10 days after:

(i) it files a notice of removal; or

(ii) it is served with a notice of removal filed by another party.

(d) Law Applicable.

(1) *State Law.* When these rules refer to state law, the term "law" includes the state's statutes and the state's judicial decisions.

(2) *District of Columbia.* The term "state" includes, where appropriate, the District of Columbia. When these rules provide for state law to apply, in the District Court for the District of Columbia:

(A) the law applied in the District governs; and

(B) the term "federal statute" includes any Act of Congress that applies locally to the District.

RULE 82. JURISDICTION AND VENUE UNAFFECTED

These rules do not extend or limit the jurisdiction of the district courts or the venue of actions in those courts. An admiralty or maritime claim under Rule 9(h) is not a civil action for purposes of 28 U.S.C. §§ 1391-1392.

RULE 83. RULES BY DISTRICT COURTS; JUDGE'S DIRECTIVES

(a) Local Rules.

(1) *In General.* After giving public notice and an opportunity for comment, a district court, acting by a majority of its district judges, may adopt and amend rules governing its practice. A local rule must be consistent with--but not duplicate--federal statutes and rules adopted under 28 U.S.C. §§ 2072 and 2075, and must conform to any uniform numbering system prescribed by the Judicial Conference of the United States. A local rule takes effect on the date specified by the district court and remains in effect unless amended by the court or abrogated by the judicial council of the circuit. Copies of rules and amendments must, on their adoption, be furnished to the judicial council and the Administrative Office of the United States Courts and be made available to the public.

(2) *Requirement of Form.* A local rule imposing a requirement of form must not be enforced in a way that causes a party to lose any right because of a nonwillful failure to comply.

(b) Procedures When There is No Controlling Law. A judge may regulate practice in any manner consistent with federal law, rules adopted under 28 U.S.C. §§ 2072 and 2075, and the district's local rules. No sanction or other disadvantage may be imposed for noncompliance with any requirement not in federal law, federal rules, or the local rules unless the alleged violator has been furnished in the particular case with actual notice of the requirement.

RULE 84. FORMS

The forms in the Appendix suffice under these rules and illustrate the simplicity and brevity that these rules contemplate.

RULE 85. TITLE

These rules may be cited as the Federal Rules of Civil Procedure.

RULE 86. EFFECTIVE DATES

(a) In General. These rules and any amendments take effect at the time specified by the Supreme Court, subject to 28 U.S.C. § 2074. They govern:

(1) proceedings in an action commenced after their effective date; and

(2) proceedings after that date in an action then pending unless:

(A) the Supreme Court specifies otherwise; or

(B) the court determines that applying them in a particular action would be infeasible or work an injustice.

(b) December 1, 2007 Amendments. If any provision in Rules 1-5.1, 6-73, or 77-86 conflicts with another law, priority in time for the purpose of 28 U.S.C. § 2072(b) is not affected by the amendments taking effect on December 1, 2007.

FORMS NOT ATTACHED

APPENDIX M

INTERAGENCY GUIDANCE ON NONTRADITIONAL MORTGAGE PRODUCT RISKS

DEPARTMENT OF THE TREASURY

Office of the Comptroller of the Currency
[Docket No. 06–11]

BOARD OF GOVERNORS OF THE FEDERAL RESERVE SYSTEM
[Docket No. OP–1246]
FEDERAL DEPOSIT INSURANCE CORPORATION
DEPARTMENT OF THE TREASURY

Office of Thrift Supervision
[No. 2006–35]
NATIONAL CREDIT UNION ADMINISTRATION

Interagency Guidance on Nontraditional Mortgage Product Risks[1]

AGENCIES: Office of the Comptroller of the Currency, Treasury (OCC); Board of Governors of the Federal Reserve System (Board); Federal Deposit Insurance Corporation (FDIC); Office of Thrift Supervision, Treasury (OTS); and National Credit Union Administration (NCUA).

ACTION: Final guidance.

SUMMARY: The OCC, Board, FDIC, OTS, and NCUA (the Agencies), are issuing final Interagency Guidance on Nontraditional Mortgage Product Risks (guidance). This guidance has been developed to clarify how institutions can offer nontraditional mortgage products in a safe and sound manner, and in a way that clearly discloses the risks that borrowers may assume.

FOR FURTHER INFORMATION CONTACT:
OCC: Gregory Nagel, Credit Risk Specialist, Credit and Market Risk, (202) 874–5170; or Michael S. Bylsma, Director, or Stephen Van Meter, Assistant Director, Community and Consumer Law Division, (202) 874– 5750.
Board: Brian Valenti, Supervisory Financial Analyst, (202) 452–3575; or Virginia Gibbs, Senior Supervisory Financial Analyst, (202) 452–2521; or Sabeth I. Siddique, Assistant Director,
(202) 452–3861, Division of Banking Supervision and Regulation; Kathleen C. Ryan, Counsel, Division of Consumer and Community Affairs, (202) 452– 3667; or Andrew Miller, Counsel, Legal Division, (202) 452–3428. For users of Telecommunications Device for the Deaf (''TDD'') only, contact (202) 263–4869.
FDIC: Suzy S. Gardner, Examination Specialist, (202) 898–3640, or April Breslaw, Chief, Compliance Section, (202) 898–6609, Division of Supervision and Consumer Protection; or Ruth R. Amberg, Senior Counsel, (202) 898– 3736, or Richard Foley, Counsel, (202) 898–3784, Legal Division.
OTS: William Magrini, Senior Project Manager, Examinations and Supervision Policy, (202) 906–5744; or Fred Phillips-Patrick, Director, Credit Policy, (202) 906–7295; or Glenn Gimble, Senior Project Manager, Compliance and Consumer Protection, (202) 906–7158.
NCUA: Cory Phariss, Program Officer, Examination and Insurance, (703) 518– 6618.

SUPPLEMENTARY INFORMATION:

---

[1] http://www.occ.treas.gov/fr/fedregister/71fr58609.pdf (last visited June 24, 2008).

I. BACKGROUND

The Agencies developed this guidance to address risks associated with the growing use of mortgage products that allow borrowers to defer payment of principal and, sometimes, interest. These products, referred to variously as "nontraditional", "alternative", or "exotic" mortgage loans (hereinafter referred to as nontraditional mortgage loans), include "interest-only" mortgages and "payment option" adjustable-rate mortgages. These products allow borrowers to exchange lower payments during an initial period for higher payments during a later amortization period.

While similar products have been available for many years, the number of institutions offering them has expanded rapidly. At the same time, these products are offered to a wider spectrum of borrowers who may not otherwise qualify for more traditional mortgages. The Agencies are concerned that some borrowers may not fully understand the risks of these products. While many of these risks exist in other adjustable-rate mortgage products, the Agencies concern is elevated with nontraditional products because of the lack of principal amortization and potential for negative amortization. In addition, institutions are increasingly combining these loans with other features that may compound risk. These features include simultaneous second-lien mortgages and the use of reduced documentation in evaluating an applicant's creditworthiness.

In response to these concerns, the Agencies published for comment proposed Interagency Guidance on Nontraditional Mortgage Products, 70 FR 77249 (Dec. 29, 2005). The Agencies proposed guidance in three primary areas: "Loan Terms and Underwriting Standards", "Portfolio and Risk Management Practices", and "Consumer Protection Issues". In the first section, the Agencies sought to ensure that loan terms and underwriting standards for nontraditional mortgage loans are consistent with prudent lending practices, including credible consideration of a borrower's repayment capacity. The portfolio and risk management practices section outlined the need for strong risk management standards, capital levels commensurate with the risk, and an allowance for loan and lease losses (ALLL) that reflects the collectability of the portfolio. Finally, the consumer protection issues section recommended practices to ensure consumers have clear and balanced information prior to making a product choice. Additionally, this section described control systems to ensure that actual practices are consistent with policies and procedures.

The Agencies together received approximately 100 letters in response to the proposal.[1] Comments were received from financial institutions, trade associations, consumer and community organizations, state financial regulatory organizations, and other members of the public.

II. OVERVIEW OF PUBLIC COMMENTS

The Agencies received a full range of comments. Some commenters applauded the Agencies' initiative in proposing the guidance, while others questioned whether guidance is needed.

A majority of the depository institutions and industry groups that commented stated that the guidance is too prescriptive. They suggested institutions should have more flexibility in determining appropriate risk management practices. A number observed that nontraditional mortgage products have been offered successfully for many years. Others opined that the guidance would stifle innovation and result in qualified borrowers not being approved for these loans. Further, many questioned whether the guidance is an appropriate mechanism for addressing the Agencies' consumer protection concerns.

A smaller subset of commenters argued that the guidance does not go far enough in regulating or restricting nontraditional mortgage products. These commenters included consumer organizations, individuals, and several community bankers. Several stated these products contribute to speculation and unsustainable appreciation in the housing market. They expressed concern that severe problems will occur if and when there is a downturn in the economy. Some also argued that these products are harmful to borrowers and that borrowers may not understand the associated risks.

FN[1]Nine of these letters requested a thirty-day extension of the comment period, which the Agencies granted.

Many commenters voiced concern that the guidance will not apply to all lenders, and thus federally regulated financial institutions will be at a competitive disadvantage. The Agencies note that both State financial regulatory organizations that commented on the proposed guidance—the Conference of State Bank Supervisors (CSBS) and the State Financial Regulators Roundtable (SFRR)—committed to working with State regulatory agencies to distribute guidance that is similar in nature and scope to the financial service providers under their jurisdictions.[2] These commenters noted their interest in addressing the potential for inconsistent regulatory treatment of lenders based on whether or not they are supervised solely by state agencies. Subsequently, the CSBS, along with a national organization representing state residential mortgage regulators, issued a press release confirming their intent to offer guidance to State regulators to apply to their licensed residential mortgage brokers and lenders.[3]

III. FINAL JOINT GUIDANCE

The Agencies made a number of changes to the proposal to respond to commenters' concerns and to provide additional clarity. Significant comments on the specific provisions of the proposed guidance, the Agencies'' responses, and changes to the proposed guidance are discussed as follows.

Scope of the Guidance

Many financial institution and trade group commenters raised concerns that the proposed guidance did not adequately define ''nontraditional mortgage products''. They requested clarification of which products would be subject to enhanced scrutiny. Some suggested that the guidance focus on products that allow negative amortization, rather than interest-only loans. Others suggested excluding certain products with nontraditional features, such as reverse mortgages and home equity lines of credit (HELOCs). Those commenting on interest-only loans noted that they do not present the same risks as products that allow for negative amortization. Those that argued that HELOCs should be excluded noted that they are already covered by interagency guidance issued in 2005. They also noted that the principal amount of these loans is generally lower than that for first mortgages. As for reverse mortgages, the commenters pointed out that they were developed for a specific market segment and do not present the same concerns as products mentioned in the guidance.

> FN2 Letter to J. Johnson, Board Secretary, *et al.* from
> N. Milner, President & CEO, Conference of State Bank Supervisors (Feb. 14, 2006); Letter to J. Johnson, Board Secretary, *et al.*, from B. Kent, Chair, State Financial Regulators Roundtable.
> FN3 Media Release, CSBS & American Association of Residential Mortgage Regulators, ''CSBS and AARMR Consider Guidance on Nontraditional Mortgage Products for State-Licensed Entities'' (June 7, 2006), available at *http://www.csbs.org/ Content/NavigationMenu/PublicRelations/ PressReleases/News_Releases.htm*. The press release stated:
> The guidance being developed by CSBS and AARMR is based upon proposed guidance issued in December 2005 by the Office of the Comptroller of the Currency, the Board of Governors of the Federal Reserve System, the Federal Deposit Insurance Corporation, the Office of Thrift Supervision, and the National Credit Union Administration.
> The Federal guidance, when finalized, will only apply to insured financial institutions and their affiliates. CSBS and AARMR intend to develop a modified version of the guidance which will primarily focus on residential mortgage underwriting and consumer protection. The guidance will be offered to State regulators to apply to their licensed residential mortgage brokers and lenders.

To address these concerns, the Agencies are clarifying the types of products covered by the guidance. In general, the guidance applies to all residential mortgage loan products that allow borrowers to defer repayment of principal or interest. This includes all interest-only products and negative amortization mortgages, with the exception of HELOCs. The Agencies decided not to include HELOCs in this guidance, other than as discussed in the Simultaneous Second-Lien Loans section, since they are already covered by the May 2005 Interagency *Credit Risk Management Guidance for Home Equity Lending*. The Agencies are amending the May 2005 guidance, however, to address the consumer disclosure recommendations included in the nontraditional mortgage guidance.

The Agencies decided against focusing solely on negative amortization products. Many of the interest-only products pose risks similar to products that allow negative amortization, especially when combined with high leverage and reduced documentation. Accordingly, they present similar concerns from a risk management and consumer protection standpoint. The Agencies did, however, agree that reverse mortgages do not present the types of concerns that are addressed in the guidance and should be excluded.

LOAN TERMS AND UNDERWRITING STANDARDS

Qualifying Borrowers

The Agencies proposed that for all nontraditional mortgage products, the analysis of borrowers' repayment capacity should include an evaluation of their ability to repay the debt by final maturity at the fully indexed rate, assuming a fully amortizing repayment schedule. In addition, the proposed guidance stated that for products that permit negative amortization, the repayment analysis should include the initial loan amount plus any balance increase that may accrue from negative amortization. The amount of the balance increase is tied to the initial terms of the loan and estimated assuming the borrower makes only the minimum payment.

Generally, banks and industry groups believed that the proposed underwriting standards were too prescriptive and asked for more flexibility. Consumer groups generally supported the proposed underwriting standards, warning that deteriorating underwriting standards are bad for individual borrowers and poor public policy.

A number of commenters suggested that industry practice is to underwrite payment option adjustable-rate mortgages at the fully indexed rate, assuming a fully amortizing payment. Yet several commenters argued that this standard should not be required when risks are adequately mitigated. Moreover, many commenters opposed assuming a fully amortizing payment for interest-only loans with extended interest-only periods. They argued that the average life span of most mortgage loans makes it unlikely that many borrowers will experience the higher payments associated with amortization. Additionally, many commenters opposed the assumption of minimum payments during the deferral period for products that permit negative amortization on the ground that this assumption suggests that lenders assume a worst-case scenario.

The Agencies believe that institutions should maintain qualification standards that include a credible analysis of a borrower's capacity to repay the full amount of credit that may be extended. That analysis should consider both principal and interest at the fully indexed rate. Using discounted payments in the qualification process limits the ability of borrowers to demonstrate sufficient capacity to repay under the terms of the loan. Therefore, the proposed general guideline of qualifying borrowers at the fully indexed rate, assuming a fully amortizing payment, including potential negative amortization amounts, remains in the final guidance.

Regarding interest-only loans with extended interest-only periods, the Agencies note that since the average life of a mortgage is a function of the housing market and interest rates, the average may fluctuate over time. Additionally, the Agencies were concerned that excluding these loans from the underwriting standards could cause some creditors to change their market offerings to avoid application of the guidance. Accordingly, the final guidance does not exclude interest-only loans with extended interest-only periods.

Finally, regarding the assumption for the amount that the balance may increase due to negative amortization, the Agencies have revised the language to respond to commenters' requests for clarity. The basic standard, however, remains unchanged. The Agencies expect a borrower to demonstrate the capacity to repay the full loan amount that may be advanced.[4] This includes the initial loan amount plus any balance increase that may accrue from the negative amortization provision. The final document contains guidance on determining the amount of any balance increase that may accrue from the negative amortization provision, which does not necessarily equate to the full negative amortization cap for a particular loan.

The Agencies requested comment on whether the guidance should address consideration of future income or other future events in the qualification standards. The commenters generally agreed that there is no reliable method for considering future income or other future events in the underwriting process. Accordingly, the Agencies have not modified the guidance to address these issues.

Collateral-Dependent Loans

Commenters that specifically addressed this aspect of the guidance concurred that it is unsafe and unsound to rely solely on an individual borrower's ability to sell or refinance once amortization commences. However, many expressed concern about the possibility that the term "collateral-dependent", as it is used in the guidance, would be interpreted to apply to stated income and other reduced documentation loans.

To address this concern, the Agencies provided clarifying language in a footnote to this section. The final guidance provides that a loan will not be determined to be collateral-dependent solely because it was underwritten using reduced documentation.

> FN4 This is similar to the standard in the Agencies' May 2005 *Credit Risk Management Guidance for Home Equity Lending* recommending that, for interest-only and variable rate HELOCs, borrowers should demonstrate the ability to amortize the fully drawn line over the loan term.

Risk Layering

Financial institution and industry group commenters were generally critical of the risk layering provisions of the proposed guidance on the grounds that they were too prescriptive. These commenters argued that institutions should have flexibility in determining factors that mitigate additional risks presented by features such as reduced documentation and simultaneous second-lien loans. A number of commenters, however, including community and consumer organizations, financial institutions, and industry associations, suggested that reduced documentation loans should not be offered to subprime borrowers. Others questioned whether stated income loans are appropriate under any circumstances, when used with nontraditional mortgage products, or when used for wage earners who can readily provide standard documentation of their wages. Several commenters argued that simultaneous second-lien loans should be paired with nontraditional mortgage loans only when borrowers will continue to have substantial equity in the property.

The Agencies believe that the guidance provides adequate flexibility in the methods and approaches to mitigating risk, with respect to risk layering. While the Agencies have not prohibited any of the practices discussed, the guidance uniformly suggests strong quality control and risk mitigation factors with respect to these practices.

The Agencies declined to provide guidance recommending reduced documentation loans be limited to any particular set of circumstances. The final guidance recognizes that mitigating factors may determine whether such loans are appropriate but reminds institutions that a credible analysis of both a borrower's willingness and ability to repay is consistent with sound and prudent lending practices. The final guidance also cautions that institutions generally should be able to readily document income for wage earners through means such as W–2 statements, pay stubs, or tax returns.

Portfolio and Risk Management Practices

Many financial institution and industry group commenters opposed provisions of the proposed guidance for the setting of concentration limits. Some commenters advocated active monitoring of concentrations of diversification strategies as more appropriate approaches. The intent of the guidance was not to set hard concentration limits for nontraditional mortgage products. Instead, institutions with concentrations in these products should have well-developed monitoring systems and risk management practices. The guidance was clarified to reiterate this point.

Additionally, a number of financial institution and industry association commenters opposed the provisions regarding third-party originations. They argued that the proposal would force lenders to have an awareness and control over third-party practices that is neither realistic nor practical. In particular, many of these commenters argued that lenders should not be responsible for overseeing the marketing and borrower disclosure practices of third parties.

Regarding controls over third-party practices, the Agencies clarified their expectations that institutions should have strong systems and controls for establishing and maintaining relationships with third parties. Reliance on third-party relationships can significantly increase an institution's risk profile. The guidance, therefore, emphasizes the need for institutions to exercise appropriate due diligence prior to entering into a third-party relationship and to provide ongoing, effective oversight and controls. In practice, an institution's risk management system should reflect the complexity of its third-party activities and the overall level of risk involved.

A number of commenters urged the Agencies to remove language in the proposed guidance relating to implicit recourse for loans sold in the secondary market. They expressed concern that the proposal added new capital requirements. The Agencies clarified the language in the guidance addressing this issue. The Agencies do not intend to establish new capital requirements. Instead, the Agencies' intent is to reiterate existing guidelines regarding implicit recourse under the Agencies' risk-based capital rules.

Consumer Protection Issues
Communications With Consumers
Many financial institution and trade group commenters suggested that the Agencies' consumer protection goals would be better accomplished through generally applicable regulations, such as Regulation Z (Truth in Lending) [5] or Regulation X (Real Estate Settlement Procedures). [6] Some commenters stated that the proposed guidance would add
burdensome new disclosure requirements and cause a confusing overlap with current Regulation Z requirements. They also expressed concern that the guidance would contribute to an overload of information currently provided to consumers. Additionally, some argued that implementing the disclosure provisions might trigger Regulation Z requirements concerning advertising. [7] Some commenters also urged the Agencies to adopt model disclosure forms or other descriptive materials to assist in compliance with the guidance.
        FN7 *See* 12 CFR part 226.24(c) (2006).

Some commenters voiced concern that the Agencies are attempting to establish a suitability standard similar to that used in the securities context. These commenters argued that lenders are not in a position to determine which products are most suitable for borrowers, and that this decision should be left to borrowers themselves.

Finally, several community and consumer organization commenters questioned whether additional disclosures are sufficient to protect borrowers and suggested various additional measures, such as consumer education and counseling.

The Agencies carefully considered the commenters' argument that consumer protection issues—particularly, disclosures—would be better addressed through generally applicable regulations. The Agencies determined, however, that given the growth in this market, guidelines are needed now to ensure that consumers will receive the information they need about the material features of nontraditional mortgages as soon as possible.

The Agencies also gave careful consideration to the commenters' concerns that the guidelines will overlap with Regulation Z, add to the disclosure burden on lenders, and contribute to information overload. While the Agencies are sensitive to these concerns, we do not believe they warrant significant changes to the guidance. The guidance focuses on providing information to consumers during the pre-application shopping phase and post-closing with any monthly statements lenders choose to provide to consumers. Moreover, the Agencies do not anticipate that the information outlined in the guidance will result in additional lengthy disclosures. Rather, the Agencies contemplate that the information can be provided in brief narrative format and through the use of examples based on hypothetical loan transactions.[8] We have, however, revised the guidance to make clear that transaction-specific disclosures are not required. Institutions will still need to ensure that their marketing materials promoting their products comply with Regulation Z, as applicable.

As previously discussed, some commenters, including industry trade associations, asked the Agencies to include model or sample disclosures or other descriptive materials as part of the guidance to assist lenders, including smaller institutions, in following the recommended practices for communications with consumers. The Agencies have determined not to include required model or sample disclosures in the guidance. Instead, the guidance provides a set of recommended practices to assist institutions in addressing particular risks raised by nontraditional mortgage products.

> FN8 *See* elsewhere in today's issue of the Federal Register. (Proposed Illustrations of Consumer Information for Nontraditional Mortgage Products).

The Agencies have determined that it is desirable to first seek public comment on potential model disclosures, and in a Federal Register notice accompanying this guidance are seeking comment on proposed illustrations of consumer information for nontraditional mortgage products that are consistent with the recommendations contained in the guidance. The Agencies appreciate that some institutions, including community banks, following the recommendations set forth in the guidance may prefer not to incur the costs and other burdens of developing their own consumer information documents. The Agencies are, therefore, requesting comment on illustrations of the type of information contemplated by the guidance.

The Agencies disagree with the commenters who expressed concern that the guidance appears to establish a suitability standard, under which lenders would be required to assist borrowers in choosing products that are suitable to their needs and circumstances. It was not the Agencies' intent to impose such a standard, nor is there any language in the guidance that does so. In any event, the Agencies have revised certain statements in the proposed guidance that could have been interpreted to suggest a requirement to ensure that borrowers select products appropriate to their circumstances.

Control Systems

Several commenters requested more flexibility in designing appropriate control systems. The Agencies have revised the ''Control Systems'' portion of the guidance to clarify that we are not requiring any particular means of monitoring adherence to an institution's policies, such as call monitoring or mystery shopping. Additional changes have also been made to clarify that the Agencies do not expect institutions to assume an unwarranted level of responsibility for the actions of third parties. Rather, the control systems that are expected for loans purchased from or originated through third parties are consistent with the Agencies' current supervisory policies. As previously discussed, the Agencies have also made changes to the portfolio and risk management practices portion of the final guidance to clarify their expectations concerning oversight and monitoring of third-party originations.

IV. TEXT OF FINAL JOINT GUIDANCE

The text of the final Interagency Guidance on Nontraditional Mortgage Product Risks follows:

Interagency Guidance on Nontraditional Mortgage Product Risks

Residential mortgage lending has traditionally been a conservatively managed business with low delinquencies and losses and reasonably stable underwriting standards. In the past few years consumer demand has been growing, particularly in high priced real estate markets, for closed-end residential mortgage loan products that allow borrowers to defer repayment of principal and, sometimes, interest. These mortgage products, herein referred to as nontraditional mortgage loans, include such products as "interest-only" mortgages where a borrower pays no loan principal for the first few years of the loan and "payment option" adjustable-rate mortgages (ARMs) where a borrower has flexible payment options with the potential for negative amortization.[1]

> FN1 Interest-only and payment option ARMs are variations of conventional ARMs, hybrid ARMs, and fixed rate products. Refer to the Appendix for additional information on interest-only and payment option ARM loans. This guidance does not apply to reverse mortgages; home equity lines of credit ("HELOCs"), other than as discussed in the Simultaneous Second-Lien Loans section; or fully amortizing residential mortgage loan products.

While some institutions have offered nontraditional mortgages for many years with appropriate risk management and sound portfolio performance, the market for these products and the number of institutions offering them has expanded rapidly. Nontraditional mortgage loan products are now offered by more lenders to a wider spectrum of borrowers who may not otherwise qualify for more traditional mortgage loans and may not fully understand the associated risks.

Many of these nontraditional mortgage loans are underwritten with less stringent income and asset verification requirements ("reduced documentation") and are increasingly combined with simultaneous second-lien loans.[2] Such risk layering, combined with the broader marketing of nontraditional mortgage loans, exposes financial institutions to increased risk relative to traditional mortgage loans.

Given the potential for heightened risk levels, management should carefully consider and appropriately mitigate exposures created by these loans. To manage the risks associated with nontraditional mortgage loans, management should:

Ensure that loan terms and underwriting standards are consistent with prudent lending practices, including consideration of a borrower's repayment capacity;

Recognize that many nontraditional mortgage loans, particularly when they have risk-layering features, are untested in a stressed environment. As evidenced by experienced institutions, these products warrant strong risk management standards, capital levels commensurate with the risk, and an allowance for loan and lease losses that reflects the collectibility of the portfolio; and

Ensure that consumers have sufficient information to clearly understand loan terms and associated risks prior to making a product choice.

The Office of the Comptroller of the Currency (OCC), the Board of Governors of the Federal Reserve System (Board), the Federal Deposit Insurance Corporation (FDIC), the Office of Thrift Supervision (OTS) and the National Credit Union Administration (NCUA) (collectively, the Agencies) expect institutions to effectively assess and manage the risks associated with nontraditional mortgage loan products.[3]

Institutions should use this guidance to ensure that risk management practices adequately address these risks. The Agencies will carefully scrutinize risk management processes, policies, and procedures in this area. Institutions that do not adequately manage these risks will be asked to take remedial action.

> FN2 Refer to the Appendix for additional information on reduced documentation and simultaneous second-lien loans.
> FN3 Refer to Interagency Guidelines Establishing Standards for Safety and Soundness. For each Agency, those respective guidelines are addressed in: 12 CFR part 30 Appendix A (OCC); 12 CFR part 208 Appendix D–1 (Board); 12 CFR part 364 Appendix A (FDIC); 12 CFR part 570 Appendix A (OTS); and 12 U.S.C. 1786 (NCUA).

The focus of this guidance is on the higher risk elements of certain nontraditional mortgage products, not the product type itself. Institutions with sound underwriting, adequate risk management, and acceptable portfolio performance will not be subject to criticism merely for offering such products.

Loan Terms and Underwriting Standards
When an institution offers nontraditional mortgage loan products, underwriting standards should address the effect of a substantial payment increase on the borrower's capacity to repay when loan amortization begins. Underwriting standards should also comply with the agencies' real estate lending standards and appraisal regulations and associated guidelines.[4]

Central to prudent lending is the internal discipline to maintain sound loan terms and underwriting standards despite competitive pressures. Institutions are strongly cautioned against ceding underwriting standards to third parties that have different business objectives, risk tolerances, and core competencies. Loan terms should be based on a disciplined analysis of potential exposures and compensating factors to ensure risk levels remain manageable.

> FN4 Refer to 12 CFR part 34—Real Estate Lending and Appraisals, OCC Bulletin 2005–3— Standards for National Banks' Residential Mortgage Lending, AL 2003–7—Guidelines for Real Estate Lending Policies and AL 2003–9—Independent Appraisal and Evaluation Functions (OCC); 12 CFR 208.51 subpart E and Appendix C and 12 CFR part 225 subpart G (Board); 12 CFR part 365 and Appendix A, and 12 CFR part 323 (FDIC); 12 CFR 560.101 and Appendix and 12 CFR part 564 (OTS). Also, refer to the 1999 Interagency Guidance on the "Treatment of High LTV Residential Real Estate Loans" and the 1994 "Interagency Appraisal and Evaluation Guidelines". Federally Insured Credit Unions should refer to 12 CFR part 722—Appraisals and NCUA 03–CU–17— Appraisal and Evaluation Functions for Real Estate Related Transactions (NCUA).

Qualifying Borrowers—Payments on nontraditional loans can increase significantly when the loans begin to amortize. Commonly referred to as payment shock, this increase is of particular concern for payment option ARMs where the borrower makes minimum payments that may result in negative amortization. Some institutions manage the potential for excessive negative amortization and payment shock by structuring the initial terms to limit the spread between the introductory interest rate and the fully indexed rate. Nevertheless, an institution's qualifying standards should recognize the potential impact of payment shock, especially for borrowers with high loan-to-value (LTV) ratios, high debt-to-income (DTI) ratios, and low credit scores. Recognizing that an institution's underwriting criteria are based on multiple factors, an institution should consider these factors jointly in the qualification process and may develop a range of reasonable tolerances for each factor. However, the criteria should be based upon prudent and appropriate underwriting standards, considering both the borrower's characteristics and the product's attributes.

For all nontraditional mortgage loan products, an institution's analysis of a borrower's repayment capacity should include an evaluation of their ability to repay the debt by final maturity at the fully indexed rate,[5] assuming a fully amortizing repayment schedule.[6] In addition, for products that permit negative amortization, the repayment analysis should be based upon the initial loan amount plus any balance increase that may accrue from the negative amortization provision.[7]

> FN5 The fully indexed rate equals the index rate prevailing at origination plus the margin that will apply after the expiration of an introductory interest rate. The index rate is a published interest rate to which the interest rate on an ARM is tied. Some commonly used indices include the 1-Year Constant Maturity Treasury Rate (CMT), the 6-Month London Interbank Offered Rate (LIBOR), the 11th District Cost of Funds (COFI), and the Moving Treasury Average (MTA), a 12-month moving average of the monthly average yields of U.S. Treasury securities adjusted to a constant maturity of one year. The margin is the number of percentage points a lender adds to the index value to calculate

the ARM interest rate at each adjustment period. In different interest rate scenarios, the fully indexed rate for an ARM loan based on a lagging index (e.g., MTA rate) may be significantly different from the rate on a comparable 30-year fixed-rate product. In these cases, a credible market rate should be used to qualify the borrower and determine repayment capacity.

FN6 The fully amortizing payment schedule should be based on the term of the loan. For example, the amortizing payment for a loan with a 5-year interest only period and a 30-year term would be calculated based on a 30-year amortization schedule. For balloon mortgages that contain a borrower option for an extended amortization period, the fully amortizing payment schedule can be based on the full term the borrower may choose.

FN7 The balance that may accrue from the negative amortization provision does not necessarily equate to the full negative amortization cap for a particular loan. The spread between the introductory or ''teaser'' rate and the accrual rate will determine whether or not a loan balance has the potential to reach the negative amortization cap before the end of the initial payment option period (usually five years). For example, a loan with a 115 percent negative amortization cap but a small spread between the introductory rate and the accrual rate may only reach a 109 percent maximum loan balance before the end of the initial payment option period, even if only minimum payments are made. The borrower could be qualified based on this lower maximum loan balance.

Furthermore, the analysis of repayment capacity should avoid over-reliance on credit scores as a substitute for income verification in the underwriting process. The higher a loan's credit risk, either from loan features or borrower characteristics, the more important it is to verify the borrower's income, assets, and outstanding liabilities.

Collateral-Dependent Loans— Institutions should avoid the use of loan terms and underwriting practices that may heighten the need for a borrower to rely on the sale or refinancing of the property once amortization begins. Loans to individuals who do not demonstrate the capacity to repay, as structured, from sources other than the collateral pledged are generally considered unsafe and unsound.[8] Institutions that originate collateral-dependent mortgage loans may be subject to criticism, corrective action, and higher capital requirements.

Risk Layering—Institutions that originate or purchase mortgage loans that combine nontraditional features, such as interest only loans with reduced documentation or a simultaneous second-lien loan, face increased risk. When features are layered, an institution should demonstrate that mitigating factors support the underwriting decision and the borrower's repayment capacity. Mitigating factors could include higher credit scores, lower LTV and DTI ratios, significant liquid assets, mortgage insurance or other credit enhancements. While higher pricing is often used to address elevated risk levels, it does not replace the need for sound underwriting.

Reduced Documentation—Institutions increasingly rely on reduced documentation, particularly unverified income, to qualify borrowers for nontraditional mortgage loans. Because these practices essentially substitute assumptions and unverified information for analysis of a borrower's repayment capacity and general creditworthiness, they should be used with caution. As the level of credit risk increases, the Agencies expect an institution to more diligently verify and document a borrower's income and debt reduction capacity. Clear policies should govern the use of reduced documentation. For example, stated income should be accepted only if there are mitigating factors that clearly minimize the need for direct verification of repayment capacity. For many borrowers, institutions generally should be able to readily document income using recent W–2 statements, pay stubs, or tax returns.

FN8 A loan will not be determined to be ''collateral-dependent'' solely through the use of reduced documentation.

Simultaneous Second-Lien Loans— Simultaneous second-lien loans reduce owner equity and increase credit risk. Historically, as combined loan-to-value ratios rise, so do defaults. A delinquent borrower with minimal or no equity in a property may have little incentive to work with a lender to bring the loan current and avoid foreclosure. In addition, second-lien home equity lines of credit (HELOCs) typically increase borrower exposure to increasing interest rates and monthly payment burdens. Loans with minimal or no owner equity generally should not have a payment structure that allows for delayed or negative amortization without other significant risk mitigating factors.

Introductory Interest Rates—Many institutions offer introductory interest rates set well below the fully indexed rate as a marketing tool for payment option ARM products. When developing nontraditional mortgage product terms, an institution should consider the spread between the introductory rate and the fully indexed rate. Since initial and subsequent monthly payments are based on these low introductory rates, a wide initial spread means that borrowers are more likely to experience negative amortization, severe payment shock, and an earlier-than-scheduled recasting of monthly payments. Institutions should minimize the likelihood of disruptive early recastings and extraordinary payment shock when setting introductory rates.

Lending to Subprime Borrowers— Mortgage programs that target subprime borrowers through tailored marketing, underwriting standards, and risk selection should follow the applicable interagency guidance on subprime lending.[9] Among other things, the subprime guidance discusses circumstances under which subprime lending can become predatory or abusive. Institutions designing nontraditional mortgage loans for subprime borrowers should pay particular attention to this guidance. They should also recognize that risk-layering features in loans to subprime borrowers may significantly increase risks for both the institution and the borrower.

> FN9 Interagency Guidance on Subprime Lending, March 1, 1999, and Expanded Guidance for Subprime Lending Programs, January 31, 2001. Federally insured credit unions should refer to 04–CU–12—Specialized Lending Activities (NCUA).

Non-Owner-Occupied Investor Loans—Borrowers financing non-owner-occupied investment properties should qualify for loans based on their ability to service the debt over the life of the loan. Loan terms should reflect an appropriate combined LTV ratio that considers the potential for negative amortization and maintains sufficient borrower equity over the life of the loan. Further, underwriting standards should require evidence that the borrower has sufficient cash reserves to service the loan, considering the possibility of extended periods of property vacancy and the variability of debt service requirements associated with nontraditional mortgage loan products.[10]

> FN10 Federally insured credit unions must comply with 12 CFR part 723 for loans meeting the definition of member business loans.

Portfolio and Risk Management Practices

Institutions should ensure that risk management practices keep pace with the growth and changing risk profile of their nontraditional mortgage loan portfolios and changes in the market. Active portfolio management is especially important for institutions that project or have already experienced significant growth or concentration levels. Institutions that originate or invest in nontraditional mortgage loans should adopt more robust risk management practices and manage these exposures in a thoughtful, systematic manner. To meet these expectations, institutions should:

Develop written policies that specify acceptable product attributes, production and portfolio limits, sales and securitization practices, and risk management expectations;
Design enhanced performance measures and management reporting that provide early warning for increasing risk;

Establish appropriate ALLL levels that consider the credit quality of the portfolio and conditions that affect collectibility; and

Maintain capital at levels that reflect portfolio characteristics and the effect of stressed economic conditions on collectibility. Institutions should hold capital commensurate with the risk characteristics of their nontraditional mortgage loan portfolios.

Policies—An institution's policies for nontraditional mortgage lending activity should set acceptable levels of risk through its operating practices, accounting procedures, and policy exception tolerances. Policies should reflect appropriate limits on risk layering and should include risk management tools for risk mitigation purposes. Further, an institution should set growth and volume limits by loan type, with special attention for products and product combinations in need of heightened attention due to easing terms or rapid growth.

Concentrations—Institutions with concentrations in nontraditional mortgage products should have well-developed monitoring systems and risk management practices. Monitoring should keep track of concentrations in key portfolio segments such as loan types, third-party originations, geographic area, and property occupancy status.

Concentrations also should be monitored by key portfolio characteristics such as loans with high combined LTV ratios, loans with high DTI ratios, loans with the potential for negative amortization, loans to borrowers with credit scores below established thresholds, loans with risk-layered features, and non-owner-occupied investor loans. Further, institutions should consider the effect of employee incentive programs that could produce higher concentrations of nontraditional mortgage loans. Concentrations that are not effectively managed will be subject to elevated supervisory attention and potential examiner criticism to ensure timely remedial action.

Controls—An institution's quality control, compliance, and audit procedures should focus on mortgage lending activities posing high risk. Controls to monitor compliance with underwriting standards and exceptions to those standards are especially important for nontraditional loan products. The quality control function should regularly review a sample of nontraditional mortgage loans from all origination channels and a representative sample of underwriters to confirm that policies are being followed. When control systems or operating practices are found deficient, business-line managers should be held accountable for correcting deficiencies in a timely manner. Since many nontraditional mortgage loans permit a borrower to defer principal and, in some cases, interest payments for extended periods, institutions should have strong controls over accruals, customer service and collections. Policy exceptions made by servicing and collections personnel should be carefully monitored to confirm that practices such as re-aging, payment deferrals, and loan modifications are not inadvertently increasing risk. Customer service and collections personnel should receive product-specific training on the features and potential customer issues with these products.

Third-Party Originations—Institutions often use third parties, such as mortgage brokers or correspondents, to originate nontraditional mortgage loans. Institutions should have strong systems and controls in place for establishing and maintaining relationships with third parties, including procedures for performing due diligence. Oversight of third parties should involve monitoring the quality of originations so that they reflect the institution's lending standards and compliance with applicable laws and regulations.

Monitoring procedures should track the quality of loans by both origination source and key borrower characteristics. This will help institutions identify problems such as early payment defaults, incomplete documentation, and fraud. If appraisal, loan documentation, credit problems or consumer complaints are discovered, the institution should take immediate action. Remedial action could include more thorough application reviews, more frequent re-underwriting, or even termination of the third-party relationship.[11]

Secondary Market Activity—The sophistication of an institution's secondary market risk management practices should be commensurate with the nature and volume of activity. Institutions with significant secondary market activities should have comprehensive, formal strategies for managing risks.[12] Contingency planning should include how the institution will respond to reduced demand in the secondary market.

> FN11 Refer to OCC Bulletin 2001–47—Third-Party Relationships and AL 2000–9—Third-Party Risk (OCC). Federally insured credit unions should refer to 01–CU–20 (NCUA), Due Diligence over Third Party Service Providers. Savings associations should refer to OTS Thrift Bulletin 82a—Third Party Arrangements.
>
> FN12 Refer to "Interagency Questions and Answers on Capital Treatment of Recourse, Direct Credit Substitutes, and Residual Interests in Asset Securitizations", May 23, 2002; OCC Bulletin 2002– 22 (OCC); SR letter 02–16 (Board); Financial Institution Letter (FIL–54–2002) (FDIC); and CEO Letter 163 (OTS). *See* OCC's Comptroller Handbook for Asset Securitization, November 1997. *See* OTS Examination Handbook Section 221, Asset-Backed Securitization. The Board also addressed risk management and capital adequacy of exposures arising from secondary market credit activities in SR letter 97–21. Federally insured credit unions should refer to 12 CFR Part 702 (NCUA).

While third-party loan sales can transfer a portion of the credit risk, an institution remains exposed to reputation risk when credit losses on sold mortgage loans or securitization transactions exceed expectations. As a result, an institution may determine that it is necessary to repurchase defaulted mortgages to protect its reputation and maintain access to the markets. In the agencies' view, the repurchase of mortgage loans beyond the selling institution's contractual obligation is implicit recourse. Under the agencies' risk-based capital rules, a repurchasing institution would be required to maintain risk-based capital against the entire pool or securitization.[13] Institutions should familiarize themselves with these guidelines before deciding to support mortgage loan pools or buying back loans in default.

Management Information and Reporting—Reporting systems should allow management to detect changes in the risk profile of its nontraditional mortgage loan portfolio. The structure and content should allow the isolation of key loan products, risk-layering loan features, and borrower characteristics. Reporting should also allow management to recognize deteriorating performance in any of these areas before it has progressed too far. At a minimum, information should be available by loan type (*e.g.*, interest-only mortgage loans and payment option ARMs); by risk-layering features (*e.g.*, payment option ARM with stated income and interest-only mortgage loans with simultaneous second-lien mortgages); by underwriting characteristics (*e.g.*, LTV, DTI, and credit score); and by borrower performance (*e.g.*, payment patterns, delinquencies, interest accruals, and negative amortization).

Portfolio volume and performance should be tracked against expectations, internal lending standards and policy limits. Volume and performance expectations should be established at the subportfolio and aggregate portfolio levels. Variance analyses should be performed regularly to identify exceptions to policies and prescribed thresholds. Qualitative analysis should occur when actual performance deviates from established policies and thresholds. Variance analysis is critical to the monitoring of a portfolio's risk characteristics and should be an integral part of establishing and adjusting risk tolerance levels.

> FN13 Refer to 12 CFR part 3 Appendix A, Section 4 (OCC); 12 CFR parts 208 and 225, Appendix A, III.B.3 (FRB); 12 CFR part 325, Appendix A, II.B (FDIC); 12 CFR 567 (OTS); and 12 CFR part 702 (NCUA) for each Agency's capital treatment of recourse.

Stress Testing—Based on the size and complexity of their lending operations, institutions should perform sensitivity analysis on key portfolio segments to identify and quantify events that may increase risks in a segment or the entire portfolio. The scope of the analysis should generally include stress tests on key performance drivers such as interest rates, employment levels, economic growth, housing value fluctuations, and other factors beyond the institution's immediate control. Stress tests typically assume rapid deterioration in one or more factors and attempt to estimate the potential influence on default rates and loss severity. Stress testing should aid an institution in identifying, monitoring and managing risk, as well as developing appropriate and cost-effective loss mitigation strategies. The stress testing results should provide direct feedback in determining underwriting standards, product terms, portfolio concentration limits, and capital levels.

Capital and Allowance for Loan and Lease Losses—Institutions should establish an appropriate allowance for loan and lease losses (ALLL) for the estimated credit losses inherent in their nontraditional mortgage loan portfolios. They should also consider the higher risk of loss posed by layered risks when establishing their ALLL.

Moreover, institutions should recognize that their limited performance history with these products, particularly in a stressed environment, increases performance uncertainty. Capital levels should be commensurate with the risk characteristics of the nontraditional mortgage loan portfolios. Lax underwriting standards or poor portfolio performance may warrant higher capital levels.

When establishing an appropriate ALLL and considering the adequacy of capital, institutions should segment their nontraditional mortgage loan portfolios into pools with similar credit risk characteristics. The basic segments typically include collateral and loan characteristics, geographic concentrations, and borrower qualifying attributes. Segments could also differentiate loans by payment and portfolio characteristics, such as loans on which borrowers usually make only minimum payments, mortgages with existing balances above original balances, and mortgages subject to sizable payment shock. The objective is to identify credit quality indicators that affect collectability for ALLL measurement purposes. In addition, understanding characteristics that influence expected performance also provides meaningful information about future loss exposure that would aid in determining adequate capital levels.

Institutions with material mortgage banking activities and mortgage servicing assets should apply sound practices in valuing the mortgage servicing rights for nontraditional mortgages. In accordance with interagency guidance, the valuation process should follow generally accepted accounting principles and use reasonable and supportable assumptions.14

Consumer Protection Issues
While nontraditional mortgage loans provide flexibility for consumers, the Agencies are concerned that consumers may enter into these transactions without fully understanding the product terms. Nontraditional mortgage products have been advertised and promoted based on their affordability in the near term; that is, their lower initial monthly payments compared with traditional types of mortgages. In addition to apprising consumers of the benefits of nontraditional mortgage products, institutions should take appropriate steps to alert consumers to the risks of these products, including the likelihood of increased future payment obligations. This information should be provided in a timely manner—before disclosures may be required under the Truth in Lending Act or other laws—to assist the consumer in the product selection process.

Concerns and Objectives—More than traditional ARMs, mortgage products such as payment option ARMs and interest-only mortgages can carry a significant risk of payment shock and negative amortization that may not be fully understood by consumers. For example, consumer payment obligations may increase substantially at the end of an interest-only period or upon the "recast" of a payment option ARM. The magnitude of these payment increases may be affected by factors such as the expiration of promotional interest rates, increases in the interest rate index, and negative amortization. Negative amortization also results in lower levels of home equity as compared to a traditional amortizing mortgage product. When borrowers go to sell or refinance the property, they may find that negative amortization has substantially reduced or eliminated their equity in it even when the property has appreciated. The concern that consumers may not fully understand these products would be exacerbated by marketing and promotional practices that emphasize potential benefits without also providing clear and balanced information about material risks.

> FN14 Refer to the "Interagency Advisory on Mortgage Banking", February 25, 2003, issued by the bank and thrift regulatory agencies. Federally Insured Credit Unions with assets of $10 million or more are reminded they must report and value nontraditional mortgages and related mortgage servicing rights, if any, consistent with generally accepted accounting principles in the Call Reports they file with the NCUA Board.

In light of these considerations, communications with consumers, including advertisements, oral statements, promotional materials, and monthly statements, should provide clear and balanced information about the relative benefits and risks of these products, including the risk of payment shock and the risk of negative amortization. Clear, balanced, and timely communication to consumers of the risks of these products will provide consumers with useful information at crucial decision-making points, such as when they are shopping for loans or deciding which monthly payment amount to make. Such communication should help minimize potential consumer confusion and complaints, foster good customer relations, and reduce legal and other risks to the institution.

Legal Risks—Institutions that offer nontraditional mortgage products must ensure that they do so in a manner that complies with all applicable laws and regulations. With respect to the disclosures and other information provided to consumers, applicable laws and regulations include the following:

Truth in Lending Act (TILA) and its implementing regulation, Regulation Z.
Section 5 of the Federal Trade Commission Act (F.T.C. Act). TILA and Regulation Z contain rules governing disclosures that institutions must provide for closed-end mortgages in advertisements, with an application,[15] before loan consummation, and when interest rates change. Section 5 of the F.T.C. Act prohibits unfair or deceptive acts or practices.[16]

Other Federal laws, including the fair lending laws and the Real Estate Settlement Procedures Act (RESPA), also apply to these transactions. Moreover, the Agencies note that the sale or securitization of a loan may not affect an institution's potential liability for violations of TILA, RESPA, the F.T.C. Act, or other laws in connection with its origination of the loan. State laws, including laws regarding unfair or deceptive acts or practices, also may apply.

> FN15 These program disclosures apply to ARM products and must be provided at the time an application is provided or before the consumer pays a nonrefundable fee, whichever is earlier.
> FN16 The OCC, the Board, and the FDIC enforce this provision under the F.T.C. Act and section 8 of the FDI Act. Each of these agencies has also issued supervisory guidance to the institutions under their respective jurisdictions concerning unfair or deceptive acts or practices. *See* OCC Advisory Letter 2002–3—Guidance on Unfair or Deceptive Acts or Practices, March 22, 2002; Joint Board and FDIC Guidance on Unfair or Deceptive Acts or Practices by State-Chartered Banks, March 11, 2004. Federally insured credit unions are prohibited from using any advertising or promotional material that is inaccurate, misleading, or deceptive in any way concerning its products, services, or financial condition. 12 CFR 740.2. The OTS also has a regulation that prohibits savings associations from using advertisements or other representations that are inaccurate or misrepresent the services or contracts offered. 12 CFR 563.27. This regulation supplements its authority under the F.T.C. Act.

Recommended Practices
Recommended practices for addressing the risks raised by nontraditional mortgage products include the following:[17]

Communications with Consumers— When promoting or describing nontraditional mortgage products, institutions should provide consumers with information that is designed to help them make informed decisions when selecting and using these products. Meeting this objective requires appropriate attention to the timing, content, and clarity of information presented to consumers. Thus, institutions should provide consumers with information at a time that will help consumers select products and choose among payment options. For example, institutions should offer clear and balanced product descriptions when a consumer is shopping for a mortgage—such as when the consumer makes an inquiry to the institution about a mortgage product and receives information about nontraditional mortgage products, or when marketing relating to nontraditional mortgage products is provided by the institution to the consumer—not just upon the submission of an application or at consummation.[18] The provision of such information would serve as an important supplement to the disclosures currently required under TILA and Regulation Z or other laws.[19]

> FN17 Institutions also should review the recommendations relating to mortgage lending practices set forth in other supervisory guidance from their respective primary regulators, as applicable, including guidance on abusive lending practices.
>
> FN18 Institutions also should strive to: (1) Focus on information important to consumer decision making; (2) highlight key information so that it will be noticed; (3) employ a user-friendly and readily navigable format for presenting the information; and (4) use plain language, with concrete and realistic examples. Comparative tables and information describing key features of available loan products, including reduced documentation programs, also may be useful for consumers considering the nontraditional mortgage products and other loan features described in this guidance.
>
> FN19 Institutions may not be able to incorporate all of the practices recommended in this guidance when advertising nontraditional mortgages through certain forms of media, such as radio, television, or billboards. Nevertheless, institutions should provide clear and balanced information about the risks of these products in all forms of advertising.

Promotional Materials and Product Descriptions. Promotional materials and other product descriptions should provide information about the costs, terms, features, and risks of nontraditional mortgages that can assist consumers in their product selection decisions, including information about the matters discussed below.

Payment Shock. Institutions should apprise consumers of potential increases in payment obligations for these products, including circumstances in which interest rates or negative amortization reach a contractual limit. For example, product descriptions could state the maximum monthly payment a consumer would be required to pay under a hypothetical loan example once amortizing payments are required and the interest rate and negative amortization caps have been reached.[20] Such information also could describe when structural payment changes will occur (*e.g.*, when introductory rates expire, or when amortizing payments are required), and what the new payment amount would be or how it would be calculated. As applicable, these descriptions could indicate that a higher payment may be required at other points in time due to factors such as negative amortization or increases in the interest rate index.

Negative Amortization. When negative amortization is possible under the terms of a nontraditional mortgage product, consumers should be apprised of the potential for increasing principal balances and decreasing home equity, as well as other potential adverse consequences of negative amortization. For example, product descriptions should disclose the effect of negative amortization on loan balances and home equity, and could describe the potential consequences to the consumer of making minimum payments that cause the loan to negatively amortize. (One possible consequence is that it could be more difficult to refinance the loan or to obtain cash upon a sale of the home).

Prepayment Penalties. If the institution may impose a penalty in the event that the consumer prepays the mortgage, consumers should be alerted to this fact and to the need to ask the lender about the amount of any such penalty.[21]

Cost of Reduced Documentation Loans. If an institution offers both reduced and full documentation loan programs and there is a pricing premium attached to the reduced documentation program, consumers should be alerted to this fact.

> FN20 Consumers also should be apprised of other material changes in payment obligations, such as balloon payments.
> FN21 Federal credit unions are prohibited from imposing prepayment penalties. 12 CFR 701.21(c)(6).

Monthly Statements on Payment Option ARMs. Monthly statements that are provided to consumers on payment option ARMs should provide information that enables consumers to make informed payment choices, including an explanation of each payment option available and the impact of that choice on loan balances. For example, the monthly payment statement should contain an explanation, as applicable, next to the minimum payment amount that making this payment would result in an increase to the consumer's outstanding loan balance. Payment statements also could provide the consumer's current loan balance, what portion of the consumer's previous payment was allocated to principal and to interest, and, if applicable, the amount by which the principal balance increased. Institutions should avoid leading payment option ARM borrowers to select a non-amortizing or negatively-amortizing payment (for example, through the format or content of monthly statements).

Practices to Avoid. Institutions also should avoid practices that obscure significant risks to the consumer. For example, if an institution advertises or promotes a nontraditional mortgage by emphasizing the comparatively lower initial payments permitted for these loans, the institution also should provide clear and comparably prominent information alerting the consumer to the risks. Such information should explain, as relevant, that these payment amounts will increase, that a balloon payment may be due, and that the loan balance will not decrease and may even increase due to the deferral of interest and/or principal payments. Similarly, institutions should avoid promoting payment patterns that are structurally unlikely to occur.[22] Such practices could raise legal and other risks for institutions, as described more fully above.

> FN22 For example, marketing materials for payment option ARMs may promote low predictable payments until the recast date. Such marketing should be avoided in circumstances in which the minimum payments are so low that negative amortization caps would be reached and higher payment obligations would be triggered before the scheduled recast, even if interest rates remain constant.

Institutions also should avoid such practices as: Giving consumers unwarranted assurances or predictions about the future direction of interest rates (and, consequently, the borrower's future obligations); making one-sided representations about the cash savings or expanded buying power to be realized from nontraditional mortgage products in comparison with amortizing mortgages; suggesting that initial minimum payments in a payment option ARM will cover accrued interest (or principal and interest) charges; and making misleading claims that interest rates or payment obligations for these products are ''fixed''.

Control Systems—Institutions should develop and use strong control systems to monitor whether actual practices are consistent with their policies and procedures relating to nontraditional mortgage products. Institutions should design control systems to address compliance and consumer information concerns as well as the safety and soundness considerations discussed in this guidance. Lending personnel should be trained so that they are able to convey information to consumers about product terms and risks in a timely, accurate, and balanced manner. As products evolve and new products are introduced, lending personnel should receive additional training, as necessary, to continue to be able to convey information to consumers in this manner. Lending personnel should be monitored to determine whether they are following these policies and procedures. Institutions should review consumer complaints to identify potential compliance, reputation, and other risks. Attention should be paid to appropriate legal review and to using compensation programs that do not improperly encourage lending personnel to direct consumers to particular products.

With respect to nontraditional mortgage loans that an institution makes, purchases, or services using a third party, such as a mortgage broker, correspondent, or other intermediary, the institution should take appropriate steps to mitigate risks relating to compliance and consumer information concerns discussed in this guidance. These steps would ordinarily include, among other things, (1) Conducting due diligence and establishing other criteria for entering into and maintaining relationships with such third parties, (2) establishing criteria for third-party compensation designed to avoid providing incentives for originations inconsistent with this guidance, (3) setting requirements for agreements with such third parties, (4) establishing procedures and systems to monitor compliance with applicable agreements, bank policies, and laws, and (5) implementing appropriate corrective actions in the event that the third party fails to comply with applicable agreements, bank policies, or laws.

Appendix: Terms Used in This Document

Interest-only Mortgage Loan—A nontraditional mortgage on which, for a specified number of years (*e.g.*, three or five years), the borrower is required to pay only the interest due on the loan during which time the rate may fluctuate or may be fixed. After the interest-only period, the rate may be fixed or fluctuate based on the prescribed index and payments include both principal and interest.

Payment Option ARM—A nontraditional mortgage that allows the borrower to choose from a number of different payment options. For example, each month, the borrower may choose a minimum payment option based on a ''start'' or introductory interest rate, an interest-only payment option based on the fully indexed interest rate, or a fully amortizing principal and interest payment option based on a 15-year or 30-year loan term, plus any required escrow payments. The minimum payment option can be less than the interest accruing on the loan, resulting in negative amortization. The interest-only option avoids negative amortization but does not provide for principal amortization. After a specified number of years, or if the loan reaches a certain negative amortization cap, the required monthly payment amount is recast to require payments that will fully amortize the outstanding balance over the remaining loan term.

Reduced Documentation—A loan feature that is commonly referred to as ''low doc/no doc'', ''no income/no asset'', ''stated income'' or ''stated assets''. For mortgage loans with this feature, an institution sets reduced or minimal documentation standards to substantiate the borrower's income and assets.

Simultaneous Second-Lien Loan—A lending arrangement where either a closed-end second-lien or a home equity line of credit (HELOC) is originated simultaneously with the first lien mortgage loan, typically in lieu of a higher down payment.

Dated: September 25, 2006.
John C. Dugan,
Comptroller of the Currency.
By order of the Board of Governors of the Federal Reserve System, September 27, 2006.
Jennifer J. Johnson,
Secretary of the Board.
Dated at Washington, DC, this 27th day of September, 2006. Federal Deposit Insurance Corporation.
Robert E. Feldman,
Executive Secretary.

Dated: September 28, 2006.

By the Office of Thrift Supervision. John M. Reich, *Director.*

By the National Credit Union Administration on September 28, 2006.

JoAnn M. Johnson,

Chairman.

[FR Doc. 06–8480 Filed 10–3–06; 8:45 am]

BILLING CODE 4810–33–P, 6210–01–P, 6714–01–P, 6720–01–P, 7535–01–P

APPENDIX N

F.T.C. POLICY STATEMENT OF DECEPTION

F.T.C. POLICY STATEMENT ON DECEPTION[1]
Appended to <u>Cliffdale Associates, Inc.</u>, 103 F.T.C. 110, 174 (1984).

FEDERAL TRADE COMMISSION
WASHINGTON, D.C. 20580

October 14, 1983

The Honorable John D. Dingell
Chairman
Committee on Energy and Commerce
U.S. House of Representatives
Washington, D.C. 20515

Dear Mr. Chairman:

This letter responds to the Committee's inquiry regarding the Commission's enforcement policy against deceptive acts or practices.[1] We also hope this letter will provide guidance to the public.

Section 5 of the F.T.C. Act declares unfair or deceptive acts or practices unlawful. Section 12 specifically prohibits false ads likely to induce the purchase of food, drugs, devices or cosmetics. Section 15 defines a false ad for purposes of Section 12 as one which is "misleading in a material respect."[2] Numerous Commission and judicial decisions have defined and elaborated on the phrase "deceptive acts or practices" under both Sections 5 and 12. Nowhere, however, is there a single definitive statement of the Commission's view of its authority. The Commission believes that such a statement would be useful to the public, as well as the Committee in its continuing review of our jurisdiction.

We have therefore reviewed the decided cases to synthesize the most important principles of general applicability. We have attempted to provide a concrete indication of the manner in which the Commission will enforce its deception mandate. In so doing, we intend to address the concerns that have been raised about the meaning of deception, and thereby attempt to provide a greater sense of certainty as to how the concept will be applied.[3]

I. SUMMARY

Certain elements undergird all deception cases. First, there must be a representation, omission or practice that is likely to mislead the consumer.[4] Practices that have been found misleading or deceptive in specific cases include false oral or written representations, misleading price claims, sales of hazardous or systematically defective products or services without adequate disclosures, failure to disclose information regarding pyramid sales, use of bait and switch techniques, failure to perform promised services, and failure to meet warranty obligations.[5]

Second, we examine the practice from the perspective of a consumer acting reasonably in the circumstances. If the representation or practice affects or is directed primarily to a particular group, the Commission examines reasonableness from the perspective of that group.

---

[1] http://www.ftc.gov/bcp/policystmt/ad-decept.htm (last visited June 23, 2008).

Third, the representation, omission, or practice must be a "material" one. The basic question is whether the act or practice is likely to affect the consumer's conduct or decision with regard to a product or service. If so, the practice is material, and consumer injury is likely, because consumers are likely to have chosen differently but for the deception. In many instances, materiality, and hence injury, can be presumed from the nature of the practice. In other instances, evidence of materiality may be necessary.

Thus, the Commission will find deception if there is a representation, omission or practice that is likely to mislead the consumer acting reasonably in the circumstances, to the consumer's detriment. We discuss each of these elements below.

II. THERE MUST BE A REPRESENTATION, OMISSION, OR PRACTICE THAT IS LIKELY TO MISLEAD THE CONSUMER.

Most deception involves written or oral misrepresentations, or omissions of material information. Deception may also occur in other forms of conduct associated with a sales transaction. The entire advertisement, transaction or course of dealing will be considered. The issue is whether the act or practice is likely to mislead, rather than whether it causes actual deceptions.

Of course, the Commission must find that a representation, omission, or practice occurred in cases of express claims, the representation itself establishes the meaning. In cases of implied claims, the Commission will often be able to determine meaning through an examination of the representation itself, including an evaluation of such factors as the entire document, the juxtaposition of various phrases in the document, the nature of the claim, and the nature of the transactions.[7] In other situations, the Commission will require extrinsic evidence that reasonable consumers reach the implied claims.[8] In all instances, the Commission will carefully consider any extrinsic evidence that is introduced.

Some cases involve omission of material information, the disclosure of which is necessary to prevent the claim, practice, or sale from being misleading.[9] Information may be omitted from written[10] or oral[11] representations or from the commercial transaction.12

In some circumstances, the Commission can presume that consumers are likely to reach false beliefs about the product or service because of an omission. At other times, however, the Commission may require evidence on consumers' expectations.[13]

Marketing and point-of-sales practices that are likely to mislead consumers are also deceptive. For instance, in bait and switch cases, a violation occurs when the offer to sell the product is not a bona fide offer.[14] The Commission has also found deception where a sales representative misrepresented the purpose of the initial contact with customers.[15] When a product is sold, there is an implied representation that the product is fit for the purposes for which it is sold. When it is not, deception occurs.[16] There may be a concern about the way a product or service is marketed, such as where inaccurate or incomplete information is provided.[17] A failure to perform services promised under a warranty or by contract can also be deceptive.[18]

III. THE ACT OR PRACTICE MUST BE CONSIDERED FROM THE PERSPECTIVE OF THE REASONABLE CONSUMER

The Commission believes that to be deceptive the representation, omission or practice must be likely to mislead reasonable consumers under the circumstances.[19] The test is whether the consumer's interpretation or reaction is reasonable.[20] When representations or sales practices are targeted to a specific audience, the Commission determines the effect of the practice on a reasonable member of that group. In evaluating a particular practice, the Commission considers the totality of the practice in determining how reasonable consumers are likely to respond.

A company is not liable for every interpretation or action by a consumer. In an advertising context, this principle has been well-stated:

An advertiser cannot be charged with liability with respect to every conceivable misconception, however outlandish, to which his representations might be subject among the foolish or feeble-minded. Some people, because of ignorance or incomprehension, may be misled by even a scrupulously honest claim. Perhaps a few misguided souls believe, for example, that all "Danish pastry" is made in Denmark. Is it therefore an actionable deception to advertise "Danish pastry" when it is made in this country.? Of course not, A representation does not become "false and deceptive" merely because it will be unreasonably misunderstood by an insignificant and unrepresentative segment of the class of persons to whom the representation is addressed. Heinz W. Kirchner, 63 F.T.C. 1282, 1290 (1963).

To be considered reasonable, the interpretation or reaction does not have to be the only one.[21] When a seller's representation conveys more than one meaning to reasonable consumers, one of which is false, the seller is liable for the misleading interpretation.[22] An interpretation will be presumed reasonable if it is the one the respondent intended to convey.

The Commission has used this standard in its past decisions. The test applied by the Commission is whether the interpretation is reasonable in light of the claim."[23] In the Listerine case, the Commission evaluated the claim from the perspective of the "average listener."[24] In a case involving the sale of encyclopedias, the Commission observed "[i]n determining the meaning of an advertisement, a piece of promotional material or a sales presentation, the important criterion is the net impression that it is likely to make on the general populace."[25] The decisions in American Home Products, Bristol Myers, and Sterling Drug are replete with references to reasonable consumer interpretations.[26] In a land sales case, the Commission evaluated the oral statements and written representations "in light of the sophistication and understanding of the persons to whom they were directed."[27] Omission cases are no different: the Commission examines the failure to disclose in light of expectations and understandings of the typical buyer[28] regarding the claims made.

When representations or sales practices are targeted to a specific audience, such as children, the elderly, or the terminally ill, the Commission determines the effect of the practice on a reasonable member of that group.[29] For instance, if a company markets a cure to the terminally ill, the practice will be evaluated from the perspective of how it affects the ordinary member of that group. Thus, terminally ill consumers might be particularly susceptible to exaggerated cure claims. By the same token, a practice or representation directed to a well-educated group, such as a prescription drug advertisement to doctors, would be judged in light of the knowledge and sophistication of that group.[30]

As it has in the past, the Commission will evaluate the entire advertisement, transaction, or course of dealing in determining how reasonable consumers are likely to respond. Thus, in advertising the Commission will examine "the entire mosaic, rather than each tile separately."[31] As explained by a court of appeals in a recent case:

The Commission's right to scrutinize the visual and aural imagery of advertisements follows from the principle that the Commission looks to the impression made by the advertisements as a whole. Without this mode of examination, the Commission would have limited recourse against crafty advertisers whose deceptive messages were conveyed by means other than, or in addition to, spoken words. American Home Products, 695 F.2d 681, 688 (3d Cir. Dec. 3, 1982).[32]

In a case involving a weight loss product, the Commission observed:

It is obvious that dieting is the conventional method of losing weight. But it is equally obvious that many people who need or want to lose weight regard dieting as bitter medicine. To these corpulent consumers the promises of weight loss without dieting are the Siren's call, and advertising that heralds unrestrained consumption while muting the inevitable need for temperance, if not abstinence, simply does not pass muster. Porter & Dietsch, 90 F.T.C. 770, 864-865 (1977), 605 F.2d 294 (7th Cir. 1979), cert. denied, 445 U.S. 950 (1980).

Children have also been the specific target of ads or practices. In *Ideal Toy*, the Commission adopted the Hearing Examiner's conclusion that:

False, misleading and deceptive advertising claims beamed at children tend to exploit unfairly a consumer group unqualified by age or experience to anticipate or appreciate the possibility that representations may he exaggerated or untrue. *Ideal Toy*, 64 F.T.C. 297, 310 (1964).

See also, *Avalon Industries Inc.*, 83 F.T.C. 1728, 1750 (1974).

In a subsequent case, the Commission explained that "[i]n evaluating advertising representations, we are required to look at the complete advertisement and formulate our opinions on them on the basis of the net general impression conveyed by them and not on isolated excerpts." *Standard Oil of Calif*, 84 F.T.C. 1401, 1471 (1974), *aff'd as modified*, 577 F.2d 653 (9th Cir. 1978), *reissued*, 96 F.T.C. 380 (1980).

The Third Circuit stated succinctly the Commission's standard. "The tendency of the advertising to deceive must be judged by viewing it as a whole, without emphasizing isolated words or phrases apart from their context." *Beneficial Corp. v. FTC*, 542 F.2d 611, 617 (3d Cir. 1976), *cert denied*, 430 U.S. 983 (1977).

Commission cases reveal specific guidelines. Depending on the circumstances, accurate information in the text may not remedy a false headline because reasonable consumers may glance only at the headline.[33] Written disclosures or fine print may be insufficient to correct a misleading representations.[34] Other practices of the company may direct consumers' attention away from the qualifying disclosures.[35] Oral statements, label disclosures or point-of-sale material will not necessarily correct a deceptive representation or omission.[36] Thus, when the first contact between a seller and a buyer occurs through a deceptive practice, the law may be violated even if the truth is subsequently made known to the purchaser.[37] Pro forma statements or disclaimers may not cure otherwise deceptive messages or practices.[38]

Qualifying disclosures must be legible and understandable. In evaluating such disclosures, the Commission recognizes that in many circumstances, reasonable consumers do not read the entirety of an ad or are directed away from the importance of the qualifying phrase by the acts or statements of the seller. Disclosures that conform to the Commission's Statement of Enforcement Policy regarding clear and conspicuous disclosures, which applies to television advertising, are generally adequate, CCH Trade Regulation Reporter, ¶ 7569.09 (Oct. 21, 1970). Less elaborate disclosures may also suffice.[39]

Certain practices, however, are unlikely to deceive consumers acting reasonably. Thus, the Commission generally will not bring advertising cases based on subjective claims (taste, feel, appearance, smell) or on correctly stated opinion claims if consumers understand the source and limitations of the opinion.[40] Claims phrased as opinions are actionable, however, if they are not honestly held, if they misrepresent the qualifications of the holder or the basis of his opinion or if the recipient reasonably interprets them as implied statements of fact.[41]

The Commission generally will not pursue cases involving obviously exaggerated or puffing representations, *i.e.*, those that the ordinary consumers do not take seriously.42 Some exaggerated claims, however, may be taken seriously by consumers and are actionable. For instance, in rejecting a respondent's argument that use of the words "electronic miracle" to describe a television antenna was puffery, the Commission stated:

Although not insensitive to respondent's concern that the term miracle is commonly used in situations short of changing water into wine, we must conclude that the use of "electronic miracle" in the context of respondent's grossly exaggerated claims would lead consumers to give added credence to the overall suggestion that this device is superior to other types of antennae. *Jay Norris*, 91 F.T.C. 751, 847 n.20 (1978), *aff'd*, 598 F.2d 1244 (2d Cir.), *cert. denied*, 444 U.S. 980 (1979).

Finally, as a matter of policy, when consumers can easily evaluate the product or service, it is inexpensive, and it is frequently purchased, the Commission will examine the practice closely before issuing a complaint based on deception. There is little incentive for sellers to misrepresent (either by an explicit false statement or a deliberate false implied statement) in these circumstances since they normally would seek to encourage repeat purchases. Where, as here, market incentives place strong constraints on the likelihood of deception, the Commission will examine a practice closely before proceeding.

In sum, the Commission will consider many factors in determining the reaction of the ordinary consumer to a claim or practice. As would any trier of fact, the Commission will evaluate the totality of the ad or the practice and ask questions such as: how clear is the representation? how conspicuous is any qualifying information? how important is the omitted information? do other sources for the omitted information exist? how familiar is the public with the product or service?[43]

IV. THE REPRESENTATION, OMISSION OR PRACTICE MUST BE MATERIAL

The third element of deception is materiality. That is, a representation, omission or practice must be a material one for deception to occur.[44] A "material" misrepresentation or practice is one which is likely to affect a consumer's choice of or conduct regarding a product.[45] In other words, it is information that is important to consumers. If inaccurate or omitted information is material, injury is likely.[46]

The Commission considers certain categories of information presumptively material.[47] First, the Commission presumes that express claims are material.[48] As the Supreme Court stated recently, "[i]n the absence of factors that would distort the decision to advertise, we may assume that the willingness of a business to promote its products reflects a belief that consumers are interested in the advertising."[49] Where the seller knew, or should have known, that an ordinary consumer would need omitted information to evaluate the product or service, or that the claim was false, materiality will be presumed because the manufacturer intended the information or omission to have an effect.[50] Similarly, when evidence exists that a seller intended to make an implied claim, the Commission will infer materiality.[51]

The Commission also considers claims or omissions material if they significantly involve health, safety, or other areas with which the reasonable consumer would be concerned. Depending on the facts, information pertaining to the central characteristics of the product or service will be presumed material. Information has been found material where it concerns the purpose,[52] safety,[53] efficacy,[54] or cost,[55] of the product or service. Information is also likely to be material if it concerns durability, performance, warranties or quality. Information pertaining to a finding by another agency regarding the product may also be material.[56]

Where the Commission cannot find materiality based on the above analysis, the Commission may require evidence that the claim or omission is likely to be considered important by consumers. This evidence can be the fact that the product or service with the feature represented costs more than an otherwise comparable product without the feature, a reliable survey of consumers, or credible testimony.[57]

A finding of materiality is also a finding that injury is likely to exist because of the representation, omission, sales practice, or marketing technique. Injury to consumers can take many forms.[58] Injury exists if consumers would have chosen differently but for the deception. If different choices are likely, the claim is material, and injury is likely as well. Thus, injury and materiality are different names for the same concept.

V. CONCLUSION

The Commission will find an act or practice deceptive if there is a misrepresentation, omission, or other practice, that misleads the consumer acting reasonably in the circumstances, to the consumer's detriment. The Commission will not generally require extrinsic evidence concerning the representations understood by reasonable consumers or the materiality of a challenged claim, but in some instances extrinsic evidence will be necessary.

The Commission intends to enforce the F.T.C. Act vigorously. We will investigate, and prosecute where appropriate, acts or practices that are deceptive. We hope this letter will help provide you and the public with a greater sense of certainty concerning how the Commission will exercise its jurisdiction over deception. Please do not hesitate to call if we can be of any further assistance.

By direction of the Commission, Commissioners Pertschuk and Bailey dissenting, with separate statements attached and with separate response to the Committee's request for a legal analysis to follow.

/s/James C. Miller III
Chairman

cc: Honorable James T. Broyhill
Honorable James J. Florio
Honorable Norman F. Lent

Endnotes:

[1]S. Rep. No. 97-451, 97th Cong., 2d Sess. 16; H.R. Rep. No. 98-156, Part I, 98th Cong., 1st Sess. 6 (1983). The Commission's enforcement policy against unfair acts or practices is set forth in a letter to Senators Ford and Danforth, dated December 17, 1980.

[2]In determining whether an ad is misleading, Section 15 requires that the Commission take into account "representations made or suggested" as well as "the extent to which the advertisement fails to reveal facts material in light of such representations or material with respect to consequences which may result from the use of the commodity to which the advertisement relates under the conditions prescribed in said advertisement, or under such conditions as are customary or usual." 15 U.S.C. 55. If an act or practice violates Section 12, it also violates Section 5. *Simeon Management Corp.*, 87 F.T.C. 1184, 1219 (1976), *aff'd*, 579 F.2d 1137 (9th Cir. 1978); *Porter & Dietsch*, 90 F.T.C. 770, 873-74 (1977), *aff'd*, 605 P.2d 294 (7th Cir. 1979), *cert. denied*, 445 U.S. 950 (1980).

[3]Chairman Miller has proposed that Section 5 be amended to define deceptive acts. Hearing Before the Subcommittee for Consumers of the Committee on Commerce, Science, and Transportation, United States Senate, 97th Cong., 2d Sess. *FTCs Authority Over Deceptive Advertising*, July 22,1982, Serial No. 97-134, p. 9. Three Commissioners believe a legislative definition is unnecessary. *Id*. at 45 (Commissioner Clanton), at 51 (Commissioner Bailey) and at 76 (Commissioner Pertschuk). Commissioner Douglas supports a statutory definition of deception. Prepared statement by

Commissioner George W. Douglas, Hearing Before the Subcommittee for Consumers of the Committee on Commerce, Science and Transportation, United States Senate, 98th Cong. lst Sess. (March 16, 1983) p. 2.

[4]A misrepresentation is an express or implied statement contrary to fact. A misleading omission occurs when qualifying information necessary to prevent a practice, claim, representation, or reasonable expectation or belief from being misleading is not disclosed. Not all omissions are deceptive, even if providing the information would benefit consumers. As the Commission noted in rejecting a proposed requirement for nutrition disclosures, "In the final analysis, the question whether an advertisement requires affirmative disclosure would depend on the nature and extent of the nutritional claim made in the advertisement.". ITT Continental Baking Co. Inc., 83 F.T.C. 865, 965 (1976). In determining whether an omission is deceptive, the Commission will examine the overall impression created by a practice, claim, or representation. For example, the practice of offering a product for sale creates an implied representation that it is fit for the purposes for which it is sold. Failure to disclose that the product is not fit constitutes a deceptive omission. [See discussion below at 5-6) Omissions may also be deceptive where the representations made are not literally misleading, if those representations create a reasonable expectation or belief among consumers which is misleading, absent the omitted disclosure.

Non-deceptive emissions may still violate Section 5 if they are unfair. For instance, the R-Value Rule, 16 C.F.R. 460.5 (1983), establishes a specific method for testing insulation ability, and requires disclosure of the figure in advertising. The Statement of Basis and Purpose, 44 FR 50,242 (1979), refers to a deception theory to support disclosure requirements when certain misleading claims are made, but the rule's general disclosure requirement is based on an unfairness theory. Consumers could not reasonably avoid injury in selecting insulation because no standard method of measurement existed.

[5]Advertising that lacks a reasonable basis is also deceptive. *Firestone*, 81 F.T.C. 398, 451-52 (1972), *aff'd*, 481 F.2d 246 (6th Cir.), *cert. denied*, 414 U.S. 1112 (1973). *National Dynamics*, 82 F.T.C. 488, 549-50 (1973); *aff'd and remanded on other grounds*, 492 F.2d 1333 (2d Cir.), *cert. denied*, 419 U.S. 993 (1974), *reissued*, 85 F.T.C. 391 (1976). *National Comm'n on Egg Nutrition*, 88 F.T.C. 89, 191 (1976), *aff'd*, 570 P.2d 157 (7th Cir.), *cert. denied*, 439 U.S. 821, *reissued*, 92 F.T.C. 848 (1978). The deception theory is based on the fact that most ads making objective claims imply, and many expressly state, that an advertiser has certain specific grounds for the claims. If the advertiser does not, the consumer is acting under a false impression. The consumer might have perceived the advertising differently had he or she known the advertiser had no basis for the claim. This letter does not address the nuances of the reasonable basis doctrine, which the Commission is currently reviewing. 48 FR 10,471 (March 11, 1983)

[6]In *Beneficial Corp. v. FTC*, 542 F.2d 611, 617 (3d Cir. 1976), the court noted "the likelihood or propensity of deception is the criterion by which advertising is measured."

[7]On evaluation of the entire document:

The Commission finds that many of the challenged Anacin advertisements, when viewed in their entirety, did convey the message that the superiority of this product has been proven [footnote omitted]. It is immaterial that the word "established", which was used in the complaint, generally did not appear in the ads; the important consideration is the net impression conveyed to the public. *American Home Products*, 98 F.T.C. 136, 374 (1981), *aff'd*, 695 F.2d (3d Cir. 1982).

On the juxtaposition of phrases:

On this label, the statement "Kills Germs By Millions On Contact" immediately precedes the assertion "For General Oral Hygiene Bad Breath, Colds and Resultant Sore Throats" [footnote omitted]. By placing these two statements in close proximity, respondent has conveyed the message that since Listerine can kill millions of germs, it can cure, prevent and ameliorate colds and sore throats [footnote omitted]. *Warner Lambert*, 86F.T.C. 1398, 1489-90 (1975), *aff'd*, 562 F.2d 749 (D.C. Cir. 1977), *cert. denied*, 435 U.S. 950 (1978) (emphasis in original).

On the nature of the claim, *Firestone* is relevant. There the Commission noted that the alleged misrepresentation concerned the safety of respondent's product, "an issue of great significance to consumers. On this issue, the Commission has required scrupulous accuracy in advertising claims, for obvious reasons." 81 F.T.C. 398,456 (1972), *aff'd*, 481 F.2d 246 (6th Cir.), *cert. denied*, 414 U.S. IU2 (1973).

In each of these cases, other factors, including in some instances surveys, were in evidence on the meaning of the ad.

[8]The evidence can consist of expert opinion, consumer testimony (particularly in cases involving oral representations), copy tests, surveys, or any other reliable evidence of consumer interpretation.

[9]As the Commission noted in the Cigarette rule, "The nature, appearance, or intended use of a product may create the impression on the mind of the consumer . . . and if the impression is false, and if the seller does not take adequate steps to correct it, he is responsible for an unlawful deception." Cigarette Rule Statement of Basis and Purpose, 29 FR 8324, 8352 (July 2, 1964).

[10]*Porter & Dietsch*, 90 F.T.C. 770, 873-74 (1977), *aff'd.* 605 F.2d 294 (7th Cir. 1979), *cert. denied*, 445 U.S. 950 (1980); *Simeon Management Corp.*, 87 F.T.C. 1184, 1230 (1976), *aff'd*, 579 F.2d 1137 (9th Cir. 1978).

[11]*See, e.g., Grolier*, 91 F.T.C. 315,480 (1978), *remanded on other grounds*, 615 F.2d 1215 (9th Cir. 1980), *modified on other grounds*, 98 FM 882 (1981), *reissued*, 99 F.T.C. 379 (1982).

[12]In *Peacock Buick*, 86 F.T.C. 1532 (1975), *aff'd*, 553 F.2d 97 (4th Cir. 1977), the Commission held that absent a clear and early disclosure of the prior use of a late model car, deception can result from the setting in which a sale is made and the expectations of the buyer ... *Id* at 1555.

Even in the absence of affirmative misrepresentations, it is misleading for the seller of late model used cars to fail to reveal the particularized uses to which they have been put... When a later model used car is sold at close to list price ... the assumption likely to be made by some purchasers is that, absent disclosure to the contrary, such car has not previously been used in a way that might substantially impair its value. In such circumstances, failure to disclose a disfavored prior use may tend to mislead. *Id* at 1557-58.

[13]In *Leonard Porter*, the Commission dismissed a complaint alleging that respondents' sale of unmarked products in Alaska led consumers to believe erroneously that they were handmade in Alaska by natives. Complaint counsel had failed to show that consumers of Alaskan craft assumed respondents' products were handmade by Alaskans in Alaska. The Commission was unwilling, absent evidence, to infer from a viewing of the items that the products would tend to mislead consumers.

By requiring such evidence, we do not imply that elaborate proof of consumer beliefs or behavior is necessary, even in a case such as this, to establish the requisite capacity to deceive. However, where visual inspection is inadequate, some extrinsic testimony evidence must be added. 88 F.T.C. 546, 626, n.5 (1976).

[14]*Bait and Switch Policy Protocol*, December 10, 1975; Guides Against Bait Advertising, 16 C.F.R. 238.0 (1967). 32 PR 15,540.

[15]*Encyclopedia Britannica* 87 F.T.C. 421, 497 (1976), *aff'd*, 605 F.2d 964 (7th Cir. 1979), *cert. denied*, 445 U.S. 934 (1980), *modified*, 100 F.T.C. 500 (1982).

[16]See the complaints in *BayleySuit*, C-3117 (consent agreement) (September 30,1983) [102 F.T.C. 1285]; *Figgie International, Inc.*, D. 9166 (May 17, 1983).

[17]The Commission's complaints in *Chrysler Corporation*, 99 F.T.C. 347 (1982), and *Volkswagen of America*, 99 F.T.C. 446 (1982), alleged the failure to disclose accurate use and care instructions for replacing oil filters was deceptive. The complaint in *Ford Motor Co.*, D. 9154, 96 F.T.C. 362 (1980), charged Ford with failing to disclose a "piston scuffing" defect to purchasers and owners which was allegedly widespread and costly to repair. *See also General Motors*, D. 9145 (provisionally accepted consent agreement, April 26, 1983). [102 F.T.C. 1741]

[18]*See Jay Norris Corp.*, 91 F.T.C. 751 (1978), *aff'd with modified language in order*, 598 P.2d 1244 (2d Cir. 1979), *cert. denied*, 444 U.S. 980 (1979) (failure to consistently meet guarantee claims of "immediate and prompt" delivery as well as money back guarantees); *Southern States Distributing Co.*, 83 F.T.C. 1126 (1973) (failure to honor oral and written product maintenance guarantees, as represented); *Skylark Originals, Inc.*, 80 F.T.C. 337 (1972), *aff'd*, 475 F.2d 1396 (3d Cir. 1973) (failure to promptly honor moneyback guarantee as represented in advertisements and catalogs); *Capitol Manufacturing Corp.*, 73 F.T.C. 872 (1968) (failure to fully, satisfactorily and promptly meet all obligations and requirements under terms of service guarantee certificate).

[19]The evidence necessary to determine how reasonable consumers understand a representation is discussed in Section II of this letter.

[20]An interpretation may be reasonable even though it is not shared by a majority of consumers in the relevant class, or by particularly sophisticated consumers. A material practice that misleads a significant minority of reasonable consumers is deceptive. *See Heinz W. Kirchner*, 63 F.T.C. 1282 (1963).

[21]A secondary message understood by reasonable consumers is actionable if deceptive even though the primary message is accurate. *Sears, Roebuck & Co.*, 95 F.T.C. 406, 511 (1980), *aff'd* 676 F.2d 385, (9th Cir. 1982); *Chrysler*, 87 F.T.C. 749 (1976), *aff'd*, 561 F.2d 357 (D.C. Cir.), *reissued* 90 F.T.C. 606 (1977); *Rhodes Pharmacal Co.*, 208 F.2d 382, 387 (7th Cir. 1953), *aff'd*, 348 U.S. 940 (1955).

[22]*National Comm'n on Egg Nutrition*, 88 F.T.C. 89, 185 (1976), *enforced in part*, 570 F.2d 157 (7th Cir. 1977); *Jay Norris Corp.*, 91 F.T.C. 751, 836 (1978), *aff'd*, 598 F.2d 1244 (2d Cir. 1979).

[23]*National Dynamics*, 82 F.T.C. 488, 524, 548 (1973), *aff'd*, 492 P.2d 1333 (2d Cir.), *cert. denied*, 419 U.S. 993 (1974), *reissued* 85 F.T.C. 39-1 (1976).

[24]*Warner-Lambert*, 86 F.T.C. 1398, 1415 n.4 (1975), *aff'd*, 562 F.2d 749 (D.C. Cir. 1977), *cert denied*, 435 U.S. 950 (1978).

[25]*Grolier*, 91 F.T.C. 315, 430 (1978), *remanded on other grounds*, 615 F.2d 1215 (9th Cir. 1980), *modified on other grounds*, 98 F.T.C. 882 (1981), *reissued*, 99 F.T.C. 379 (1982).

[26]*American Home Products*, 98 F.T.C. 136 (1981), *aff'd* 695 F.2d 681 (3d Cir. 1982). consumers may be led to expect, quite reasonably..." (at 386); "... consumers may reasonably believe..." (*Id.* n.52); "... would reasonably have been understood by consumers...." (at 371); "the record shows that consumers could reasonably have understood this language . . ." (at 372). See also, pp. 373, 374, 375. *Bristol-Myers*, D. 8917 (July 5, 1983), appeal docketed, No. 83-4167 (2nd Cir. Sept. 12,1983)...... ads must be judged by the impression they make on reasonable members of the public . . . " (Slip Op. at 4); ". . . consumers could reasonably have understood . . ." (Slip Op. at 7); ". . . consumers could reasonably infer . . ." (Slip Op. at 11) [102 F.T.C. 21 (1983)]. *Sterling Drug, Inc.*, D. 8919 (July 5,1983), appeal docketed, No. 83-7700 (9th Cir. Sept. 14,1983)...... consumers could reasonably assume . . ." (Slip Op. at 9); ". . . consumers could reasonably interpret the ads . . ." (Slip Op. at 33). [102 F.T.C. 395 (1983)]

[27]*Horizon Corp.*, 97 F.T.C. 464, 810 n.13 (1981).

[28]*Simeon Management*, 87 F.T.C. 1184, 1230 (1976).

[29]The listed categories are merely examples. Whether children, terminally ill patients, or any other subgroup of the population will be considered a special audience depends on the specific factual context of the claim or the practice.

The Supreme Court has affirmed this approach. "The determination whether an advertisement is misleading requires consideration of the legal sophistication of its audience." *Bates v. Arizona*, 433 U.S. 350, 383 n.37 (1977).

[30]In one case, the Commission's complaint focused on seriously ill persons. The ALJ summarized: According to the complaint, the frustrations and hopes of the seriously ill and their families were exploited, and the representation had the tendency and capacity to induce the seriously ill to forego conventional medical treatment worsening their condition and in some cases hastening death, or to cause them to spend large amounts of money and to undergo the inconvenience of traveling for a non-existent "operation." *Travel King*, 86 F.T.C. 715, 719 (1975).

[31]*F.T.C. v. Sterling Drug*, 317 F.2d 669, 674 (2d Cir. 1963).

[32]Numerous cases exemplify this point. For instance, in *Pfizer*, the Commission ruled that "the net impression of the advertisement, evaluated from the perspective of the audience to whom the advertisement is directed, is controlling." 81 F.T.C. 23, 58 (1972).

[33]In *Litton Industries*, the Commission held that fine print disclosures that the surveys included only "Litton authorized" agencies were inadequate to remedy the deceptive characterization of the survey population in the headline. 97 F.T.C. 1, 71, n.6 (1981), *aff'd as modified*, 676 F.2d 364 (9th Cir. 1982). Compare the Commission's note in the same case that the fine print disclosure "Litton and one other brand" was reasonable to quote the claim that independent service technicians had been surveyed, "[F]ine print was a reasonable medium for disclosing a qualification of only limited relevance." 97 F.T.C. 1, 70, n.5 (1981).

In another case, the Commission held that the body of the ad corrected the possibly misleading headline because in order to enter the contest, the consumer had to read the text, and the text would eliminate any false impression stemming from the headline. *D.L. Blair*, 82 F.T.C. 234, 255,256 (1973).

In one case respondent's expert witness testified that the headline (and accompanying picture) of an ad would be the focal point of the first glance. He also told the administrative law judge that a consumer would spend [t]ypically a few seconds at most" on the ads at issue. *Crown Central*, 84 F.T.C. 1493, 1543 nn. 14-15 (1974),

[34]In *Giant Food*, the Commission agreed with the examiner that the fine-print disclaimer was inadequate to correct a deceptive impression. The Commission quoted from the examiner's finding that "very few if any of the persons who would read Giant's advertisements would take the trouble to, or did, read the fine print disclaimer." 61 F.T.C. 326, 348 (1962).

Cf. Beneficial Corp. v. FTC, 542 P.2d 611, 618 (3d Cir. 1976), where the court reversed the Commission's opinion that no qualifying language could eliminate the deception stemming from use of the slogan "Instant Tax Refund."

[35]"Respondents argue that the contracts which consumers signed indicated that credit life insurance was not required for financing, and that this disclosure obviated the possibility of deception. We disagree. It Is clear from consumer testimony that oral deception was employed in some instances to cause consumers to ignore the warning in their sales agreement. . ." *Peacock Buick*, 86 F.T.C. 1532, 1558-59 (1974).

[36]*Exposition Press*, 295 F.2d $69, 873 (2d Cir. 1961); *Gimbel Bros.*, 61 F.T.C. 1051, 1066 (1962); *Carter Products*, 186 F.2d 821, 824 (1951).

By the same token, money-back guarantees do not eliminate deception. In *Sears*, the Commission observed:

A money-back guarantee is no defense to a charge of deceptive advertising.... A money-back guarantee does not compensate the consumer for the often considerable time and expense incident to returning a major-ticket item and obtaining a replacement.

Sears, Roebuck and Co., 95 F.T.C. 406, 518 (1980), *aff'd*, 676 F.2d 385 (9th Cir. 1982). However, the existence of a guarantee, if honored, has a bearing on whether the Commission should exercise its discretion to prosecute. *See* Deceptive and Unsubstantiatcd Claims Policy Protocol, 1975.

[37]*See American Home Products*, 98 F.T.C. 136, 370 (1981), *aff'd*, 695 F.2d 681, 688 (3d Cir. Dec. 3, 1982), Whether a disclosure on the label cures deception in advertising depends on the circumstances:

... it is well settled that dishonest advertising is not cured or excused by honest labeling [footnote emitted]. Whether the ill-effects of deceptive nondisclosure can be cured by a disclosure requirement limited to labeling, or whether a further requirement of disclosure in advertising should be imposed, is essentially a question of remedy. As such it is a matter within the sound discretion of the Commission [footnote omitted]. The question of whether in a particular case to require disclosure in advertising cannot be answered by application of any hard-and-fast principle. The test is simple and pragmatic: Is it likely that, unless such disclosure is made, a substantial body of consumers will be misled to their detriment? *Statement of Basis and Purpose for the Cigarette Advertising and Labeling Trade Regulation Rule*, 1965, pp. 89-90. 29 FR 8325 (1964).

Misleading "door openers" have also been found deceptive (Encyclopedia Britannica, 87 F.T.C. 421 (1976), *aff'd*, 605 P.2d 964 (7th Cir. 1979), *cert. denied*, 445 U.S. 934 (1980), *as modified*, 100 F.T.C. 500 (1982)), as have offers to sell that are not bona fide offers (*Seekonk Freezer Meats, Inc.*, 82 F.T.C. 1025 (1973)). In each of these instances, the truth is made known prior to purchase.

[38]In the Listerine case, the Commission held that pro forma statements of no absolute prevention followed by promises of fewer colds did not cure or correct the false message that Listerine will prevent colds. *Warner Lambert* 86 F.T.C. 1398, 1414 (1975), *aff'd*, 562 F.2d 749 (D.C. Cir. 1977), *cert. denied*, 435 U.S. 950 (1978).

[39]*Chicago Metropolitan Pontiac Dealers' Ass'n*, C. 3110 (June 9,1983). [101 F.T.C. 854 (1983)]

[40]An opinion is a representation that expresses only the behalf of the maker, without certainty, as to the existence of a fact, or his judgement as to quality, value, authenticity, or other matters of judgement. American Law Institute, Restatement on Torts, Second ¶ 538 A.

[41]*Id.* ¶ 539. At common law, a consumer can generally rely on an expert opinion. *Id.*, ¶ 542(a). For this reason, representations of expert opinion will generally be regarded as representations of fact.

[42]"[T]here is a category of advertising themes, in the nature of puffing or other hyperbole, which do not amount to the type of affirmative product claims for which either the Commission or the consumer would expect documentation." *Pfizer, Inc*, 81 F.T.C. 23, 64 (1972).

The term "Puffing" refers generally to an expression of opinion not made as a representation of fact. A seller has some latitude in puffing his goods, but he is not authorized to misrepresent them or to assign to them benefits they do not possess [cite omitted]. Statements made for the purpose of deceiving prospective purchasers cannot properly be characterized as mere puffing. *Wilmington Chemical*, 69 F.T.C. 828, 865 (1966).

[43]In *Avalon Industries*, the ALJ observed that the "'ordinary person with a common degree of familiarity with industrial civilization' would expect a reasonable relationship between the size of package and the size of quantity of the contents. He would have no reason to anticipate slack filling." 83 F.T.C. 1728, 1750 (1974) (I.D.).

[44]"A misleading claim or omission in advertising will violate Section 5 or Section 12, however, only if the omitted information would be a material factor in the consumer's decision to purchase the product." *American Home Products Corp.*, 98 F.T.C. 136,368 (1981), *aff'd*, 695 F.2d 681 (3d Cir. 1982). A claim is material if it is likely to affect consumer behavior. "Is it likely to affect the average consumer in deciding whether to purchase the advertised product-is there a material deception, in other words?" Statement of Basis and Purpose, *Cigarette Advertising and Labeling Rule*, 1965, pp. 86-87. 29 FR 8325 (1964).

[45]Material information may affect conduct other than the decision to purchase a product. The Commission's complaint in *Volkswagen of America*, 99 F.T.C. 446 (1982), for example, was based on provision of inaccurate instructions for oil filter installation. In its *Restatement on Torts, Second*, the American Law Institute defines a material misrepresentation or

omission as one which the reasonable person would regard as important in deciding how to act, or one which the maker knows that the recipient, because of his or her own peculiarities, is likely to consider important. Section 538(2). The Restatement explains that a material fact does not necessarily have to affect the finances of a transaction. "There are many more-or-less sentimental considerations that the ordinary man regards as important." Comment on Clause 2(a)(d).

[46]In evaluating materiality, the Commission takes consumer preferences as given. Thus, if consumers prefer one product to another, the Commission need not determine whether that preference is objectively justified. *See Algoma Lumber*, 291 U.S. 54, 78 (1933). Similarly, objective differences among products are not material if the difference is not likely to affect consumer choices.

[47]The Commission will always consider relevant and competent evidence offered to rebut presumptions of materiality.

[48]Because this presumption is absent for some implied claims, the Commission will take special caution to ensure materiality exists in such cases.

[49]*Central Hudson Gas & Electric Co. v. PSC*, 447 U.S. 557, 567 (1980).

[50]*Cf. Restatement on Contracts, Second* ¶ 162(1).

[51]In *American Home Products*, the evidence was that the company intended to differentiate its products from aspirin. The very fact that AHP sought to distinguish its products from aspirin strongly implies that knowledge of the true ingredients of those products would be material to purchasers." *American Home Products*, 98 F.T.C. 136, 368 (1981), *aff'd*, 695 F.2d 681 (3d. Cir. 1982).

[52]In *Fedders*, the ads represented that only Fedders gave the assurance of cooling on extra hot, humid days. "Such a representation is the raison d'etre for an air conditioning unit-it is an extremely material representation." 85 F.T.C. 38, 61 (1975) (I.D.), *petition dismissed*, 529 F.2d 1398 (2d Cir.), *cert. denied*, 429 U.S. 818 (1976).

[53]"We note at the outset that both alleged misrepresentations go to the issue of the safety of respondent's product, an issue of great significance to consumers." *Firestone*, 81 F.T.C. 398, 456 (1972), *aff'd*, 481 P.2d 246 (6th Cir.), *cert. denied*, 414 U.S. 1112 (1973).

[54]The Commission found that information that a product was effective in only the small minority of cases where tiredness symptoms are due to an iron deficiency, and that it was of no benefit in all other cases, was material. *J.B. Williams Co.*, 68 F.T.C. 481, 546 (1965), *aff'd*, 381 F.2d 884 (6th Cir. 1967).

[55]As the Commission noted in *MacMillan, Inc.*:

In marketing their courses, respondents failed to adequately disclose the number of lesson assignments to be submitted in a course. These were material facts necessary for the student to calculate his tuition obligation, which was based on the number of lesson assignments he submitted for grading. The nondisclosure of these material facts combined with the confusion arising from LaSalle's inconsistent use of terminology had the capacity to mislead students about the nature and extent of their tuition obligation. *MacMillan, Inc.*, 96 F.T.C. 208, 303-304 (1980).

See also, Peacock Buick, 86 F.T.C. 1532, 1562 (1975), *aff'd*, 553 F.2d 97 (4th Cir. 1977).

[56]*Simeon Management Corp.*, 87 F.T.C. 1184 (1976), *aff'd*, 579 P.2d 1137, 1168, n.10 (9th Cir. 1978).

[57]In *American Home Products*, the Commission approved the ALJ's finding of materiality from an economic perspective:

If the record contained evidence of a significant disparity between the prices of Anacin and plain aspirin, it would form a further basis for a finding of materiality. That is, there is a reason to believe consumers are willing to pay a premium for a product believed to contain a special analgesic ingredient but not for a product whose analgesic is ordinary aspirin. *American Home Products*, 98 F.T.C. 136, 369 (1981), *aff'd*, 695 F.2d 681 (3d Cir. 1982).

[58]The prohibitions of Section 5 are intended to prevent injury to competitors as well as to consumers. The Commission regards injury to competitors as identical to injury to consumers. Advertising and legitimate marketing techniques are intended to "lure" competitors by directing business to the advertiser. In fact, vigorous competitive advertising can actually benefit consumers by lowering prices, encouraging product innovation, and increasing the specificity and amount of information available to consumers. Deceptive practices injure both competitors and consumers because consumers who preferred the competitor's product are wrongly diverted.

APPENDIX O

F.T.C. POLICY STATEMENT ON UNFAIRNESS

F.T.C. POLICY STATEMENT ON UNFAIRNESS[1]

Appended to <u>International Harvester Co.</u>, 104 F.T.C. 949, 1070 (1984). <u>See</u> 15 U.S.C. § 45(n).

FEDERAL TRADE COMMISSION
WASHINGTON, D. C. 20580

December 17, 1980

The Honorable Wendell H. Ford
Chairman, Consumer Subcommittee
Committee on Commerce, Science, and Transportation
Room 130 Russell Office Building
Washington, D.C. 20510

The Honorable John C. Danforth
Ranking Minority Member, Consumer Subcommittee
Committee on Commerce, Science, and Transportation
Room 130 Russell Office Building
Washington, D.C. 20510

Dear Senators Ford and Danforth:

This is in response to your letter of June 13, 1980, concerning one aspect of this agency's jurisdiction over "unfair or deceptive acts or practices." You informed us that the Subcommittee was planning to hold oversight hearings on the concept of "unfairness" as it has been applied to consumer transactions. You further informed us that the views of other interested parties were solicited and compiled in a Committee Print earlier this year.[1] Your letter specifically requested the Commission's views on cases under Section 5 "not involving the content of advertising," and its views as to "whether the Commission's authority should be limited to regulating false or deceptive commercial advertising." Our response addresses these and other questions related to the concept of consumer unfairness.

We are pleased to have this opportunity to discuss the future work of the agency. The subject that you have selected appears to be particularly timely. We recognize that the concept of consumer unfairness is one whose precise meaning is not immediately obvious, and also recognize that this uncertainty has been honestly troublesome for some businesses and some members of the legal profession. This result is understandable in light of the general nature of the statutory standard. At the same time, though, we believe we can respond to legitimate concerns of business and the Bar by attempting to delineate in this letter a concrete framework for future application of the Commission's unfairness authority. We are aided in this process by the cumulative decisions of this agency and the federal courts, which, in our opinion, have brought added clarity to the law. Although the administrative and judicial evolution of the consumer unfairness concept has still left some necessary flexibility in the statute, it is possible to provide a reasonable working sense of the conduct that is covered.

In response to your inquiry we have therefore undertaken a review of the decided cases and rules and have synthesized from them the most important principles of general applicability. Rather than merely reciting the law, we have attempted to provide the Committee with a concrete indication of the manner in which the Commission has enforced, and will continue to enforce, its unfairness mandate. In so doing we intend to

---

[1] http://www.ftc.gov/bcp/policystmt/ad-unfair.htm (last visited June 25, 2008).

address the concerns that have been raised about the meaning of consumer unfairness, and thereby attempt to provide a greater sense of certainty about what the Commission would regard as an unfair act or practice under Section 5.

This letter thus delineates the Commission's views of the boundaries of its consumer unfairness jurisdiction and is subscribed to by each Commissioner. In addition, we are enclosing a companion Commission statement that discusses the ways in which this body of law differs from, and supplements, the prohibition against consumer deception, and then considers and evaluates some specific criticisms that have been made of our enforcement of the law.[2] Since you have indicated a particular interest in the possible application of First Amendment principles to commercial advertising, the companion statement will include discussions relevant to that question. The companion statement is designed to respond to the key questions raised about the unfairness doctrine. However, individual Commissioners may not necessarily endorse particular arguments or particular examples of the Commission's exercise of its unfairness authority contained in the companion statement.

Commission Statement of Policy on the Scope of the Consumer Unfairness Jurisdiction

Section 5 of the F.T.C. Act prohibits, in part, "unfair ... acts or practices in or affecting commerce."[3] This is commonly referred to as the Commission's consumer unfairness jurisdiction. The Commission's jurisdiction over "unfair methods of competition" is not discussed in this letter.[4] Although we cannot give an exhaustive treatment of the law of consumer unfairness in this short statement, some relatively concrete conclusions ran nonetheless be drawn.

The present understanding of the unfairness standard is the result of an evolutionary process. The statute was deliberately framed in general terms since Congress recognized the impossibility of drafting a complete list of unfair trade practices that would not quickly become outdated or leave loopholes for easy evasion.[5] The task of identifying unfair trade practices was therefore assigned to the Commission, subject to judicial review,[6] in the expectation that the underlying criteria would evolve and develop over time. As the Supreme Court observed as early as 1931, the ban on unfairness "belongs to that class of phrases which do not admit of precise definition, but the meaning and application of which must be arrived at by what this court elsewhere has called 'the gradual process of judicial inclusion and exclusion.'"[7]

By 1964 enough cases had been decided to enable the Commission to identify three factors that it considered when applying the prohibition against consumer unfairness. These were: (1) whether the practice injures consumers; (2) whether it violates established public policy; (3) whether it is unethical or unscrupulous.[8] These factors were later quoted with apparent approval by the Supreme Court in the 1972 case of *Sperry & Hutchinson*.[9] Since then the Commission has continued to refine the standard of unfairness in its cases and rules, and it has now reached a more detailed sense of both the definition and the limits of these criteria.[10]

Consumer injury

Unjustified consumer injury is the primary focus of the F.T.C. Act, and the most important of the three *S&H* criteria. By itself it can be sufficient to warrant a finding of unfairness. The Commission's ability to rely on an independent criterion of consumer injury is consistent with the intent of the statute, which was to "[make] the consumer who may be injured by an unfair trade practice of equal concern before the law with the merchant injured by the unfair methods of a dishonest competitor."[11]

The independent nature of the consumer injury criterion does not mean that every consumer injury is legally "unfair," however. To justify a finding of unfairness the injury must satisfy three tests. It must be substantial; it must not be outweighed by any countervailing benefits to consumers or competition that the practice produces; and it must be an injury that consumers themselves could not reasonably have avoided.

First of all, the injury must be substantial. The Commission is not concerned with trivial or merely speculative harms.[12] In most cases a substantial injury involves monetary harm, as when sellers coerce consumers into purchasing unwanted goods or services[13] or when consumers buy defective goods or services on credit but are unable to assert against the creditor claims or defenses arising from the transaction.[14] Unwarranted health and safety risks may also support a finding of unfairness.[15] Emotional impact and other more subjective types of harm, on the other hand, will not ordinarily make a practice unfair. Thus, for example, the Commission will not seek to ban an advertisement merely because it offends the tastes or social beliefs of some viewers, as has been suggested in some of the comments.[16]

Second, the injury must not be outweighed by any offsetting consumer or competitive benefits that the sales practice also produces. Most business practices entail a mixture of economic and other costs and benefits for purchasers. A seller's failure to present complex technical data on his product may lessen a consumer's ability to choose, for example, but may also reduce the initial price he must pay for the article. The Commission is aware of these tradeoffs and will not find that a practice unfairly injures consumers unless it is injurious in its net effects.[17] The Commission also takes account of the various costs that a remedy would entail. These include not only the costs to the parties directly before the agency, but also the burdens on society in general in the form of increased paperwork, increased regulatory burdens on the flow of information, reduced incentives to innovation and capital formation, and similar matters.[18] Finally, the injury must be one which consumers could not reasonably have avoided.[19] Normally we expect the marketplace to be self-correcting, and we rely on consumer choice-the ability of individual consumers to make their own private purchasing decisions without regulatory intervention--to govern the market. We anticipate that consumers will survey the available alternatives, choose those that are most desirable, and avoid those that are inadequate or unsatisfactory. However, it has long been recognized that certain types of sales techniques may prevent consumers from effectively making their own decisions, and that corrective action may then become necessary. Most of the Commission's unfairness matters are brought under these circumstances. They are brought, not to second-guess the wisdom of particular consumer decisions, but rather to halt some form of seller behavior that unreasonably creates or takes advantage of an obstacle to the free exercise of consumer decisionmaking.[20]

Sellers may adopt a number of practices that unjustifiably hinder such free market decisions. Some may withhold or fail to generate critical price or performance data, for example, leaving buyers with insufficient information for informed comparisons.[21] Some may engage in overt coercion, as by dismantling a home appliance for "inspection" and refusing to reassemble it until a service contract is signed.[22] And some may exercise undue influence over highly susceptible classes of purchasers, as by promoting fraudulent "cures" to seriously ill cancer patients.[23] Each of these practices undermines an essential precondition to a free and informed consumer transaction, and, in turn, to a well-functioning market. Each of them is therefore properly banned as an unfair practice under the F.T.C. Act.[24]

Violation of public policy

The second *S&H* standard asks whether the conduct violates public policy as it has been established by statute, common law, industry practice, or otherwise. This criterion may be applied in two different ways. It may be used to test the validity and strength of the evidence of consumer injury, or, less often, it may be cited for a dispositive legislative or judicial determination that such injury is present.

Although public policy was listed by the *S&H* Court as a separate consideration, it is used most frequently by the Commission as a means of providing additional evidence on the degree of consumer injury caused by specific practices. To be sure, most Commission actions are brought to redress relatively clear-cut injuries, and those determinations are based, in large part, on objective economic analysis. As we have indicated before, the Commission believes that considerable attention should be devoted to the analysis of whether substantial net harm has occurred, not only because that is part of the unfairness test, but also because the focus on injury is the best way to ensure that the Commission acts responsibly and uses its resources wisely. Nonetheless, the Commission wishes to emphasize the importance of examining outside statutory policies and established judicial principles for assistance in helping the agency ascertain whether a particular form of conduct does in fact tend to harm consumers. Thus the agency has referred to First Amendment decisions upholding consumers' rights to receive information, for example, to confirm that restrictions on advertising tend unfairly to hinder the informed exercise of consumer choice.[25]

Conversely, statutes or other sources of public policy may affirmatively allow for a practice that the Commission tentatively views as unfair. The existence of such policies will then give the agency reason to reconsider its assessment of whether the practice is actually injurious in its net effects.[26] In other situations there may be no clearly established public policies, or the policies may even be in conflict. While that does not necessarily preclude the Commission from taking action if there is strong evidence of net consumer injury, it does underscore the desirability of carefully examining public policies in all instances.[27] In any event, whenever objective evidence of consumer injury is difficult to obtain, the need to identify and assess all relevant public policies assumes increased importance.

Sometimes public policy will independently support a Commission action. This occurs when the policy is so clear that it will entirely determine the question of consumer injury, so there is little need for separate analysis by the Commission. In these cases the legislature or court, in announcing the policy, has already determined that such injury does exist and thus it need not be expressly proved in each instance. An example of this approach arose in a case involving a mail-order firm.[28] There the Commission was persuaded by an analogy to the due-process clause that it was unfair for the firm to bring collection suits in a forum that was unreasonably difficult for the defendants to reach. In a similar case the Commission applied the statutory policies of the Uniform Commercial Code to require that various automobile manufacturers and their distributors refund to their customers any surplus money that was realized after they repossessed and resold their customer's cars.[29] The Commission acts on such a basis only where the public policy is suitable for administrative enforcement by this agency, however. Thus it turned down a petition for a rule to require fuller disclosure of aerosol propellants, reasoning that the subject of fluorocarbon safety was currently under study by other scientific and legislative bodies with more appropriate expertise or jurisdiction over the subject.[30]

To the extent that the Commission relies heavily on public policy to support a finding of unfairness, the policy should be clear and well-established. In other words, the policy should be declared or embodied in formal sources such as statutes, judicial decisions, or the Constitution as interpreted by the courts, rather than being ascertained from the general sense of the national values. The policy should likewise be one that is widely shared, and not the isolated decision of a single state or a single court. If these two tests are not met the policy cannot be considered as an "established" public policy for purposes of the S&H criterion. The Commission would then act only on the basis of convincing independent evidence that the practice was distorting the operation of the market and thereby causing unjustified consumer injury.

Unethical or unscrupulous conduct

Finally, the third *S&H* standard asks whether the conduct was immoral, unethical, oppressive, or unscrupulous. This test was presumably included in order to be sure of reaching all the purposes of the underlying statute, which forbids "unfair" acts or practices. It would therefore allow the Commission to reach conduct that violates generally recognized standards of business ethics. The test has proven, however, to be largely duplicative. Conduct that is truly unethical or unscrupulous will almost always injure consumers or violate public policy as well. The Commission has therefore never relied on the third element of *S&H* as an independent basis for a finding of unfairness, and it will act in the future only on the basis of the first two.

We hope this letter has given you the information that you require. Please do not hesitate to call if we can be of any further assistance. With best regards,

/s/Michael Pertschuk Chairman

/s/Paul Rand Dixon Commissioner

/s/David A. Clanton Commissioner

/s/Robert Pitofsky Commissioner

/s/Patricia P. Bailey Commissioner

---

[1]Unfairness: Views on Unfair Acts and Practices in Violation of the Federal Trade Commission Act (1980) (hereinafter referred to as "Committee Print").

[2]Neither this letter nor the companion statement addresses ongoing proceedings, but the Commission is prepared to discuss those matters separately at an appropriate time.

[3]The operative sentence of Section 5 reads in full as follows: "Unfair methods of competition in or affecting commerce, and unfair or deceptive acts or practices in or affecting commerce, are declared unlawful." 15 U.S.C. 45(a)(1).

[4]In fulfilling its competition or antitrust mission the Commission looks to the purposes, policies, and spirit of the other antitrust laws and the F.T.C. Act to determine whether a practice affecting competition or competitors is unfair. *See, e.g., F.T.C. v. Brown Shoe Co.,* 384 U.S. 316 (1966). In making this determination the Commission is guided by the extensive legislative histories of those statutes and a considerable body of antitrust case law. The agency's jurisdiction over "deceptive acts or practices" is likewise not discussed in this letter.

[5]*See* H.R. Conf. Rep. No. 1142, 63d Cong., 2d Sess., at 19 (1914) (If Congress "were to adopt the method of definition, it would undertake an endless task"). In 1914 the statute was phrased only in terms of "unfair methods of competition," and the reference to "unfair acts or practices" was not added until the Wheeler-Lee Amendment in 1938. The initial language was still understood as reaching most of the conduct now characterized as consumer unfairness, however, and so the original legislative history remains relevant to the construction of that part of the statute.

[6]The Supreme Court has stated on many occasions that the definition of "unfairness" is ultimately one for judicial determination. *See, e.g., F.T.C. v. Sperry & Hutchinson Co.,* 405 U.S. 233, 249 (1972); *F.T.C. v. R..F. Keppel & Bro.,* 291 U.S. 304, 314 (1934).

[7]*F.T.C. v. Raladam Co.,* 283 U.S. 643, 648 (1931). *See also F.T.C. v. R.F. Keppel & Bro.,* 291 U.S. 304, 310 (1934) ("Neither the language nor the history of the Act suggests that Congress intended to confine the forbidden methods to fixed and unyielding categories").

[8]The Commission's actual statement of the criteria was as follows:

(1) whether the practice, without necessarily having been previously considered unlawful, offends public policy as it has been established by statutes, the common law, or otherwise-whether, in other words, it is within at least the penumbra of some common- law, statutory, or other established concept of unfairness; (2) whether it is immoral, unethical, oppressive, or unscrupulous; (3) whether it causes substantial injury to consumers (or competitors or other businessmen).

Statement of Basis and Purpose, Unfair or Deceptive Advertising and Labeling of Cigarettes in Relation to the Health Hazards of Smoking, 29 Fed. Reg. 8324, 8355 (1964).

[9]*F.T.C. v. Sperry & Hutchinson C..,* 405 U.S. 223, 244-45 n.5 (1972). The Circuit Courts have concluded that this quotation reflected the Supreme Court's own views. *See Spiegel, Inc. v. FTC,* 540 F.2d 287, 293 n.8 (7th Cir. 1976); *Heater v. FTC,* 503 F.2d 321, 323 (9th Cir. 1974). The application of these factors to antitrust matters is beyond the scope of this letter.

[10]These standards for unfairness are generally applicable to both advertising and non-advertising cases.

[11]83 Cong. Rec. 3255 (1938) (remarks of Senator Wheeler).

[12]An injury may be sufficiently substantial, however, if it does a small harm to a large number of people, or if it raises a significant risk of concrete harm.

[13]*See, e.g., Holland Furnace Co. v. FTC,* 295 F.2d 302 (7th Cir. 1961) (seller's servicemen dismantled home furnaces and then refused to reassemble them until the consumers had agreed to buy services or replacement parts).

[14]Statement of Basis and Purpose, Preservation of Consumers' Claims and Defenses, 40 Fed. Reg. 53,506, 53522-23 (1975).

[15]For an example *see Philip Morris, Inc.,* 82 F.T.C. 16 (1973) (respondent had distributed free-sample razor blades in such a way that they could come into the hands of small children) (consent agreement). Of course, if matters involving health and safety are within the primary jurisdiction of some other agency, Commission action might not be appropriate.

[16]*See, e.g.,* comments of Association of National Advertisers, Committee Print at 120. In an extreme case, however, where tangible injury could be clearly demonstrated, emotional effects might possibly be considered as the basis for a finding of unfairness. *Cf.* 15 U.S.C. 1692 *et seq.* (Fair Debt Collection Practices Act) (banning, eg., harassing late-night telephone calls).

[17]*See Pftzer, Inc.,* 81 F.T.C. 23, 62-63 n. 13 (1972); Statement of Basis and Purpose, Disclosure Requirements and Prohibitions Concerning Franchising and Business Opportunity Ventures, 43 Fed. Reg. 59614, 59636 n.95 (1978).

When making this determination the Commission may refer to existing public policies for help in ascertaining the existence of consumer injury and the relative weights that should be assigned to various costs and benefits. The role of public policy in unfairness determinations will be discussed more generally below.

[18]For example, when the Commission promulgated the Holder Rule it anticipated an overall lowering of economic costs to society because the rule gave creditors the incentive to police sellers, thus increasing the likelihood that those selling defective goods or services would either improve their practices or leave the marketplace when they could not obtain financing. These benefits, in the Commission's judgment, outweighed any costs to creditors and sellers occasioned by the rule. See Statement of Basis and Purpose, Preservation of Consumers' Claims and Defenses, 40 Fed. Reg. 53506, 53522-23 (1975).

[19]In some senses any injury can be avoided--for example, by hiring independent experts to test all products in advance, or by private legal actions for damages-but these courses may be too expensive to be practicable for individual consumers to pursue.

[20]This emphasis on informed consumer choice has commonly been adopted in other statutes as well. *See, e.g.,* Declaration of Policy, Fair Packaging and Labeling Act, 15 U.S.C. 1451 ("Informed consumers are essential to the fair and efficient functioning of a free market economy".)

[21]*See, e.g.,* Statement of Basis and Purpose, Labeling and Advertising of Home Insulation, 44 Fed. Reg. 50218, 50222-23 (1979); Statement of Basis and Purpose, Posting of Minimum Octane Numbers on Gasoline Dispensing Pumps, 36 Fed. Reg. 23871,23882 (1971). *See also Virginia State Board of Pharmacy v. Virginia Citizens Consumer Council,* Inc., 425 U.S. 748 (1976).

[22]*See Holland Furnace Co. v. ETC,* 295 F.2d 302 (7th Cir. 1961); *cf Arthur Murray Studio, Inc. v.* EW, 458 F.2d 622 (5th Cir. 1972) (emotional high-pressure sales tactics, using teams of salesmen who refused to let the customer leave the room until a contract was signed). *See also* Statement of Basis and Purpose, Cooling-Off Period for Door-to-Door Sales, 37 Fed. Reg. 22934, 22937-38 (1972).

[23]*See, e.g., Travel King,* Inc., 86 F.T.C. 715, 774 (1975). The practices in this rase primarily involved deception, but the Commission noted the special susceptibilities of such patients as one reason for banning the ads entirely rather than relying on the remedy of fuller disclosure. The Commission recognizes that "undue influence" in advertising and promotion is difficult to define, and therefore exercises its authority here only with respect to substantial coercive-like practices and significant consumer injury.

[24]These few examples are not exhaustive, but the general direction they illustrate is clear. As the Commission stated in promulgating its Eyeglasses Rule, the inquiry should begin, at least, by asking "whether the acts or practices at issue inhibit the functioning of the competitive market and whether consumers are harmed thereby." Statement of Basis and Purpose, Advertising of 0phthalmic Goods and Services, 43 Fed. Reg. 23992,24001 (1978).

[25]*See* Statement of Basis and Purpose, Advertising of ophthalmic Goods and Services, 43 Fed. Reg. 23992,24001 (1978), *citing Virginia State Board of Pharmacy v. Virginia Citizens Consumer Council,* 425 U.S. 748 (1976).

[26]*Cf.* Statement of Basis and Purpose, Advertising of ophthalmic Goods and Services, *supra; see also n.17 supra.*

[27]The analysis of external public policies is extremely valuable but not always definitive. The legislative history of Section 5 recognizes that new forms of unfair business practices may arise which, at the time of the Commission's involvement, have not yet been generally proscribed. See page 4, *supra.* Thus a review of public policies established independently of Commission action may not be conclusive in determining whether the challenged practices should be prohibited or otherwise restricted. At the same time, however, we emphasize the importance of examining public policies, since a thorough analysis can serve as an important check on the overall reasonableness of the Commission's actions.

[28]*Spiegel, Inc. v. FTC,* 540 F.2d 287 (7th Cir. 1976). In this case the Commission did inquire into the extent of the resulting consumer injury, but under the rationale involved it presumably need not have done so. *See also F.T.C. v. R.F. Keppel & Bro.,* 291 U.S. 304 (1934) (firm had gained a marketing advantage by selling goods through a lottery technique that violated state gambling policies); *cf. Simeon Management Corp.,* 87 F.T.C. 1184, 1231 (1976), *aff'd,* 579 F.2d 1137 (9th Cir. 1978) (firm advertised weight-loss program that used a drug which could not itself be advertised under FDA regulations) (alternative ground). Since these public-policy cases are based on legislative determinations, rather than on a judgment within the Commission's area of special economic expertise, it is appropriate that they can reach a relatively wider range of consumer injuries than just those associated with impaired consumer choice.

[29]A surplus occurs when a repossessed car is resold for more than the amount owed by the debtor plus the expenses of repossession and resale. The law of 49 states requires that creditors refund surpluses when they occur, but if creditors systematically refuse to honor this obligation, consumers have no practical way to discover that they have been deprived of money to which they are entitled. *See Ford Motor Co.,* 94 F.T.C. 564, 618 (1979) *appeal pending,* Nos. 79-7649 and 79-7654 (9th Cir.); *Ford Motor Co.,93* F.T.C. 402 (1979) (consent decree); *General Motors Corp.,* D. 9074 (Feb., 1980) (consent decree). By these latter two consent agreements the Commission, because of its unfairness jurisdiction, has been able to secure more than $2 million for consumers allegedly deprived of surpluses to which they were entitled.

[30]See Letter from John F. Dugan, Acting Secretary, to Action on Smoking and Health (January 13, 1977). *See* also letter from Charles A. Tobin, Secretary, to Prof. Page and Mr. Young (September 17,1973) (denying petition to exercise § 6(b) subpoena powers to obtain consumer complaint information from cosmetic fu-ms and then to transmit the data to FDA for that agency's enforcement purposes).

APPENDIX P

OCC ADVISORY LETTER ON PREDATORY LENDING

OCC Advisory Letter AL 2003-2

Comptroller of the Currency
Administrator of National Banks

SUBJECT: Guidelines for National Banks to Guard Against Predatory and Abusive Lending Practices

TO: Chief Executive Officers of All National Banks and National Bank Operating Subsidiaries, Department and Division Heads, and All Examining Personnel

INTRODUCTORY STATEMENT

The Office of the Comptroller of the Currency (OCC) has received inquiries as to whether state laws and local initiatives addressing certain types of abusive lending practices can apply to national banks under the principles of federal preemption that have been articulated by the federal courts. Inquiries have also been made about the standards of conduct that the OCC expects national banks to observe in this area.

Because these inquiries raise issues of broad public interest, the OCC believes it appropriate to set forth in this advisory letter supervisory guidance concerning lending practices that have been criticized as "predatory" or "abusive." Such practices are inconsistent with important national objectives, including the goals of fair access to credit, community development, and stable homeownership by the broadest spectrum of America. Any lending practices that take unfair advantage of borrowers, or that have a detrimental impact on communities, also conflict with the high standards expected of national banks.

Many abusive lending practices are already unlawful under existing federal laws and regulations.[1] But even where the particular attributes of a loan are not subject to a specific prohibition, loans reflecting abusive practices nevertheless can involve unfair and deceptive conduct and present significant safety and soundness, reputation, and other risks to national banks.[2]

Although the OCC does not have reason to believe that national banks or their operating subsidiaries (collectively referred to herein as "national banks") generally are engaged in predatory lending practices, it expects that national banks will take appropriate steps to ensure that they do not become involved in predatory lending.[3]

---

[1] *See, e.g.,* Home Ownership and Equity Protection Act, 15 USC 1639.

[2] *See, e.g.,* OCC Advisory Letter 2002-3, "Guidance on Unfair or Deceptive Acts or Practices" (March 22, 2002); OCC Bulletin 2001-47, "Third Party Relationships," (November 1, 2001); OCC Bulletin 2001-6, "Expanded Guidance for Subprime Lending Programs" (January 31, 2001); OCC Advisory Letter 2000-11, "Title Loan Programs" (November 27, 2000); and OCC Advisory Letter 2000-10, "Payday Lending" (November 27, 2000).

[3] National banks and their subsidiaries face significant risks of indirectly and inadvertently facilitating predatory lending practices through the use of third-party loan brokers and in connection with loan purchases. Therefore, the OCC has also issued guidance stating its expectation that national banks will establish appropriate due diligence and monitoring procedures adequate to address such risks. *See* OCC Advisory Letter 2003-3, "Avoiding Predatory and Abusive Lending Practices in Brokered and Purchased Loans" (February 21, 2003).

This guidance provides examples of practices that may be abusive, and provides advice on how national banks should avoid engaging in such practices.

The advisory also describes how certain abusive lending can involve unfair or deceptive practices and thus violate section 5 of the Federal Trade Commission Act (F.T.C. Act).[4] The OCC will review credible evidence that a national bank has engaged in abusive lending practices and, where such practices are found to violate an applicable law or safety and soundness standards, will take appropriate supervisory action.

BACKGROUND

The terms "abusive lending" or "predatory lending" are most frequently defined by reference to a variety of lending practices.[5] Although it is generally necessary to consider the totality of the circumstances to assess whether a loan is predatory, a fundamental characteristic of predatory lending is the aggressive marketing of credit to prospective borrowers who simply cannot afford the credit on the terms being offered. Typically, such credit is underwritten predominantly on the basis of the liquidation value of the collateral, without regard to the borrower's ability to service and repay the loan according to its terms absent resorting to that collateral. This abusive practice leads to "equity stripping." When a loan has been made based on the foreclosure value of the collateral, rather than on a determination that the borrower has the capacity to make the scheduled payments under the terms of the loan, based on the borrower's current and expected income, current obligations, employment status, and other relevant financial resources, the lender is effectively counting on its ability to seize the borrower's equity in the collateral to satisfy the obligation and to recover the typically high fees associated with such credit. Not surprisingly, such credits experience foreclosure rates higher than the norm.

While such disregard of basic principles of loan underwriting lies at the heart of predatory lending, a variety of other practices may also accompany the marketing of such credit:

Loan "flipping" – frequent refinancings that result in little or no economic benefit to the borrower and are undertaken with the primary or sole objective of generating additional loan fees, prepayment penalties, and fees from the financing of credit-related products;
Refinancings of special subsidized mortgages that result in the loss of beneficial loan terms;
"Packing" of excessive and sometimes "hidden" fees in the amount financed;
Using loan terms or structures – such as negative amortization – to make it more difficult or impossible for borrowers to reduce or repay their indebtedness;
Using balloon payments to conceal the true burden of the financing and to force borrowers into costly refinancing transactions or foreclosures;
Targeting inappropriate or excessively expensive credit products to older borrowers,[6] to persons who are not financially sophisticated or who may be otherwise vulnerable to abusive practices, and to persons who could qualify for mainstream credit products and terms;

---

[4] 15 USC 45(a)(1).
[5] *See, e.g.,* OCC Advisory Letter 2000-7, "Abusive Lending Practices" (July 25, 2000).
[6] *See* AARP "Subprime Mortgage Lending and Older Americans," (March 2001) (predatory lending practices often are targeted at older homeowners), available at http://www.research.aarp.org/consume/dd57_lending.html.

Inadequate disclosure of the true costs, risks and, where necessary, appropriateness to the borrower of loan transactions;
The offering of single premium credit life insurance; and
The use of mandatory arbitration clauses.

LEGAL AND SUPERVISORY RISKS ASSOCIATED WITH ABUSIVE LENDING PRACTICES

Safety and Soundness Concerns

As noted above, a departure from fundamental principles of loan underwriting generally forms the basis of abusive lending: lending without a determination that a borrower can reasonably be expected to repay the loan from resources other than the collateral securing the loan, and relying instead on the foreclosure value of the borrower's collateral to recover principal, interest, and fees. A national bank that makes a loan to a consumer based predominantly on the liquidation value of the borrower's collateral, rather than on a determination of the borrower's repayment ability, including current and expected income, current obligations, employment status, and other relevant financial resources, is engaging in a fundamentally unsafe and unsound banking practice that is inconsistent with established lending standards.[7] This practice not only increases the risk to the bank that the loan will default but may also increase the bank's potential loss exposure upon default.

Safety and soundness concerns can also arise when a bank's lending practices effectively foreclose access to a secondary market. Major government-sponsored enterprises (GSEs) active in the secondary market for mortgage loans have taken a number of affirmative steps to reduce the possibility that they will purchase abusive loans.[8] These steps include a refusal to purchase mortgage loans:

In which the lender has not adequately determined the borrower's ability to repay the debt;
Subject to the Home Ownership and Equity Protection Act (HOEPA);[9]
With points and fees in excess of 5 percent of the loan amount, except in cases where a higher amount of fees was justified to prevent the loan from being unprofitable; and
In which a prepaid single premium credit insurance policy was included in the amount financed.

These GSEs also restrict the use of prepayment penalties. In addition, these entities require monthly borrower payments on loans they have purchased to be reported to the major credit-reporting bureaus. National banks and their operating subsidiaries whose business practices are

---

[7] *See* 12 CFR 30, Appendix A. *See also* 12 CFR 34, D, Appendix A.
[8] *See, e.g.,* Freddie Mac "Protecting Borrowers from Predatory Lending Practices," (1997; revised 2003), available at [http://www.freddiemac.com/corporate/affordhouse/predlend/apl_fact.html]; Fannie Mae, "Fannie Mae Chairman Announces New Loan Guidelines to Combat Predatory Lending Practices," News Release (April 11, 2000), available at [http://www.fanniemae.com/newsreleases/2000/0710.jhtml]. These secondary market guidelines can serve as a useful guide for national banks in developing their own lending policies.
[9] HOEPA loans are closed-end loans secured by a consumer's principal dwelling, other than a reverse mortgage or a loan to finance the acquisition or initial construction of the home, that are high-cost because they exceed specified statutory and regulatory interest-rate or fee thresholds. Such loans are subject to specific disclosure requirements and substantive restrictions in federal law. *See* 15 USC 1602(aa)(1) and 12 CFR 226.32.

inconsistent with these guidelines, therefore, run the risk of losing an important source of funding for their operations, and of thereby exposing themselves to greater default risk and risk of loss.

Violations of the F.T.C. Act

National banks are subject to section 5 of the F.T.C. Act, which makes unlawful "unfair or deceptive acts or practices" in commerce.[10] The OCC has the authority to enforce section 5 with respect to national banks and to impose sanctions for violations in individual cases.[11] Such practices as loan flipping, equity stripping, and the refinancing of special subsidized mortgage loans may be indicative of unfair or deceptive practices that violate section 5 of the F.T.C. Act. The OCC believes that application of the standards of section 5 and use of the OCC's authority to enforce compliance with those standards in individual cases is a particularly appropriate approach to ensure that abusive lending practices are not occurring in the national banking system.

While such determinations are inherently fact-specific, the OCC has issued detailed guidance on the standards it will generally employ in determining whether an act or practice is unfair or deceptive under the F.T.C. Act.[12] Practices may be found to be *deceptive* and, therefore, unlawful under section 5 of the F.T.C. Act if each of the following factors are present:

First, there is a representation, omission, act, or practice that is likely to mislead;
Second, the act or practice would be likely to mislead a reasonable consumer (*a reasonable member of the group targeted by the acts or practices in question*); and
Third, the representation, omission, act, or practice is likely to mislead in a material way.

A practice may be found to be *unfair* and, therefore, unlawful under section 5 of the F.T.C. Act if each of the following factors are present:

First, the practice causes substantial consumer injury, such as monetary harm;
Second, the injury is not outweighed by benefits to the consumer or to competition; and
Third, the injury caused by the practice is one that consumers could not reasonably have avoided.

Loan "Flipping" and the Refinancing of Special Subsidized Mortgages as Unfair or Deceptive Practices Under the F.T.C. Act

Loan "flipping" is generally understood to mean the repeated refinancing of a loan under circumstances that result in little or no economic benefit to the borrower, with the objective of generating additional loan points, loan fees, prepayment penalties, and fees from financing the sale of credit-related products. In addition, the practice is frequently targeted to consumers with limited

---

[10] 15 USC 45(a)(1).

[11] Congress gave the OCC broad powers to compel national banks to comply with any "law, rule, or regulation." 12 USC 1818(b)(1). This includes the ability to issue cease and desist orders when the OCC determines that a national bank is violating or has violated section 5 of the F.T.C. Act. The other federal banking agencies have comparable authority to enforce section 5 of the F.T.C. Act with respect to the banks they regulate. *See, e.g.,* FDIC Financial Institution Letter, FIL 57-2002 (May 30, 2002), available at [http://www.fdic.gov/news/news/financial/2002/fil0257.html]. *See also* Letter from Alan Greenspan, Chairman, Board of Governors of the Federal Reserve System to Rep. John J. LaFalce (May 30, 2002), available at [http://www.federalreserve.gov/boarddocs/press/bcreg/2002/2002530/attachment.pdf].

[12] *See* OCC Advisory Letter 2002-3, "Guidance on Unfair or Deceptive Acts or Practices" (March 22, 2002).

financial options. Ascertaining whether a lender has engaged in loan "flipping" is a highly fact-specific determination, but the practice generally involves sequential refinancing transactions where, among other things, there is *little or no economic benefit to the borrower*. Therefore, "flipping" should be thought of as a limited, discrete subset of refinancing transactions. Depending upon the totality of the circumstances, loan flipping may be an unfair or deceptive practice in violation of the F.T.C. Act. The OCC will take supervisory action as appropriate to address such violations.

For example, loan flipping may constitute an *unfair* practice under the F.T.C. Act. The practice can result in substantial borrower injury resulting from the substantial fees imposed and from the fact that the transaction may increase debt burdens, decrease home equity, enhance the likelihood of foreclosure, and adversely affect the borrower's credit history. [13] In addition, loan flipping fails to generate benefits to the consumer that would outweigh this harm. The benefits to competition from this practice – such as lower consumer costs – also seem to be lacking. The harm from loan flipping also may not be "reasonably avoidable," for example, if the costs, terms, and risks have not been described in a way that the consumer can reasonably be expected to understand and be able to act upon.[14] As a general matter, many terms or practices associated with loan flipping carry risks that the borrower cannot reasonably be expected to appreciate in the absence of clear and understandable explanatory information.

Even a single refinancing transaction can be abusive and unfair or deceptive, such as in cases involving the refinancing of a special subsidized mortgage. These mortgages, often originated under programs sponsored by governmental or nonprofit organizations, generally contain below-market interest rates or other nonstandard terms beneficial to the borrower. The refinancing of such loans generally entails the loss of one or more of the beneficial loan terms, and thus, carries a particularly high risk of being detrimental to the borrower.

"Equity Stripping" as an Unfair or Deceptive Practice Under the F.T.C. Act

"Equity stripping" is identified as a predatory lending practice because it is associated with significant harm to consumers, including an increase in debt burdens and the loss of home equity with little or no compensating benefit to the borrower. Home equity stripping typically involves making loans with excessively high, up-front fees that are financed and secured by the borrower's home, often with an excessively high penalty upon prepayment of the loan, for the sole or primary objective of stripping the borrower's home equity. It can also result from loan flipping, and from the practice of making a loan predominantly on the basis of the liquidation value of the collateral, without regard to the borrower's ability to service and repay the loan according to its terms absent resort to that collateral. Whether a bank has engaged in "equity stripping" also is a highly fact-specific determination involving a finding of consumer abuse. It is to be distinguished from transactions in which home equity decreases may be an integral part of an informed consumer's

---

[13] In addition, there may be balloon payments in the new loan that may force another refinancing involving additional fees that will add to the ultimate cost of the credit, decrease home equity, and increase both the debt burden and the likelihood of foreclosure.

[14] A review of such information also will be relevant to a determination of whether the transaction also involved *deception* under the F.T.C. Act.

purpose for entering into the transaction.[15] Depending upon the totality of the circumstances, equity stripping may be an unfair or deceptive practice in violation of the F.T.C. Act. The OCC will take supervisory action as appropriate to address such violations involving equity stripping.

For example, equity stripping may constitute an *unfair* practice under the F.T.C. Act. Equity-stripping practices will almost always involve substantial consumer injury. Such practices decrease the borrower's wealth, either immediately or over time, and can cause the borrower to lose his or her home. In addition, equity stripping will almost always fail to generate benefits to the consumer or to competition that would outweigh these substantial consumer harms. As with loan flipping, whether the practice was reasonably avoidable by a consumer would depend on the specific facts and circumstances of the transaction and entail a review of the adequacy of information provided to the consumer.[16] This review would include an examination of whether and how the borrower was informed about particular terms or practices associated with equity stripping that carry risks the borrower cannot reasonably be expected to appreciate in the absence of clear and understandable explanatory information. Without adequate information about the effect of these terms and practices, a borrower may not be reasonably able to avoid the injury that may ensue from them.

Violations of Other Applicable Laws

Predatory lending practices also may violate other laws, such as HOEPA, which covers certain high-cost mortgage loans. Among other things, HOEPA prohibits negative amortization, increases in the interest rate upon default, and balloon payments for covered loans with a term of less than five years. It also restricts the use of prepayment penalties and due-on-demand clauses in covered loans.[17] HOEPA also prohibits the refinancing of a covered loan to another covered loan in the first year of the loan, unless the refinancing is in the borrower's interest. In addition, HOEPA prohibits lenders from engaging in a pattern or practice of making covered loans based on the borrower's collateral without regard to the borrower's ability to repay, including the borrower's current and expected income, current obligations, and employment.[18]

Moreover, certain predatory lending practices involve unlawful discrimination. If a national bank engages in the practice of "steering" a borrower to a loan with higher costs rather than to a comparable loan offered by the bank with lower costs for which the borrower could qualify, and does this on the basis of the borrower's race, national origin, age, or gender, for example, the OCC will take appropriate enforcement action under the federal fair lending laws.[19]

---

[15] For example, some consumers may take out a home equity loan to finance improvements that will enhance the home's value, or to finance other expenditures such as college tuition. Borrowers also may knowingly accept terms that risk the depletion of equity, such as prepayment penalties, in exchange for countervailing economic benefits such as a lower interest rate.

[16] This review also will be relevant to a determination of whether the transaction involved *deception* under the F.T.C. Act.

[17] *See* 12 CFR 226.32.

[18] *See* 12 CFR 226.34.

[19] *See* 15 USC 1691; 42 USC 3601 *et seq.* Some government studies, for example, have concluded that certain abusive lending practices have been targeted to, and harm, low-income and predominantly minority neighborhoods and the elderly. *See* U.S. Department of Treasury and U.S. Department of Housing and Urban Development, "Curbing Predatory Home Mortgage Lending: A Joint Report" (June 2000), available at [http://www.treas.gov/press/releases/reports/treasrpt.pdf].

Impact of Certain Abusive Lending Practices on CRA Evaluations and Ratings

Because Community Reinvestment Act (CRA) performance must be considered in connection with various applications for deposit facilities, including branch applications and bank merger transactions, predatory lending also may impede a bank's strategic plans to expand its operations or to combine with another organization. Under the CRA regulations, abusive lending practices that violate the federal fair lending laws, the F.T.C. Act, or HOEPA, or that evidence other illegal credit practices, adversely affect an institution's CRA performance.[20] When such conduct comes to the attention of the OCC, it will be taken into account in the OCC's evaluation of the bank's CRA performance.

Furthermore, a national bank that engages in a pattern or practice of extending credit based predominantly on the liquidation value of the collateral, or otherwise without regard to the borrower's ability to service and repay the loan — in addition to violating HOEPA in some circumstances — is not helping to meet the credit needs of the community consistent with safe and sound operations, and has acted contrary to the OCC's safety and soundness regulatory guidelines.[21] Such an activity or practice also may adversely affect the OCC's evaluation of the bank's CRA performance.

RECOMMENDATIONS FOR AVOIDING PREDATORY AND ABUSIVE LENDING PRACTICES

In order to safeguard the interests of the bank and its customers, national banks are advised to have policies and procedures in place to prevent the bank and any of its subsidiaries from engaging in practices that might be considered predatory or abusive. Such policies and procedures should be fashioned to ensure that the bank's lending complies with applicable safety and soundness standards and consumer protection laws.

Establishment of Policies and Procedures

Underwriting policies

As noted above, when a loan has been made based on the foreclosure value of the collateral rather than on a determination that the borrower has the capacity to service and repay the loan without resort to the collateral, the lender is effectively counting on its ability to seize the borrower's collateral and use the borrower's equity in the collateral to satisfy the obligation, and is thus engaging in an unsafe and unsound banking practice.

National banks are advised to adopt policies and procedures to ensure that an appropriate determination has been made that the borrower has the capacity to make scheduled payments to

---

[20] *See* 12 CFR 25.28(c). *See also* Interagency Questions and Answers Regarding Community Reinvestment, Q&A ___.28(c)-1, 66 Fed. Reg. 36620, 36640 (July 12, 2001).
[21] *See* 12 CFR 30, Appendix A.

service and repay the loan, including principal, interest, insurance, and taxes,[22] based on a consideration of the borrower's:

Current and expected income;
Other relevant financial resources;
Employment status; and
Financial obligations, including other indebtedness. [23]

Such policies also should address debt-to-income and loan-to-value ratios, as necessary to mitigate the risk of lending without regard to ability to repay.

Policies addressing risk of abusive practices

National banks should also consider articulating clear policies and procedures to specify, if applicable, whether and under what circumstances the bank will make loans involving features or circumstances that have been associated with abusive lending practices, including the following:

Frequent, sequential refinancings;
Refinancings of special subsidized mortgages that contain terms favorable to the borrower;
Single-premium credit life insurance or similar products;
Negative amortization;
Balloon payments in short-term transactions;
Prepayment penalties that are not limited to the early years of a loan;
Financing points, fees, penalties, and other charges;
Interest rate increases upon default;
Mandatory arbitration clauses; and
Making loans subject to HOEPA.[24]

As noted above, transactions involving these features may be appropriate in many circumstances and may contribute to legitimate business objectives. However, to avoid the risk that a transaction could be deemed to involve unfair or deceptive practices, a primary objective of such policies and procedures should be to prevent customer misunderstanding of the terms and relative costs, risks, and benefits of their loan transaction. Borrowers should be provided with the information that is sufficient to draw the borrower's attention to these key terms, and to enable them to determine whether the loan meets their particular financial circumstances and needs. National banks also should have policies to help ensure that interest rates and other pricing terms for their loans reasonably reflect the costs and risks of making such loans and are consistent with OCC regulations.[25] Furthermore, to promote credit access where borrowers demonstrate a good record of

---

[22] OCC safety and soundness regulatory guidelines require a national bank to "establish and maintain loan documentation practices that . . . [i]dentify the . . . source of repayment, and assess the ability of the borrower to repay the indebtedness in a timely manner." 12 CFR 30, Appendix A.

[23] In addition, as appropriate, policies should address the use of multiple borrowers to satisfy debt-service coverage ratios to protect against reliance on the income of third-party guarantors or other obligors whose relationship to the borrower or to the collateral suggests that they may not, in fact, be relied upon to repay the loan as structured, if necessary, to prevent default or foreclosure.

[24] *See* footnote 8.

[25] *See* 12 CFR 7.4002.

performance in handling credit, national banks are encouraged to adopt policies and procedures that provide for reporting of good credit histories to the major credit reporting bureaus.

Policies concerning appropriateness of certain transactions

In addition, as noted above, some practices may be unfair or deceptive, and abusive, depending upon the consumers that are affected or that are the target audience. Therefore, bank policies may need to specifically address such circumstances. The bank may face significant risks when it offers to borrowers who are elderly, vulnerable, or not financially sophisticated, loan products that contain features that have been associated with abusive lending. Thus, banks are advised to adopt policies and procedures that ensure that lending practices reflect the degree of care that is appropriate to the risk, considering such factors as:

The sophistication or expertise of the borrower in credit transactions, if known or apparent;
The need for, and proposed use of, the loan proceeds, if known or stated;
The borrower's understanding of how the loan meets the borrower's particular financial circumstances and needs; and
The bank's assessment of the terms and conditions of the loan relative to those needs.

Loan Quality Control Reviews and Corrective Action

As a general matter, banks should periodically perform a documentation review on a random sampling of transactions to ensure that transactions comply with bank policies and legal requirements. In addition, in appropriate circumstances, such as when a particular risk has been identified, banks should conduct a more comprehensive review. For example, documentation reviews may indicate problems involving potential fraud or abuse such as significant and unexplained variations between the preliminary disclosures required to be provided to customers under the Truth in Lending Act or the Real Estate Settlement Procedures Act and the final charges appearing on closing documents; fees that appear to be duplicative or unearned; or evidence of materially misleading statements or omissions with respect to the costs, benefits, risks, and burdens of the transaction. In such circumstances, the bank should take all steps appropriate, including corrective action, to address the deficiencies and to address any borrower injury.

CONCLUSION

The OCC encourages national banks to adopt policies and procedures to address, and in practice to avoid, engaging in loan practices that may be abusive, unfair, or deceptive – practices that raise legal risks and serious supervisory concerns and that, if not remedied, could result in supervisory action, injury to the bank's reputation, and financial loss.

For further information concerning the matters discussed in this advisory letter, please contact the Community and Consumer Law Division at (202) 874-5750, the Compliance Division at (202) 874-4428, or the appropriate supervisory office.

David Hammaker
Deputy Comptroller for Compliance

APPENDIX Q

FAIR DEBT COLLECTION PRACTICES ACT

THE FAIR DEBT COLLECTION PRACTICES ACT

As amended by Pub. L. 109-351, §§ 801-02, 120 Stat. 1966 (2006)

As a public service, the staff of the Federal Trade Commission (FTC) has prepared the following complete text of the Fair Debt Collection Practices Act (FDCPA), 15 U.S.C. §§ 1692-1692p.

Please note that the format of the text differs in minor ways from the U.S. Code and West's U.S. Code Annotated. For example, this version uses FDCPA section numbers in the headings. In addition, the relevant U.S. Code citation is included with each section heading. Although the staff has made every effort to transcribe the statutory material accurately, this compendium is intended as a convenience for the public and not a substitute for the text in the U.S. Code.

Table of Contents

15 USC 1601 note

§ 801. Short Title

This title may be cited as the "Fair Debt Collection Practices Act."

§ 802. Congressional findings and declaration of purpose

(a) There is abundant evidence of the use of abusive, deceptive, and unfair debt collection practices by many debt collectors. Abusive debt collection practices contribute to the number of personal bankruptcies, to marital instability, to the loss of jobs, and to invasions of individual privacy.

(b) Existing laws and procedures for redressing these injuries are inadequate to protect consumers.

(c) Means other than misrepresentation or other abusive debt collection practices are available for the effective collection of debts.

(d) Abusive debt collection practices are carried on to a substantial extent in interstate commerce and through means and instrumentalities of such commerce. Even where abusive debt collection practices are purely intrastate in character, they nevertheless directly affect interstate commerce.

(e) It is the purpose of this title to eliminate abusive debt collection practices by debt collectors, to insure that those debt collectors who refrain from using abusive debt collection practices are not competitively disadvantaged, and to promote consistent State action to protect consumers against debt collection abuses.

15 USC 1692a
§ 803. Definitions
As used in this title—

(1) The term "Commission" means the Federal Trade Commission.

(2) The term "communication" means the conveying of information regarding a debt directly or indirectly to any person through any medium.

(3) The term "consumer" means any natural person obligated or allegedly obligated to pay any debt.

(4) The term "creditor" means any person who offers or extends credit creating a debt or to whom a debt is owed, but such term does not include any person to the extent that he receives an assignment or transfer of a debt in default solely for the purpose of facilitating collection of such debt for another.

(5) The term "debt" means any obligation or alleged obligation of a consumer to pay money arising out of a transaction in which the money, property, insurance or services which are the subject of the transaction are primarily for personal, family, or household purposes, whether or not such obligation has been reduced to judgment.

(6) The term "debt collector" means any person who uses any instrumentality of interstate commerce or the mails in any business the principal purpose of which is the collection of any debts, or who regularly collects or attempts to collect, directly or indirectly, debts owed or due or asserted to be owed or due another. Notwithstanding the exclusion provided by clause (F) of the last sentence of this paragraph, the term includes any creditor who, in the process of collecting his own debts, uses any name other than his own which would indicate that a third person is collecting or attempting to collect such debts. For the purpose of section 808(6), such term also includes any person who uses any instrumentality of interstate commerce or the mails in any business the principal purpose of which is the enforcement of security interests. The term does not include—

(A) any officer or employee of a creditor while, in the name of the creditor, collecting debts for such creditor;

(B) any person while acting as a debt collector for another person, both of whom are related by common ownership or affiliated by corporate control, if the person acting as a debt collector does so only for persons to whom it is so related or affiliated and if the principal business of such person is not the collection of debts;

(C) any officer or employee of the United States or any State to the extent that collecting or attempting to collect any debt is in the performance of his official duties;

(D) any person while serving or attempting to serve legal process on any other person in connection with the judicial enforcement of any debt;

(E) any nonprofit organization which, at the request of consumers, performs bona fide consumer credit counseling and assists consumers in the liquidation of their debts by receiving payments from such consumers and distributing such amounts to creditors; and

(F) any person collecting or attempting to collect any debt owed or due or asserted to be owed or due another to the extent such activity

(i) is incidental to a bona fide fiduciary obligation or a bona fide escrow arrangement;

(ii) concerns a debt which was originated by such person;

(iii) concerns a debt which was not in default at the time it was obtained by such person; or

(iv) concerns a debt obtained by such person as a secured party in a commercial credit transaction involving the creditor.

(7) The term "location information" means a consumer's place of abode and his telephone number at such place,
or his place of employment.

(8) The term "State" means any State, territory, or possession of the United States, the District of Columbia, the
Commonwealth of Puerto Rico, or any political subdivision of any of the foregoing.

§ 804 15 USC 1692b
§ 804. Acquisition of location information

Any debt collector communicating with any person other than the consumer for the purpose of acquiring location information about the consumer shall—

(1) identify himself, state that he is confirming or correcting location information concerning the consumer, and, only if expressly requested, identify his employer;

(2) not state that such consumer owes any debt;

(3) not communicate with any such person more than once unless requested to do so by such person or unless the debt collector reasonably believes that the earlier response of such person is erroneous or incomplete and that such person now has correct or complete location information;

(4) not communicate by post card;

(5) not use any language or symbol on any envelope or in the contents of any communication effected by the mails or telegram that indicates that the debt collector is in the debt collection business or that the communication relates to the collection of a debt; and

(6) after the debt collector knows the consumer is represented by an attorney with regard to the subject debt and has knowledge of, or can readily ascertain, such attorney's name and address, not communicate with any person other than that attorney, unless the attorney fails to respond within a reasonable period of time to the communication from the debt collector.

§ 805 15 USC 1692c

§ 805. Communication in connection with debt collection

(a) COMMUNICATION WITH THE CONSUMER GENERALLY. Without the prior consent of the consumer given directly to the debt collector or the express permission of a court of competent jurisdiction, a debt collector may not communicate with a consumer in connection with the collection of any debt—

(1) at any unusual time or place or a time or place known or which should be known to be inconvenient to the consumer. In the absence of knowledge of circumstances to the contrary, a debt collector shall assume that the convenient time for communicating with a consumer is after 8 o'clock antimeridian and before 9 o'clock postmeridian, local time at the consumer's location;

(2) if the debt collector knows the consumer is represented by an attorney with respect to such debt and has knowledge of, or can readily ascertain, such attorney's name and address, unless the attorney fails to respond within a reasonable period of time to a communication from the debt collector or unless the attorney consents to direct communication with the consumer; or

(3) at the consumer's place of employment if the debt collector knows or has reason to know that the consumer's employer prohibits the consumer from receiving such communication.

(b) COMMUNICATION WITH THIRD PARTIES. Except as provided in section 804, without the prior consent of the consumer given directly to the debt collector, or the express permission of a court of competent jurisdiction, or as reasonably necessary to effectuate a post judgment judicial remedy, a debt collector may not communicate, in connection with the collection of any debt, with any person other than a consumer, his attorney, a consumer reporting agency if otherwise permitted by law, the creditor, the attorney of the creditor, or the attorney of the debt collector.

(c) CEASING COMMUNICATION. If a consumer notifies a debt collector in writing that the consumer refuses to pay a debt or that the consumer wishes the debt collector to cease further communication with the consumer, the debt collector shall not communicate further with the consumer with respect to such debt, except—

(1) to advise the consumer that the debt collector's further efforts are being terminated;

(2) to notify the consumer that the debt collector or creditor may invoke specified remedies which are ordinarily invoked by such debt collector or creditor; or

(3) where applicable, to notify the consumer that the debt collector or creditor intends to invoke a specified remedy. If such notice from the consumer is made by mail, notification shall be complete upon receipt.

(d) For the purpose of this section, the term "consumer" includes the consumer's spouse, parent (if the consumer is a minor), guardian, executor, or administrator.

15 USC 1692d

§ 806. Harassment or abuse

A debt collector may not engage in any conduct the natural consequence of which is to harass, oppress, or abuse any person in connection with the collection of a debt. Without limiting the general application of the foregoing, the following conduct is a violation of this section:

(1) The use or threat of use of violence or other criminal means to harm the physical person, reputation, or property of any person.

(2) The use of obscene or profane language or language the natural consequence of which is to abuse the hearer or reader.

(3) The publication of a list of consumers who allegedly refuse to pay debts, except to a consumer reporting agency or to persons meeting the requirements of section 603(f) or 604(3) of this Act.

(4) The advertisement for sale of any debt to coerce payment of the debt.

(5) Causing a telephone to ring or engaging any person in telephone conversation repeatedly or continuously with intent to annoy, abuse, or harass any person at the called number.

(6) Except as provided in section 804, the placement of telephone calls without meaningful disclosure of the caller's identity.

15 USC 1692e

§ 807. False or misleading representations

A debt collector may not use any false, deceptive, or misleading representation or means in connection with the collection of any debt. Without limiting the general application of the foregoing, the following conduct is a violation of this section:

(1) The false representation or implication that the debt collector is vouched for, bonded by, or affiliated with the United States or any State, including the use of any badge, uniform, or facsimile thereof.

(2) The false representation of—

(A) the character, amount, or legal status of any debt; or

(B) any services rendered or compensation which may be lawfully received by any debt collector for the collection of a debt.

(3) The false representation or implication that any individual is an attorney or that any communication is from an attorney.

(4) The representation or implication that nonpayment of any debt will result in the arrest or imprisonment of any person or the seizure, garnishment, attachment, or sale of any property or wages of any person unless such action is lawful and the debt collector or creditor intends to take such action.

(5) The threat to take any action that cannot legally be taken or that is not intended to be taken.

(6) The false representation or implication that a sale, referral, or other transfer of any interest in a debt shall cause the consumer to—

(A) lose any claim or defense to payment of the debt; or

(B) become subject to any practice prohibited by this title.

(7) The false representation or implication that the consumer committed any crime or other conduct in order to disgrace the consumer.

(8) Communicating or threatening to communicate to any person credit information which is known or which should be known to be false, including the failure to communicate that a disputed debt is disputed.

(9) The use or distribution of any written communication which simulates or is falsely represented to be a document authorized, issued, or approved by any court, official, or agency of the United States or any State, or which creates a false impression as to its source, authorization, or approval.

(10) The use of any false representation or deceptive means to collect or attempt to collect any debt or to obtain information concerning a consumer.

(11) The failure to disclose in the initial written communication with the consumer and, in addition, if the initial communication with the consumer is oral, in that initial oral communication, that the debt collector is attempting to collect a debt and that any information obtained will be used for that purpose, and the failure to

disclose in subsequent communications that the communication is from a debt collector, except that this paragraph shall

not apply to a formal pleading made in connection with a legal action.

(12) The false representation or implication that accounts have been turned over to innocent purchasers for value.

(13) The false representation or implication that documents are legal process.

(14) The use of any business, company, or organization name other than the true name of the debt collector's business, company, or organization.

(15) The false representation or implication that documents are not legal process forms or do not require action by the consumer.

(16) The false representation or implication that a debt collector operates or is employed by a consumer reporting agency as defined by section 603(f) of this Act.

15 USC 1692f

§ 808. Unfair practices

A debt collector may not use unfair or unconscionable means to collect or attempt to collect any debt. Without limiting the general application of the foregoing, the following conduct is a violation of this section:

(1) The collection of any amount (including any interest, fee, charge, or expense incidental to the principal obligation)

unless such amount is expressly authorized by the agreement creating the debt or permitted by law.

(2) The acceptance by a debt collector from any person of a check or other payment instrument postdated by more than five days unless such person is notified in writing of the debt collector's intent to deposit such check or instrument not more than ten nor less than three business days prior to such deposit.

(3) The solicitation by a debt collector of any postdated check or other postdated payment instrument for the purpose of threatening or instituting criminal prosecution.

(4) Depositing or threatening to deposit any postdated check or other postdated payment instrument prior to the date on such check or instrument.

(5) Causing charges to be made to any person for communications by concealment of the true propose of the communication. Such charges include, but are not limited to, collect telephone calls and telegram fees.

(6) Taking or threatening to take any nonjudicial action to effect dispossession or disablement of property if—

(A) there is no present right to possession of the property claimed as collateral through an enforceable security interest;

(B) there is no present intention to take possession of the property; or

(C) the property is exempt by law from such dispossession or disablement.

(7) Communicating with a consumer regarding a debt by post card.

(8) Using any language or symbol, other than the debt collector's address, on any envelope when communicating with a consumer by use of the mails or by telegram, except that a debt collector may use his business name if such name does not indicate that he is in the debt collection business.

15 USC 1692G

§ 809. Validation of debts

(a) Within five days after the initial communication with a consumer in connection with the collection of any debt, a debt collector shall, unless the following information is contained in the initial communication or the consumer has paid the debt, send the consumer a written notice containing—

(1) the amount of the debt;

(2) the name of the creditor to whom the debt is owed;

(3) a statement that unless the consumer, within thirty days after receipt of the notice, disputes the validity of the debt, or any portion thereof, the debt will be assumed to be valid by the debt collector;

(4) a statement that if the consumer notifies the debt collector in writing within the thirty-day period that the debt, or any portion thereof, is disputed, the debt collector will obtain verification of the debt or a copy of a

judgment against the consumer and a copy of such verification or judgment will be mailed to the consumer by the debt collector; and

(5) a statement that, upon the consumer's written request within the thirty-day period, the debt collector will provide the consumer with the name and address of the original creditor, if different from the current creditor.

(b) If the consumer notifies the debt collector in writing within the thirty-day period described in subsection (a) that the debt, or any portion thereof, is disputed, or that the consumer requests the name and address of the original creditor, the debt collector shall cease collection of the debt, or any disputed portion thereof, until the debt collector obtains verification of the debt or any copy of a judgment, or the name and address of the original creditor, and a copy of such verification or judgment, or name and address of the original creditor, is mailed to the consumer by the debt collector. Collection activities and communications that do not otherwise violate this title may continue during the 30-day period referred to in subsection (a) unless the consumer has notified the debt collector in writing that the debt, or any portion of the debt, is disputed or that the consumer requests the name and address of the original creditor. Any collection activities and communication during the 30-day period may not overshadow or be inconsistent with the disclosure of the consumer's right to dispute the debt or request the name and address of the original creditor.

(c) The failure of a consumer to dispute the validity of a debt under this section may not be construed by any court as an admission of liability by the consumer.

(d) A communication in the form of a formal pleading in a civil action shall not be treated as an initial communication for purposes of subsection (a).

(e) The sending or delivery of any form or notice which does not relate to the collection of a debt and is expressly required by the Internal Revenue Code of 1986, title V of Gramm-Leach-Bliley Act, or any provision of Federal or State law relating to notice of data security breach or privacy, or any regulation prescribed under any such provision of law, shall not be treated as an initial communication in connection with debt collection for purposes of this section.

15 USC 1692h
§ 810. Multiple debts
If any consumer owes multiple debts and makes any single payment to any debt collector with respect to such debts, such debt collector may not apply such payment to any debt which is disputed by the consumer and, where applicable, shall apply
such payment in accordance with the consumer's directions.

15 USC 1692i
§ 811. Legal actions by debt collectors
(a) Any debt collector who brings any legal action on a debt against any consumer shall—

(1) in the case of an action to enforce an interest in real property securing the consumer's obligation, bring such action only in a judicial district or similar legal entity in which such real property is located; or

(2) in the case of an action not described in paragraph (1), bring such action only in the judicial district or similar

legal entity—

(A) in which such consumer signed the contract sued upon; or

(B) in which such consumer resides at the commencement of the action.

(b) Nothing in this title shall be construed to authorize the bringing of legal actions by debt collectors.

15 USC 1692j
§ 812. Furnishing certain deceptive forms
(a) It is unlawful to design, compile, and furnish any form knowing that such form would be used to create the false belief in a consumer that a person other than the creditor of such consumer is participating in the collection of or in an attempt to collect a debt such consumer allegedly owes such creditor, when in fact such person is not so participating.

(b) Any person who violates this section shall be liable to the same extent and in the same manner as a debt collector is liable under section 813 for failure to comply with a provision of this title.

15 USC 1692k

§ 813. Civil liability

(a) Except as otherwise provided by this section, any debt collector who fails to comply with any provision of this title with respect to any person is liable to such person in an amount equal to the sum of—

(1) any actual damage sustained by such person as a result of such failure;

(2) (A) in the case of any action by an individual, such additional damages as the court may allow, but not exceeding $1,000; or

(B) in the case of a class action,

(i) such amount for each named plaintiff as could be recovered under subparagraph (A), and

(ii) such amount as the court may allow for all other class members, without regard to a minimum individual recovery, not to exceed the lesser of $500,000 or 1 per centum of the net worth of the debt collector; and

(3) in the case of any successful action to enforce the foregoing liability, the costs of the action, together with a reasonable attorney's fee as determined by the court. On a finding by the court that an action under this section was brought in bad faith and for the purpose of harassment, the court may award to the defendant attorney's fees reasonable in relation to the work expended and costs.

(b) In determining the amount of liability in any action under subsection (a), the court shall consider, among other relevant factors—

(1) in any individual action under subsection (a)(2)(A), the frequency and persistence of noncompliance by the debt collector, the nature of such noncompliance, and the extent to which such noncompliance was intentional; or

(2) in any class action under subsection (a)(2)(B), the frequency and persistence of noncompliance by the debt collector, the nature of such noncompliance, the resources of the debt collector, the number of persons adversely affected, and the extent to which the debt collector's noncompliance was intentional.

(c) A debt collector may not be held liable in any action brought under this title if the debt collector shows by a preponderance of evidence that the violation was not intentional and resulted from a bona fide error notwithstanding the maintenance of procedures reasonably adapted to avoid any such error.

(d) An action to enforce any liability created by this title may be brought in any appropriate United States district court without regard to the amount in controversy, or in any other court of competent jurisdiction, within one year from the date on which the violation occurs.

(e) No provision of this section imposing any liability shall apply to any act done or omitted in good faith in conformity with any advisory opinion of the Commission, notwithstanding that after such act or omission has occurred, such opinion is amended, rescinded, or determined by judicial or other authority to be invalid for any reason.

15 USC 1692l

§ 814. Administrative enforcement

(a) Compliance with this title shall be enforced by the Commission, except to the extent that enforcement of the requirements imposed under this title is specifically committed to another agency under subsection (b). For purpose of the exercise by the Commission of its functions and powers under the Federal Trade Commission Act, a violation of this title shall be deemed an unfair or deceptive act or practice in violation of that Act. All of the functions and powers of the Commission under the Federal Trade Commission Act are available to the Commission to enforce compliance by any person with this title, irrespective of whether that person is engaged in commerce or meets any other jurisdictional tests in the Federal Trade Commission Act, including the power to enforce the provisions of this title in the same manner as if the violation had been a violation of a Federal Trade Commission trade regulation rule.

(b) Compliance with any requirements imposed under this title shall be enforced under—

(1) section 8 of the Federal Deposit Insurance Act, in the case of—

(A) national banks, by the Comptroller of the Currency;

(B) member banks of the Federal Reserve System (other than national banks), by the Federal Reserve Board; and

(C) banks the deposits or accounts of which are insured by the Federal Deposit Insurance Corporation (other than members of the Federal Reserve System), by the Board of Directors of the Federal Deposit Insurance Corporation;

(2) section 5(d) of the Home Owners Loan Act of 1933, section 407 of the National Housing Act, and sections 6(i) and 17 of the Federal Home Loan Bank Act, by the Federal Home Loan Bank Board (acting directing or through the Federal Savings and Loan Insurance Corporation), in the case of any institution subject to any of those provisions;

(3) the Federal Credit Union Act, by the Administrator of the National Credit Union Administration with respect to any Federal credit union;

(4) subtitle IV of Title 49, by the Interstate Commerce Commission with respect to any common carrier subject to such subtitle;

(5) the Federal Aviation Act of 1958, by the Secretary of Transportation with respect to any air carrier or any foreign air carrier subject to that Act; and

(6) the Packers and Stockyards Act, 1921 (except as provided in section 406 of that Act), by the Secretary of Agriculture with respect to any activities subject to that Act.

(c) For the purpose of the exercise by any agency referred to in subsection (b) of its powers under any Act referred to in that subsection, a violation of any requirement imposed under this title shall be deemed to be a violation of a requirement imposed under that Act. In addition to its powers under any provision of law specifically referred to in subsection (b), each of the agencies referred to in that subsection may exercise, for the purpose of enforcing compliance with any requirement imposed under this title any other authority conferred on it by law, except as provided in subsection (d).

(d) Neither the Commission nor any other agency referred to in subsection (b) may promulgate trade regulation rules or other regulations with respect to the collection of debts by debt collectors as defined in this title.

15 USC 1692m
§ 815. Reports to Congress by the Commission

(a) Not later than one year after the effective date of this title and at one-year intervals thereafter, the Commission shall make reports to the Congress concerning the administration of its functions under this title, including such recommendations as the Commission deems necessary or appropriate. In addition, each report of the Commission shall include its assessment of the extent to which compliance with this title is being achieved and a summary of the enforcement actions taken by the Commission under section 814 of this title.

(b) In the exercise of its functions under this title, the Commission may obtain upon request the views of any other Federal agency which exercises enforcement functions under section 814 of this title.

15 USC 1692n
§ 816. Relation to State laws

This title does not annul, alter, or affect, or exempt any person subject to the provisions of this title from complying with the laws of any State with respect to debt collection practices, except to the extent that those laws are inconsistent with any provision of this title, and then only to the extent of the inconsistency. For purposes of this section, a State law is not inconsistent with this title if the protection such law affords any consumer is greater than the protection provided by this title.

15 USC 1692o
§ 817. Exemption for State regulation

The Commission shall by regulation exempt from the requirements of this title any class of debt collection practices within any State if the Commission determines that under the law of that State that class of debt collection practices is subject to requirements substantially similar to those imposed by this title, and that there is adequate provision for enforcement.

15 USC 1692p

§ 818. Exception for certain bad check enforcement programs operated by private entities

(a) In General.—

(1) TREATMENT OF CERTAIN PRIVATE ENTITIES.—

Subject to paragraph (2), a private entity shall be excluded from the definition of a debt collector, pursuant to the exception provided in section 803(6), with respect to the operation by the entity of a program described in paragraph (2)(A) under a contract described in paragraph (2)(B).

(2) CONDITIONS OF APPLICABILITY.—Paragraph (1) shall apply if—

(A) a State or district attorney establishes, within the jurisdiction of such State or district attorney and with respect to alleged bad check violations that do not involve a check described in subsection (b), a pretrial diversion program for alleged bad check offenders who agree to participate voluntarily in such program to avoid criminal prosecution;

(B) a private entity, that is subject to an administrative support services contract with a State or district attorney and operates under the direction, supervision, and control of such State or district attorney, operates the pretrial diversion program described in subparagraph (A); and

(C) in the course of performing duties delegated to it by a State or district attorney under the contract, the private entity referred to in subparagraph (B)—

(i) complies with the penal laws of the State;

(ii) conforms with the terms of the contract and directives of the State or district attorney;

(iii) does not exercise independent prosecutorial discretion;

(iv) contacts any alleged offender referred to in subparagraph (A) for purposes of participating in a program referred to in such paragraph—

(I) only as a result of any determination by the State or district attorney that probable cause of a bad check violation under State penal law exists, and that contact with the alleged offender for purposes of participation in the program is appropriate; and

(II) the alleged offender has failed to pay the bad check after demand for payment, pursuant to State law, is made for payment of the check amount;

(v) includes as part of an initial written communication with an alleged offender a clear and conspicuous statement that—

(I) the alleged offender may dispute the validity of any alleged bad check violation;

(II) where the alleged offender knows, or has reasonable cause to believe, that the alleged bad check violation is the result of theft or forgery of the check, identity theft, or other fraud that is not the result of the conduct of the alleged offender, the alleged offender may file a crime report with the appropriate law enforcement agency; and

(III) if the alleged offender notifies the private entity or the district attorney in writing, not later than 30 days after being contacted for the first time pursuant to clause (iv), that there is a dispute pursuant to this subsection, before further restitution efforts are pursued, the district attorney or an employee of the district attorney authorized to make such a determination makes a determination that there is probable cause to believe that a crime has been committed; and

(vi) charges only fees in connection with services under the contract that have been authorized by the contract with the State or district attorney.

(b) Certain Checks Excluded.—A check is described in this subsection if the check involves, or is subsequently found to involve—

(1) a postdated check presented in connection with a payday loan, or other similar transaction, where the payee of the check knew that the issuer had insufficient funds at the time the check was made, drawn, or delivered;

(2) a stop payment order where the issuer acted in good faith and with reasonable cause in stopping payment on the check;

(3) a check dishonored because of an adjustment to the issuer's account by the financial institution holding such account without providing notice to the person at the time the check was made, drawn, or delivered;

(4) a check for partial payment of a debt where the payee had previously accepted partial payment for such debt;

(5) a check issued by a person who was not competent, or was not of legal age, to enter into a legal contractual obligation at the time the check was made, drawn, or delivered; or

(6) a check issued to pay an obligation arising from a transaction that was illegal in the jurisdiction of the State or district attorney at the time the check was made, drawn, or delivered.

(c) Definitions.—For purposes of this section, the following definitions shall apply:

(1) STATE OR DISTRICT ATTORNEY.—The term "State or district attorney" means the chief elected or appointed prosecuting attorney in a district, county (as defined in section 2 of title 1, United States Code), municipality, or comparable jurisdiction, including State attorneys general who act as chief elected or appointed prosecuting attorneys in a district, county (as so defined), municipality or comparable jurisdiction, who may be referred to by a variety of titles such as district attorneys, prosecuting attorneys, commonwealth's attorneys, solicitors, county attorneys, and state's attorneys, and who are responsible for the prosecution of State crimes and violations of jurisdiction-specific local ordinances.

(2) CHECK.—The term "check" has the same meaning as in section 3(6) of the Check Clearing for the 21st Century Act.

(3) BAD CHECK VIOLATION.—The term "bad check violation" means a violation of the applicable State criminal law relating to the writing of dishonored checks.

15 USC 1692r

§ 819. Effective date

This title takes effect upon the expiration of six months after the date of its enactment, but section 809 shall apply only with respect to debts for which the initial attempt to collect occurs after such effective date.

15 USC 1692 note
Legislative History

House Report: No. 95-131 (Comm. on Banking, Finance, and Urban Affairs)

Senate Report: No. 95-382 (Comm. on Banking, Housing and Urban Affairs)

Congressional Record, Vol. 123 (1977)

April 4, House considered and passed H.R. 5294.

Aug. 5, Senate considered and passed amended version of H.R. 5294.

Sept. 8, House considered and passed Senate version.

Enactment: Public Law 95-109 (Sept. 20, 1977)

Amendments: Public Law Nos.

99-361 (July 9, 1986)

104-208 (Sept. 30, 1996)

109-351 (Oct. 13, 2006)

APPENDIX R

AFFILIATED BUSINESS ARRANGEMENT DISCLOSURE STATEMENT

To:
From:
Property:
Date:

This is to give you notice that [referring party] has a business relationship with [settlement services providers(s)]. [Describe the nature of the relationship between the referring party and the providers(s), including percentage of ownership interest, if applicable.] Because of this relationship, this referral may provide [referring party] a financial or other benefit.

[A.] Set forth below is the estimated charge or range of charges for the settlement services listed. You are NOTrequired to use the listed provider(s) as a condition for [settlement of your loan on] [or] [purchase, sale, or refinance of] the subject property. THERE ARE FREQUENTLY OTHER SETTLEMENT SERVICE PROVIDERS AVAILABLE WITH SIMILAR SERVICES. YOU ARE FREE TO SHOP AROUND TO DETERMINE THAT YOU ARE RECEIVING THE BEST SERVICES AND THE BEST RATE FOR THESE SERVICES.

[provider and settlement service] [charge or range of charges]

_____

_____

[B.] Set forth below is the estimated charge or range of charges for the settlement services of an attorney, credit reporting agency, or real estate appraiser that we, as your lender, will require you to use, as a condition of your loan on this property, to represent our interests in the transaction.

[provider and settlement service][charge or range of charges]

_____

_____

ACKNOWLEDGMENT

I/we have read this disclosure form, and understand that [referring party] is referring me/us to purchase the above-described settlement service(s) and may receive a financial or other benefit as the result of this referral.

.......[signature]

[INSTRUCTIONS TO PREPARER:] [Use paragraph A for referrals other than those by a lender to an attorney, a credit reporting agency, or a real estate appraiser that a lender is requiring a borrower to use to represent the lender's interests in the transaction. Use paragraph B for those referrals to an attorney, credit reporting agency, or real estate appraiser that a lender is requiring a borrower to use to represent the lender's interests in the transaction. When applicable, use both paragraphs. Specific timing rules for delivery of the affiliated business disclosure statement are set forth in 24 CFR 3500.15(b)(1) of Regulation X.] These INSTRUCTIONS TO PREPARERS should not appear on the statement.

[61 FR 58477, Nov 15, 1996]

FORECLOSURE AUDIT FORM

This form is for attorneys who know foreclosure law, but want a reminder to ensure each defense is reviewed.

Foreclosure Audit

Audit Information			

[Attorney Name] Today's Date: [Date]

Home owner name(s): [Enter Name(s) Here]

Property Address: [Enter Property Address Here]

Lender in Mtg/HUD 1: [Lender Name]

Current Servicer: [Servicer Name]

Mortgage Broker: [Broker Name]

Date Loan Closed: [Date Here]

Loan Information:

☐ Owner Occupied ☐ Investment ☐ Second Home

☐ Purchase ☐ ☐ Refinance with Cash Out ☐

Loan Terms: [Terms Here] Loan Amount: [Amt Here]

Property Information:

☐ ☐ ☐

Borrower 1 & 2 Information:

☐ Single ☐ Married ☐ ☐ English as 1st Language

☐ Apparently Verified ☐ SISA ☐ NINA ☐ SIVA

Audit Review Checklist (Condensed)							
1	ABA Disclosures	2	TILA APR	3		4	TILA Rescission Notice
5	C/P Notice Mailed	6	FHA C/P	7	ECOA	8	Notice to Spouse
9	Prop ID Check	10	Lost Note	11	Note Impossible	12	Mortgage Impossible
13	Unconscionability	14	Standing	15	Invalid Assignment	16	Forced Insurance
17	Breach of Contract	18	MERS	19	State Laws	20	RESPA KB's
21	BK Issues	22	FDCPA	23	Atty Fees	24	Flood Disclosures

Quick Recommendation	

☐ Rescission Possible ☐

☐ Stat. Damages Possible ☐ Common Law Defenses

INDEX

ABOUT THE AUTHOR

Troy Doucet owned a mortgage firm for several years, fighting tirelessly to save homeowners money. In 2004, *Broker* magazine featured him as its cover story when he proposed the mortgage industry eliminate junk fees from all mortgages. Mr. Doucet eliminated all junk fees from his company's loans early on, and grew the firm quickly. In 2006, Mr. Doucet left the industry to pursue academic goals. He completed a course in paralegal studies in 2006, and started law school in 2007.

Mr. Doucet assists attorneys throughout the United States in their efforts to combat foreclosure. He regularly audits loans for TILA and HOEPA violations, as well as for the other defenses contained in this book. For Mr. Doucet, this book represents another step in his efforts to combat abusive lending. He hopes you find it helpful.

Cover design by **YAXELStudio®**, http://www.yaxel.com

Cover image by Nikolay Mamluke, http://www.junial.com, as published by http://www.dreamstime.com